# COLLEGE
# STUDENT
# RETENTION

# COLLEGE
# STUDENT
# RETENTION
## Formula for Student Success

Edited by Alan Seidman

Foreword by Vincent Tinto

AMERICAN COUNCIL ON EDUCATION
PRAEGER
Series on Higher Education

Library of Congress Cataloging-in-Publication Data

College student retention : formula for student success / edited by Alan Seidman;
    foreword by Vincent Tinto.
    p. 1 cm.—(ACE/Praeger series on higher education)
    Includes bibliographical references and index.
    ISBN 0–275–98193–2 (alk. paper)
    1. College attendance—United States.   2. College dropouts—United States.   3.
Academic achievement—United States.   I. Seidman, Alan.   II. Title.   III. Series:
American Council on Education/Praeger series on higher education.
    LC148.2.C65    2005
    378.1'619—dc22        2004028152

British Library Cataloguing in Publication Data is available.

Library of Congress Catalog Card Number: 2004028152
ISBN: 0–275–98193–2

First published in 2005

Praeger Publishers, 88 Post Road West, Westport, CT 06881
An imprint of Greenwood Publishing Group, Inc.
www.praeger.com

Printed in the United States of America

The paper used in this book complies with the
Permanent Paper Standard issued by the National
Information Standards Organization (Z39.48–1984).

10  9  8  7  6  5  4  3  2  1

For my wife, Barbara
my inspiration

# CONTENTS

# FOREWORD
## College Student Retention: Formula for Student Success

Research on student retention is voluminous. It is easily one of the most widely studied topics in higher education over the past thirty years. Over that time considerable attention has been paid to developing and testing theories of student retention that seek to explain why some students leave and others persist. Although there is still some disagreement over the details of differing theories, the broad dimensions of a theory of student retention are starting to emerge. Among other things, we can say with a good deal of confidence that academic preparation, commitments, and involvement matter.

Despite all the research that has been conducted to date, little work has been devoted to the development of a model of student persistence that would provide guidelines to institutions for creating policies, practices, and programs to enhance student success. The absence of such a model is not the result of a lack of research but rather of the failure of past research to translate its many findings into forms that would guide institutional action. In this regard a significant gap remains between what researchers know about the nature of student retention and what practitioners need to know to enhance student retention. This volume represents an effort to address that gap.

Today it is more important than ever for institutions to respond to the challenge of increasing student success. Forced to cope with tight, if not shrinking, budgets, institutions face mounting pressure to improve their rates of student retention and graduation. In many cases, this pressure reflects the movement of states to include graduation rates in a system of institutional accountability. In other cases, this pressure reflects the impact of widely publicized ranking systems that include graduation rates as one measure of "quality." In still other cases, this pressure mirrors the reality that increased student retention is critical to the stability of institutional budgets. Whatever its source, it is evident that institutions of higher education are increasingly concerned about the persistence and graduation of their students and therefore especially interested in finding useful models of student success that can guide their actions. This edited volume is directed to the development of such models.

*Vincent Tinto*
*Syracuse University*

# INTRODUCTION

I t can be said that education is the great equalizer. No matter what economic stratum a person is born into, he or she can acquire the skills necessary to succeed through education. A strong, vibrant, varied, and expanding national economy depends in part on the educational attainment of its citizens. A nation that values and promotes the educational attainment of its citizens is a nation that is concerned with its ability to compete in the global economy.

Goldstein (1995) points out in his review of literature on college choice that change is constant in our lives. As the average age of the U.S. population increases, as that population continues to participate in a growing global economic community, and as technology advances, people are discovering that continuous learning may be not only desirable but also necessary. Indeed, in order to make choices that involve critical thinking skills, a citizenry must become knowledgeable.

In a technological society with ever-increasing use of the Internet and other modes of communication and commerce, we must continually enhance our skill sets if we want to remain knowledgeable and competitive. Those unwilling or unable to obtain the necessary skills to compete in an ever-complex workplace are doomed to stay in low-skill, low-paying jobs. When our nation has to look abroad for workers skilled in mathematics, quantitative reasoning, and the sciences, perhaps it is a sign that our educational system is failing to provide those skills at the level necessary to continue to advance our country. Those turned off to education, not willing to continue their cultural and intellectual growth, will surely become a burden to society. We cannot afford to waste our precious human capital.

Federal and state governments realize that education is important to the vitality and success of our country. The federal and state governments have virtually mandated the accessibility of higher education for all of their citizens. This mandate has been demonstrated for more than 150 years by cooperation between the federal and state governments, from the development of the Land Grant College of the nineteenth century to the development of the open admissions, low-cost community college in the beginning of the twentieth century. The opportunity for higher education is available for most of our citizens who want to take advantage of it.

Even though access to higher education is becoming universally available to all, many students who start in a higher education program drop out prior to completing a degree or achieving their individual academic and social goals. This is not a recent phenomenon. For years a number of students have been unsuccessful in attaining their academic and personal goals. In response to student attrition, colleges developed intervention programs and services to try to retain students. Over the years, colleges have spent vast amounts of money on programs and services for a variety of groups who may need extra services to develop the skills necessary to graduate.

To retain students, colleges have provided programs for the economically disadvantaged, programs for underrepresented students (minorities), programs and services for students with disabilities, women, and older adults reentering college or beginning college for the first time. Counseling programs have been strengthened to try to meet the needs of students. Job and career centers have been established to help students decide on career options and to provide a place for potential employers to meet students. The U.S. and state governments have made financial aid more readily available to a wider range of students, even though aid is now provided as loans rather than outright grants except to the neediest students.

In spite of these programs and services, retention from first to second year has not improved over time. The data also show that graduation rates have not improved over time. Logic dictates that the addition of programs and services should improve the retention of students, but in reality this seems not to be the case.

The knowledge of student behaviors and ways we can alter them will help students achieve their academic and social goals and perhaps develop a thirst for lifelong learning. To remain competitive in the ever-changing and challenging world, people will have to take the initiative to seek out educational opportunities. If a person is turned off to the educational system because of a poor experience, he or she may never be inclined to avail himself or herself of the opportunity to advance with additional education. That person in turn may not encourage others to take advantage of additional education. As we move ahead at a breakneck speed technologically, we must continue to encourage our citizens to learn new and different things.

This book examines a number of areas critical to the retention of students. Chapter 1 explores the history of the retention movement in the United States. Although we think of retention research going back over seventy years as old, in the scheme of the United States' educational history, retention research is very new indeed. The reader will learn in this book when the retention movement began and when we started to measure attrition and graduation rates and develop theories. Chapter 2 gives us measures of persistence from a number of perspectives. The reader will note that the data set used by researchers to study retention varies and can create different results for the same problem studied. In Chapter 3 we look at the various retention theories and look at expanding our currently accepted theories to match the different avenues students use to pursue education. In Chapter 4 we explore our definitions of retention and how important those definitions are. Without a standardized definition of retention, we may not be able to establish comparisons within the educational system. The argument can be made for a nationally accepted definition for some types of comparisons, but local definition may be best when a college looks at its own retention. Chapter 5 examines reliable retention research that posits positive, neutral, and negative results. The authors of that chapter choose a number of studies that must meet specific criteria for thirteen propositions to yield reliable knowledge. The reader will have to judge whether or not fewer than the acceptable number of studies or number of positive results will alter his or her thinking about the propositions. Chapter 6 looks at the little-studied area of retention and graduation beyond the first year. Most colleges front-load, that is, put most of their retention programs and services into the first term and year, and have seen positive results from that approach. But what happens after the first year? How students choose pathways to achieving a four-year degree is explored in Chapter 7, and nine themes of student retention are examined in Chapter 8. These chapters reaffirm our knowledge about college student retention, showing how complicated the path to earning a degree truly is for some students. The effects of income, race, gender, and institutional type on student retention are examined in Chapter 9. Chapter 10 focuses on the financial implications of student retention. Tying all this information together is the Seidman formula for student success, which is presented in Chapter 11. This formula creates an action plan and explains what colleges can do now to effect change and to retain students until they complete their academic and personal goals. Perhaps now is a time for action to help our populace achieve its academic and personal goals, instead of a time for study to come up with additional theories about why students leave college. In the Epilogue, Vincent Tinto reiterates the need to move away from theory to action.

This book could not have been completed without the enthusiasm of the contributors. Each one worked tirelessly to develop a chapter that is meaningful and educational and contains their latest thinking on the topic. The contributors to this volume are truly the most influential teachers and practitioners in the field today. I am grateful to them for their willingness to participate in this endeavor. I cannot thank Susan Slesinger, editor at Greenwood Publishing, enough for her comments, suggestions, and encouragement through the publication process. I would like to thank the American Council on Education for permitting me to go forward with this book from an idea to completion. I dedicate this book to my wife Barbara, who never stops believing in me and my abilities and commitment to college student retention.

## REFERENCE

Goldstein, A. S. (1995). The factors that influence "college choice decision-making" as perceived by the "older adult undergraduate student." Doctoral dissertation, Syracuse University, Syracuse, New York.

# CHAPTER 1

## Past to Present

### A Historical Look at Retention

*Joseph B. Berger and Susan C. Lyon*

### INTRODUCTION

This chapter examines the history of retention with an emphasis on how our understanding of and attention to retention have changed over time. After a review of historical antecedents, we describe the beginnings of concern with retention in American higher education and its changes over time and up through the present. More specifically, this chapter answers questions such as:

- When did retention first become an issue and interest to colleges?
- How has the view of retention changed over time?
- What is the current thinking about retention?
- What is the future for studying retention?

We begin with an overview of the various contextual issues that have shaped the nature of retention and the ways higher education has addressed the issues. We then move to a brief discussion of the different ways in which retention and related terms are defined (see Chapter 4 of this volume for a more thorough treatment of these definitions). In the remainder of the chapter, we cover the historical overview of retention in a substantive chronological narrative and conclude with some thoughts on the nature of retention over the years.

## CONTEXTUAL INFLUENCES ON RETENTION

The main purpose of this chapter is to provide an overview on the historical development of retention. The history of retention is presented in a chronological fashion through the identification of major eras, each of which is characterized by different issues, concerns, and approaches to retention. However, prior to proceeding to the historical overview, it is important to set the context by summarizing some key definitions, assumptions, issues, and sources of influence on the ways educators have thought about, studied, and addressed student retention in higher education. These contextual factors—students, campuses, educational roles, socioeconomic contexts, policies and interventions, knowledge bases, and the conceptualization of retention—have all evolved over time and are intertwined within each era in ways that define the unique stage of development for retention at different points in time. The following discussion provides a concise overview of these factors and their relationship to the historical development of retention in American higher education.

### Students

First and foremost, retention is about students. The supply of and types of students served by colleges and universities in our country have changed over time, moving from a small, selective, generally homogenous group of privileged individuals to a diverse spectrum of individuals numbering in the millions. As the student population has grown and diversified, so have retention issues. The numbers of students entering college at different times have impacted retention. In the early portions of the history of American higher education, student demand for higher education was low, as were aspirations for earning degrees. As a result of a lack of student interest in higher education and in earning a postsecondary degree, retention was unimportant until the last few decades. Once demand increased and student bodies diversified, colleges responded by paying more attention to retention. Such interest was general at first but increasingly became more nuanced and complex as campuses focused on retaining a more diverse range of students in terms of ability, preparation, and background. Levels of preparation, motivations, and other individual characteristics shape the reasons why students attend college and directly impact the chances that students will be retained at particular types of institutions and ultimately persist to earn a postsecondary degree.

## Campuses

Retention is also a campus-based phenomenon. By definition, retention is the ability of a particular college or university to successfully graduate the students that initially enroll at that institution. The number and types of campuses that comprise the loosely coupled system of higher education in America has changed over time as well, resulting in a diversified contemporary collection of campuses that is composed of more than 3,600 institutions.

Specific kinds of campuses tend to attract different types of students. Some campuses, such as highly selective private institutions that are considered more prestigious, recruit and enroll students who are more likely to be retained given their family backgrounds, exposure to the expectations of college, and level of educational preparation. In contrast, less selective institutions tend to attract students who are less likely to be retained given their backgrounds. It is well documented that most students who enroll in courses at community colleges do not intend to earn degrees, so retention varies widely by type of program within community colleges. Some campuses do a better job of retaining certain types of students—women's colleges and historically Black colleges and universities (HBCUs) have been shown to be more successful at retaining female and Black students, respectively. Differences in retention rates are not only a function of the types of students attracted by certain kinds of institutions, but also a function of the type of environment provided by the institution and how well that particular environment is designed to fit the needs of students enrolled at that institution (Astin 1990). As the concept of retention has evolved over time, so has the recognition that one size does not fit all in terms of retention rates and the types of policies and interventions needed to improve retention on any one campus. Hence, as the study of retention has developed, so too has awareness that each institution must tailor retention to fit the specific needs of its students and the context of that particular institutional environment.

## Educational Roles

The roles of faculty and other educators, such as student affairs professionals, has also evolved, and the evolution of professional roles has both impacted and been impacted by retention issues. Early campuses were composed entirely of faculty members (sometimes one or two individuals) who were generalists and were responsible not only for all instructional activities, but also for all other professional roles and activities on campuses. As campuses grew and disciplinary fields became more specialized, so too did the roles of the professionals on campus. Faculty became more specialized in particular fields and administrative roles became distinct. In particular, the growth of student affairs administrators, admissions officers, and enrollment management specialists was driven by, and helped develop, retention efforts across the spectrum of American higher education. However, more recent trends have seen retention increasingly recognized as the responsibility of all educators on campus, faculty and staff, even when there are specialized staff members solely dedicated to improving retention on campus.

## Socioeconomic Contexts

The larger social, economic, and political contexts in which higher education is embedded have also played a key role in retention at different points in history. As mentioned in several places throughout this chapter, the sociocultural context of American society has shaped who has been served and in what ways they have been served during different points in history. The demands placed by society on higher education and the need for college graduates with earned degrees have grown over time. This pattern of increasing importance for individuals to possess a college degree has led to increased concern about retention as higher education has grown on one hand and become a more competitive market for students on the other. Demographic and economic shifts have accounted for much of the increased attention to retention over the last thirty years or so. For example, the relative stabilization (or even the anticipation of enrollment pool stagnation or decrease) of traditional pools of high school graduates increased concern about how to keep students who had already enrolled on a campus, rather than focusing solely on recruiting new students to maintain desired student body sizes and tuition revenue. The economy has had similar effects, with economic downturns creating larger college enrollments, and times of economic prosperity leading to more value being placed on the attainment of a college degree in the competitive workforce market. More specifically, the soaring costs of higher education in conjunction with decreased ability of institutions to raise tuition and fees created more pressure for institutions to retain students already enrolled rather than spending greater resources on attracting new students. Individual institutions have not been alone in feeling increased economic pressures over the latter part of the twentieth century to improve retention. State-funded public postsecondary educational systems have also been paying more attention to retention as policymakers have increased demands for publicly funded systems and institutions to strive for and document better performance on key outcome indicators such as retention. Material resources have not been the only source of resource dependency for postsecondary institutions. The symbolic prestige of high rankings in nationally known publications such as *U.S. News & World Report* has increasingly created greater public awareness about and institutional responsiveness to retention rates. As a result, campuses around the country have become increasingly concerned about retention rates as a source of prestige that can be converted into other kinds of symbolic, material, and human resources—particularly in the competition for more and better students.

## Policies and Interventions

Policies and interventions have emerged in response to concerns about retention and have shaped the ways in which retention has developed as well. Policies and interventions at the federal and state levels have impacted retention as well as trends in types of campus interventions. The federal government has initiated over time a number of policy initiatives—such as the Morrill Act, GI Bill, Civil Rights Act, financial aid—that increased the importance of and access to higher education. As higher percentages of individuals went to college under such programs, the goal of earning a degree, not merely attending college, became more desirable. As the completion of a college degree became more important for individuals, it also became more important for postsecondary campuses to demonstrate that they could help individual students realize that goal. The role of state-level policy initiatives has also increased over time. While states historically have played a limited role in this regard, the end of the twentieth century and beginning of the twenty-first century have seen many states implement accountability systems in which retention has been used as a key criterion for success and often as a factor in determining funding for state campuses.

## Knowledge Base

Our base of empirical and conceptual knowledge about retention has grown and shaped retention efforts throughout higher education. The earliest studies on student mortality, as student attrition was originally conceptualized, began in the 1930s. Prior to the 1960s the study of retention, and even the higher education enterprise as a whole, was still developing. In the late 1960s, a more systematic knowledge base, a synthesis of existing studies, began to emerge. A series of studies in the late 1960s, notably Feldman and Newcomb's (1969) pioneering work on the impact of college on students, and more specifically the work of Alexander Astin and William Spady, spurred a more focused study of what came to be known as retention. Building upon these earlier works, Vincent Tinto published his interactionalist model of student retention in 1975. Tinto's model spurred tremendous interest in the study of retention. Other important studies included Astin's (1977, 1985) theory of involvement, and the work of Kamens (1974) and Bean (1980, 1983), which made noteworthy contributions to the theoretical foundations of the study of retention. The emergence of a theory base spurred a proliferation of studies that now number in the thousands, making undergraduate retention one of the most studied fields in higher education. The development of new theories has slowed as the number of studies has expanded, but knowledge has continued to be refined and further developed. Many studies have applied the existing models to the examination of retention in different types of postsecondary institutions and for different types of students. There has also been a movement to integrate various theories to develop more comprehensive models, and some studies have used constructs from other disciplines and theories to elaborate upon the existing retention models.

Early retention studies focused primarily on single-institution studies, and the growth of theory-driven research initially emphasized more generic models that could explain causes of attrition and suggestions for retention as a general phenomenon. Many recent studies now focus on how specific types of students (e.g., students from different types of racial or ethnic backgrounds, socioeconomic statuses, etc.) fare in terms of retention at specific types of institutional settings (e.g., community colleges or selective institutions). Berger (2000a) has proposed, for example, that students who come from different socioeconomic strata are more or less likely to be retained at different types of campuses and that future research should focus on a number of midrange theories that explain the interaction between specific types of students and specific types of campuses, rather than continuing to search for more macro-oriented theories that try to explain retention for all types of students at all types of campuses.

## Conceptualization of Retention

Finally understanding how retention and its related issues have been conceptualized and defined is important as a contextual issue that must be considered in any historical analysis of retention. Therefore, before moving to the substance of this chapter, it is important to understand that the conceptualization of retention has not been consistent. Various aspects of student departure from college has been a topic of great interest to educators and researchers for some time, but the terminology used to explain this phenomenon has changed over time and includes descriptors such as student mortality (McNeely 1937; Gekowski & Schwartz 1961), college dropouts (Summerskill 1962; Spady 1971; Tinto 1975), student attrition (Sexton 1965; Panos & Astin 1967; Pantages & Creedon 1978; Tinto 1993), college retention (Iffert 1957; Tinto 1990; Berger 2002; Braxton & Mundy 2002), and student persistence (Berger & Milem 1999; Berger 2002). While these terms are closely related, they are not synonymous. Given the centrality of these key concepts to the phenomena being studied, they are briefly defined and distinguished from one another in the following bullets:

- Attrition—refers to students who fail to reenroll at an institution in consecutive semesters.
- Dismissal—refers to a student who is not permitted by the institution to continue enrollment.
- Dropout—refers to a student whose initial educational goal was to complete at least a bachelor's degree but who did not complete it.
- Mortality—refers to the failure of students to remain in college until graduation.
- Persistence—refers to the desire and action of a student to stay within the system of higher education from beginning year through degree completion.
- Retention—refers to the ability of an institution to retain a student from admission to the university through graduation.
- Stopout—refers to a student who temporarily withdraws from an institution or system.
- Withdrawal—refers to the departure of a student from a college or university campus.

When discussing student departure, it is important to distinguish between *voluntary* and *involuntary* withdrawal as well as *institutional* and *system* departure. *Voluntary* departure occurs when the student decides not to reenroll; *involuntary* departure occurs when the institution does not permit the student to reenroll. *Institutional* departure describes the process of leaving a particular institution, whereas *system* departure refers to the departure from the higher education system.

The contextual issues—student trends, diversity of campuses, educational roles, socioeconomic external contexts, policies and interventions, and bases of knowledge—are interwoven throughout the remainder of the chapter as key considerations in each of the nine historical eras described below.

## HISTORICAL OVERVIEW

American colleges have existed for over 300 years and continue to be among the most well-respected postsecondary institutions in the world. Throughout the course of its life, American higher education has withstood changes in mission, curriculum, students, and financing. These changes have affected the nature of retention in terms of patterns of retention, institutional concern about retention, the ways in which retention has been conceptualized and studied, and the range and types of strategies that have been used to try to improve retention.

An examination of published reports and articles on the historical development of retention provides a basis for identifying distinct historical stages that map how retention has evolved over time in American higher education. The historical eras described below are one way to organize how we view and understand important developments in retention. The time periods that comprise each era are not uniform in terms of the number of years within each chronological segment. Rather, each era represents common themes that evolved over time.

For the purposes of this chapter, we have divided the development of retention into nine eras, as follows:

1. Retention Prehistory (1600s–mid-1800s)
2. Evolving toward Retention (mid-1800s–1900)
3. Early Developments (1900–1950)
4. Dealing with Expansion (1950s)
5. Preventing Dropouts (1960s)
6. Building Theory (1970s)
7. Managing Enrollments (1980s)
8. Broadening Horizons (1990s)
9. Current and Future Trends (early twenty-first century)

The first four eras cover the precedents that led to the emergence of retention as a distinct issue to be addressed, studied, and improved throughout higher education. These first four eras cover almost 330 years, most of which are covered by the era labeled "Retention Prehistory" as there was little concern with retention in any systematic way until the beginning of the twentieth century. The last five eras cover the last thirty years or so, the period of time in which retention became a universal concern across the higher education landscape and in which the practical, theoretical, and knowledge bases became more fully developed. Each of the nine eras are discussed in chronological order throughout the remainder of the chapter. The subsection covering each of the eras includes an overview of each contextual issue discussed above and summarizes the key advancements that characterized these time periods.

## Retention Prehistory (1600s–Mid-1800s)

Currently, retention of college students is of paramount interest to institutions of higher education. For many centuries there was no need to consider the issue because so few students attended colleges and very few students were interested in graduating. Indeed, colleges in colonial America struggled to maintain even small enrollments and were primarily interested in attracting students with little or no concern about persistence toward graduation with a degree. College degrees had little or no importance in early American society, and higher education was such a small enterprise that there was no reason to consider persistence toward a degree as an issue. Moreover, these early postsecondary institutions catered to very specific populations. For example, the earliest American colleges, Harvard (1636), William and Mary (1693), and Yale (1701), were established as extensions of their respective churches with the goal of educating young men to satisfy the local demand for pastors and missionaries among various Christian religions. Over two-thirds of the graduates during the seventeenth century became ministers (Geiger 1999). Early colleges were predominantly denominational. As the colonies developed and expanded, however, community pressure to allow freedom of worship in higher education prevailed. As demand for ministers lessened and a need for more professionally trained men emerged, colleges expanded their curriculum to prepare men from elite families for vocations in law and public life. The continued demand for ministers was filled primarily by farmers' sons, and this fueled the growth of numerous extremely small colleges serving rural boys and young men. These institutions were not very stable; most did not even stay open long enough to develop a graduating class. It might be said that in most cases campus survival needed to be established before college officials could even begin to worry about student mortality. This trend continued well into the mid-nineteenth century.

Throughout this period of time, higher education had multiple forces to compete with. The massive expansion of the American frontier brought instant material gratification which afforded many the opportunities to prosper. It was difficult for families to forgo this material reward to allow their sons to attend college. For the majority of colonial families, college was a luxury, not a necessity, and since there were no formal admission requirements, it was something that could wait. In addition, the distances that needed to be traveled to attend these institutions served as barriers to early adoption. The largest class to graduate from Harvard prior to the American Revolution was the class of 1771, with a total of sixty-three graduates (Rudolph 1990). By 1776, colonial colleges enrolled nearly 750 students, over half of whom were sons of farmers destined for the ministry, the others being sons of elite gentlemen with aspirations of careers in law and public life (Geiger 1999).

After the American Revolution, colleges were chartered in the newly free states including Maryland, South Carolina, North Carolina, and Vermont; however, it would be years before the infrastructures of these institutions, as well as the colonial colleges, would be organized well enough to attract significant numbers of students. Between 1775 and 1800 a decrease in college attendance was experienced. The overall number of male students attending college and graduating was still so small that any thought of retention was premature.

The early 1800s was a time of rapid expansion of the American college. Private denominational colleges emerged and enrollments grew by over 80 percent (Geiger 1999). By 1820 enrollments outpaced the population growth and male enrollments were back up to 1 percent. The number of men enrolling in college continued to rise significantly with the establishment of denominational colleges (Geiger 1999). This period was also a time of great turmoil as institutions struggled to define what they were and whom they served. The Yale Report of 1828 restored to universities the notion of classical instruction, which focused on providing students with a foundation for learning. The report also called for an examination of admissions standards to distinguish a college from an academy.

College enrollment expanded furiously throughout the 1820s and 1830s. The rapid rise of denominational colleges was responsible for enrollment increases of nearly 80 percent in each of these decades. This rapid growth continued until the 1840s, when hard economic times changed the outlook of the country in relation to college education. The crash of 1837 sparked discourse on the current state of education, as education was viewed to cater to the professional class and ignore working class families.

## Evolving Toward Retention (Mid-1800s–1900)

As noted in the previous section, retention did not exist as a concept in early American colleges because actual degree attainment was rare. Retention was still not a concern in the late nineteenth century, but this period of time was nevertheless marked by increases in degree attainment and by expansion of curricular and co-curricular options that provided a more complete collegiate experience. The development of a more comprehensive collegiate experience was in response to external conditions that stimulated the increased importance of degree attainment and helped make the completion of college a more desirable option. As a college degree became more desirable, academic offerings and campus life improved and became more conducive to sustained periods of attendance.

By the mid-nineteenth century, colleges admitted men of all religious denominations across a wide range of ages. The most well-established early institutions educated young men ranging in age from their early teens through late twenties, mainly children of elite families with goals of attaining skills comparable to those of their fathers. The curricula of these early colleges were developed to provide students with a liberal education that included classical languages, ethics, metaphysics, and natural philosophy or science. The students at these early colleges did not take their studies seriously and a majority did not graduate. There is no evidence that progress toward the attainment of a degree was even expected by the faculty at these colleges. The time spent at college was idiosyncratic, depending more on the wishes and needs of the students' family than on the requirements of the institution.

In addition to academics, college life became an important part of the student experience during this time. College life was created by students as a way to test authority. At Harvard, for example, students participated in organized social events, and it was customary for men to be found playing card games, drinking, and "stealing the turnkeys of their Cambridge neighbors" (Horowitz 1987) as a bonding ritual. At William and Mary and at Yale, literary societies were used as supplements to classroom learning. Students would participate in open debates and writing competitions which provided a forum for further expansion of the mind.

With the rise in the number of students attending college, the importance of student life began to be realized. Institutions created programs and promoted a well-balanced academic and social curriculum for differentiation and recruitment purposes. Student affairs took on importance as student life changed dramatically. During this time, extracurricular activities emerged and were used to create loyalty to the campus. No evidence exists to tell us whether such efforts improved retention; retention rates were not tracked and higher education was still decades away from such concerns.

During the early 1800s, expansion to the west also began with the average size of a western college averaging fifty-six students. Oberlin College was the first college to admit women, although very few women attended that institution. The majority of women were educated in academies, as colleges resisted pressure to admit women until the second half of the nineteenth century.

By 1850, the average size of a college was 174 students. Collegiate education continued to expand from an elite institution serving only privileged White males to a more diverse student body which included women. Between 1850 and 1900, over forty women's institutions were chartered, including Vassar, Smith, and Wellesley. The primary goal of women's colleges at that time was to prepare women for their eventual roles as housewives, mothers, and elementary school teachers. During the same time period, German influence emerged in American colleges, most notably in the form of research and graduate education. The opening of Johns Hopkins University is a notable event in this era.

One of the most defining moments for American higher education occurred in 1862 with the signing of the Morrill Land Grant Act. The act was responsible for massive expansion of the number of institutions. The act called for at least one college in every state to offer programs in agriculture and engineering. This act transformed the "college" into the "university" and focused efforts on equal access. The act, however, was not predicated upon student demand, and enrollments actually decreased at the same time that the number of universities dramatically increased. The shrinking demand for college reflected the fact that earning a college degree was not yet a widespread priority for students or postsecondary institutions.

The first 250 years in higher education focused more on institutional survival than on student persistence and retention. While many factors contributed to this situation, two are particularly noteworthy. First, most colleges were small and campus openings and closings occurred continuously. Second, students generally were not going to college to earn degrees. As we will see in the next section, these trends changed, leading to the first embryonic movements toward retention.

## Early Developments (1900–1950)

Not until the early 1900s did the number of institutions opened remain constant while enrollments increased. In 1895 the largest institutions recorded enrollments of 2,000 students, in 1910 that number had doubled to 4,000, and by 1915 the number grew to 5,000 students (Geiger 1999). Across the country there were 110,000 students attending just over 1,000 institutions (Goodchild 1999). The growth and stability of institutions was the result of the convergence of another set of larger societal issues. The nation had become firmly industrialized and increasingly urban, both of which increased the need for college education as a means of producing managers and professionals to run the increasingly organized and complex work of the nation.

The rapid growth in college enrollments allowed institutions to create selective admissions policies. For the first time in history, colleges had enough interest from prospective students that some campuses could afford to be more selective about the type and quality of students who attended their institutions. Students from elite families were given preferential treatment and were used to help create the image of elite institutions. As these institutions began to define themselves as elitist, their national recruitment efforts increased in order to attract the best students from across the country. The rise of selective admissions policies developed not only to ensure that students were academically qualified, but also to weed out "undesirables." Increased desire to attend college coupled with increasingly selective admissions policies led to the creation of many new institutions. Many were coeducational or women's colleges as women became an increasingly large part of the undergraduate student population. Institutions were also created, some with substantial financial backing, to serve Jewish, Catholic, and African American students who were prohibited as undesirables in many of the well-established institutions. Many less selective colleges, including large numbers of private and public junior colleges, also arose at this time to serve students who otherwise would not have access to a postsecondary education.

Antecedents of retention began to emerge out of this growth in the undergraduate population and the increasing numbers of diverse types of colleges and universities. The enhanced nature of student differentiation across the different types of institutions greatly exacerbated existing differences across institutions with regard to the extent to which students would be likely to complete their studies and earn a postsecondary degree. This trend was further fueled by slowly increasing expectations that a college degree was a valuable asset in the competition for entry into higher paying professional positions over merely having a high school diploma along with some college education. The more selective end of the institutional spectrum began to view a certain amount of attrition as a hallmark of institutional success; that competition for academic success would inevitably lead to failure for some students. The vast majority of institutions, however, continued to be more concerned with attracting students than with keeping them.

The increasing importance of the college degree along with the increased awareness of different attrition rates led to the first documented studies that clearly focused on what would come to be called retention. The first studies of "student mortality" emerged in the 1930s. One of the first widespread studies to examine multiple issues related to the departure of students at multiple institutions was conducted by John McNeely and published in 1938 on behalf of the U.S. Department of the Interior and the Office of Education. This study used data from sixty institutions across the country. Entitled "College Student Mortality," this study examined the extent of attrition, average time to degree completion, points in the academic career in which attrition was most prevalent, impact of institutional size, impact of other factors (gender, age at entrance, location of home, type of lodging, participation in extracurricular activities, and engagement in part-time work), and reasons for departure (academic dismissal, financial difficulties, illness and death, lack of interest, and being called home by parents). This pioneering work was remarkable for the breadth and depth with which it covered the extent and patterns of student attrition. McNeely's work was clearly a forerunner of the more comprehensive studies that would become common some thirty years later. The Great Depression and World War II, however, turned the nation's resources and interests away from postsecondary education for the next ten years. The post–World War II boom began higher education's golden age of expansion and provided the genesis for renewed interest in student access and degree attainment.

## Dealing with Expansion (1950s)

Despite two world wars and an economic depression, enrollments largely stayed constant and even grew. The end of this period saw an American society that was sending over 2 million students to over 1,800 colleges. Most growth in student enrollments occurred in the last few years in the post–World War II period of the late 1940s. The growth in enrollment had begun in the early part of the century as college became increasingly desirable in an increasingly industrial and technologically oriented society. Government policy, in response to key events such as the Great Depression and World War II, was a major contributor to the enrollment boom that began at the close of the 1940s and that shaped the rapid expansion of the 1950s. Immediately prior to this period, the

National Youth Administration was developed in 1935 to help counter the effects of the Depression and funded postsecondary educational opportunities to hundreds of thousands of students who otherwise would not have gone to college. The GI Bill had an even greater impact, creating a tremendous surge in enrollment as soldiers returned home from war to attend college en masse. The primary purpose of the GI Bill was to help returning soldiers acquire skills necessary to reengage in civilian life. Over 1.1 million ex-GIs took the opportunity to further their education. Harvard received over 60,000 applications (Geiger 1999) and enrollment numbers exceeded capacity at many institutions. Finally, the launch of Sputnik triggered the passage of subsequent federal policy interventions such as the National Defense Education Act of 1958 and the Higher Education Act of 1965. These acts encouraged college attendance and promoted education as necessary for the stability of the United States. These acts also defined the role the federal government would play in financially supporting higher education.

Expansion created the need to persist as a high school degree became less sufficient for future economic and social attainment. College education became necessary for mobility to occur. Students became more committed to their studies and to graduating with the hope of bettering themselves. The explosion of higher education offered different avenues of access to the masses as well. During this time, community colleges grew in importance. These institutions, open to all high school graduates, served a diverse student body and were often-times used to gain access to more selective four-year institutions. The importance of community colleges continued through the 1960s, evident by their rapid growth and increased enrollments.

As the number of students enrolled across many types of institutions increased, institutions of higher education began to think about the retention issue, although it was not until predictions of a decrease in enrollment of students in the early 1970s that retention became a major focus of educators, researchers, and institutions alike. However, attention was increasingly being paid to why some students were not successfully earning their college degrees. Most of the emphasis in the practice and in study of these issues focused on understanding patterns of academic failure.

## Preventing Dropouts (1960s)

By the beginning of the 1960s, higher education was dealing with a myriad of consequences that arose from the post–World War II expansion of higher education. The rapid growth of student enrollment, not only in terms of larger enrollments but also in terms of increasingly diverse student bodies, created many challenges for the expanding roster of college and university campuses across the country. The rapid growth of campuses created many new physical structures in the form of academic buildings and residence halls, but campus expansion also created the need for new infrastructure to cope with the bourgeoning enrollments and increased needs of larger and more diverse student bodies.

The movement toward access that had begun in the late 1940s and continued throughout the 1950s included the civil rights movement, which created postsecondary opportunities that had not previously been widely available for African Americans and other racial and ethnic minority groups. Attempts to promote access and diversity on college campuses led to many challenges, some of which were directly associated with the retention of students. Many campuses were unprepared to deal with a more diverse student body, and many were unable or unwilling to create supportive environments for students of color. Additionally, many students from underrepresented minority groups that were now allowed greater access to higher education had not been provided adequate educational preparation, given the inequities in school systems throughout America. As a result, retention rates were quite low for minority students.

Lack of preparation was not limited to students of color. On campus, the composition of the student body was changing. The great expansion of the 1950s permitted greater access to higher education for all students. State and federal funding allowed more middle and lower class students to attend. The economy forced changes in the curriculum to prepare students for jobs and careers. Pressures arose to get good grades so that one could continue to advanced degrees in professions such as law. During this time students began to move from learning as the primary goal of their education to making the grades that would help them in their future. This thinking was unsettling to many on campus, and students expressed their dissatisfaction with the new direction of the curricula. Students protested and demanded a return to "intellectual challenge, flexibility, and the recognition of individuality" (Horowitz 1987).

In general, higher education was changing so rapidly at this time that many students and institutions were not adequately prepared to improve access to degree attainment. Many students were now enrolling in colleges with educational backgrounds that had not prepared them for the academic expectations and social norms of college. At the same time, many institutions were unprepared and lacking knowledge about how best to meet the needs of a more diverse student body.

Student dissatisfaction with the political and functional aspects of campus life grew as the higher education enterprise expanded in size and scope throughout the 1960s. This decade was a period of change for higher education, marked with student unrest. It was an era which brought with it increased student activism and campus rebellion. Many simultaneous events during this time caused dissention, beginning with the civil rights movement and culminating with the Vietnam war. This era stands out because unlike at any other time of student dissention, the student movement in this era involved radical tactics such as sit-ins, strikes, and protests. These events coincided with growing recognition that student satisfaction with and departure from college was more complicated than a simple matter of academic fit and success. The early 1960s focused on individual characteristics associated with academic failure, but the latter part of the decade saw some initial efforts to understand the role that affective characteristics and social contexts played in student departure. This was in response to growing concerns about college completion and given growing recognition of the impact of greater student diversity.

While individual campuses had begun to regularly monitor enrollments in the 1950s, there had only been limited attempts to systematically assess patterns of student persistence. Mostly psychological approaches were used in any studies that attempted to do more than report existing patters of departure or look at demographic characteristics as sources of variation in departure patterns. Many of these early research studies on college student departure were conducted through the psychological lens (Summerskill 1962) which focused on the personality attributes (maturity, motivation, disposition) of students as the main reasons for persistence or nonpersistence.

Spady (1971) notes that there were six major types of studies—philosophical, census, autopsy, case, descriptive, and predictive—most of which were conducted at the tail end of the 1950s and throughout the 1960s. Philosophical studies (also known as theoretical studies) were usually built on assumptions that dropout from college should be prevented, and consisted of recommendations for preventing this type of attrition. Census studies attempted to describe the extent of attrition, dropout, and transfer rates within and across institutions. Autopsy studies provided self-reported data regarding the reasons students left college. Case studies generally tracked students identified as at-risk upon entry to see what led to their success or failure to graduate from college. Descriptive approaches provided overviews of the characteristics of dropout students and their experiences. Finally, predictive studies attempted to identify admissions criteria that could be used to generate forecasts about the potential for students to succeed in college. Despite all of these studies, Spady noted an absence of what he called analytical-exploratory studies that synthesized existing knowledge in order to systematically develop a coherent body of empirically based knowledge that could better inform efforts to understand and improve undergraduate retention. As we shall see in the next section, Spady's initial model and his call for this type of knowledge development was the beginning of an ongoing movement in which retention would become a major focus of theory, research, policy, and practice throughout American higher education.

Spady's (1971) model emphasized the interaction between individual student characteristics and key aspects of the campus environment. Moreover, this model was derived from existing empirical evidence and designed to be a conceptual framework for developing a more coherent understanding of the student departure process. Spady's work was notable for several reasons. First, it was the first attempt to synthesize existing empirical work into a cohesive conceptual framework. Second, most of the previous studies had been grounded in psychology rather than sociology. Third, it served as a precursor to Tinto's model that would soon become "near-paradigmatic" (Braxton, Sullivan, & Johnson 1997) in the study of research.

Spady's (1971) contribution was made possible by an emerging body of work that provided him with the evidence that served as the foundations for his observations and synthesis. In fact, earlier attempts (e.g., Knoell 1966; Marsh 1966) to synthesize early dropout studies were acknowledged precursors to Spady's work. Additionally, by the late 1960s a few large-scale studies (e.g., Panos & Astin 1967; Bayer 1968; Trent & Medsker 1965) had emerged and had begun a shift toward a more comprehensive and systematic examination of college withdrawal and persistence. These studies were either largely atheoretical or focused primarily on demographic and psychological characteristics, however. While these studies improved on the body of single institution studies that had begun to be conducted on campuses in the 1950s, they contained little emphasis on the interaction of student and campus characteristics and included no real attempt to collectively build knowledge on attrition and retention in a systematic manner.

## Building Theory (1970s)

By 1970, retention had become an increasingly common topic within and among college and university campuses. The concerns about student dropout and satisfaction became increasingly crystallized throughout the 1960s, and the 1970s dawned with greater efforts to systematically identify causes and solutions to the challenge of retention. Enough studies and reports were published at this time so that researchers could begin to construct a knowledge base to inform retention concerns and issues throughout most of higher education.

In many ways, this era really begins with the publication of William Spady's seminal article, "Dropouts from Higher Education: An Interdisciplinary Review and Synthesis" (1971). In this article Spady reviews the empirical literature that had been expanding throughout the 1960s on the dropout process asking for future research to focus on the interaction between student attributes and the university environment. Spady's sociological model of student departure begins to explain the process as an interaction between the student and the college environment. Throughout this interaction a student's attributes (values, interests, skills, attitudes, etc.) are exposed to norms of an environment (faculty, peers, administrators). If the student and the environment are congruent in their norms, the student will assimilate both socially and academically, increasing the likelihood of persistence.

Not long after, Vincent Tinto built upon and enhanced Spady's model with other emerging sources of evidence about the nature of the student departure process. Tinto's interactionalist theory of student departure became one of the best known, and most often cited, theories relating to student departure. In its basic form, Tinto's interactionalist theory incorporates elements of both the psychological and organizational theoretical models. It purports that a student's entry characteristics coupled with the student's initial commitment to the institution and commitment to graduation influence student departure decisions. The theory also suggests that early and continued institutional commitment will impact both academic and social integration within the university, both important factors in college student retention (Tinto 1975, 1993).

Another early sociological perspective comes from the work of David Kamens (1971, 1974). Kamens (1971) uses multi-institutional data to demonstrate how institutions with greater size and complexity, coupled with a superior capacity to place graduates in prestigious social and occupational roles, have lower rates of attrition than do other types of post-secondary institutions. Kamens provides an open systems view of organizational behavior in higher education and emphasizes how colleges and universities with highly institutionalized social charters (Meyer 1970) are able to use their elevated role in the field of higher education to enact a stronger influence on student persistence. In a later work, Kamens (1974) introduces elements of the symbolic dimension as he demonstrates how the use of legitimized myths in postsecondary institutional settings helps to reinforce the social charter of an institution, thereby strengthening the ability of an institution to retain students.

Alexander Astin and his colleagues at UCLA had also been studying retention since the late 1960s using large national databases collected from hundreds of colleges. Astin concluded from extensive analysis of these data that involvement was the key to retention. Simply put, the more students were involved in their academic endeavors and in college life, the more likely they were to be retained. Astin (1977, 1985) suggested that the amount of physical and psychological energy that a student invests in the collegiate experience (both social and academic) directly influenced departure decisions. The simplicity of this model made it easy to use, and it served as the basis for many retention interventions on campuses throughout the country.

By the end of the 1970s, theory was well established, and Tinto's work in particular was driving a more rigorous and systematic examination of retention. Numerous empirical studies, mostly conducted by Ernest Pascarella and Patrick Terenzini, developed operational measures of the core constructs from Tinto's models. This empirical work was a noteworthy contribution, because it provided a foundation of research that led to an explosion of studies and a more systematic understanding of retention. This developing knowledge base would become the basis for a wave of studies and more systematic approaches to studying retention in the following decade and beyond.

## Managing Enrollments (1980s)

The study of retention expanded rapidly in the 1980s. This expansion was fueled in part by the conceptual and empirical contributions to knowledge that had been made in the 1970s, but the practical realities of demographic shifts were the main drivers of sustained and expanding interest in retention. By the mid-1970s enrollments in higher education had exceeded 11 million; however, this growth was becoming stagnant. The anticipation of a leveling off of the supply of students led campus leaders at colleges and universities to further explore better ways for attracting and retaining students on their campuses. Previously, only limited connections had been made between efforts to recruit and enroll new students through the admissions process and efforts to retain those students once they were successfully enrolled. This separation between admissions and retention changed rapidly after the mid-1970s as campuses became increasingly aware that the enrollment boom of the previous few decades was about over.

In an effort to more effectively maintain optimally sized student bodies, in terms of both quantity and quality, the concept of enrollment management was born. The roots of enrollment management had begun in the early 1970s, but the first known use of the term came in 1976 when Jack Maguire, the dean of enrollment at Boston College, began disseminating information about efforts on his campus to align the admissions, financial aid, registration, and institutional research areas in order to better control enrollment. Maguire used the term *enrollment management* (Hossler 2002), and the concept spread rapidly, gradually becoming institutionalized throughout the American higher education system.

More specifically, enrollment management can be defined as

> both an organizational concept as well as a systematic set of activities designed to enable educational institutions to exert more influence over their student enrollments. This is accomplished by the use of institutional research in the areas of student college choice, student attrition, and student outcomes to guide institutional practices in the areas of new student recruitment and financial aid, student support services, as well as curriculum development and other academic areas which affect the enrollment and persistence of students. (Hossler 1988)

Although the term *enrollment management* is a critical concept and is formal in definition and theory, colleges and universities have implemented its practice to varying degrees. The enrollment management classifications typically employed by universities fall into one of the following four categories: the enrollment management committee, the enrollment management coordinator, the enrollment management matrix, and the enrollment management division. Each of these categories gets progressively more formal in terms of structure, authority, and effectiveness (Kemerer, Baldridge, & Green 1982). The enrollment management committee is often a university's first attempt to integrate enrollment management. The committee is typically made up of faculty members and midlevel administrators. While the committee is a first step, many members are not intimately familiar with the enrollment process, turnover inhibits any true accomplishments of the group, and there is no formal authority to enact changes in policy. The appointment of an enrollment management coordinator can be effective if the person appointed is well networked and well regarded among leadership in the university. As with the committee, the coordinator has no formal authority or impact on policy, so connections are critical if this position is to effect change. Under the enrollment management matrix, a senior-level vice president brings together key players from admissions, financial aid, and career planning on a regular basis. This model has many advantages, including authority of the senior-level manager to impact change as well as ongoing and increased dialogue between key offices. The implementation of an enrollment management division is the most formal and centralized system. Under this system the major departments that impact enrollment management report to one senior manager. This organizational structure affords the greatest impact for change because the person in charge has authority and is able to address issues from a systems perspective (Kemerer et al. 1982).

While the emergence of enrollment management dominated the practice of retention at this time, advances in the study of retention were being built on the successful contributions of the previous decade. For example, Bean (1980, 1983) offered a new theoretical perspective on retention that used concepts adapted from organizational studies of worker turnover (Price & Mueller 1981) that were helpful in explaining student departure and that were subsequently used in other studies of undergraduate persistence (Braxton & Brier 1989; Berger & Braxton 1998). Bean's (1980, 1983) model examines how organizational attributes and reward structures affect student satisfaction and persistence, and studies using this model have found that student perceptions of organizational routinization, participation, communication, and rewards influence levels of student satisfaction, which in turn affect student persistence.

By the end of the 1980s a number of models and theories had become well established in the literature, and a substantial body of empirical studies had been conducted across a wide range of institutional settings. This continually developing body of work provided a foundation for a new generation of models and studies in the 1980s and 1990s. These new models and studies elaborated on and integrated theories and concepts from various existing frameworks and studies. Scholars have elaborated on Tinto's theory from a number of different perspectives (Braxton et al. 1997), including psychological, environmental, economic, and organizational. These attempts to elaborate on Tinto's theory provide evidence that Tinto's model, as initially conceptualized, benefited from the addition of constructs from other theoretical perspectives that improve the explanatory power of the model and provide information about sources of social and academic integration for undergraduate students.

The spread of knowledge through increased writing and research was being matched by increased communication across campuses, and major associations concerned with admissions and student life began to feature retention as an important theme at regional and national conferences. The expanding knowledge base provided a stronger basis for professionals on campuses who were concerned with retention and enrollment management to be more intentional about their efforts to improve retention. The development of a variety of campus-based initiatives in turn provided campus professionals with a wealth of strategies and interventions that could be shared across campuses as part of a national dialogue. The study and practice of retention had grown into a topic of national attention. The emergence of a wider variety of more specific programs also created a growing body of literature on the evaluation of the effectiveness of these efforts. As a result, in addition to the growth in theory-driven studies, more research was being published about the wide variety of campus-based practices being implemented on campuses across the country.

At the same time, retention was becoming increasingly diversified in terms of the types of students who were applying to college, the types of institutions that were concerned with retention, and the types of students that campuses were trying to retain. More studies were being conducted on and campus-based strategies were being implemented for different types of students from varying racial and ethnic backgrounds, first-generation college students, and non-traditionally aged students. Retention was becoming a concern at a wider range of campuses, a trend that was coming to include community colleges to a greater extent than ever before. The concept of retention even moved into graduate student retention, after a long history of focusing only on the retention of undergraduates.

## Broadening Horizons (1990s)

The 1990s were a time of continued expansion of research, knowledge, and strategies that continued the trend in which retention had become a dynamic and full-fledged area of study and had become permanently established as an educational priority throughout American higher education. It was also a time at which retention as a field of study had become well enough established to begin taking stock of the vast amounts of knowledge that had been amassed through thousands of published and unpublished studies.

Although many future researchers studied retention using Tinto's interactional model, very little empirical evidence existed relating to the internal consistency of each of these propositions. To assess the internal consistency of Tinto's theoretical model, Braxton et al. (1997) empirically tested the model's fifteen propositions. Based on results of single-institution research studies, four propositions were found to be "logically interconnected." The four propositions are defined as (Braxton 2000):

1. Students bring to college different entry characteristics which will impact their initial commitment to the institution.
2. A student's initial commitment to the institution will impact the student's future commitment to the institution.
3. Students' continued commitment to the institution is enhanced by the level of *social integration* they realize early on.
4. The greater the level of commitment to the institution, the higher the likelihood of the student being retained through graduation.

These data suggest that social integration, not academic integration, is key to understanding student departure. Braxton et al. (1997) recommended that future researchers explore additional psychological, social, and organizational influences that impact both social integration and commitment (institution and graduation) as a way to improve upon Tinto's theory. Subsequent studies have begun to take on this challenge, and other studies have continued to search for other explanatory factors that might help solve the departure puzzle.

While the need for financial aid and the important role it played on campus had been well established in practice for years, the role of finances in retention was one area that began to receive more attention as a field of study in the 1990s. A series of earlier studies by Alberto Cabrera, Amaury Nora, Edward St. John, Michael Paulsen, and others laid the groundwork for increasing recognition that the ability to pay for college was increasingly important and the recognition of financial barriers was an essential part of studying ways to improve retention.

There was also a reemphasis on academics and student learning. It was increasingly recognized that greater emphasis needed to be placed not only on retention but also on student learning. Initiatives such as the Student Learning Imperative were developed by student affairs professionals to emphasize the centrality of learning as the primary goal of college. Many retention efforts reflected the renewed emphasis on student learning through the development of learning communities in which students who lived together also took classes together. These trends emphasized the overlap between involvement in the academic and social spheres of campus rather than focusing on them as separate sources of influence on retention.

Greater attention was also being paid to student diversity and the challenges of retaining students of color and students from disadvantaged backgrounds. Many critiques emerged about the dominant cultures on predominantly White campuses that created additional challenges for students of color and others to succeed. Some of these same critiques questioned much of the theory base that had been developed on assumptions that students must adopt the values and norms of a particular campus in order to succeed. Laura Rendon and others developed alternative models focusing on ways in which college campuses could validate the experiences and knowledge of students of color as an effective means for improving the retention and academic success for students of color who had traditionally been marginalized in mainstream higher education.

The 1990s might also be called the era of the emergence of "persistence." Recognition that persistence and retention are distinct concepts began to fully emerge in the late 1990s. More and more, scholars and practitioners had begun to realize that while retention is an important concept for many students and for campuses themselves, many students attend more than one college to earn an undergraduate degree. Increasingly, student success has been recognized as the ability to persist to the completion of a degree at one or more colleges.

## Current and Future Trends (Early Twenty-First Century)

The early twenty-first century has dawned with retention fully entrenched as a major policy issue and a well-established professional realm that has brought researchers and practitioners together in widespread efforts to better serve and retain college students throughout the country. Retention efforts are well established on virtually every campus in the nation, retention is used as a key indicator of institutional effectiveness, there are literally thousands of studies on this topic, and the field has even recently developed its own academic journal, the *Journal of College Student Retention: Research, Theory & Practice*, devoted solely to this important topic.

Yet, there are many unresolved issues. Retention rates remain lower than most campus officials would like on most campuses across the country. A report by American College Testing states that nationwide 25.9 percent of freshmen at four-year institutions do not return to school the following year. At highly selective institutions the dropout rate is 8 percent, and at less selective institutions it is as high as 35 percent. At open-enrollment institutions, the departure rate is nearly 50 percent (Devarics & Roach 2000). These numbers indicate that better knowledge is still needed and that much work remains to be accomplished on college campuses throughout the nation. The numbers are worse when one considers the retention rates for students from underrepresented minority groups, first-generation backgrounds, and lower socioeconomic backgrounds. Efforts to improve these patterns are essential to the success of individual students and campuses. As higher education becomes increasingly important for success in a society that has become knowledge- and technology-oriented, retention and persistence are more important than ever. The large number of studies and initiatives developed over the past few decades are a strong foundation for furthering this important work.

The increasing trend toward accountability in higher education also has important implications for the future of retention. The past fifteen years have seen accountability become a more important mandate in higher education. Retention rates have been mandated as a core indicator by accrediting agencies for some time, but most states now review the retention rates of public institutions, and some states even tie resource allocations to such indicators. On a related note, most national rankings, such as the U.S. News & World Report and others, use retention numbers to help rank institutions. These rankings are increasingly serving as a source of information to guide families in choosing colleges for their children, creating a consumer-driven form of accountability. These trends appear to be here to stay, and they make paying attention to retention more important than ever. The continued increase of competition for resources in higher education will make retention even more important in the future.

New issues continue to arise. The emergence of distance learning and alternative modes of instructional delivery provide new opportunities and new challenges for promoting access to higher education and opportunities for degree attainment. However, there are many concerns about how these new instructional strategies impact retention. Thus far, most studies have focused on retention within distance-learning courses. More research is needed on how online learning impacts persistence toward a degree. This will become increasingly important as online learning continues to grow in traditional and nontraditional sectors of higher education.

In conclusion, retention has evolved over time. While little attention was paid to retention for much of the first few hundred years of American higher education, the study of retention has developed over the last thirty-five years at a rapid pace. Retention has become one of the core indicators and main fields of study within higher education. As higher education and earning a college degree have become more important in society, retention has become more important in higher education. A review of the history of retention clearly indicates that we should expect that the more we study and learn about the retention, the more we will recognize the complexities involved in helping the diverse array of students succeed in our equally diverse system of higher education. The future of retention promises to be as important and dynamic as its past.

## REFERENCES

Astin, A. W. (1977). *Four critical years.* San Francisco: Jossey-Bass.

———. (1985). *Achieving academic excellence.* San Francisco: Jossey-Bass.

———. (1990). *Assessment for excellence: The philosophy and practice of assessment and evaluation in higher education.* New York: Macmillan.

———. (1997). *What matters in college: Four critical years revisited.* San Francisco: Jossey-Bass.

Bayer, A. (1968). The college dropout: Factors affecting senior college completion. *Sociology of Education* 41: 305–316.

Bean, J. (1980). Dropouts and turnover: The synthesis and test of a causal model of student attrition. *Research in Higher Education* 12: 155–187.

———. (1983). The application of a model of turnover in work organizations to the student attrition process. *Review of Higher Education* 6: 129–148.

Berger, J. B. (2000a). Optimizing capital, social reproduction, and undergraduate persistence: A sociological perspective. In *Rethinking the departure puzzle: New theory and research on student retention,* ed. J. M. Braxton, 95–126. Nashville: Vanderbilt University Press.

———. (2000b). Organizational behavior at colleges and student outcomes: A new perspective on college impact. *Review of Higher Education* 23(1): 61–83.

———. (2002). Understanding the organizational nature of student persistence: Empirically-based recommendations for practice. *Journal of College Student Retention* 3(1): 3–21.

Berger, J. B., & Braxton, J. M. (1998). Revising Tinto's interactionalist theory of student departure through theory elaboration: Examining the role of organizational attributes in the persistence process. *Research in Higher Education* 39(2): 103–120.

Berger, J. B., & Milem, J. F. (1999). The role of student involvement and perceptions of integration in a causal model of student persistence. *Research in Higher Education* 40(6): 641–664.

Braxton, J. M., ed. (2000). *Reworking the student departure puzzle.* Nashville, TN: Vanderbilt University Press.

Braxton, J. M., & Brier, E. M. (1989). Melding organizational and interactional theories of student attrition: A path analytic study. *Review of Higher Education* 13(1): 47–61.

Braxton, J. M., & Mundy, M. E. (2002). Powerful institutional levers to reduce college student departure. *Journal of College Student Retention* 3(1): 91–118.

Braxton, J. M., Sullivan, A. S., & Johnson, R. (1997). Appraising Tinto's theory of college student departure. In *Higher education: Handbook of theory and research*, Vol. 12, ed. J. S. Smart, 107–164. New York: Agathon.

Demitroff, J. F. (1974). Student persistence. *College and University* 49: 553–557.

Devarics, C., & Roach, R. (2000). Fortifying the federal presence in retention. *Black Issues in Higher Education* 17(3): 20–25.

Feldman, K. A., and Newcomb, T. M. (1969). *The impact of college on students*. San Francisco: Jossey-Bass.

Geiger, R. (1999). *American higher education in the twenty-first century: Social, political and economic challenges*, ed. Altbach, Berdahl, & Gumport, 38–65. Baltimore: Johns Hopkins University Press.

Gekowski, N., & Schwartz, S. (1961). Student mortality and related factors. *Journal of Educational Research* 54: 192–194.

Goodchild, L. F. (1999). Transformations of the American college idea: Six historic ways of learning. *New Directions for Higher Education* 27(1): 7–23.

Horowitz, H. L. (1987). *Campus life: Undergraduate cultures from the end of the eighteenth century to the present*. New York: Random House.

Hossler, D. (1988). Admissions and enrollment management. In *Student affairs functions in higher education*, ed. A. L. Rentz & G. L. Saddlemire, 41–67. Springfield, IL: Charles C. Thomas.

———. (2002). Enrollment management. In *Higher education in the United States: An encyclopedia, volume 1*, ed. J.J.F. Forest & K. Kinser, Santa Barbara, CA: ABC-CLIO.

Iffert, R. E. (1957). *Retention and withdrawal of college students*. U.S. Office of Education, Bulletin 1957, no. 1. Washington, DC: U.S. Government Printing Office.

Kamens, D. H. (1971). The college "charter" and college size: Effects on occupational choice and college attrition. *Sociology of Education* 44 (Summer): 270–296.

———. (1974). Colleges and elite formation: The case of prestigious American Colleges. *Sociology of Education* 47 (Summer): 354–378.

Kemerer, F. R., Baldridge, J. V., & Green, K. C. (1982). *Strategies for effective enrollment management*. Washington, DC: American Association of State Colleges and Universities.

Knoell, D. M. (1966). A critical review of research on the college dropout. In *The college dropout and utilization of talent*, ed. L. A. Pervin, L. E. Reik, & W. Dalrymple, 63–81. Princeton: Princeton University Press.

Library of Congress. (1975). The charter of the president and fellows of Harvard College.

Marsh, L. M. (1966). College dropout: A review. *Personnel and Guidance Journal* 44: 475–481.

McNeely, J. H. (1937). *College student mortality*. U.S. Office of Education, Bulletin 1937, no. 11. Washington, DC: U.S. Government Printing Office.

Meyer, J. W. (1970). The charter: Conditions of diffuse socialization in schools. In *Social Processes and Social Structure: An Introduction to Sociology*, ed. W. R. Scott. New York: Henry Holt.

Milem, J. F., & Berger, J. B. (1997). A modified model of college student persistence: The relationship between Astin's theory of involvement and Tinto's theory of student departure. *Journal of College Student Development* 38(4): 387–400.

Panos, R. J., & Astin, A. W. (1967). Attrition among college students. *ACE Research Reports* 2(4).

Pantages, T. J., & Creedon, C. F. (1978). Studies of college attrition: 1950–1975. *Review of Educational Research* 48(1): 49–101.

Price, J. L., & Mueller, C. W. (1981). A causal model of turnover for nurses. *Academy of Management Journal* 24: 543–565.

Rudolph, F. (1990). *The American college and university: A history*. Athens: University of Georgia Press.

Sexton, V. S. (1965). Factors contributing to attrition in college populations: Twenty-five years of research. *Journal of General Psychology* 72: 301–326.

Spady, W. (1971). Dropouts from higher education: An interdisciplinary review and synthesis. *Interchange* 1: 64–85.

Summerskill, J. (1962). In *The American college*, ed. N. Sanford, 627–657. New York: Wiley.

Tinto, V. (1975). Dropouts from higher education: A theoretical synthesis of recent research. *Review of Educational Research* 45: 89–125.

———. (1990). Principles of effective retention. *Journal of the Freshman Year Experience* 2 (1): 35–48.

———. (1993). *Leaving college: Rethinking the causes and cures of student attrition*. Chicago: University of Chicago Press.

Trent, J. W., & Medsker, L. L. (1965). *Beyond high school*. San Francisco: Jossey-Bass.

# CHAPTER 2

# Measurements of Persistence

*Thomas G. Mortenson*

## INTRODUCTION

Voluntary school or college enrollment is not capricious. Students (or their parents) must consciously act to maintain their status in education, as it gets ever more costly to do so. Because of these costs, those who choose voluntary school or college enrollment must see school enrollment benefits outweighing these costs to persist in the educational system. This student-initiated decision is persistence, or from the institutional perspective, this is retention. It is measured through a series of status-to-status ratios. These may be called transition ratios, persistence rates, retention rates, completion rates, cohort survival rates, or graduation rates. They may also be used to measure dropout rates, transfer rates, and other measures of change in student status. These data are gathered to assess educational performance. How well are students moving through the education pipeline? Who is doing well and who else is doing poorly? Are students persisting longer? Where does student persistence need to be improved?

To answer these questions, data are gathered on the enrollment status of specific groups of students at successive points in time. Educational progress, or lack thereof, is noted. This persistence measurement activity is essential to understanding the progress of groups of students in the education pipeline. Cohorts of students are tracked from one status through transition to the next status level. The resulting rates describe the proportion of the original cohort reaching whatever the future status point happens to be, typically the next year or level of school or graduation.

The measurement of student persistence in education is complicated by the many ways students move through the education pipeline in the United States. Quite likely very few or none of the millions of voluntarily enrolled postsecondary students pursue education in exactly the same way. Thus the measurement systems struggle to define and count student progress in ways that provide useful information to users. Among the major persistence or retention measurement problems are student transfers between institutions, student progression at different rates, and stopouts.

Users are also likely to have their own particular uses for persistence data such as:

- Institutional users are most likely to be interested in institutional retention and graduation rates. How well have admitted cohorts of students succeeded in their institutions? Have rates increased or decreased? How well does one institution compare to peer institutions?

- State users may be more interested in data accumulated to the state level. For instance, how many of those who start high school or college eventually graduate? Inter-institutional transfers may be irrelevant at the state level, although they reduce institutional graduation rates. Can persistence rates be used to project high school enrollment? High school graduates? College freshmen? College graduates?

- Users at the national level may be indifferent to institutional and state persistence and may be satisfied with gross measures of high school and college graduation and attainment.

- Most users will be interested in population disaggregation by race or ethnicity, geography, gender, family income, and other demographic characteristics as well.

- All users should be interested in population disaggregation by academic characteristics of students, for example, high school grades and class rank and other measures of academic preparation, ACT or SAT test scores, credit loads, and others.

- In experiments, data users are likely to want to control for institutional interventions believed to influence persistence, such as where and with whom a student lives and what academic support services are used.

Here we follow students through the education pipeline along baselines of time and age to observe and measure their progress and persistence behaviors. There are a very few simple but essential guidelines to follow, and we begin with these concepts and definitions.

## KEY TERMS

The three foundations for the measurement of student persistence are definitions for cohorts, denominators, and numerators.

*Cohorts*. Persistence measurement begins with the careful identification of a clearly defined group or cohort of students at one point in time and place and with specific demographic and enrollment characteristics. Examples might be all ninth-grade students in a particular high school in the fall of a particular year, or all Black male first-time, full-time degree-seeking freshmen beginning college at a particular institution in a particular term.

Because persistence and graduation rates are often descriptive and comparative, defining cohorts is especially important. Among the demographic cohort descriptors are gender, race or ethnicity, age, and geographic location (state, county). Academic descriptors might include year of matriculation, academic (high school grades, class rank, ACT or SAT test scores), credits accumulated, and college GPA.

*Denominators*. The identification of a cohort of a certain number of students in time and place and with specific demographic and enrollment characteristics fixes the denominator of whatever rate is being studied.

It is important that this number remain fixed in subsequent use. The most egregious misuses of persistence and graduation rates occur when this number is subsequently revised (always reduced) to adjust for some student enrollment behaviors, such as student transfers out of the school, institution, or system being monitored. Doing so amounts to manipulating the data to inflate and overstate results. These discredited adjustments have consequences when exposed.

*Numerators*. As the original cohort is tracked over time, the numbers shrink. All students eventually drop out, stop out, transfer, die, or graduate, or in some way leave the original group. This attrition occurs over time. The measurement of the survivors at subsequent points in time provides the numerator for the persistence, retention, or graduation rate. While the primary objective of the data collection is to measure these rates for cohort survivors, in fact, collecting data on departures may be more important than is collecting data on persisters, particularly if these data are gathered to measure educational performance and success with an eye toward improvement.

**Figure 2.1**
**School Enrollment Rates for Age 3 to 65 and Over, 2002**

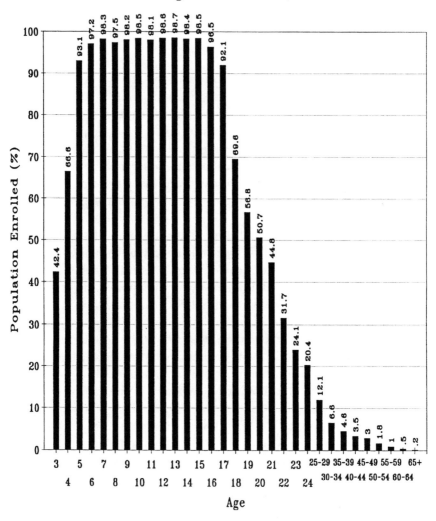

Source: U.S. Census Bureau.

## HIGH SCHOOL PERSISTENCE AND GRADUATION

In nearly all states, school enrollment is compulsory through a student's sixteenth birthday. Thereafter attendance is voluntary and attrition begins. Figure 2.1 shows the proportion of the U.S. civilian

**Figure 2.2**
**Various High School Graduation Rates, 1967–2000**

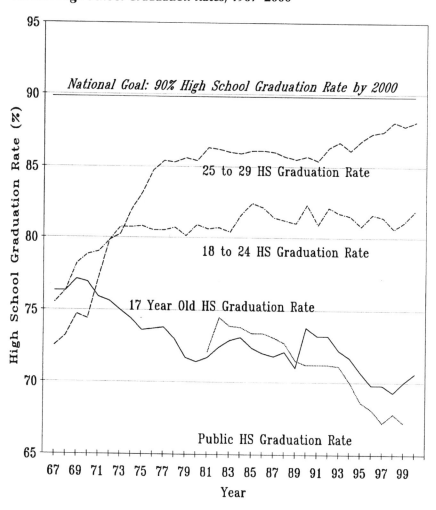

Sources: NCES and U.S. Census Bureau.

noninstitutional population enrolled in a formal school or college by age in 2002.

The measurement of high school student persistence and attrition is often badly understood because it is so poorly recorded and misleadingly reported. Figure 2.2 shows that high school graduation rates in the United States may be increasing, stable, or decreasing over the last thirty years depending on the data source used. The widely used Census Bureau data include as a graduate high school dropouts who completed a General Education Diploma (GED) test or other form of "equivalent" certification. This combined rate rises with age as young adults who did not complete high school and receive their diploma instead take and pass the GED test some time after leaving high school. The Census Bureau's reported high school graduate rate among 25- to 29-year-olds has risen, from 78 percent in 1970 to 88 percent by 2000.

If one looks at the high school graduation rate among 17-year-olds, however, this rate has declined from 77 percent in 1970 to about 71 percent by 2000. And the ratio of public high school regular diploma recipients to ninth graders four years earlier has declined from about 74 percent in 1982 to 67 percent by 1999.

One measurement problem is the shifting form of high school completion from persistence through twelfth grade, culminating in the award of a regular high school diploma to dropping out of high school and passing the GED test. But other problems are developing also. One of these is the shifting of reported data from high school graduation (with specific definition) to high school completion that may not include graduation (i.e., certificates of completion for those who do not complete course requirements for graduation, Individual Educational Program [IEP] diplomas). Another is home schooling, without graduation. A third results from immigration and the interpretation of foreign education credentials.

In 1982 the report *A Nation at Risk* recommended significantly strengthening the high school curriculum to prepare students for college and work. States then added significantly to high school graduation requirements. As states have added to public high school graduation requirements, the share of public high school ninth graders meeting these higher graduation standards has steadily declined.[1]

## COLLEGE FRESHMAN-TO-SOPHOMORE PERSISTENCE RATES

Student persistence and graduation in higher education are measured in two ways: *institutional* persistence and graduation, and *summary* persistence and graduation. The difference is the result of student "swirling," that is, enrollment in more than one institution between matriculation and graduation. The sum of institutional graduation rates, in particular, will be lower than summary graduation rates because of student transfers between institutions, and to some degree this affects persistence measurement as well.

**Figure 2.3**
**Freshman-to-Sophomore Persistence Rates at Public and Private Four-Year Institutions, 1983–2001**

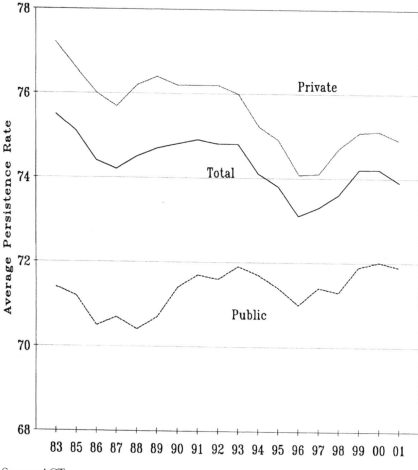

Source: ACT.

Freshman-to-sophomore persistence measurement is important both because of student vulnerability at the beginning of college and because institutions can react quickly with interventions. Figure 2.3 shows mean freshman-to-sophomore persistence rates for about 1,680 equally weighted four-year public and private colleges and universities since 1983 based on data collected by American College Testing (ACT). Institutional freshman-to-sophomore persistence rates have declined slightly

Figure 2.4
Freshman-to-Sophomore Persistence Rates at Public and Private Two-Year
Institutions, 1983–2001

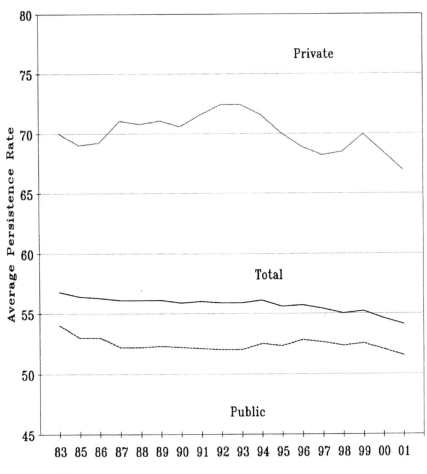

Source: ACT.

between 1983 and 2001. Figure 2.4 shows these data for about 850 public and private two-year colleges also using data collected by ACT.

Figures 2.3 and 2.4 also show that institutional persistence rates vary
by institutional control. Persistence is somewhat greater in private institutions than it is in public colleges and universities. Persistence rates also
vary between two-year and four-year institutions.

Of critical importance, institutional persistence rates also vary directly
with the academic selectivity of the institution. Institutions that prac-

**Figure 2.5**
**Freshman-to-Sophomore Persistence Rates by Admissions Selectivity at Four-Year Institutions, 2001**

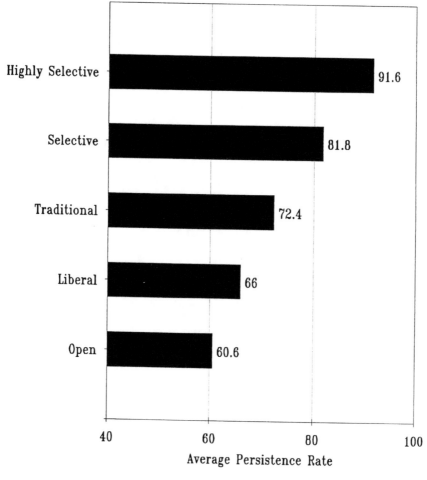

Source: ACT.

tice more selective admissions tend to have higher freshman-to-sophomore persistence rates than do colleges that practice less selective admissions. Students with the most successful academic records in high school are also most likely to be academically successful in college. And colleges that enroll these students are more likely to have higher persistence rates than do other colleges that are less academically selective in their admissions. Figure 2.5 shows average freshman-to-sophomore

**Figure 2.6**
**Change in Freshman-to-Sophomore Persistence Rates by Admissions Selectivity, 1991–2001**

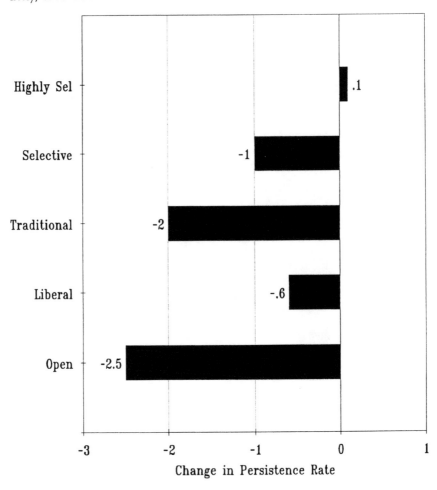

Source: ACT.

persistence rates at 1,680 public and private four-year colleges and universities in 2001 according to their admissions selectivity. In 2001, first-year to second-year persistence rates ranged from 60.6 percent at the open admissions institutions to 91.6 percent at the highly selective institutions. Figure 2.6 shows how these persistence rates have changed between 1991 and 2001.

As shown in Figure 2.7 private institutions generally have a small edge

**Figure 2.7**
**Freshman-to-Sophomore Persistence Rates by Admissions Selectivity and Control at Four-Year Institutions, 2001**

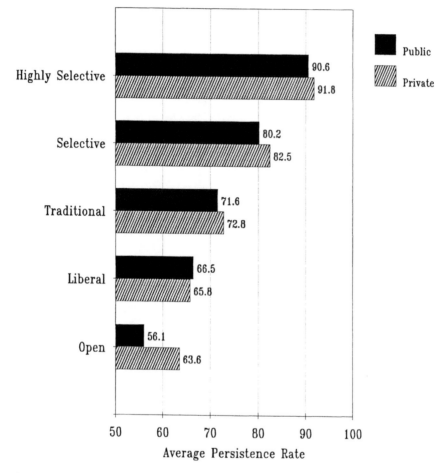

Source: ACT.

over public institutions in freshman-to-sophomore persistence rates when admissions selectivity is controlled. However, between 1991 and 2001 public colleges had some success increasing freshman persistence in highly selective, selective, and liberal admissions institutions. In private institutions, by contrast, persistence rates declined slightly at all levels of admissions selectivity as shown in Figure 2.8.

Over the last ten years of these data collected and reported by ACT, there have been changes in freshman-to-sophomore persistence rates

**Figure 2.8**
**Change in Freshman-to-Sophomore Persistence Rates by Academic Selec-
tivity and Control at Four-Year Institutions, 1991–2001**

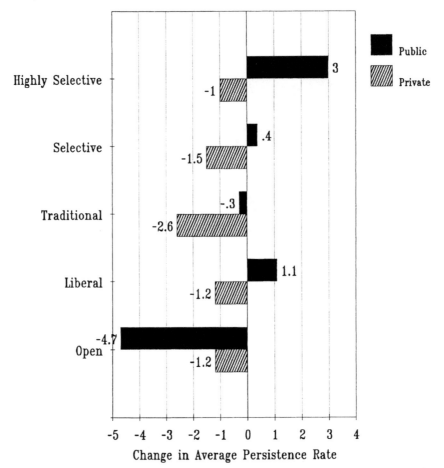

Source: ACT.

across levels of admissions selectivity. The most obvious finding in Figure 2.6 is that persistence rates have declined the most at the least selective institutions.

When political control and highest degree offered are added as controls, doctoral granting institutions have a slight edge over institutions
offering bachelor's or master's degrees as their highest degree offerings as
shown in Figures 2.9 and 2.10.

**Figure 2.9**
**Freshman-to-Sophomore Persistence Rates at Public Four-Year Institutions by Level and Selectivity, 2001**

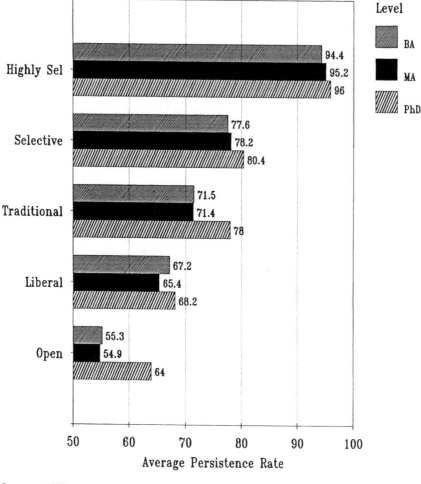

Source: ACT.

## BACHELOR'S DEGREE GRADUATION RATES

College graduation rates for those who start college may be decreasing or increasing, depending on the data set used. Or, if one uses the longest data set (from the Census Bureau), college graduation rates may be unchanged over the last fifty years. The answer depends on the data set referenced and the particular definitions associated with each data set.

**Figure 2.10**
**Freshman-to-Sophomore Persistence Rates at Private Four-Year Institutions by Level and Selectivity, 2001**

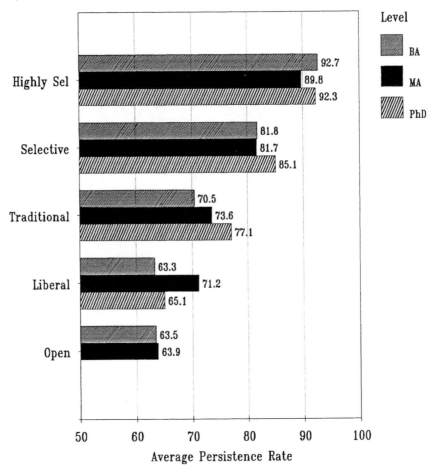

Source: ACT.

These data are particularly affected by lengthening time to degree and student enrollment at multiple institutions during their undergraduate careers. Figure 2.11 shows how three important data sets can yield conflicting results.

- The ACT data gathered from 1,450 public and private four-year colleges and universities show declining five-year institutional graduation rates, from 57.5 percent in 1983 to 51.6 percent by 2003.

**Figure 2.11**
**Bachelor's Degree Graduation Rates, 1983–2003**

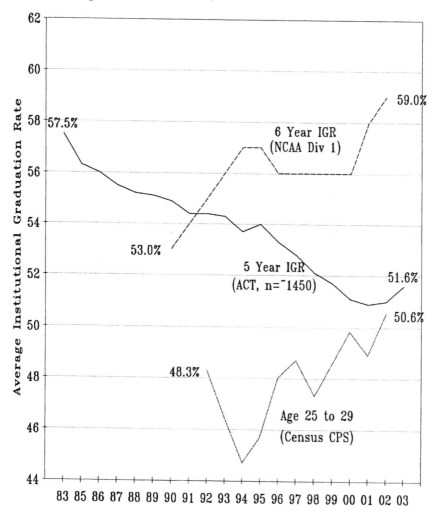

Sources: ACT; U.S. Census Bureau; National Collegiate Athletic Association.

- The National Collegiate Athletic Association (NCAA) data gathered from 327 Division I colleges and universities show six-year institutional graduation rates increasing from 53 percent in 1984 to 59 percent by 1996.
- The Census Bureau's data gathered from a national sample of about 60,000 households show a graduation rate increasing from 48.3 percent among 25- to 29-year-olds in 1992 to 50.6 percent by 2002.

**Figure 2.12**
**Bachelor's Degree Completion Rate by Age 25 to 29 for Those Who Have Entered College, 1947–2002**

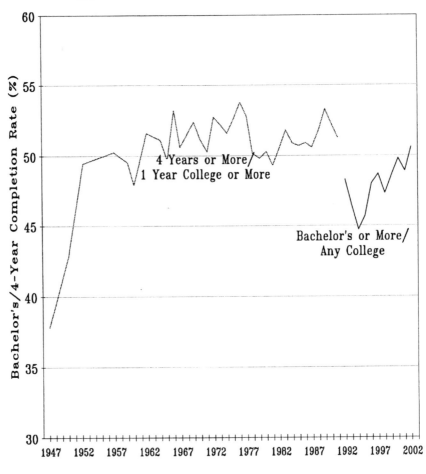

Source: U.S. Census Bureau.

Not only are the results different, but so too are the trends evident in these relatively short time spans. The NCAA and Census Bureau data show increasing graduation rates, while the ACT data show decreasing rates. When older Census Bureau data (with different data definitions) are used, the 2003 graduation rate of 50.6 percent is nearly identical to the 50.2 percent reported in 1957. This trend is flat as shown in Figure 2.12.

The details of these four different calculations explain some of the differences, although the explanations still fall short of a consistent and satisfactory answer. In these three widely used data sets there are differences in time frames, definitions, samples, methods of data collection, units of measure, and perhaps reliability of reported status data. The following list highlights these differences.

- The ACT data have been collected in an annual survey of about 1,680 public and private four-year colleges and universities since 1983. At that time a five-year graduation rate was requested from institutions, and for consistency ACT has continued to ask for five-year data. However, as time to degree completion has lengthened among undergraduates, this measure has been replaced elsewhere by the six-year graduation rate. Even that now falls short as a recent National Center for Educational Statistics (NCES) study reported that only about two-thirds of all bachelor's degrees were awarded by age 24.

- The NCAA data are gathered to assess the graduation of student athletes on financial assistance compared to other students of the same gender and race or ethnicity on the same campuses. These students are found most frequently at the 327 Division I institutions. Thus the student athlete data are useful only for the aided athletes. The real value is in the six-year graduation rate data for all undergraduates disaggregated by gender and race or ethnicity. The sample, of course, is limited to the 327 Division I institutions.

- The Census Bureau data are collected each March in the Current Population Survey. This is a sample of about 60,000 households and the reported data are limited to the civilian, noninstitutional population. The most useful reported data are on 25- to 29-year-olds, after most students have completed their bachelor's degrees. These data capture the transfers that started out in one institution and graduated from another and thus are lost to institutional graduation rates.

Each data set offers useful insights into college graduation rates although no individual data set provides all answers. The major advantages and disadvantages of each data set include the following:

- The unit of analysis for the ACT data is the institution. ACT gathers additional data on institutional characteristics for institutions that make its detailed reports especially valuable. In particular ACT's tabulation and reporting of average institutional graduation rates by admissions selectivity, highest degree offered, and control, along with standard deviations of cell means since 1983, make these reports unique. The major drawback to the current ACT report is five-year institutional graduation rates, something ACT has announced it will change.

- The NCAA data provide six-year graduation rates for students disaggregated by gender and race or ethnicity for thirteen years. The ACT data do not provide these breakdowns. These data, however, are limited to the 327 NCAA Division I institutions.

- The Census Bureau data, while based on a population sample, have the advantage of capturing students who start out at one institution but graduate from another.

The following figures illustrate some of the stories told about graduation rates in data reported by the Census Bureau for 25- to 29-year-olds. Unless noted otherwise (prior to 1992) these graduation rates are the ratio of those 25- to 29-year-olds with a bachelor's degree or higher from college divided by the number of 25- to 29-year-olds with any college experience at all.

Figure 2.13 shows bachelor's degree completion rates by race or ethnicity and gender. For all 25- to 29-year-olds, 50.6 percent of those with any college experience had completed a bachelor's degree in 2002. These rates ranged from 28.8 percent for Hispanics to 69.7 percent for Asian/Pacific Islanders. Completion rates are somewhat higher for females (51.7 percent) than for males (49.3 percent).

Figure 2.14 shows the associate degree–only completion rates by these same gender and racial or ethnic categories. For all 25- to 29-year-olds in 2002, 14.2 percent of those with any college experience had an associate's degree and no more from higher education. Completion rates ranged from 7.6 percent for Asian/Pacific Islanders to 19.5 percent for Hispanics, a flip-flop of the bachelor's degree range for these groups. Women were slightly more likely than men to report having completed an associate's degree.

Bachelor's degree completion rates by age in 2002 are shown in Figure 2.15. These rates peak quickly at age 25 to 29 years, although over time they might rise somewhat further as some adults in their 30s or older complete their bachelor's level educations. These data also suggest that about half of those who start college eventually complete a bachelor's degree.

Figures 2.16 through 2.22 show bachelor's and associate's degree completion rates overall, by gender, and by racial ethnic group for the years 1992 through 2002. This spans the years of the Census Bureau's most recent definition of educational attainment: highest degree completed divided by those with any college experience. (Prior to 1992 the Census Bureau reported four years or more of college divided by those with one

**Figure 2.13**
**Bachelor's or Higher Degree Completion by Age 25 to 29 for Those Who Have Entered College, 2002**

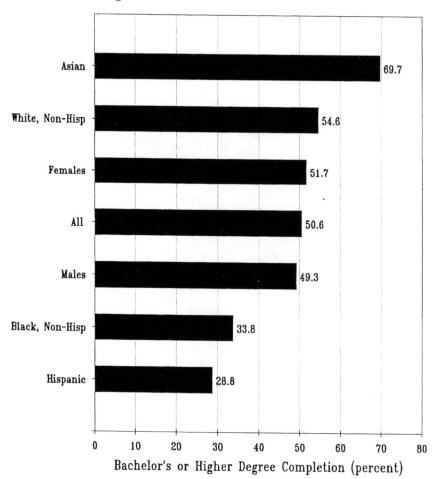

Source: U.S. Census Bureau.

year or more of college.) During this relatively short time span, bachelor's degree completion rates have tended upward (at least since 1994) for all groups except Hispanics. The picture is more mixed for associate's degree completion rates.

Finally, the bachelor's degree completion rates for each population subgroup may be compared to the rates for the population to create equity

**Figure 2.14**
**Associate's Degree Completion by Age 25 to 29 for Those Who Have Entered College, 2002**

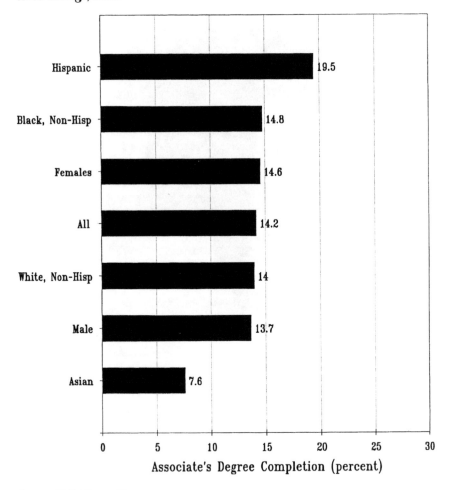

Associate's Degree Completion (percent)

Source: U.S. Census Bureau.

**Figure 2.15**
**Bachelor's or Higher Degree Completion by Age for Those Who Have Entered College, 2002**

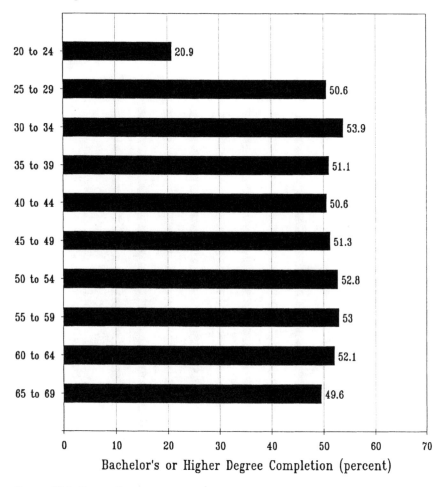

Bachelor's or Higher Degree Completion (percent)

Source: U.S. Census Bureau.

**Figure 2.16**
**Undergraduate Degree Completion by Age 25 to 29 for Those Entering College, 1992–2002**

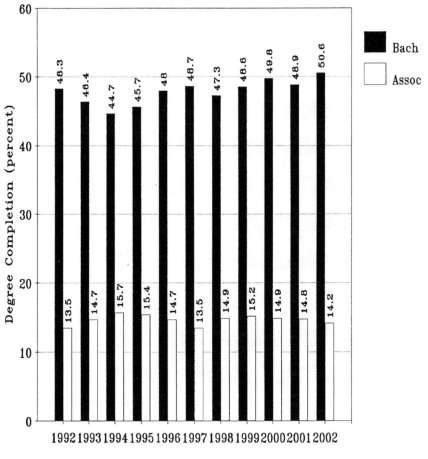

Source: U.S. Census Bureau.

**Figure 2.17**
**Undergraduate Degree Completion for Males by Age 25 to 29 for Those Entering College, 1992–2002**

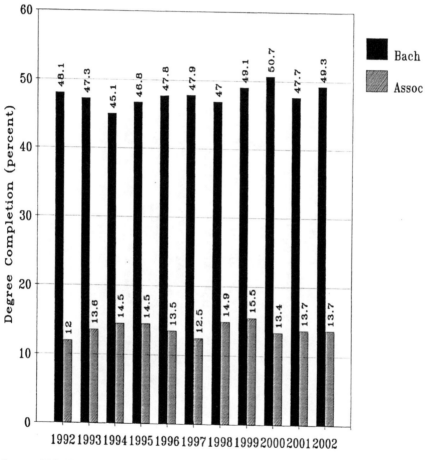

Source: U.S. Census Bureau.

**Figure 2.18**
**Undergraduate Degree Completion for Females by Age 25 to 29 for Those Entering College, 1992–2002**

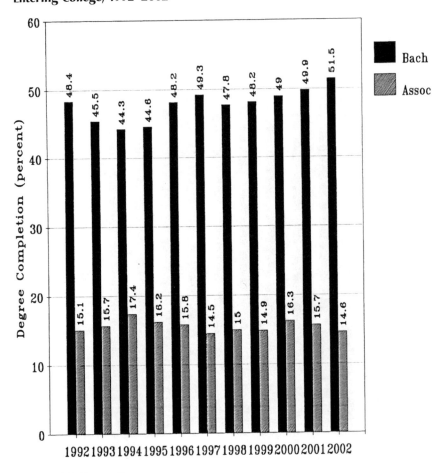

Source: U.S. Census Bureau.

**Figure 2.19**
**Undergraduate Degree Completion for White Non-Hispanics by Age 25 to 29 for Those Entering College, 1992–2002**

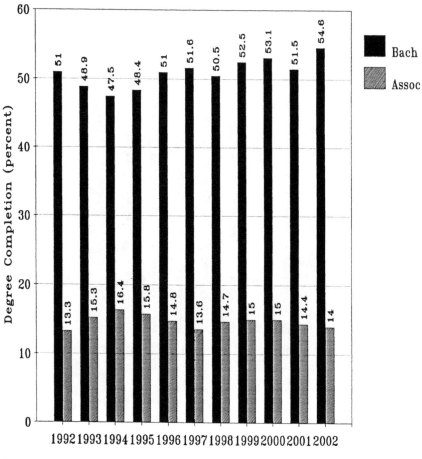

55

**Figure 2.20**
**Undergraduate Degree Completion for Black Non-Hispanics by Age 25 to 29 for Those Entering College, 1992–2002**

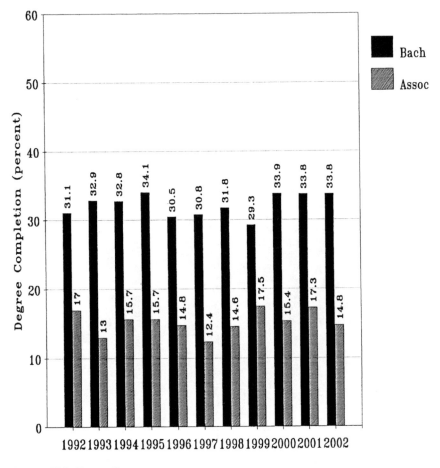

Source: U.S. Census Bureau.

indices. Figure 2.23 compares the bachelor's degree completion rate to the completion rate for the population for each year 1992 through 2002. Here trends over time are clarified:

- The bachelor's degree completion rates for some groups are improving relative to the group average between 1992 and 2002. These groups include Asian/Pacific Islanders, White non-Hispanics, females, and Black non-Hispanics.

**Figure 2.21**
**Undergraduate Degree Completion for Asian/Pacific Islanders by Age 25 to 29 for Those Entering College, 1992–2002**

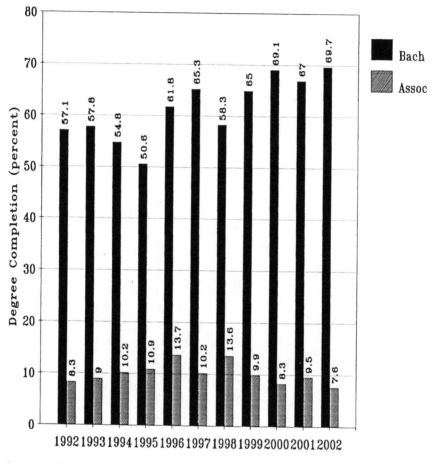

Source: U.S. Census Bureau.

- For other groups, however, relative completion rates have deteriorated. These groups include males and Hispanics.

These data tell important stories about what is happening to students as they move through the education pipeline toward adulthood and independence. Definably distinct groups of students move at different rates. These data do not explain why, just that there are differences across time and between groups of students in the education pipeline.

**Figure 2.22**
**Undergraduate Degree Completion for Hispanics by Age 25 to 29 for Those Entering College, 1992–2002**

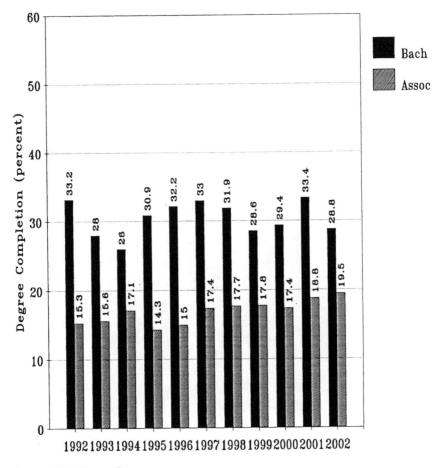

Source: U.S. Census Bureau.

These data must be used with caution as illustrated twice here. Different data can correctly say that a retention or graduation rate is moving up, is moving down, or remains flat. Differently defined data will inevitably produce different results. Data definitions and limitations must be carefully understood before findings are reported, conclusions are drawn, and recommendations are made.

**Figure 2.23**
**Bachelor's Degree Completion Equity Indices by Gender and Race or Ethnicity, 1992–2002**

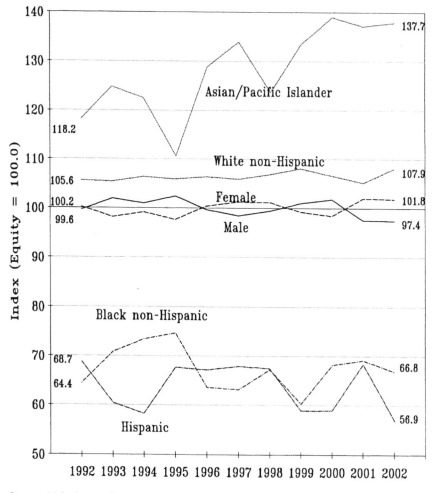

Source: U.S. Census Bureau.

## CONCLUSION

The school enrollment statistics from the Current Population Survey are based on replies to the interviewer's inquiry whether the person was enrolled in a regular school. Interviewers were instructed to count as enrolled anyone who had been enrolled at any time during the current term or school year in any type of public, parochial, or other private school in the regular school system. Such schools include nursery schools, kindergartens, elementary schools, high schools, colleges, universities, and professional schools. Attendance may be on either a full-time or part-time basis and during the day or night. *Regular schooling is that which may advance a person toward an elementary or high school diploma or a college, university, or professional school degree.* Children enrolled in nursery schools and kindergartens are included in the enrollment figures for regular schools and are also shown separately. Enrollment in schools that are not in the regular school system, such as trade schools, business colleges, and schools for the mentally handicapped, which do not advance students to regular school degrees, are not included. People enrolled in classes that do not require physical presence in school, such as correspondence courses or other courses of independent study, and in training courses given directly on the job are also excluded from the count of those enrolled in school, unless such courses are being counted for credit at a regular school. It is not surprising, therefore, that retention figures can vary depending upon which data set is used and the retention definition used.

## NOTE

1. For recent studies and tabulations on high school graduation rates for the United States and individual states, see the following:

*Census Bureau.* The Census Bureau includes GED as high school graduates. Data collected in the October *Current Population Survey* and available at http://www. census.gov/population/www/socdemo/educ-attn.html and http://www.census. gov/population/www/socdemo/school.html.

*Postsecondary Education OPPORTUNITY.* Using data collected by the National Center for Education Statistics on public school graded enrollment and regular high school graduates. Divides regular high school diplomas by ninth graders four years earlier. Available at http://www.postsecondary.org/archives/Reports/ Spreadsheets/HSGradRate.htm.

*Manhattan Institute.* Published a series of reports on urban public high school graduation rates. Available at http://www.manhattan-institute.org/html/ewp_03.htm.

# CHAPTER 3

# Theoretical Developments in the Study of College Student Departure

*John M. Braxton and Amy S. Hirschy*

## INTRODUCTION

Scholars have studied college student retention for over seventy years (Braxton 2000a). The last three decades have produced the greatest understanding of this nettlesome problem. Although researchers have conducted studies using economic (Cabrera, Stampen, & Hansen 1990; St. John & Noell 1989), organizational (Bean 1980, 1982), psychological (Brower 1992; Stage 1989), and sociological (Rootman 1972) theoretical perspectives, Tinto's interactionalist theory of college student departure enjoys paradigmatic stature (Braxton, Hirschy, & Mc-Clendon 2004). Yet critics identify limitations of Tinto's theory, and a full understanding of the problem of student departure remains obscure.

A multitheoretical approach to reducing institutional rates of student persistence is needed because college student departure is best characterized as an ill-structured problem (Braxton & Mundy 2001–2002). Ill-structured problems defy a single solution and require a number of possible strategies which still may not alleviate them (Kitchener 1986; Wood 1983). Economic, psychological, organizational, and sociological theories (Tinto 1986) may be used to explain student departure. This chapter first offers a cursory review of conceptual models using economic, psychological, organizational, and sociological theories to account for student departure. This review is not intended to include all theories of student persistence; instead, it presents examples of conceptual models grounded in a range of disciplinary literature bases. Next, we describe

Tinto's theory and its empirical validity based on research findings. We then offer two theoretical perspectives on student departure: a revision of Tinto's theory for understanding student departure from residential colleges and universities and a new theory for understanding student attrition at commuter institutions.

## THEORY REVIEW

### Economic

Weighing the costs and benefits of attending a given college or university by the individual student constitutes the crux of an economic perspective on college student departure (Tinto 1986). Human capital theory offers that personal investments in education, training, or other learning opportunities can bring returns on the individual's investment of time, money, and energy (Becker 1964). Thus, departure likely results if a student perceives that the costs of attending a particular college or university exceed the benefits of attendance (Braxton 2003). Studies on college student departure using an economic perspective concentrate on the costs of attending a particular college or university and an individual's ability to pay. A student's ability to pay and the student's perceptions of the costs of his or her education influence persistence (Cabrera & Nora 1994; Cabrera, Nora, & Castaneda 1993; Cabrera et al. 1990; St. John 1994; St. John, Paulson, & Starkey 1996; Stampen & Cabrera 1988). St. John, Cabrera, Nora, and Asker (2000) proffer a broad discussion of economic factors related to the college student departure puzzle.

### Organizational

The role of organizational structure and organizational behavior in the college student departure process constitutes the organizational perspective on student departure (Berger & Braxton 1998; Tinto 1986). An example of a theory with organizational constructs follows.

#### Bean's Model of Work Turnover to Student Attrition

Bean (1980, 1983) adapted Price and Mueller's (1981) model of employee turnover in work organizations to the problem of student departure from colleges and universities. In Bean's theoretical model, ten exogenous variables influence satisfaction, which in turn influences a student's intent to leave. Intent to leave then has a direct impact on a student's decision to persist in college. Influences on satisfaction include five variables identical to Price and Mueller's model: routinization, participation, instrumental communication, integration, and distributive justice. The constructs of participation, communication, and distributive justice are organizationally based. Bean added the following five variables which influence satisfaction: grades, practical value, development (which represent Price and Mueller's concept of pay or rewards), courses (job content), and membership in campus organizations (professionalism).

All the variables have a positive effect on satisfaction except for routinization. Two additional variables influence a student's intent to leave and his or her departure decision. The first is derived from Price and Mueller's variable of kinship responsibility, which Bean terms "marriage." Put differently, the likelihood of marriage increases the likelihood of a student's intent to leave and drop out. The final determinant of intent to leave and drop out is opportunity. Bean defines this as the student's opportunity to transfer to another college.

## Psychological

The role of psychological characteristics and psychological processes in the departure of college students reflects the psychological orientation to understanding this phenomenon (Tinto 1986, 1993). Psychological characteristics and processes that distinguish between students who persist and those who depart are at the level of the individual student and at the level of the environment of a college or university. Such environments may be at the level of the college or university as an organization (Baird 2000) or at the suborganizational level (Braxton 2000a).

Psychological characteristics and processes that may affect student departure include academic aptitude and skills, motivational states, personality traits, and student development theories. Examples of persistence theories that focus on the influence of such psychological characteristics and processes are presented below.

### Bean and Eaton's Psychological Model of College Student Retention

Founded on Bentler and Speckart's (1979) adaptation of Fishbein and Ajzen's (1975) psychological theory of attitudes, intentions, and behaviors, Bean and Eaton (2000) integrate four psychological theories into their model of student departure. Student entry characteristics, such as past behavior, beliefs, and normative beliefs, shape how students perceive the college or university environment. Interactions with the institutional environment then result in psychological processes that affect a student's motivation. The psychological processes include positive self-efficacy, declining stress, increasing efficacy, and internal locus of control. Students experience ongoing adjustments of these internal processes as they experience both the college and external environment, such as parental or spousal influences. The psychological processes lead to academic and social integration, institutional fit and loyalty, intent to persist, and persistence.

## Astin's Theory of Involvement

Astin (1984) states that "student involvement refers to the amount of physical and psychological energy a student devotes to the academic experience" (297). Involvement pertains to the behaviors students engage in while attending college, which influence student outcomes, including persistence. Astin's theory comprises five basic tenets. First, involvement can be generalized (e.g., the student experience) or specific (e.g., preparing for a test). Next, involvement occurs along a continuum which is distinct for each student at a particular time. Involvement also possesses quantitative and qualitative aspects. Further, the amount of student learning and personal development associated with any educational program is directly influenced by the quality and quantity of student involvement in that program. Finally, the effectiveness of educational policy or practice is directly related to its capacity to increase student involvement (298).

## Sociological

The sociological perspective illuminates the influence of social structure and social forces on college student departure (Braxton 2000b; Tinto 1986). College student peers, family socioeconomic status, mechanisms of anticipatory socialization, and the support of significant others constitute important social forces that influence college student departure decisions. Four sociological lenses on college student persistence are described.

## Nontraditional Student Attrition

Bean and Metzner (1985) posit a model of the college departure process for the older or nontraditional student that is influenced by one or more of the following variables: academic performance, intent to leave, previous performance and educational goals, and environmental variables. The researchers indicate that environmental variables (such as finances, hours of employment, outside encouragement, family responsibilities, and opportunity to transfer) have a greater impact on departure decisions of adult students than academic variables (e.g., study habits, academic advising, absenteeism, major certainty, and course availability). The authors suggest that environmental factors that influence persistence can compensate for weak academic support. Moreover, Bean and Metzner (1985) posit that the most important (retention) variables are likely to differ for subgroups such as older students, part-time students, ethnic minorities, women, or academically underprepared students at different types of institutions (529).

## Capital, Social Reproduction, and Undergraduate Persistence

Berger (2000) applies Bourdieu's (1973, 1977) concept of cultural capital to the college student departure process. Cultural capital refers to a symbolic resource that can be used by an individual to maintain and advance one's social status. Examples include informal interpersonal skills, manners, linguistics, and educational credentials (Bourdieu 1973, 1977). Students demonstrate varying levels of cultural capital and attempt to optimize this resource as part of the social reproduction process. According to Berger (2000), social reproduction manifests itself at both the individual level and the organizational level. Phrased differently, educational institutions also possess cultural capital, as evidenced by selectivity in the admissions process and perceived success of graduates.

Berger's four main propositions to test a social reproductive lens on the student persistence reflect a congruence (or mismatch) between a student's cultural capital and the level of cultural capital at the particular college or university. First, institutions with higher levels of cultural capital will have the highest retention rates. Second, students with higher levels of cultural capital are more likely to persist, across all types of institutions, than are students with less access to cultural capital. Third, students with higher levels of cultural capital are most likely to persist at institutions with correspondingly high levels of organizational cultural capital. Finally, students with access to lower levels of cultural capital are most likely to persist at institutions with correspondingly low levels of organizational cultural capital (113–116).

## Cultural Propositions Related to Premature Student Departure

Kuh and Love (2000) also consider a cultural perspective to help understand issues related to college student persistence. They provide eight propositions that relate a student's individual cultures of origin with the cultural milieu of existing peer groups. Identified in the following list, the propositions address multiple influences of culture: integration, differentiation, and fragmentation (Martin 1992).

1. The college experience, including a decision to leave college, is mediated through a student's cultural meaning-making system.
2. One's cultures of origin (or cultural backgrounds) mediate the importance attached to attending college and earning a college degree.
3. Knowledge of a student's cultures of origin and the cultures of immersion is needed to understand a student's ability to successfully negotiate the institution's cultural milieu.
4. The probability of persistence is inversely related to the cultural distance between a student's culture(s) of origin and cultures of immersion.
5. Students who traverse a long cultural distance must become acclimated to dominant cultures of immersion or join one or more enclaves.
6. The amount of time a student spends in one's cultures of origin after matriculating is positively related to cultural stress and reduces the chances they will persist.
7. The likelihood a student will persist is related to the extensity and intensity of one's sociocultural connections to the academic program and to affinity groups.
8. Students who belong to one or more enclaves in the cultures of immersion are more likely to persist, especially if group members value achievement and persistence. (Kuh & Love 2000, 201)

As mentioned at the start of this chapter, Tinto's theory (1975, 1986, 1993) on student departure is the most studied, tested, revised, and critiqued in the literature. Put differently, Tinto's theory holds the predominate position as indexed in more than 775 citations (Braxton et al. 2004).

## TINTO'S INTERACTIONALIST THEORY

Tinto extended Spady's (1970) work on connecting Durkheim's (1951) theory of suicide to the study of college student persistence. Tinto views student departure as a longitudinal process that occurs because of the meanings the individual students ascribe to their interactions with the formal and informal dimensions of a given college or university (Braxton, Sullivan, & Johnson 1997; Tinto 1986, 1993). Such interactions occur between the individual student and the academic and social systems of a college or university.

More specifically, Tinto (1975) posits that various individual characteristics (for example, family background, individual attributes, and pre-college schooling experiences) that students possess as they enter college directly influence their departure decisions, as well as their initial commitments to the institution and to the goal of college graduation. Initial commitment to the institution and initial commitment to the goal of graduation influence the level of a student's integration into the academic and social systems of the college or university.

According to Tinto (1975, 104), academic integration consists of structural and normative dimensions. Structural integration entails meeting the explicit standards of the college or university, whereas normative integration pertains to an individual's identification with the normative structure of the academic system. Social integration pertains to the extent of congruency between the individual student and the social system of a college or university. Tinto holds that social integration occurs both at the level of the college or university and at the level of subcultures of an institution (1975, 107).

Tinto postulates that academic and social integration influence a student's subsequent commitments to the institution and to the goal of college graduation. The greater the student's level of academic integration, the greater the level of subsequent commitment to the goal of college graduation. Also, the greater the student's level of social integration, the greater the level of subsequent commitment to the focal college or university (Tinto 1975, 110). The student's initial level of commitments—institutional and graduation goal—also influence the student's level of subsequent commitments. In turn, the greater the levels of both subsequent institutional commitment and commitment to the goal of college graduation, the greater the likelihood the individual will persist in college.

Tinto clarifies and refines his foundational theory on student attrition (1982, 1986) and further develops the theory in his book, *Leaving Col-*

*lege: Rethinking the Causes and Cures of Student Attrition* (1987, 1993). The revisions in the 1975 model acknowledge the influences of financial resources, connection with an external community (such as family and/or work), and classroom experiences on a student's decision to persist.

## FURTHER THEORETICAL DEVELOPMENT ON THE STUDENT DEPARTURE PUZZLE

Despite the paradigmatic stature of Tinto's interactionalist theory, scholars such as Attinasi (1989, 1992) and Tierney (1992) offer conceptual criticisms of it. Moreover, the empirical validity of this theory also looms problematic with important differences between residential and commuter colleges and universities. Empirical tests conducted in residential colleges and universities afford strong support for five of the thirteen propositions derived from Tinto's formulations (Braxton et al. 1997). In contrast, only two of the thirteen propositions receive strong empirical backing from tests conducted in commuter colleges and universities (Braxton et al. 1997).

Partial support for Tinto's theory in residential institutions indicates a need to revise Tinto's theory to account for student departure in residential colleges and universities (Braxton et al. 2004). In contrast, the problematic nature of support for this theory in commuter institutions justifies its abandonment for application in this institutional setting. Consequently, Braxton, Hirschy, and McClendon (2004) put forth a revision of Tinto's theory to account for student departure from residential colleges and universities. They also advance a theory of student departure from commuter colleges and universities.

Although basically different, these two theoretical statements share some common attributes. We present these common attributes before describing the theories of student departure from residential and commuter institutions.

### Common Attributes

The two theoretical perspectives presented in this chapter share four attributes. These common attributes are as follows:

1. The two theoretical formulations spring from the process of inductive theory construction. Inductive theory construction uses the findings of empirical research to derive new concepts, patterns of understanding,

and generalizations (Wallace 1971). Put differently, new concepts, patterns of understanding, and empirical generalizations emerge from a "conceptual factor analysis" of the results of empirical research (Braxton 2000b).

2. These two theoretical statements are theories of the middle range (Braxton et al. 2004). Merton (1968) differentiated between grand and middle-range theory. Grand theory seeks to explain a wide range of phenomena, whereas middle-range theories endeavor to explain a limited range of phenomena. In the case of these theoretical statements, one seeks to explain student departure in residential colleges and universities, whereas the other attempts to account for departure from commuter colleges and universities.

3. College student departure takes the form of an ill-structured problem (Braxton & Mundy 2001–2002). Ill-structured problems defy a single solution; instead, ill-structured problems generate alternative solutions, approaches that may not alleviate the problem (Kitchener 1986; Wood 1983). As a consequence, a multitheoretical approach to accounting for student departure is needed (Braxton & Mundy 2001–2002). Both of the theoretical perspectives we describe in this chapter incorporate constructs exhibiting economic, organizational, psychological, and sociological orientations toward student departure.

4. Both of these theoretical formulations meet three criteria for a good theory (Braxton et al. 2004). First, both theories account for extant research findings (Chafetz 1978). Both theories derive their formulations from research on the college student departure process. Second, the operationalization of the propositions of both theories is possible. Thus, both theories are amenable to empirical testing (Chafetz 1978). Parsimony is a desirable trait of theories (Chafetz 1978). Put differently, a theory should be explained with the fewest number of constructs and propositions possible. Both of the theories described in this chapter are relatively parsimonious. The propositions included in each theory are needed to account for relevant findings from research.

## New Theoretical Perspectives

We now describe the theoretical formulations for student departure from residential institutions and for departure from commuter colleges and universities. Given the need for many colleges and universities to reduce their student departure rates, we then offer some guidelines to guide the day-to-day professional practice of college and university administrators and faculty members. Finally, we offer some specific recommendations for institutional policy and practice.

## THEORY OF STUDENT DEPARTURE FROM RESIDENTIAL COLLEGES AND UNIVERSITIES

Braxton, Sullivan, and Johnson's (1997) review of empirical support for Tinto's theory in residential colleges and universities revealed five strongly supported propositions. Thus, Tinto's theory receives partial support for understanding departure from residential institutions. Four of the five strongly supported propositions are logically interrelated and lead directly or indirectly to persistence. These propositions form the foundation for revising Tinto's theory. Braxton (2000b) proposes that theory revision should utilize reliable empirical relationships as well as an inductive review of findings from a variety of theoretical perspectives. Braxton, Hirschy, and McClendon (2004) employ such methods to revise Tinto's theory, using empirical findings from organizational, psychological, economic, and sociological perspectives to create new constructs. Finally, this revision identifies factors that influence social integration, a central construct in Tinto's theory that is strongly supported by empirical findings (Braxton et al. 1997). Thus, a major contribution of this revision involves identifying antecedents to social integration. A summary of the revised theory for student departure from residential colleges and universities and the concomitant propositions follows (see Figure 3.1).[1]

In residential institutions, student entry characteristics shape the student's initial commitment to the goal of attaining a degree (GC-1) and the student's initial commitment to the institution (IC-1). Entry characteristics include the student's gender, racial or ethnic background, socioeconomic status, academic ability, high school academic preparation, parental education, and the ability to pay for college. The student's initial commitment to the institution (IC-1) in turn influences the student's perceptions of several institutional dimensions: the institution's commitment to the welfare of students, the integrity of the institution, and the potential for social community with peers. Institutional commitment to the welfare of students is defined as an abiding concern for the growth and development of students. Institutional integrity refers to the degree to which the actions of faculty, administrators, and staff members of a college or university community are congruent with the stated mission, goals, and values of the school. Communal potential is the extent to which a student believes that a subgroup of students exists within the college or university community with whom the student shares similar

**Figure 3.1**
**Tinto's Theory Revised for Student Departure in Residential Colleges and Universities**

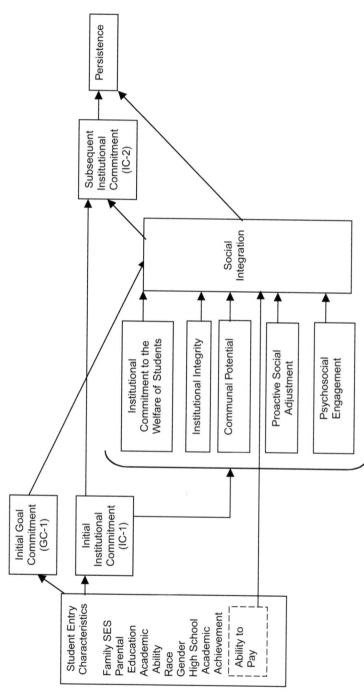

Source: Adapted from Braxton, Hirschy, & McClendon (2004).

values, beliefs, and goals. The greater the student's level of initial commitment to the institution (IC-1), the more favorable his or her perceptions of the three institutional characteristics (Braxton & Hirschy 2004).

The student's initial commitment to the institution (IC-1) also affects two psychological dimensions: a student's proactive social adjustment and psychosocial engagement. Proactive social adjustment refers to a student's propensity to approach the demands and pressures of social interaction in a positive manner. Psychosocial engagement denotes the level of psychological energy a student devotes to his or her interactions with peers and to involvement in activities at the chosen college or university. The greater the student's level of initial commitment to the institution (IC-1), the greater the student's levels of proactive social adjustment and psychosocial engagement.

This theory offers seven antecedents to social integration. Social integration refers to the extent a student perceives a sense of normative congruence and social affiliation with members of the social communities of a college or university (Tinto 1975). The five constructs described above which are shaped by a student's initial commitment to the institution (IC-1) serve as antecedents to social integration. To elaborate, a student's perception of each of the two organizational constructs—institutional commitment to student welfare and institutional integrity—affects the student's level of social integration. In other words, students who perceive that faculty, administrators, and staff promote student success and demonstrate that they value and respect students are more likely to affiliate with members of the institution. In contrast, students who perceive that campus policies, practices, and programs are incongruent with the espoused mission and values of the institution may feel dissonance with the campus community; thus, they will experience lower levels of social integration. The next antecedent to social integration stems from a sociological perspective: communal potential, which focuses on a student's assessment of how likely he or she will find meaningful social relationships with peers on campus. The potential social connection does not have to be with the dominant student culture; instead, students can perceive the possibility of relationships with a smaller affinity group or cultural enclave (Kuh & Love 2000). Phrased differently, it is not the scope of the larger student community culture that matters as an antecedent to social integration as much as the qualities that students perceive among the student body that offer potential for social connection.

Two psychological constructs—proactive social adjustment and psychosocial engagement—also significantly influence the student's level of social integration. Students who recognize their need for social affiliation and anticipate membership in a group by learning its values, norms, and attitudes display attributes of proactive social adjustment. Regarding psychosocial engagement, students who invest time and psychological energy into interacting with others in the college community are more likely to have greater levels of social integration (Astin 1984; Berger & Milem 1999). In sum, greater levels of each of these five constructs lead to higher levels of social integration.

The remaining antecedents to social integration are ability to pay and initial goal commitment (IC-2). First, a student who is more satisfied with the costs of attending his or her institution is more likely to persist (Cabrera et al. 1990), as students who suffer from ongoing financial concerns are less likely to be actively engaged in the campus social community. Alleviating or reducing financial stress leads to higher levels of social integration. Ability to pay reflects an economic theoretical perspective. Finally, students at residential institutions who display high levels of commitment to earn a college education are more likely to immerse themselves in the social realm of the institution with other students and with faculty. It follows that the higher the student's initial commitment to attain a degree (GC-1), the greater the student's level of social integration.

Both social integration and a student's initial commitment to the institution affect the student's subsequent institutional commitment (IC-2). The greater the level of subsequent commitment to the institution, the more likely the student will persist in college. Due to the central role of social integration on residential colleges and universities, it also has a direct effect on persistence.

## THEORY OF STUDENT DEPARTURE FROM COMMUTER COLLEGES AND UNIVERSITIES

Because few of Tinto's original propositions gathered strong support in studies conducted in commuter colleges and universities (Braxton et al. 1997), a new theory construction is offered. Similar to the theory revision offered for residential institutions, the following theory was created by an inductive review of empirical findings. In contrast, most of the propositions for this theory emerged from research conducted primarily at commuter colleges and universities.

A wide variety of students attend commuter colleges and universities. Enrollees can include traditionally aged students who live at home with their parents, older students, students with family obligations, working students, part-time students, and full-time students (Bean & Metzner 1985; Stewart & Rue 1983). Whereas many traditionally aged students in residential institutions choose to attend college "instead" of something else, most adult students attend college "in addition" to their other day-to-day involvements and obligations, such as family and work (Tinto 1993, 126). As such, commuter students typically hold their primary social memberships with family, friends, and colleagues off campus. As a result, the influences of the campus and external environments in commuter colleges and universities differ from those of residential institutions.

The basic elements of the theory of student departure from commuter colleges and universities include student entry characteristics, the environments within and external to campus, and the student's academic integration on campus. Each of these elements influences the student's subsequent institutional commitment (IC-2) or the student's decision to persist at the focal commuter institution. Figure 3.2 shows a graphical representation of the theory, and a narrative summary follows.

## Student Entry Characteristics

Student entry characteristics wield a direct force on a student's decision to depart and indirectly influence persistence through students' initial commitments to the institution and how students adjust to campus and external environments. A student's family background, academic ability, high school academic preparation, and gender exemplify student entry characteristics. Additionally, students enroll with several traits that influence their decisions to remain enrolled or not. For example, students who value the purpose of attending college and feel dedicated to attain a degree show signs of motivation, which increases their likelihood of persisting. Likewise, students who strongly believe that they are capable of earning a degree through their own efforts are less likely to depart commuter colleges and universities.

## External Environment

Because students at commuter colleges and universities typically balance multiple commitments off campus in addition to their role on campus, the external environment plays a significant role in enrollment decisions. The influences can be positive and negative, depending on several factors. Students with high levels of personal empathy tend to be sensitive to how their actions affect others. Therefore, individuals who perceive that their student roles create hardship for their families (e.g., financial stress or limited time spent at home) are less likely to continue

**Figure 3.2**
**Theory of Student Departure in Commuter Colleges and Universities**

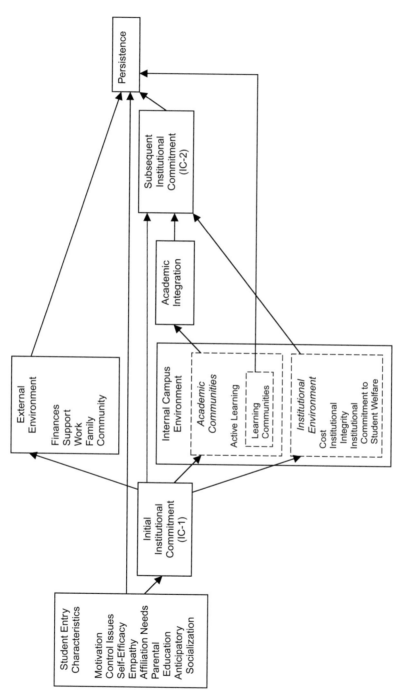

Source: Adapted from Braxton, Hirschy, & McClendon (2004).

in school. If the costs of attending the institution are minimized, then the student is more likely to persist. Similarly, if family members encourage the student to continue his or her educational path, then the student is less likely to depart. Support or discouragement from friends, work colleagues, and members of community organizations also serve as external influences that affect students.

## Internal Campus Environment

Competing time demands minimize social involvement at commuter institutions, as students devote their campus time to academic pursuits of attending class, meeting with faculty, or fulfilling degree requirements (Tinto 1993). Students spend their time efficiently on campus, hurrying to class and leaving afterward to be at the next place that requires their presence, often work or home. An aerial view of the campus might resemble a transportation center, with frequent arrivals and departures of cars, buses, and other vehicles. The various forms of rushed comings and goings create a "buzzing confusion" (Braxton et al. 2004, 45). Amid this activity, the daily schedule of class meeting times provides order.

To expound on various relevant factors within the commuter campus environment, we offer propositions from several theoretical perspectives. The theory's propositions emerged through psychological, sociological, organizational, and economic lenses.

## Psychological Influences

Students who are very motivated and feel a high degree of self-efficacy are more likely to persist in commuter environments. In contrast, some students find the activity confusing and chaotic. Moreover, the stress of managing the demands of work or home life can be additional sources of complexity and uncertainty. Thus, the greater the student's need for order and control in his or her life, the lower the student's level of subsequent institutional commitment.

## Sociological Influences

Due to the well-worn paths between the parking lots and the classrooms and the reality that students who attend commuter colleges and universities often rely on social communities off campus, the social realm of commuter institutions is not as strong as in residential institutions. Unfortunately, some students may experience difficult adjustments to weak, unstructured social communities. For example, parental education level can influence a student's expectations for what a college environment should be. Students whose parents attended college are more likely to expect social engagement with peers, based on their understanding of the college experience from their parents. Thus, the higher the level of parental education, the less likely a student feels subsequent commitment to the institution. Likewise, as parental education increases, there is a higher likelihood of student departure from a commuter institution (Hagedorn, Maxwell, and Hampton 2001–2002; Halpin 1990). Anticipatory socialization behaviors such as forming early expectations for college and participating in orientation activities play a role in how a student perceives the college environment (Nora, Attinasi, & Matonak 1990). The greater the level of anticipatory socialization a student experiences, the weaker the student's subsequent institutional commitment. Further, students who have higher needs for social affiliation may feel isolated and insufficiently connected on commuter campuses, leading to lower subsequent institutional commitments and, in turn, greater levels of departure.

## Organizational Influences

Two organizational characteristics of the campus environment influence a student's subsequent commitment to the institution: institutional integrity and institutional commitment to student welfare (Braxton & Hirschy 2004). Over time, students perceive institutional integrity, a sense of congruence between the day-to-day actions of faculty, administrators, and staff and the espoused mission and values of the institution. The greater the perceived institutional integrity, the higher the level of subsequent commitment to the institution. Institutional actors who are committed to student welfare display an abiding concern for the growth and development of students. By showing that they care about, respect, and fairly treat students, members of the campus community demonstrate that they support student success. The greater a student's perception of institutional commitment to student welfare, the higher the probability of greater subsequent institutional commitment.

## Economic Influence

Students weigh the costs and benefits of investing their time and economic resources on higher education (Braxton 2003; Tinto 1986). Institutions that minimize the costs associated with enrollment and maximize the perceived value of the student's investment can influence persistence decisions. The lower the costs of college attendance incurred by students, the greater the probability of persistence.

## Academic Communities

Without strong social communities on commuter campuses, the academic realm of the institution holds primary status. Tinto (1975) postulates that academic integration influences subsequent goal commitment (GC-1), but that link is not strongly supported in the literature (Braxton et al. 1997). However, Braxton and Lien (2000) found that academic integration influences subsequent institutional commitment (IC-2) in commuter institutions. The greater the degree of a student's academic integration, the greater his or her subsequent commitment to the institution, which then leads to a higher probability of persistence.

The classroom serves as a site for the intersection of both social and academic dimensions of the student experience. Considering the classroom as a community facilitates meaningful connections between students and faculty and among peers. Faculty who intentionally involve class members in the learning process and engage critical thinking about course materials contribute to student persistence. Forms of active learning include role plays, debates, collaborative learning projects, and peer group work (Bonwell & Eison 1991). In the context of a commuter institution, active learning in classrooms may satisfy some students' needs for high levels of social affiliation. Further, students who take courses that feature active learning methods are more likely to experience greater degrees of subsequent institutional commitment.

Along the same line, students involved in learning communities benefit the most from the academic dimension of commuter campuses (Tinto 1997). Students who share a set of themed courses with a cohort of peers, also called block scheduling, experience a powerful synergy of academic and social interaction with peers and faculty. Students engaged in learning committees in community colleges and universities are more likely to persist.

## SUMMARY

While both theories presented include propositions that address indirect and direct paths to persistence, the nature of the two institutional types requires separate approaches. Put differently, the profound differences in the student demographics and the campus environments necessitate distinct theories for residential and commuter institutions. Likewise, the following guidelines and recommendations include suggestions that can be applied to both commuter and residential institutions and some that are best applied in only one of the two settings.

## Guidelines for Institutional Practice

Day-to-day professional practice by college and university administrators and faculty members must rest on a foundation of deep understanding. Such deep understanding comes from knowledge of theory and research findings. We offer two guidelines for the decisions and actions of administrators and faculty members in residential and commuter colleges and universities. Adherence to these two guidelines should increase the probability of favorably shaping student perceptions regarding the commitment of the institution to student welfare and institutional integrity.

1. College and university administrators and faculty members should embrace a commitment to safeguarding the welfare of the student. This guideline stems from the construct *Commitment of the Institution to Student Welfare* posited in both of the theoretical perspectives previously described in this chapter. Such an abiding commitment should manifest itself in the major decisions and day-to-day activities of college and university presidents, chief academic affairs officers, and chief student affairs officers. A commitment to the welfare of students should also guide the decisions and actions of other college and university administrative officers, student affairs practitioners, and individual faculty members. Public speeches, college and university documents, and letters and memoranda should exhibit, when appropriate, the institution's commitment to the welfare of its students. Similarly, recruitment materials for prospective students, faculty, administrators, and staff should reflect this commitment.

   When making decisions, such individuals should consider the effects of decision alternatives on the growth and development of students served by the institution. When possible, decisions made should communicate the high value placed on students by the institution. Moreover, administrators, faculty, and staff members should treat students equally and with respect in their day-to-day interactions with them.

2. The decisions and day-to-day actions of college and university administrators and individual faculty members must resonate with the mission, goals, and values espoused by their college or university. Put

differently, decisions and actions should not conflict with the mission, goals, and values embraced by the institution. This guideline flows from the construct *Institutional Integrity* postulated in both of the theoretical perspectives previously presented in this chapter.

In their day-to-day behaviors and in particular their interactions with students, administrators and faculty members should act in accordance with the mission, goals, and values of their institution. When making decisions, such institutional stakeholders should assess whether various decision alternatives are congruent with the mission, goals, and values of their college or university. On occasions that students perceive dissonance between a decision and the institutional mission, goals, and values, administrators and faculty members should listen and respond to the concern in a timely, respectful manner.

## RECOMMENDATIONS FOR POLICY AND PRACTICE

We offer six overarching recommendations for both residential and commuter colleges and universities. We also present specific recommendations for residential collegiate institutions and for commuter colleges and universities. We present these various sets of recommendations as multiple policy levers. Pascarella and Terenzini (1991, 655) maintain that the achievement of institutional goals may be more likely to occur through the use of multiple policy levers rather than a single large-scale lever.

### Recommendations

1. Annual reviews of administrative performance should include an assessment of the extent to which the individual under review treats students equally and with respect in their day-to-day interactions with them. The consistency of the individual's day-to-day actions with the mission, goals, and values of the institution should also be appraised. Individual merit pay raises should be given to administrators and staff who treat students equally and with respect.

2. Student course rating instruments used to assess the teaching performance of faculty members should include items that assess the extent to which faculty treat their students equally and with respect as individuals. Items that focus on whether the actions of the faculty member uphold the values of the institution should also be included.

3. Audits of all institutional publications and documents should be conducted. Such audits would focus on the extent to which the contents of institutional publications and documents display a commitment of

the institution to student welfare. Likewise, the extent to which the contents of these documents resonate with the mission, goals, and values of the institution should also be assessed.

4. The contents of speeches and addresses made by college and university administrators must not conflict with the mission, goals, and values of the institution.

5. Institutions should implement intentional outreach programs. Brier (1999) describes a proactive program designed to encourage student commitment to the institution, to identify at-risk students, and to refer students to university resources. The telephoning of all first-year students during the early part of the fall semester is the primary medium used. Other methods of contacting students include individual contact by email and developing a listserv. The topics of the conversation center on the students' academic and social experiences. Phone calls of a similar nature are also made during the spring semester. This program clearly demonstrates a commitment of the institution to the welfare of its students.

6. The substantial dissimilarity in the departure rates of racial and ethnic minority students in contrast to White students strongly indicates a need to develop ways to reduce such departure rates (Braxton et al. 2004). Although the preceding recommendations should reduce the departure rates of both majority and minority students, some additional approaches are needed. Aside from the obvious need for colleges and universities to embrace diversity in their student body, the celebration of diversity must also occur. Speakers, programs, and workshops that honor the history and cultures of different racial and ethnic groups on campus offer media for the celebration of diversity (Braxton & McClendon 2001–2002; Braxton & Mundy 2001–2002). In addition to embracing and celebrating diversity, the recruitment and retention of a critical mass of racial and ethnic minority students should occupy center stage (Braxton et al. 2004).

## Recommendations for Commuter Institutions

In addition to the preceding six recommendations, we also propose three recommendations for implementation by commuter colleges and universities. These recommendations are as follows:

1. Administrators and individual faculty members should know the characteristics of students enrolled at their college or university. These characteristics include parental educational level, marital status, number of dependent children, and work status (Braxton et al. 2004). Such psy-

chological processes and characteristics as self-efficacy, need for affiliation, locus of control, empathy, and level of motivation to graduate
from college also influence student departure decisions from commuter
colleges and universities (Braxton et al. 2004).

Assessment of students on these various characteristics should occur
prior to their matriculation to identify students at risk for departure.
The development of policies and programs designed to reduce the likelihood of such at-risk students departing should occur.

2. The academic dimensions of commuter colleges and universities play
   an important role in student departure from this type of college (Braxton et al. 2004). As a consequence, the teaching and learning process
   in such institutions looms important. In particular, faculty members
   should use active learning in their classes. Active learning relates to
   class activities that involve students in thinking about the subject matter of a course (Bonwell & Eison 1991). We also concur with the recommendation of Braxton, Hirschy, and McClendon (2004) that
   commuter colleges and universities develop communities of learning.
   Communities of learning entail the block scheduling of courses so that
   the same group of students take some courses together. A theme may
   underlie these block-scheduled courses.

3. Appraisal of institutional policies and programs should occur to identify those policies and programs that hinder the academic progress of
   students who work, have spouses or life partners, and/or have dependent children. Such identified policies and programs should be elimi-
   nated or altered in order to lessen the stress on family life of college
   attendance.

## Recommendations for Residential Institutions

Residential colleges and universities should implement the six recommendations previously described. We also proffer three recommendations
for enactment by such collegiate institutions. Because social integration
plays a crucial part in the retention of students enrolled in residential
colleges and universities, these recommendations focus on fostering the
social integration of students in residential colleges and universities.

1. The assessment of institutional policies, practices, and activities should
   transpire to identify those that hinder the social integration of students.
   For example, dining policies that permit the purchase of fast foods or
   have inadequate seating capacities may reduce the possibility of social
   interaction among students during meal times. Also, policies that permit first- and second-year students to live off campus may also limit the
   opportunities of students to make friends. The elimination or modifi-

cation of those policies, practices, and activities judged to hinder social integration should take place.

2. Participation in orientation programs for first-year students must be mandatory (Braxton et al. 2004). Moreover, multiple opportunities for students to interact socially should also be provided during the orientation program (Braxton & McClendon 2001–2002; Braxton & Mundy 2001–2002).

3. To be sure, the most important goals of college attendance center on student learning and academic achievement. However, residential colleges and universities must provide opportunities for students to socially interact with one another (Braxton & McClendon 2001–2002; Braxton & Mundy 2001–2002). Accordingly, first-year students should be required to live on campus. Dining arrangements must give opportunities for social interaction among students. Residence halls should provide occasions for student to socially interact with others during the course of a semester (Braxton & McClendon 2001–2002).

## CLOSING REFLECTIONS

As previously indicated in this chapter, research on college student retention has been conducted for over seventy years (Braxton 2000a). However, the greatest progress in solving the puzzle of student departure has taken place since 1975 with the promulgation of Tinto's Interactionalist Theory (1975). The testing of Tinto's paradigmatic theory resulted in a deeper understanding of student departure. A promise of an even greater depth of understanding comes with the advent of the two theoretical perspectives on student departure described in this chapter. Importantly, these perspectives acknowledge fundamental differences in the departure process for students enrolled in residential colleges and universities and in commuter colleges and universities.

Although the guidelines for day-to-day practice offered in this chapter hold promise as influences on student perceptions of the commitment of their college or university to student welfare, we recommend research on such policy-relevant factors as the allocation of funds to the instructional process and student life, the range of services available to students, and the number of student affairs practitioners. Such factors may shape student perceptions of the commitment of the institution to student welfare. The verification of this view holds implications for the allocation of financial and human resources.

Student success looms as an important and challenging goal for individual colleges and universities. Adherence to the guidelines for practice, implementation of the recommendations for policy and practice advanced in this chapter, and testing of the two theoretical statements described in this chapter all may work toward reducing institutional rates of student departure and increasing the probabilities of student success.

## NOTE

1. Figures 3.1 and 3.2 graphically represent the theories and reflect updated versions from Braxton, Hirschy, and McClendon (2004).

## REFERENCES

Astin, A. W. (1984). Student involvement: A developmental theory for higher education. *Journal of College Student Personnel* 25: 297–308.

Attinasi, L. C., Jr. (1989). Getting in: Mexican Americans' perceptions of university attendance and the implications for freshman year persistence. *Journal of Higher Education* 60: 247–277.

———. (1992). Rethinking the study of the outcomes of college attendance. *Journal of College Student Development* 33: 61–70.

Baird, L. L. (2000). College climate and the Tinto model. In *Reworking the student departure puzzle*, ed. J. M. Braxton, 62–80. Nashville: Vanderbilt University Press.

Bean, J. P. (1980). Dropouts and turnover: The synthesis and test of a causal model of student attrition. *Research in Higher Education* 12: 155–187.

———. (1982). Student attrition, intentions, and confidence: Interaction effects in a path model. *Research in Higher Education* 17: 291–320.

———. (1983). The application of a model of turnover in work organizations to the student attrition process. *Review of Higher Education* 6: 129–148.

Bean, J. P., & Eaton, S. B. (2000). A psychological model of college student retention. In *Reworking the student departure puzzle*, ed. J. M. Braxton, 48–61. Nashville: Vanderbilt University Press.

Bean, J. P., & Metzner, B. S. (1985). A conceptual model of nontraditional student attrition. *Review of Educational Research* 55: 485–540.

Becker, G. S. (1964). *Human capital.* New York: National Bureau of Economic Research.

Bentler, P. M., & Speckart, G. (1979). Models of attitude-behavior relations. *Psychological Review* 86: 452–464.

Berger, J. B. (2000). Optimizing capital, social reproduction, and undergraduate persistence: A sociological perspective. In *Reworking the student departure puzzle*, ed. J. M. Braxton, 95–126. Nashville: Vanderbilt University Press.

Berger, J. B., & Braxton, J. M. (1998). Revising Tinto's interactionalist theory of student departure through theory elaboration: Examining the role of organizational attributes in the persistence process. *Research in Higher Education* 39: 103–119.

Berger, J. B., & Milem, J. F. (1999). The role of student involvement and perceptions of integration in a causal model of student persistence. *Research in Higher Education* 40: 641–664.

Bonwell, C. C., & Eison, J. A. (1991). *Active learning: Creating excitement in the classroom.* No. 1. Washington, DC: ASHE-ERIC Higher Education.

Bourdieu, P. (1973). Cultural reproduction and social reproduction. In *Knowledge, education, and cultural change,* ed. R. Brown, 189–207. London: Collier Macmillan.

———. (1977). *Outline of a theory of practice.* Trans. R. Nice. Cambridge, UK: Cambridge University Press.

Braxton, J. M. (2000a). Introduction: Reworking the student departure puzzle. In *Reworking the student departure puzzle,* ed. J. M. Braxton, 1–8. Nashville: Vanderbilt University Press.

———. (2000b). Reinvigorating theory and research on the departure puzzle. In *Reworking the student departure puzzle,* ed. J. M. Braxton, 257–274. Nashville: Vanderbilt University Press.

———. (2003). Persistence as an essential gateway to student success. In *Student services: A handbook for the profession,* 4th ed., ed. S. Komives & D. Woodard, 317–335. San Francisco: Jossey-Bass.

Braxton, J. M., & Hirschy, A. S. (2004). Reconceptualizing antecedents of social integration in student departure. In *Retention and student success in higher education,* ed. M. Yorke & B. Longden, 89–102. Buckingham, UK: Open University Press.

Braxton, J. M., Hirschy, A. S., & McClendon, S. A. (2004). *Understanding and reducing college student departure.* No. 3. ASHE-ERIC Higher Education Research Report Series. San Francisco: Jossey-Bass.

Braxton, J. M., & Lien, L. A. (2000). The viability of academic integration as a central construct in Tinto's interactionalist theory of student departure. In *Reworking the student departure puzzle,* ed. J. M. Braxton, 11–28. Nashville: Vanderbilt University Press.

Braxton, J. M., & McClendon, S. A. (2001–2002). The fostering of social integration and retention through institutional practice. *Journal of College Student Retention* 3: 57–72.

Braxton, J. M., & Mundy, M. E. (2001–2002). Powerful institutional levers to reduce college student departure. *Journal of College Student Retention* 3: 91–118.

Braxton, J. M., Sullivan, A. S., & Johnson, R. M., Jr. (1997). Appraising Tinto's theory of college student departure. In *Higher education: Handbook of theory and research,* ed. J. Smart, Vol. 12: 107–164. New York: Agathon Press.

Brier, E. M. (1999). Strategic initiatives. Paper presented at the Southern Graduate Student Association, New Orleans.

Brower, A. M. (1992). The "second half" of student integration: The effects of life task predominance on student persistence. *Journal of Higher Education* 63: 441–462.

Cabrera, A. F., & Nora, A. (1994). College students' perceptions of prejudice and discrimination and their feelings of alienation. *Review of Education, Pedagogy, and Cultural Studies* 16: 387–409.

Cabrera, A. F., Nora, A., & Castaneda, M. B. (1993). College persistence: Structural equation modeling test of an integrated model of student retention. *Journal of Higher Education* 64: 123–139.

Cabrera, A. F., Stampen, J. O., & Hansen, W. L. (1990). Exploring the effects of ability to pay on persistence in college. *Review of Higher Education* 13: 303–336.

Chafetz, J. S. (1978). *A primer on the construction and testing of theories in sociology.* Itasca, IL: F. E. Peacock.

Durkheim, E. (1951). *Suicide.* Trans. G. Simpson. Glencoe, IL: The Free Press.

Fishbein, M., & Ajzen, I. (1975). *Belief, attitude, intention, and behavior: An introduction to theory and research.* Reading, MA: Addison-Wesley.

Hagedorn, L. S., Maxwell, W., & Hampton, P. (2001–2002). Correlates of retention for African-American males in community colleges. *Journal of College Student Retention: Research, Theory and Practice* 3(3): 243–263.

Halpin, R. L. (1990). An application of the Tinto model to the analysis of freshman persistence in a community college. *Community College Review* 17: 22–32.

Kitchener, K. (1986). The reflective judgment model: Characteristics, evidence, and measurement. In *Adult cognitive development,* ed. R. Mines & K. Kitchener. New York: Praeger.

Kuh, G. D., & Love, P. G. (2000). A cultural perspective on student departure. In *Reworking the student departure puzzle: New theory and research on college student retention,* ed. J. M. Braxton, 196–212. Nashville: Vanderbilt University Press.

Martin, J. (1992). *Cultures in organizations: Three perspectives.* New York: Oxford University Press.

Merton, R. K. (1968). *Social theory and social structure.* New York: The Free Press.

Nora, A., Attinasi, L. C., & Matonak, A. (1990). Testing qualitative indicators of pre-college factors in Tinto's attrition model: A community college perspective. *Review of Higher Education* 13: 337–356.

Pascarella, E. T., & Terenzini, P. T. (1991). *How college affects students.* San Francisco: Jossey-Bass.

Price, J. L., & Mueller, C. W. (1981). A causal model of turnover for nurses. *Academy of Management Journal* 24: 543–565.

Rootman, I. (1972). Voluntary withdrawal from a total adult socializing organization: A model. *Sociology of Education* 45: 258–270.

Spady, W. (1970). Dropouts from higher education: An interdisciplinary review and synthesis. *Interchange* 1: 64–85.

St. John, E. P. (1994). *Prices, productivity, and investment: Assessing financial strategies in higher education.* ASHE-ERIC Higher Education Reports, No. 3. Washington, DC: George Washington University.

St. John, E. P., Cabrera, A. F., Nora, A., & Asker, E. H. (2000). Economic influences on persistence reconsidered: How can finance research inform the
reconceptualization of persistence models? In *Reworking the student departure puzzle*, ed. J. M. Braxton, 29–47. Nashville: Vanderbilt University
Press.

St. John, E. P., & Noell, J. (1989). The effects of student financial aid on access
to higher education: An analysis of progress with special consideration
of minority enrollment. *Research in Higher Education* 30: 563–581.

St. John, E. P., Paulson, M. B., & Starkey, J. B. (1996). The nexus between college choice and persistence. *Research in Higher Education* 37: 175–220.

Stage, F. K. (1989). Motivation, academic and social integration, and the early
dropout. *American Educational Research Journal* 26: 385–402.

Stampen, J. O., & Cabrera, A. F. (1988). The targeting and packaging of student
aid and its effect on attrition. *Economics of Education Review* 7(1): 29–46.

Stewart, S. S., & Rue, P. (1983). Commuter students: Definition and distribution. In *Commuter students: Enhancing their educational experiences*, ed.
S. S. Stewart, Vol. 24: 3–8. San Francisco: Jossey-Bass.

Tierney, W. (1992). An anthropological analysis of student participation in college. *Journal of Higher Education* 63: 603–618.

Tinto, V. (1975). Dropout from higher education: A theoretical synthesis of recent research. *Review of Educational Research* 45: 89–125.

———. (1982). Limits of theory and practice in student attrition. *Journal of
Higher Education* 53: 687–700.

———. (1986). Theories of student departure revisited. In *Higher education: A
handbook of theory and research*, ed. J. Smart, Vol. 2: 359–384. New York:
Agathon Press.

———. (1987). *Leaving college: Rethinking the causes and cures of student attrition*.
Chicago: University of Chicago Press.

———. (1993). *Leaving college: Rethinking the causes and cures of student attrition*.
2nd ed. Chicago: University of Chicago Press.

———. (1997). Classrooms as communities: Exploring the educational character of student persistence. *Journal of Higher Education* 68: 599–623.

Wallace, W. (1971). *The logic of science in sociology*. Chicago: Aldine-Atherton.

Wood, P. (1983). Inquiring systems and problem structure: Implications for cognitive development. *Human Development* 26: 249–265.

# CHAPTER 4

# How to Define Retention

## A New Look at an Old Problem

*Linda Serra Hagedorn*

### INTRODUCTION

Perhaps the two most vexing measurement issues in higher education research are how to obtain true transfer rates from community colleges to four-year universities and the correct formula for the measure of college student retention, regardless of institutional type. While this chapter will focus specifically on retention, it is important to note that the problems associated with an appropriate measurement system are common to other often-researched outcomes in higher education. Measuring college student retention is complicated, confusing, and context dependent. Higher education researchers will likely never reach consensus on the "correct" or "best" way to measure this very important outcome. The purpose of this chapter is to thoroughly review the associated problems, to discuss the methods used juxtaposed with highlights of each, and to ultimately recommend policy to reach a national consensus.

Let us begin with the most basic and noncontroversial definitions of a college persister and a nonpersister. A student who enrolls in college and remains enrolled until degree completion is a persister. A student who leaves the college without earning a degree and never returns is a nonpersister. While these definitions are simple and easy to understand, student paths are rarely this direct or straightforward. When looking at enrollment patterns that defy or at least stretch these basic definitions, we find the following student types:

- Student A—Enrolls in a university, remains enrolled for two years, and stops out to return six years later.
- Student B—Enrolls in a university, remains for one year, and transfers to another university to complete the degree.
- Student C—Enrolls in two community colleges simultaneously, ultimately earning a certificate from one of them.
- Student D—Enrolls in college but does not complete any credits. The next year the student reenrolls and remains continuously enrolled to degree completion.
- Student E—Begins in a community college and successfully transfers to a university. However, the student is not successful at the university and leaves prior to earning any credits. The next semester the student returns to the community college taking the few remaining courses necessary to earn an associate degree.
- Student F—Enrolls for a full-time load of five courses (fifteen units of college credits), but drops all but one class (three units).
- Student G—Enrolls in two courses and drops one, keeping only a physical education course.
- Student H—Enrolls in a community college for a full load of remedial courses, reenrolling in the same courses the next semester because he or she has not yet mastered the material.
- Student I—Enrolls in a full-time load of courses, but because of low GPA and lack of progress is academically suspended.
- Student J—Due to unlawful behavior, is judiciously expelled from the university.

These examples highlight the variability in student enrollment patterns that make it difficult to label one student a persister and another nonpersister. Clearly, the simple dichotomous student outcome measures often employed in quantitative analysis do not capture the complexity in student progress. Rather, retention requires a series of measures that when viewed with their complexity allow researchers and administrators to measure student progress more accurately. To further illustrate the need for certain engaged groups to have multiple descriptors of phenomena of particular interest, the example of snow is used. The English language has one word for snow that appears sufficient to describe the precipitation that falls from the sky when the weather outside dips below freezing. The Yup'ik Eskimos of Alaska, however, have multiple words for snow: a word for powdered snow, another for blowing snow, another for melted snow, and so forth (Jacobson 1984). Life in central Alaska requires and therefore recognizes the differentiation of snow types. In similar fashion, this chapter promotes the recognition and differentiation of types of college retention and promotes a more complex rather than simplistic measurement system.

## RETENTION AND DROPOUT

One of the most widely used dichotomous measures in educational research and practice is retention and dropout. Typically defined as two sides of the same coin, retention is staying in school until completion of a degree and dropping out is leaving school prematurely. It seems simplistic that retention and dropout are just purely opposites. However, more than three decades ago, Alexander Astin identified the dropout concept as a problem in his book *Predicting Academic Performance in College* (1971). According to Astin, "the term 'dropout' is imperfectly defined: the so-called dropouts may ultimately become nondropouts and vice versa. . . . But there seems to be no practical way out of the dilemma: A 'perfect' classification of dropouts versus nondropouts could be achieved only when all of the students had either died without ever finishing college or had finished college" (15). Astin added that defining "dropout" was further complicated by the prevalence of students' enrollment in several different institutions throughout their educational career (Astin 1971). According to the National Center for Education Statistics (NCES 2003a), 23.2 percent of all of the 1995–96 first-time beginning students in a four-year institution transferred to another institution by the end of the sixth year. This movement resulted in the six-year retention rate of 55.3 percent in the first institution. When subsequent institutions were considered, the retention rate rose to 62.7 percent (NCES 2003a). It is clear that retention rates can vary depending on the perspective and time at which they are measured.

The often cited Vincent Tinto (1987) agreed that there are limits to our understanding of student departure: "the label *dropout* is one of the more frequently misused terms in our lexicon of educational descriptors" (3). In fact, Tinto (1987) added that many who leave college do not see themselves as failures, but rather see their time in postsecondary instruction as a positive process of self-discovery that has resulted in individual social and intellectual maturation. John Bean (1990), agreeing with Tinto, acknowledged that students who drop out might have already achieved their goals during their limited time in college. Hence, Bean suggested that neither the student nor the college should be considered failures. Retention, as he explained, needs to be further complicated to consider student educational goals. A dropout would then be defined in comparison to student outcome versus original intent. It is only when students leave college before achieving their goals that they should be labeled a dropout.

The multiple possibilities and choices compound to make it very difficult to define retention using the simple dichotomous measure. While a dropout could be viewed as "anyone who leaves college prior to graduation," it must be accepted that a dropout may eventually return and transform into a nondropout anytime prior to death, thereby negating any earlier designations used for studies, research, or retention rates. Former dropouts may return as full-time or part-time students, return to the same institution or transfer to another institution, and remain in the same major or switch to another major.

## GRADUATION, PERSISTENCE, RETENTION, AND ATTRITION

The words *persistence* and *retention* are often used interchangeably. The National Center for Education Statistics, however, differentiates the terms by using retention as an institutional measure and persistence as a student measure. In other words, institutions retain and students persist. Another term commonly used with retention is *attrition*. Attrition is the diminution in numbers of students resulting from lower student retention.

Two important terms are *graduate* and *graduation*. Starting with a commonly used definition of a graduate—a former student who has completed a prescribed course of study in a college or university—it is clear that all graduates have persisted. However, not all persisters will graduate. Furthermore, a graduate can claim only one institution regardless of prior enrollment at other colleges or universities. While the institution from whence a student graduates will count that student as a persister, previous institutions which the student attended likely count him or her as a nonpersister or dropout. Graduation rates are clearly not the same as retention rates, but both are measures under the heading of retention. Using the preceding example, the student who transferred to another institution would negatively affect the graduation rate at the initial institution.

Further adding to the complexity of the vocabulary is variation in time spans used to measure graduation rates. Typically, colleges and universities report four-year rates, while ACT publishes five-year rates, and the National Collegiate Athletic Association reports six-year rates (U.S. Department of Education 2003). There is less agreement concerning the length of time to measure the associate degree graduation rate at community colleges. The national norms reported by Beckner, Horn, and Clune (2000) indicate that the average time between first enrollment and graduation for community college associate degree earners was about three and a half years, suggesting that the graduation rates should be measured over at least a five-year time period.

## MODELS OF RETENTION

In a quest to understand retention and its supporting terminology, we turn to the literature and proposed models of retention. The most often cited model is that of Vincent Tinto (1975), who introduced the importance of student integration (both socially and academically) in the prediction of student retention (1975, 1993). This framework was based on the work of Emile Durkheim's suicide theory (1951) that pointed to one's unsuccessful integration into society as a strong precursor of suicide. In a similar manner, Tinto's integration model suggested that retention is related to the student's ability and actions to become an involved actor in her or his institution (Tinto 1987). The integration model suggests the need for a match between the institutional environment and student commitment. A good match leads to higher student integration into the academic and social domains of college life and thus greater probability of persistence. Conversely, students are more likely to drop out or transfer to another institution when the match between the students and institution is poor.

John Bean (1990) is in full agreement of the necessity of integration—as he stated, "Retention rates are related to the interaction between the students attending the college and the characteristics of the college" (171). As the author of the student attrition model, based on the Price/Mueller model of employee turnover behavior (Bean 1980), Bean deviates from Tinto's model and stresses that students' beliefs which subsequently shape their attitudes are the predictor of their persistence. Moreover, students' beliefs are affected by the interaction between the students and different components of the institution similar to interaction between employees and corporations.

While Tinto and Bean remain the early pioneers in the retention research and model arena, the importance of the issues brought on a virtual explosion in the subsequent years. An ERIC search of the terms *college or university retention* returns in excess of 3,000 hits. A scholarly refereed quarterly journal dedicated solely to the subject, the *Journal of College Student Retention: Research, Theory & Practice*, is in operation, and new books and monographs are regularly being published. A contemporary retention researcher, John Braxton, recently edited a book where several authors reworked and examined college student retention and recommended new views on the revered theories that may more appropriately address the needs of diverse college students (2000). While the purpose of this chapter is not to review the literature, it is important to establish the firm and substantial literature base that has evolved over the last quarter-century as a testament to the importance of this issue. Curious, however, is that despite the plethora of articles and books on the topic, the concept of retention and its appropriate measurement tools remain cloaked in a significant level of ambiguity.

## MEASURING RETENTION

All colleges and universities are required to submit retention figures to federal and state governments. This task is disproportionately more difficult for community colleges because of their higher turnover rates and more diverse student enrollments, including many who attend more than one institution at a time (Hagedorn & Castro 1999). Despite the difficulty, maintaining an appropriate account of student attendance is of the utmost importance because an institution's reputation and sometimes its funding levels depend on its ability to retain a significant level of its students as proof of academic success (Tichenor & Cosgrove 1991).

In his review of retention studies in the 1960s, Summerskill (1962) showed that within each type of institution, institutional retention rates varied from 18 percent to 88 percent. Summerskill also alluded to the necessity of a standard formula for measuring retention so that the reported rates could be accurately compared. Four decades later, a standard formula has not yet been universally accepted. However, the U.S. government has established a federal definition of graduation rate as part of the Student Right-to-Know and Campus Security Act (November 8, 1990).

The Student Right-to-Know and Campus Security Act, signed November 8, 1990, requires colleges to reveal their graduation rates to enable prospective applicants to make a more informed decision regarding the suitability of the institution. The graduation rate was defined as the percentage of full-time, first-time, degree-seeking enrolled students who graduate after 150 percent of the normal time for completion, defined as six years for four-year colleges (eight semesters or twelve quarters excluding summer terms) and three years for two-year colleges (four semesters or six quarters excluding summer terms).

Although the law is an attempt to provide comparative information for prospective college students, this definition obviously excludes a large number of students enrolled in colleges and universities, including

1. Transfers from other colleges
2. Part-time students
3. Enrolled students not currently working toward a degree or certificate
4. Entering students at any other time except with the traditional fall cohort
5. Students who are undeclared in majors

Furthermore, the formula is even less appropriate for community colleges that frequently enroll very large proportions of part-time and returning students.

## Practices of Measurement

It must be noted that the federal definition is a graduation rate and not a retention rate. A search of the literature, the Internet, and numerous telephone calls and emails revealed the dominant retention and other completion measurement practices currently used.

There are two federal retention formulas employed by the National Center for Education Statistics for use in the Integrated Postsecondary Education Data System (or IPEDS): one for colleges described as "less than four-year" and another for "four-year" institutions. The only difference between the two formulas is that students finishing a program such as a short-term certificate are included in the retained proportion for colleges described as "less than four-years." The retention rate is based only on enrollment from the fall of the first year of enrollment to the fall of the next (students enrolling for the first time during the preceding summer are also included in the fall counts). Included in the calculation are only first-time, degree- or certificate-seeking students. It is important to note that the retention rate is a short-term measure that covers only one year and thus is not adjusted for students who may leave the college after the first year but before a degree is earned. Colleges submit retention rates separately for full-time and part-time students. Specifically excluded from the calculation are students who are deceased, permanently disabled, or have joined armed forces or foreign aid service of the federal government and students who are on official church missions (NCES 2003b). The currently posted formulas for retention rate (RR) are as follows:

$$\text{IPEDS RR}_{\text{less than 4-year}} =$$
$$\frac{(\text{Number of students reenrolled in the following fall} + \text{Number of students who have completed})}{(\text{Number of students in the fall cohort} - \text{Exclusions})} * 100$$

and

$$\text{IPEDS RR}_{4\text{-year}} = \frac{\text{Number of students reenrolled in the following fall}}{(\text{Number of students in the fall cohort} - \text{Exclusions}))*100}.$$

In essence, the formulas used for IPEDS lead the field as the dominant formulas used in the calculation of retention rates, as they are the formulas generally used to report to the federal and state governments, but there remains differentiation on calculations and reported values among some institutions and policymaking bodies. For example, the National Information Center for Higher Education Policymaking and Analysis (NCHEMS), a body that provides state policymakers and others with information used to make important decisions, calculates and provides multiple data on completion rates by state using measures such as three-year associate degree ($ADR_3$) and six-year bachelor degree ($BDR_6$) acquisition rates; the associate ($ADR_{100}$) and bachelor degrees ($BDR_{100}$) awarded per 100 undergraduates; and the number of degrees awarded per high school graduates three and six years earlier ($AD_{HS3}$ and $BD_{HS6}$) (NCHEMS, n.d.).

The $ADR_3$ and $BDR_6$ include only first-time, full-time, degree-seeking students and thus exclude all part-time and transfer students, while the $ADR_{100}$ and $BDR_{100}$ include all students (headcount). The $AD_{HS3}$ and $BD_{HS6}$ are also based on headcounts but at the high school level and therefore include only those students who go directly to college after high school graduation (NCHEMS, n.d.).

## Common Data Set

The Common Data Set (CDS) is a joint effort by the higher education community and publishers including the College Board, *Peterson's*, *U.S. News & World Report*, and others to establish and develop clear standard definitions on the data items to be used in educational research (Peterson's 1998). The CDS is an important initiative to improve the comparability of data reported by colleges and to assist colleges and universities to ask survey questions in a standard way. While the CDS is not a mechanism for forwarding specific measures, its popularity among institutions supports the calculations and dissemination of specific institutional measures. The Common Data Set consists of ten areas of data:

1. General information
2. Enrollment and persistence figures

3. First-time, first-year (freshman) admission

4. Transfer admission

5. Academic offerings and policies

6. Student life

7. Annual expenses

8. Financial aid

9. Instructional faculty and class size

10. Degrees conferred

The Common Data Set for 2003–2004 has approximately 120 definitions that cover terms from "tuition" to "Carnegie units." As the initiative develops, new items are added and some items are edited. The CDS measurement for persistence is the same as that reported for IPEDS for both four-year and less-than-four-year institutions and thus further serves to nationalize the calculations; however, other measures help define success in more diverse ways.

## Community Colleges

There is more variation regarding the measure of retention among community colleges. The Research and Planning Group for California (RP Group, no date) and the Transfer and Retention of Urban Community College Students Project (TRUCCS) both support the use of the successful course completion ratio (SCCR) (Hagedorn 2004). Simply stated, a course completion ratio is the proportion or percentage of courses that a student completes as compared to the number of courses in which the student enrolls. Mathematically, the calculation is

$$SCCR = \frac{\text{Number of courses with the grade of A, B, C, D, CR, or P}}{\text{Number of courses of enrollment}}.$$

Completion ratios can be computed for different periods of time (for example, semester, academic year, or over several years) and flex to accommodate the full-time or part-time student. The SCCR is a continuous measure (from 0 to 100 percent), and compares a student's progress toward her or his goals. One of the major problems associated with measuring community college student retention is that many students enter the college without the goal of continuing enrollment or of ultimate graduation. Some students have achieved their postsecondary goals by taking a course or a few courses or transferring to another institution prior to graduation. The typical measures of retention and persistence provide misleading evidence of success and nonsuccess. The SCCR makes a basic assumption: a student enrolling in a course is declaring her or his goal of completing the course. Thus, a student who enrolls in four courses and successfully completes all of them has an SCCR of 100 percent. Likewise, if the student were to complete only two courses, he or she would earn an SCCR of 50 percent. The SCCR makes sense as a tool of measurement in institutions where students may frequently "stop out" and return, have diverse academic goals, are not all degree seeking, and may be enrolled in more than one institution.

## TYPES OF RETENTION

The formulas and discussion presuppose that retention exists in one variety—that is, that students either remain at an institution or do not. The truth is that retention comes in multiple varieties. There are at least four basic types of retention: institutional, system, in the major (discipline), and in a particular course.

## Institutional Retention

Institutional retention is the most basic and easy to understand and is the type measured in the formulas discussed in this chapter. In essence, institutional retention is the measure of the proportion of students who remain enrolled at the *same* institution from year to year.

## System Retention

System retention focuses on the student and turns a blind eye on which institution a student is enrolled in. Using system persistence as a measure, a student who leaves one institution to attend another is considered a persister. Therefore, system persistence accommodates the frequent occurrence of transfer or reenrollment at another campus, in another state, or in another institutional type (for example, in a for-profit). Some states, such as Texas and New York, have coordinating boards that track students who have transferred to other universities within the state, thus keeping track of a limited type of system retention (i.e., system retention within the state university system). Nevertheless, those who transferred out of institutions governed by the coordinating board are generally not tracked. While the measure of system persistence is important to truly understand and measure student success, it requires tracking—a very expensive and difficult procedure. Currently, the only national tracking done is via the National Student Loan Clearinghouse.

The National Student Loan Clearinghouse is a nonprofit organization designed to verify degrees and standardize student loan status. Participation in the clearinghouse, at a small per-student fee, requires that participating colleges submit a student enrollment status report. While the National Loan Clearinghouse data are frequently used for system persistence measures, it must be stated that the data were not originally designed to be used in that manner and all institutions do not participate.

## Retention Within a Major or Discipline

Another type of retention takes a more limited view of the topic by viewing retention within a major area of study, discipline, or specific department. For example, a student who declares engineering as a major but then switches to biology may be retained in an institutional sense but is lost to the college of engineering. Nonpersisters in one discipline may earn a degree in another major within the institution of original entry and thus be institutionally retained but departmentally nonretained. Retention within certain majors, such as engineering, may be of special interest because of the difficulty of recruitment and the predicted shortages in the fields. Engineering has a high rate of nonretention in the major, especially among women and people of color (Daempfle 2003). Retention within the major may be tracked by specific colleges or universities but is not nationally tracked and remains difficult to measure.

## Retention Within the Course

The smallest unit of analysis with respect to retention is that measured by course completion. Studying at the course level allows the specific determination of which courses are not being completed even though a student may be retained within the institution. As specific as course retention appears to be, it is still fraught with questions of measurement. The TRUCCS Project documented large variation in course completion depending on the time of measurement (Hagedorn 2003). Course completion is much higher when using the first day of class as the marker to determine if a student attempted a course versus waiting until after the add/drop time. The add/drop period is provided to allow institutions the flexibility to close courses that have inadequate enrollments and to allow students to drop courses that may be inappropriate (too easy or too hard) and to add others that may be more suitable. Using the cessation of the add/drop period as the timing for the calculation means that an attempt is defined as a course in which a student obtained a letter grade (A, B, C, D, F, W, P, or I). While the add/drop process most certainly has a positive function from both the student and the institutional viewpoint, it must be stated that during the registration process, courses frequently close when the maximum enrollment is reached, thus barring other students who may desire to enroll in the course. When enrolled students drop the course, they leave open seats that may have been better utilized by another student who was denied enrollment. Course completion is not nationally posted or compared. Community colleges more typically measure course completion because they generally have more variation in the measure.

## PROBLEMS WITH THE CURRENT MEASURES

The current definitions and formulas do not include all students and so may provide inaccurate measures of retention. Again, as an example of exclusions and confusions, the reader is directed to the initial vignettes of students provided at the beginning of the chapter—those student activities that defy the current definitions. Furthermore, there may be a bit of university "sleight of hand" associated with practices that reflect on reported figures. For some time now the *U.S. News & World Report* has published its annual rankings of colleges and universities. The rankings serve as a prestige barometer and create an intense competition especially among top research universities. To establish the highest rankings, universities can be somewhat creative in who is counted and who is not. For example, some universities will admit only those students with the very highest admission scores (SAT or ACT) in the fall cohort while extending admission to a second group of students with slightly lower scores for the spring semester or quarter. This procedure allows the universities to post their incoming freshman average SAT scores as being higher than they would be if all admits (fall and spring) were included. While the reports of fall-to-fall retention are surely accurate, they include only those students who were admitted in the fall and are those students with the highest admissions criteria and thus are most likely to be retained.

The current formulas for retention include those students who are most likely to persist and thus may provide an inflated figure less representative of the variation of student persistence. In short, the formulas generally exclude

- Part-time students
- Returning students
- Transfers
- Students who prematurely leave after the second year of enrollment

On the other hand, the formulas for retention allow the inclusion of some students as retained who probably should not be, for example, the student who enrolls in fall, drops all courses, but reenrolls the next fall (and might drop again). The retained formula does not contain all those retained, and the dropout figures do not include all those who prematurely leave or are ambiguously enrolled. We have no descriptor or measurement for the student who takes courses in a haphazard manner such that while credits are accrued (retained), no degree progress is made. No descriptor or formula includes those who appear trapped in remedial courses and although enrolled and earning credits are not earning credits that can be counted for a college degree.

## RETENTION FROM MULTIPLE ANGLES: THE NEW PROPOSED FORMULAS

Single measures of retention do not tell the whole story of student persistence. To provide full understanding of an institution's rate of student success, multiple indicators should be calculated and reported. At a minimum, institutions should regularly report institutional persistence, transfer rates (both the proportion of students who transfer to other institutions and the proportion who transfer in from other institutions), and course completion ratios.

It is recommended that a new measure of pure institutional retention that includes part-time students, continuing students, transfer students, advanced students, and those who begin enrollment at times other than with the fall cohort be reported, perhaps juxtaposed with the fall cohort variety that is frequently but solely used. The new proposed formula for degree-seeking students that could be calculated each year is

**Pure Institutional Persistence** (performed annually) =

$$\frac{\text{Current total FTE degree-seeking enrollment} - (\text{current year newly enrolled students})}{\text{Past year's fall FTE degree-seeking enrollment} + (\text{FTE enrollment of degree-seeking spring and summer}) - \text{FTE graduates}}.$$

A system persistence formula could be similarly calculated (of course, while a formula can be proposed, actual tracking of all college students on a national level is currently not available):

**Pure System Persistence** (performed annually) =

$$\frac{\text{Current total national FTE degree-seeking enrollment} - (\text{current year newly enrolled students})}{\substack{\text{Past year's total national fall FTE degree-seeking enrollment} \\ + (\text{FTE enrollment of degree-seeking spring and summer}) \\ - \text{FTE graduates}}}.$$

Persistence by major may also be performed for most disciplines thus providing a retention measure of the students declaring their initial interest areas. The calculation should be similarly cast as above but substituting the FTE students graduating within a major of those FTEs originally declaring the major.

Two final equations are suggested to complete the picture of student retention: successful course completion ratios and graduation rates. Successful course completion ratios can be calculated globally (all courses in the college or university) and within departments to provide a final and fine-tuned measure of retention. The formula for SCCR was provided earlier in the chapter. Graduation rates provide a measure of retention along with a measure of progress. The proposed equation is similar to that currently used, except that it employs FTEs and includes transfers in:

$$\text{Graduation rate}_{4\text{-year institution}} =$$
$$\frac{\text{FTE graduates throughout the academic year}}{\substack{\text{FTE students entering academic year 6 years ago} \\ (\text{including fall, spring, and summer entrants})}}.$$

## CONCLUSION

Why are college retention and its appropriate measurement so important? According to the U.S. Census Bureau, the average household income rises $14,354 and $37,874 when the householder educational attainment increases from high school graduate to associate degree holder to bachelor degree holder, respectively (Postsecondary Education Opportunity 2002). Lower incomes generally correlate with many social problems and lower living standards (McMahon 2000). Retention not only has an impact on the individual and her or his family but also produces a ripple effect on the postsecondary institutions, the workforce, and the economy.

## College Effect

Retention is one of the most common ways students, parents, and stakeholders evaluate the effectiveness of colleges. A positive reputation increases a college's ability to attract the best students and faculty. Furthermore, when a student withdraws from college the invested institutional resources were not spent wisely, forcing the college to invest additional resources to recruit new students. Noel-Levitz (2004), acknowledging the significant institutional costs, posted their *Retention Savings Worksheet* providing a formula to calculate the amount of institutional savings when the first- to second-year dropout rate is reduced. While the formula is rather complex, the two provided examples, one for a public institution and one for a private institution, show that significant savings can be accrued when the dropout rate is reduced by even a small percentage.

## Workforce Effect

Nonpersisting students lack the college training and credentials to enter the professional workforce. Industries not finding sufficiently trained workers must either invest in their own training programs or relocate to areas where sufficiently trained workers are more available, sometimes even going overseas. There is evidence, for example, of a decline in retention to science and engineering graduate programs having a significant workforce effect (Andrade et al. 2002).

## Economic Effect

From the economic point of view, higher education attainment leads to decreases in long-term poverty, higher personal per-capita income, a higher state tax base, and a stronger economy (McMahon 2000). In short, a more educated citizenry leads to advantages on many levels.

The importance of the topic is obvious. The current measures are insufficient to understand the topic and thus hinder researchers from validly identifying the predictors. The inaccurate research prevents policymakers from constructing the best policy to increase student success. This chapter encourages colleges and universities to calculate and disseminate multiple measures of retention. Moreover, it is hoped that a national tracking system that includes all colleges and universities including accredited for-profits will be constructed to track student progress. Although such a system will be very expensive, the importance of this project speaks loudly for its necessity. The old adage attributed to Derek Bok—"If you think education is expensive, try ignorance"—may be apt.

## REFERENCES

Andrade, S. J, Stigall, S., Kappus, S. S., Ruddock, M., & Oburn, M. (2002). A model retention program for science and engineering students: Contributions of the Institutional Research Office. El Paso: University of Texas.

Astin, A. W. (1971). *Predicting academic performance in college: Selectivity data for 2300 American colleges.* New York: The Free Press.

Bean, J. P. (1980). Dropouts and turnover: The synthesis and test of a causal model of student attrition. *Research in Higher Education* 12(2): 155–187.

———. (1990). Using retention research in enrollment management. In *The strategic management of college enrollments,* ed. D. Hossler, J. P. Bean, & Associates, 170–185. San Francisco: Jossey-Bass.

Berkner, L., Horn, L., & Clune, M. (2000). *Descriptive summary of 1995–96 beginning postsecondary students: Three years later.* NCES 2000–154. Washington, DC: U.S. Department of Education.

Braxton, J. M., ed. (2000). *Reworking the student departure puzzle.* Nashville: Vanderbilt University Press.

Daempfle, P. A. (2003). An analysis of the high attrition rates among first year college science, math, and engineering, majors. *Journal of College Student Retention: Research, Theory & Practice* 5(1): 37–52.

Durkheim, E. (1951). *Suicide.* New York: The Free Press.

Hagedorn, L. S. (2003). Executive reports. Unpublished reports from the Transfer and Retention of Urban Community College (TRUCCS) Project to the Los Angeles Community College District. Los Angeles: Los Angeles Community College District.

———. (2004, April). Speaking community college: A glossary of appropriate terms. Paper presented at the meeting of Council for the Study of Community Colleges (CSCC), Minneapolis, Minnesota.

Hagedorn, L. S., & Castro, C. R. (1999). Paradoxes: California's experience with reverse transfer students. In *Understanding the impact of reverse transfer students on community colleges,* ed. B. K. Townsend, 15–26. San Francisco: Jossey-Bass.

Jacobson, S. (1984). *Yup'ik Eskimo dictionary.* Fairbanks: University of Alaska Press.

McMahon, W. W. (2000). *Education and development: Measuring the social benefits.* Oxford: Oxford University Press.

National Center for Education Statistics (NCES). (2003a). The integrated postsecondary education data system (IPEDS). http://www.nces.ed.gov/ipeds/ (accessed May 1, 2004).

———. (2003b). Instructions for enrollment. http://nces.ed.gov/ipeds/pdf/web base2003/ef_inst.pdf (accessed May 2, 2004).

National Center for Higher Education Management Systems (NCHEMS). (2002). http://www.higheredinfo.org/ (accessed April 29, 2004).

Noel-Levitz. (2004). Retention savings worksheet. http://www.noellevitz.com/pdfs/RetSvgsWkst.pdf (accessed February 15, 2004).

Peterson's. (1998). Peterson's news about the common data set. http://www.petersons.com/research/he/cds (accessed April 28, 2004).

Postsecondary Education Opportunity. (2002). Average household income by educational attainment of householder, 2002. http://www.postsecondary.org/archives/Posters/AvgHshldIncbyEd02.pdf (accessed May 5, 2004).

RP Group (n.d.). http://rpgroup.org/Projects/Oper_Definitions/definitions1.htm (accessed May 1, 2004).

State Higher Education Executive Officers (SHEEO). (2004). http://www.sheeo.org (accessed May 12, 2004).

Student-Right-To-Know and Campus Security Act. November 8, 1990. Public Law 101–542. U.S. Code 1001.

Summerskill, J. (1962). Dropouts from college. In *The American college*, ed. Nevitt Standards, New York: John Wiley and Sons.

Tichenor, R., & Cosgrove, J.J. (1991). Evaluating retention-driven marketing in a community college: An alternative approach. *New Directions for Institutional Research* 18(2): 73–81.

Tinto, V. (1975). Dropout from higher education: A theoretical synthesis of recent research. *Review of Educational Research* 65 (Winter): 89–125.

———. (1987). *Leaving college: Rethinking the causes and cures of student attrition.* Chicago: University of Chicago Press.

———. (1993). *Leaving college: Rethinking the causes and cures of student attrition.* 2nd ed. Chicago: University of Chicago Press.

U.S. Census Bureau. (2000). http://www.census.gov (accessed January 13, 2004).

U.S. Department of Education, National Center for Education Statistics. (2003). The condition of education. NCES 2003-067,1. Washington, DC: U.S. Government Printing Office, 2003.

# CHAPTER 5

# Toward Reliable Knowledge about College Student Departure

*John M. Braxton and Stephanie D. Lee*

## INTRODUCTION

Scholars have studied the college student departure process for over seventy years (Braxton 2000). The longevity of such research speaks to the nettlesome nature that this problem poses to higher education in general and to individual colleges and universities in particular. Current rates of student departure adversely affect the public's perception of the quality of colleges and universities and the stability of their enrollments and budgets (Braxton, Hirschy, & McClendon 2004). Some student departure may be in the best interests of either the individual student or the institution (Tinto 1982). However, unnecessary student departure requires attention. Rather than trial-and-error, commonsensical efforts to reduce student departure (Braxton 2001–2002), reliable knowledge must guide the development and implementation of institutional policies and programs to reduce individual student departure. Policies and programs rooted in reliable knowledge provide powerful levers for institutional action (Braxton & Mundy 2001–2002).

Given a critical need for reliable knowledge about college student departure, we identify such knowledge in this chapter. Reliability refers to consistency in measurement of variables (Babbie 2001; McMillan & Schumacher 2001). Reliable knowledge results from replications.

What is sufficient evidence of consistency in research findings? Psychologists in identifying "well-established" treatments for psychosocial problems or disorders stipulate that at least two, between-group design experiments must show that either the treatment outperforms the control group or the treatment outperforms or is equal to an already established treatment (Task Force 1995; Crits-Christoph 1998). Reliable knowledge and well-established treatments are interchangeable. Although it is possible to conduct between-group experiments to identify effective retention strategies, the study of forces that influence student departure defy experimental design with random assignment of subjects to treatment and control groups.

However, we can approximate such experiments through research studies that use multivariate statistical procedures to identify factors that influence the departure decisions of college students. Moreover, we can also require more than two affirming between-group experiments to identify knowledge as reliable. We designate a threshold of ten or more tests of the influence of a given factor as the basis for determining reliability. If seven out of ten tests yield the same result, then reliable knowledge obtains. Put differently, 70 percent of ten or more tests must yield affirming results to designate a finding as reliable knowledge. We acknowledge that some readers may prefer a different threshold of tests and percent of consistent results or tests.

## TINTO'S INTERACTIONALIST THEORY AS ORGANIZING FRAMEWORK

Pantages and Creedon (1978, 94) admonished the educational community more than twenty-five years ago that the isolation of factors or groups of factors is misguided because departure is a complicated interplay among many factors. Theory, however, gives meaning to putatively isolated factors or groups of factors because it offers an understanding of the connections among such factors. Accordingly, we use the formulations of Tinto's 1975 interactionalist theory of college student departure as a framework for the identification of reliable knowledge. We use this theory because it is paradigmatic in the study of college student departure (Braxton, Hirschy, & McClendon 2004). The more than 775 citations to this theory index the predominance of this theory (Braxton, Hirschy, & McClendon 2004). Given its paradigmatic stature, this theory has been the object of considerable empirical research, research that has tested the empirical validity of its formulations.

We use Tinto's theory solely as a framework for delineating reliable knowledge about the college student departure process. The empirical validity of this theory is not of interest. Because we use this theory as a framework for understanding the connections among the factors deemed as empirically reliable, we present Tinto's theory in narrative form.

Tinto regards student departure as a longitudinal process during which the individual student ascribes meaning to his or her interactions with the formal and informal dimensions of a given college or university (Braxton, Sullivan, & Johnson 1997; Tinto 1986, 1993). Such interactions transpire between the individual student and the academic and social systems of a college or university.

Tinto posits that various individual characteristics (e.g., family background, individual attributes, and pre-college schooling experiences) that a student possesses as he or she enters college directly influence his or her departure decision, as well as initial commitments to the institution and to the goal of college graduation (Tinto 1975). Initial commitment to the institution and initial commitment to the goal of graduation influence the level of a student's integration into the academic and social systems of the college or university.

Academic integration includes structural and normative dimensions (Tinto 1975, 104). Structural integration involves the meeting of explicit standards of the college or university, whereas normative integration relates to an individual's affiliation with the normative structure of the academic system.

Social integration concerns the degree of congruency between the individual student and the social systems of a college or university. Social integration takes place both at the level of the college or university and at the level of a subculture of an institution (Tinto 1975, 107). Social integration reflects the student's perception of his or her degree of congruence with the attitudes, values, beliefs, and norms of the social communities of a college or university.

Academic and social integration influence a student's subsequent commitments to the institution and to the goal of college graduation. The greater the student's level of academic integration, the greater the level of subsequent commitment to the goal of college graduation (Tinto 1975). In addition, the greater the student's level of social integration, the greater the level of subsequent commitment to the focal college or university (Tinto 1975, 110).

The student's initial level of institutional commitment and commitment to the goal of graduation from college also influence his or her level of subsequent commitments. The greater the levels of subsequent institutional commitment and commitment to the goal of college graduation, the greater the likelihood that the individual will persist in college.

The formulations of this theory yield thirteen testable propositions (Braxton, Sullivan, & Johnson 1997). These propositions are logically interrelated and as a set explain college student departure (Braxton, Sullivan, & Johnson 1997). We use empirical tests of each of these thirteen propositions as a basis for the identification of reliable knowledge about the process of college student departure. The thirteen propositions are as follows:

1. Student entry characteristics affect the level of initial commitment to the institution.
2. Student entry characteristics affect the level of initial commitment to the goal of graduation from college.
3. Student entry characteristics directly affect the student's likelihood of persistence in college.
4. Initial commitment to the goal of graduation from college affects the level of academic integration.
5. Initial commitment to the goal of graduation from college affects the level of social integration.
6. Initial commitment to the institution affects the level of social integration.
7. Initial commitment to the institution affects the level of academic integration.
8. The greater the degree of academic integration, the greater the level of subsequent commitment to the goal of graduation from college.
9. The greater the degree of social integration, the greater the level of subsequent commitment to the institution.
10. The initial level of institutional commitment affects the subsequent level of institutional commitment.
11. The initial level of commitment to the goal of graduation from college affects the subsequent level of commitment to the goal of graduation from college.
12. The greater the level of subsequent commitment to the goal of graduation from college, the greater the likelihood of student persistence in college.
13. The greater the level of subsequent commitment to the institution, the greater the likelihood of student persistence in college.

Tinto (1975) postulated the direction of the influence for propositions 8 to 13. However, he does not posit the direction of the influence for propositions 1 to 7. We designate support for propositions 1 to 7 if the proposition receives statistically significant support regardless of the direction of the influence.

We identified studies that test one or more of these thirteen propositions. We used only tests conducted using such multivariate statistical procedures as path analysis with linear multiple regression, LISREL, multiple discriminate analysis, or logistic regression. Such statistical procedures provide us with an appraisal of the independent effects of each of the thirteen propositions and beyond other constructs posited to influence student departure (Braxton, Sullivan, & Johnson 1997). Moreover, only tests of propositions using measures we judged as having face validity were included.

We restricted our identification of tests of these propositions to peer-reviewed studies published in refereed academic and professional journals or papers presented at the meetings of academic and professional associations. We made this restriction because peer review provides some warranty that the focal study makes a contribution and meets various scholarly criteria (Anderson & Louis 1991).

Because Tinto emphasizes that his theory strives to explain the departure process within a given college or university and "is not a systems model of departure" (Tinto 1993, 112), we use only tests of propositions that were conducted using single-institutional samples.

## DELINEATION OF RELIABLE KNOWLEDGE

Important distinctions exist between residential and commuter colleges and universities (Braxton, Hirschy, & McClendon 2004). Residential colleges and universities have well-defined social communities. In contrast, the social communities of commuter colleges and universities lack structure and clarity (Braxton, Hirschy, & McClendon 2004). Students in commuter institutions also experience conflicts between attending college and other obligations such as work and family (Tinto 1993). These critical distinctions indicate that the college student departure process may differ between residential and commuter collegiate institutions (Braxton, Hirschy, & McClendon 2004).

Consequently, we delineate those propositions deemed reliable for residential colleges and universities and those for commuter colleges and universities. We concentrate on four-year commuter colleges and universities and not on two-year colleges because of the indeterminate nature of empirical research testing Tinto's propositions in this institutional setting (Braxton, Sullivan, & Johnson 1997; Braxton, Hirschy, & McClendon 2004).

We organize our findings according to each of the thirteen propositions. For each proposition, we describe the number of tests conducted and the number of affirming tests in residential colleges and universities and in commuter colleges and universities. Because Tinto (1975) views student entry characteristics as a category of variables, we aggregate tests of family background characteristics, individual attributes, and pre-college schooling to determine whether reliable knowledge results from tests of propositions 1, 2, and 3.

Table 5.1 exhibits the tests of propositions carried out in residential colleges and universities. Table 5.2 displays the tests of propositions made in commuter colleges and universities.

*Proposition 1. Student entry characteristics affect the level of initial commitment to the institution.* In residential colleges and universities, this proposition was tested twenty-nine times. Of these twenty-nine tests, sixteen produced affirming results, or fifty-five percent of these tests. As a consequence, reliable knowledge fails to result.

Likewise, reliable knowledge fails to materialize in commuter colleges and universities. Although the four tests conducted produced confirming results, the threshold of ten tests was not met.

*Proposition 2. Student entry characteristics affect the level of initial commitment to the goal of graduation from college.* This proposition was tested six times in residential colleges and universities. Although four of these tests produced affirming results, the threshold of ten tests of this proposition was not reached. Thus, we fail to recognize this knowledge as reliable.

The number of tests of this proposition in commuter colleges and universities also fails to reach the threshold of ten tests as three tests were identified. However, these three tests produced confirming results.

*Proposition 3. Student entry characteristics directly affect the student's likelihood of persistence in college.* The number of tests of this proposition in residential colleges and universities exceeds the threshold of ten, as nineteen tests were conducted. Despite meeting the threshold, reliable knowledge does not result, as seven of the nineteen tests produced verifying results.

Reliable knowledge concerning this proposition also fails to emerge from tests conducted in commuter colleges and universities. Despite substantiating results from the four tests conducted, the minimum number of ten tests was not met.

*Proposition 4. Initial commitment to the goal of graduation from college affects the level of academic integration.* Seven tests of this proposition took

**Table 5.1**
**Propositional Tests Conducted in Residential Colleges and Universities**

| Propositions | Propositional Tests |
|---|---|
| 1. Student entry characteristics affect the level of initial commitment to the institution. | Total of 29 tests<br><br>*Supportive* (16 tests)<br>Pascarella & Terenzini (1983)<br>Terenzini, Pascarella, Theophilides, & Lorang (1985) 3 tests<br>Braxton, Bray, & Berger (2000) 5 tests<br>Berger (1997) 3 tests<br>Bray, Braxton, & Sullivan (1999)<br>Helland, Stallings, & Braxton (2001–2002) 3 tests<br><br>*Unsupportive* (13 tests)<br>Terenzini, Pascarella, Theophilides, & Lorang (1985) 6 tests<br>Braxton, Bray, & Berger (2000)<br>Berger (1997) 3 tests<br>Helland, Stallings, & Braxton (2001–2002)<br>Perry, Cabrera, & Vogt (1999) 2 tests |
| 2. Student entry characteristics affect the level of initial commitment to the goal of graduation from college. | Total of 6 tests<br><br>*Supportive* (4 tests)<br>Pascarella & Terenzini (1983) Terenzini, Pascarella, Theophilides, & Lorang (1985) 3 tests<br><br>*Unsupportive* (2 tests)<br>Terenzini, Pascarella, Theophilides, & Lorang (1985) 2 tests |
| 3. Student entry characteristics directly affect the student's likelihood of persistence in college. | Total of 19 tests<br><br>*Supportive* (7 tests)<br>Allen (1999)<br>Dubrock (2000)<br>Ott (1988)<br>Pike, Schroeder, & Berry (1997) 4 tests<br><br>*Unsupportive* (12 tests)<br>Terenzini, Pascarella, Theophilides, & Lorang (1985) 6 tests<br>Pascarella, Terenzini, & Wolfle (1986) 3 tests<br>Berger & Milem (1999) 3 tests |

**Table 5.1 (continued)**

| Propositions | Propositional Tests |
|---|---|
| 4. Initial commitment to the goal of graduation from college affects the level of academic integration. | Total of 7 tests<br><br>*Supportive* (2 tests)<br>  Peterson (1993)<br>  Pascarella & Terenzini (1983)<br><br>*Unsupportive* (5 tests)<br>  Terenzini, Pascarella, Theophilides, & Lorang (1985) 2 tests<br>  Stage (1988) 2 tests<br>  Pascarella, Terenzini, & Wolfle (1986) |
| 5. Initial commitment to the goal of graduation from college affects the level of social integration. | Total of 4 tests<br><br>*Supportive* (4 tests)<br>  Pascarella & Terenzini (1983)<br>  Peterson (1993)<br>  Terenzini, Pascarella, Theophilides, & Lorang (1985)<br>  Pascarella, Terenzini, & Wolfle (1986) |
| 6. Initial commitment to the institution affects the level of social integration. | Total of 14 tests<br><br>*Supportive* (4 tests)<br>  Peterson (1993)<br>  Stage (1988) 2 tests<br>  Bray, Braxton, & Sullivan (1999)<br><br>*Unsupportive* (10 tests)<br>  Pascarella, Terenzini, & Wolfle (1986)<br>  Terenzini, Pascarella, Theophilides, & Lorang (1985) 2 tests<br>  Braxton, Bray, & Berger (2000)<br>  Berger (1997)<br>  Milem & Berger (1997)<br>  Berger & Braxton (1998)<br>  Berger & Milem (1999)<br>  Braxton, Milem, & Sullivan (2000)<br>  Helland, Stallings, & Braxton (2001–2002) |
| 7. Initial commitment to the institution affects the level of academic integration. | Total of 9 tests<br><br>*Supportive* (1 test)<br>  Peterson (1993)<br><br>*Unsupportive* (8 tests)<br>  Pascarella & Terenzini (1983) 3 tests<br>  Pascarella, Terenzini, & Wolfle (1986)<br>  Terenzini, Pascarella, Theophilides, & Lorang (1985) |

**Table 5.1 (continued)**

| Propositions | Propositional Tests |
|---|---|
| | Braxton, Bray, & Berger (2000)<br>Milem & Berger (1997)<br>Berger & Milem (1999) |
| 8. The greater the degree of academic integration, the greater the level of subsequent commitment to the goal of graduation from college. | Total of 8 tests<br><br>*Supportive* (8 tests)<br>Aitken (1982)<br>House (1992)<br>Leppel (2001)<br>Pascarella & Terenzini (1983)<br>Pascarella, Terenzini, & Wolfle (1986)<br>Terenzini, Pascarella, Theophilides, & Lorang (1985) 2 tests<br>Thomas (2000) |
| 9. The greater the degree of social integration, the greater the level of subsequent commitment to the institution. | Total of 19 tests<br><br>*Supportive* (16 tests)<br>Aitken (1982)<br>Pascarella & Terenzini (1983)<br>Stage (1988) 2 tests<br>Pascarella, Terenzini, & Wolfle (1986)<br>Terenzini, Pascarella, Theophilides, & Lorang (1985)<br>Braxton, Bray, & Berger (2000)<br>Berger (1997)<br>Bray, Braxton, & Sullivan (1999)<br>Pike, Schroeder, & Berry (1997) 2 tests<br>Milem & Berger (1997)<br>Berger & Braxton (1998)<br>Berger & Milem (1999)<br>Braxton, Milem, & Sullivan (2000)<br>Helland, Stallings, & Braxton (2001–2002)<br><br>*Unsupportive* (3 tests)<br>Terenzini, Pascarella, Theophilides, & Lorang (1985)<br>French, Immekus, & Oakes (2002)<br>Thomas (2000) |
| 10. The initial level of institutional commitment affects the subsequent level of institutional commitment. | Total of 11 tests<br><br>*Supportive* (9 tests)<br>Pascarella & Terenzini (1983)<br>Stage (1988)<br>Pascarella, Terenzini, & Wolfle (1986)<br>Terenzini, Pascarella, Theophilides, & Lorang (1985) 2 tests<br>Braxton, Bray, & Berger (2000)<br>Berger & Milem (1999) |

## Table 5.1 (continued)

| Propositions | Propositional Tests |
|---|---|
| | Milem & Berger (1997)<br>Helland, Stallings, & Braxton (2001–2002)<br><br>*Unsupportive* (2 tests)<br>Stage (1988)<br>Berger & Braxton (1998) |
| 11. The initial level of commitment to the goal of graduation from college affects the subsequent level of commitment to the goal of graduation from college. | Total of 6 tests<br><br>*Supportive* (6 tests)<br>Pascarella & Terenzini (1983)<br>Pascarella, Terenzini, & Wolfle (1986)<br>Terenzini, Pascarella, Theophilides, & Lorang (1985)<br>  2 tests<br>Stage (1988) 2 tests |
| 12. The greater the level of subsequent commitment to the goal of graduation from college, the greater the likelihood of student persistence in college | Total of 9 tests<br><br>*Supportive* (6 tests)<br>Pascarella & Terenzini (1980)<br>Pascarella & Terenzini (1983)<br>Terenzini, Lorang & Pascarella (1981)<br>Pascarella, Terenzini, & Wolfle (1986)<br>Terenzini, Pascarella, Theophilides, & Lorang (1985)<br>  2 tests<br><br>*Unsupportive* (3 tests)<br>Brower (1992)<br>Perry, Cabrera, & Vogt (1999)<br>Thomas (2000) |
| 13. The greater the level of subsequent commitment to the institution, the greater the likelihood of student persistence in college. | Total of 13 tests<br><br>*Supportive* (11 tests)<br>Pascarella & Terenzini (1980)<br>Pascarella & Terenzini (1983)<br>Terenzini, Pascarella, & Lorang (1981)<br>Pascarella, Terenzini, & Wolfle (1986)<br>Terenzini, Pascarella, Theophilides, & Lorang (1985)<br>  2 tests<br>Pike, Schroeder, & Berry (1997)<br>Berger & Milem (1999)<br>Brower (1992)<br>Perry, Cabrera, & Vogt (1999)<br>Mallette & Cabrera (1991)<br><br>*Unsupportive* (2 tests)<br>Pike, Schroeder, & Berry (1997)<br>Thomas (2000) |

**Table 5.2**
**Propositional Tests Conducted in Commuter Colleges and Universities**

| Propositions | Propositional Tests |
|---|---|
| 1. Student entry characteristics affect the level of initial commitment to the institution. | Total of 4 tests<br><br>*Supportive* (4 tests)<br>Allen (1986)<br>Braxton, Duster, & Pascarella (1988)<br>Pascarella, Duby, & Iverson (1983)<br>Cabrera, Nora, & Castaneda (1992) |
| 2. Student entry characteristics affect the level of initial commitment to the goal of graduation from college. | Total of 3 tests<br><br>*Supportive* (3 tests)<br>Allen (1986)<br>Pascarella, Duby, & Iverson (1983)<br>Cabrera, Nora, & Castaneda (1992) |
| 3. Student entry characteristics directly affect the student's likelihood of persistence in college. | Total of 4 tests<br><br>*Supportive* (4 tests)<br>Allen (1986)<br>Pascarella, Duby, & Iverson (1983)<br>Metzner & Bean (1987)<br>Moline (1987) |
| 4. Initial commitment to the goal of graduation from college affects the level of academic integration. | Total of 2 tests<br><br>*Supportive* (2 tests)<br>Allen (1986)<br>Braxton, Duster, & Pascarella (1988) |
| 5. Initial commitment to the goal of graduation from college affects the level of social integration. | Total of 1 test<br><br>*Supportive* (1 test)<br>Allen (1986) |
| 6. Initial commitment to the institution affects the level of social integration. | Total of 4 tests<br><br>*Unsupportive* (4 tests)<br>Allen (1986)<br>Braxton, Duster, & Pascarella (1988)<br>Braxton & Brier (1989)<br>Pascarella, Duby, & Iverson (1983) |
| 7. Initial commitment to the institution affects the level of academic integration. | Total of 1 test<br><br>*Supportive* (1 test)<br>Pascarella, Duby, & Iverson (1983) |

**Table 5.2 (continued)**

| Propositions | Propositional Tests |
|---|---|
| 8. The greater the degree of academic integration, the greater the level of subsequent commitment to the goal of graduation from college. | Total of 3 tests<br><br>*Supportive* (2 tests)<br>   Allen (1986)<br>   Cabrera, Nora, & Castaneda (1992)<br><br>*Unsupportive* (1 test)<br>   Metzner & Bean (1987) |
| 9. The greater the degree of social integration, the greater the level of subsequent commitment to the institution. | Total of 3 tests<br><br>*Supportive* (2 tests)<br>   Allen (1986)<br>   Cabrera, Nora, & Castaneda (1992)<br><br>*Unsupportive* (1 test)<br>   Metzner & Bean (1987) |
| 10. The initial level of institutional commitment affects the subsequent level of institutional commitment. | Total of 5 tests<br><br>*Supportive* (5 tests)<br>   Allen (1986)<br>   Braxton & Brier (1989)<br>   Braxton, Duster, & Pascarella (1988)<br>   Pascarella, Duby, & Iverson (1983)<br>   Cabrera, Nora, & Castaneda (1992) |
| 11. The initial level of commitment to the goal of graduation from college affects the subsequent level of commitment to the goal of college graduation. | Total of 3 tests<br><br>*Supportive* (3 tests)<br>   Allen (1986)<br>   Pascarella, Duby, & Iverson (1983)<br>   Metzner & Bean (1987) |
| 12. The greater the level of subsequent commitment to the goal of graduation from college, the greater the likelihood of student persistence in college. | Total of 8 tests<br><br>*Supportive* (1 test)<br>   Cabrera, Nora, & Castaneda (1992)<br><br>*Unsupportive* (7 tests)<br>   Allen (1986)<br>   Allen & Nelson (1989)<br>   Braxton & Brier (1989)<br>   Braxton, Brier, & Hossler (1988)<br>   Braxton, Duster, & Pascarella (1988)<br>   Fox (1986)<br>   Pascarella, Duby, & Iverson (1983) |

**Table 5.2 (continued)**

| Propositions | Propositional Tests |
|---|---|
| 13. The greater the level of subsequent commitment to the institution, the greater the likelihood of student persistence in college. | Total of 6 tests<br><br>*Supportive* (6 tests)<br>  Allen & Nelson (1989)<br>  Braxton & Brier (1989)<br>  Braxton, Brier, & Hossler (1988)<br>  Braxton, Duster, & Pascarella (1988)<br>  Cabrera, Nora, & Castaneda (1992)<br>  Metzner & Bean (1987) |

place in residential colleges and universities. Because the threshold of ten tests was not reached, reliable knowledge fails to result.

Reliable knowledge also fails to emerge from tests of this proposition made in commuter colleges and universities. Although the two tests conducted produced verifying results, the target of ten tests was not reached.

*Proposition 5. Initial commitment to the goal of graduation from college affects the level of social integration.* Although each of the four tests of this proposition made in residential colleges and universities produce affirming results, reliable knowledge fails to obtain. This failure stems from not reaching the threshold of ten tests.

Because only one test of this proposition transpired in commuter colleges and universities, the minimum of ten tests is not met. As a consequence, reliable knowledge fails to emerge.

*Proposition 6. Initial commitment to the institution affects the level of social integration.* As fourteen tests of this proposition took place in residential colleges and universities, the threshold of ten tests is met. However, reliable knowledge does not result, because four of the fourteen tests produced corroborating findings.

In contrast, four tests of this proposition transpired in commuter colleges and universities. Although these four tests yielded verifying results, the target of ten tests is not reached for this proposition.

*Proposition 7. Initial commitment to the institution affects the level of academic integration.* Although nine tests of this proposition occurred in residential colleges and universities, only one test generated an affirming outcome. Moreover, the target of ten tests was not attained. Thus, reliable knowledge is not forthcoming.

In stark contrast, only one test of this proposition took place in commuter colleges and universities. This sole test produced a verifying result.

Nevertheless, reliable knowledge fails to emerge because the threshold of ten tests is not reached.

*Proposition 8. The greater the degree of academic integration, the greater the level of subsequent commitment to the goal of graduation from college.* Though each of the eight tests of this proposition conducted in residential colleges and universities spawned confirming outcomes, the minimum number of ten tests was not reached. As a consequence, reliable knowledge is not delineated.

Despite the fact that two of the three tests of this proposition made in commuter colleges and universities yielded verifying results, reliable knowledge fails to emerge. The threshold of ten studies is not attained for this proposition in commuter collegiate institutions.

*Proposition 9. The greater the degree of social integration, the greater the level of subsequent commitment to the institution.* Reliable knowledge results from the tests made of this proposition in residential colleges and universities. Of the nineteen tests performed, sixteen tests generated affirmative results.

In contrast, tests of this proposition fail to produce reliable knowledge for commuter colleges and universities. Though two of the three tests performed generated affirming findings, the threshold of ten tests is not reached.

*Proposition 10. The initial level of institutional commitment affects the subsequent level of institutional commitment.* Reliable knowledge emerges from tests of this proposition conducted in residential colleges and universities. Of the eleven tests accomplished, nine yielded concurring results.

Reliable knowledge fails to emerge from tests made of this proposition in commuter colleges and universities, however. Although each of the five tests conducted affirm this proposition, the ten-test minimum is not met.

*Proposition 11. The initial level of commitment to the goal of graduation from college affects the subsequent level of commitment to the goal of graduation from college.* Tests of this proposition conducted in residential colleges and universities do not yield reliable knowledge. The threshold of ten tests is not reached, because only six tests occurred. These six tests affirmed this proposition, however.

Likewise, tests made in commuter colleges and universities fail to produce reliable knowledge, because the threshold of ten tests is not achieved. Nevertheless, the three tests made affirmed this proposition.

*Proposition 12. The greater the level of subsequent commitment to the goal of graduation from college, the greater the likelihood of student persistence in college.* Tests of this proposition in residential colleges and universities fail by one test to reach the threshold of ten tests. Of the nine tests made, six produce verifying results. Nevertheless, reliable knowledge fails to emerge.

Reliable knowledge also does not emerge from tests of this proposition made in commuter colleges and universities. Of the eight tests conducted, only one affirms this proposition.

*Proposition 13. The greater the level of subsequent commitment to the institution, the greater the likelihood of student persistence in college.* Reliable knowledge results from tests of this proposition in residential colleges and universities. Of the thirteen tests conducted in this institutional setting, eleven tests support this proposition.

In contrast, reliable knowledge fails to arise from tests of this proposition in commuter colleges and universities. Because six tests were made, the target of ten tests is not attained. Moreover, all six of the tests bolster this proposition.

## LIMITATIONS

This effort to delineate reliable knowledge about the process of college student departure is limited in several ways. These ways are:

1. Our review of studies that test one or more of the thirteen propositions of Tinto's theory is not exhaustive. In the case of some propositions, one or two more affirming studies would give rise to reliable knowledge. However, such affirming support must stem only from propositional tests that used such multivariate statistical procedures as LISREL, multiple discriminant analysis, and path analysis with hierarchical, multiple linear regression, or logistic regression.

2. Our delineation of reliable knowledge pertains only to four-year residential and commuter colleges and universities. Two-year colleges were not included.

3. This effort does not extend to the identification of reliable knowledge concerning the departure process for different groups of students.

4. Propositions 1, 2, and 3 include student entry characteristics as a general category. We aggregated tests of family background characteristics, individual attributes, and pre-college schooling to determine whether reliable knowledge results. More specific reliable knowledge about family background characteristics, individual attributes, and pre-college schooling might result from an identification of specific entry characteristics such as parental educational level, academic aptitude, and high school academic achievement and their influence on initial institutional and goal commitments and on persistence.

# CONCLUSIONS

This effort to designate tests of propositions as reliable knowledge provides a snap-shot at this juncture in time. Tests of Tinto's propositions not designated as reliable knowledge may produce reliable knowledge with additional tests. With this caveat stated, we present the two following conclusions.

1. We designate three propositions as constituting reliable knowledge in residential colleges and universities. These three reliable relationships are logically interrelated and hold meaning, meaning provided by the formulations of Tinto's interactionalist theory. This reliable relationship takes the following form: the greater the degree of social integration, the greater the level of subsequent commitment to the institution (proposition 9). The initial level of commitment to the institution also affects the student's subsequent commitment to the college or university (proposition 10). Subsequent commitment to the institution, in turn, positively affects the likelihood of student persistence in college (proposition 13). The degree of reliability for each of these three interlocking relationships exceeds 80 percent.

2. We label none of the thirteen propositions of Tinto's theory as reliable knowledge in commuter colleges and universities. None of the thirteen propositions reached the threshold of ten tests needed to ascertain reliability. Scholars and institutional policymakers may elect to use a different minimum number of tests. A lower threshold could result in the delineation of some propositions as reliable. For example, proposition 13 received six tests, all affirming. Proposition 10 received five tests, all supportive.

# IMPLICATIONS FOR POLICY AND PRACTICE

The direct and highly reliable influence of institutional policy and practice on the forming of subsequent commitment to the institution which, in turn, wields a direct and highly reliable effect on student persistence strongly indicates that institutional policy and practice in residential collegiate institutions should endeavor to foster the social integration of students. Accordingly, we offer an overarching recommendation and specific recommendations.

As an overarching recommendation, we urge residential colleges and universities to provide first-year students with multiple opportunities to interact with other students so that friendship may form. These opportunities should occur over the course of the academic year. We present this recommendation recognizing that academic attainment constitutes the primary reason for college attendance. However, departure from a given college or university harms the possibility of student academic success.

To implement this general recommendation, we put forth two specific suggestions:

1. Orientation programs for first-year students should be mandatory (Braxton, Hirschy, & McClendon 2004). Although academic adjustment and requirements need discussion, such programs should also provide opportunities for social interaction among students (Braxton & Mundy 2001–2002).

   Orientation programs for first-year students might also continue throughout the first year. Year-long orientation programs should also provide multiple opportunities for social interaction among students.

2. Institutional policy should require first-year students to reside in college or university residence halls (Braxton & Mundy 2001–2002). Living in a residence hall provides a setting for frequent face-to-face interaction among first-year students.

   Residence hall programming should also include social activities designed to help students make friends (Braxton & Mundy 2001–2002).

## CLOSING THOUGHTS

The implementation of these specific recommendations offer promise in fostering the social integration of students in residential colleges and universities. As in efforts to determine the reliability of tests of the propositions of Tinto's theory, scholars of the college student departure process and institutional research officers should conduct multiple tests of the effects of policies and practice designed to reduce college student departure. Such multiple tests could lead to reliable knowledge about institutional practices that foster social integration.

Because we have not been able to identify reliable knowledge about student departure in commuter colleges and universities, we cannot offer recommendations springing from reliable knowledge. Consequently, we urge scholars of college student departure to continue testing theory to account for student departure in commuter colleges and universities. The validation of theory and the attainment of reliable knowledge should be the aim of such research.

Although reduction in the departure rates of individual colleges and universities may result, the collegiate experiences of students enrolled in residential colleges and universities will likewise improve as a consequence of the implementation of policies and practices designed to foster student social integration.

## REFERENCES

Aitken, N. D. (1982). College student performance, satisfaction and retention: Specification and estimation of a structural model. *Journal of Higher Education* 53(1): 32–50.

Allen, D. (1999). Desire to finish college: An empirical link between motivation and persistence. *Research in Higher Education* 40: 461–485.

Allen, D. F. (1986). Attrition at a commuter institution: A path analytic validation of Tinto's theoretical model of college withdrawal. Paper presented at the Meeting of the American College Personnel Association, Los Angeles.

Allen, D. F., & Nelson, J. M. (1989). Tinto's model of college withdrawal applied to women in two institutions. *Journal of Research and Development in Education* 22(3): 1–11.

Anderson, M. S., & Louis, K. S. (1991). The changing locus of control over faculty research: From self-regulation to dispersed influence. In *Higher education: Handbook of theory and research*, ed. J. C. Smart, Vol. 7: 57–101. New York: Agathon Press.

Babbie, E. (2001). *The practice of social research.* 9th ed. Belmont, CA: Wadsworth/Thomson Learning.

Berger, J. B. (1997). Students' sense of community in residence halls, social integration, and first-year persistence. *Journal of College Student Development* 38(5): 441–452.

Berger, J. B., & Braxton, J. M. (1998). Revising Tinto's interactionalist theory of student departure through theory elaboration: Examining the role of organizational attributes in the persistence process. *Research in Higher Education* 39(2): 103–119.

Berger, J. B., & Milem, J. F. (1999). The role of student involvement and perceptions of integration in a casual model of student persistence. *Research in Higher Education* 40: 641–664.

Braxton, J. M. (2000). Introduction: Reworking the student departure puzzle. In *Reworking the student departure puzzle*, ed. John M. Braxton, 1–8. Nashville: Vanderbilt University Press.

———. (2001–2002). Introduction to special issue: Using theory and research to improve college student retention. *Journal of College Student Retention: Research, Theory and Practice* 3(1): 1–2.

Braxton, J. M., Bray, N. J., & Berger, J. B. (2000). Faculty teaching skills and their influences on the college student departure process. *Journal of College Student Development* 41(2): 215–227.

Braxton, J. M., & Brier, E. M. (1989). Melding organizational and interactional theories of student attrition. *Review of Higher Education* 13(1): 47–61.

Braxton, J. M., Brier, E. M., & Hossler, D. (1988). The influence of student problems on student withdrawal decisions: An autopsy on "autopsy studies." *Research in Higher Education* 28(3): 241–253.

Braxton, J. M., Duster, M., & Pascarella, E. T. (1988). Causal modeling and path analysis: An introduction and an illustration in student attrition research. *Journal of College Student Development* 29: 263–272.

Braxton, J. M., Hirschy, A. S., & McClendon, S. A. (2004). *Understanding and reducing college student departure*. ASHE-ERIC Higher Education Report No. 3. San Francisco: Jossey-Bass.

Braxton, J. M., Milem, J. F., & Sullivan, A. S. (2000). The influence of active learning on the college student departure process: Toward a revision of Tinto's theory. *Journal of Higher Education* 71: 569–590.

Braxton, J. M., & Mundy, M. E. (2001–2002). Powerful institutional levers to reduce college student departure. *Journal of College Student Retention: Research, Theory and Practice* 3(1): 91–118.

Braxton, J. M., Sullivan, A. S., & Johnson, R. M. (1997). Appraising Tinto's theory of college student departure. In *Higher education: Handbook of theory and research*, ed. J. C. Smart, Vol. 12: 107–164. New York: Agathon Press.

Bray, N. J., Braxton, J. M., & Sullivan, A. S. (1999). The influence of stress-related coping strategies on college student departure decisions. *Journal of College Student Development* 40: 645–657.

Brower, A. M. (1992). The "second half" of student integration: The effects of life task predominance on student persistence. *Journal of Higher Education* 63(4): 441–462.

Cabrera, A. F., Nora, A., & Castaneda, M. B. (1992). The role of finances in the persistence process: A structural model. *Research in Higher Education* 33(5): 571–593.

Crits-Christoph, P. (1998). Training in empirically validated treatments: The Division 12 APA Task Force recommendations. In *Empirically-supported therapies: Best practices in professional psychology*, ed. K. S. Dobson & K. D. Craig, Thousand Oaks, CA: Sage Publications.

DuBrock, C. P. (2000). Financial aid and college persistence: A five-year longitudinal study of 1993 and 1994 beginning freshmen students. Paper presented at the annual forum of the Association of Institutional Research, May 21–23, Cincinnati.

Fox, R. N. (1986). Application of a conceptual model of college withdrawal to disadvantaged students. *American Educational Research Journal* 23(3): 414–424.

French, B. F., Immekus, J., & Oakes, W. (2002). College student success and persistence: The role of intrinsic motivation and institutional integration. Paper presented at the annual conference of the American Educational Research Association, New Orleans.

Helland, P. A., Stallings, H. J., & Braxton, J. M. (2001–2002). The fulfillment of expectations for college student departure decisions. *Journal of College Student Retention: Research, Theory & Practice* 3(4): 381–396.

House, J. D. (1992). The relationship between academic self concept, achievement-related expectancies, and college attrition. *Journal of College Student Development* 33(1): 5–10.

Leppel, K. (2001). The impact of major on college persistence among freshmen. *Journal of Education for Business* 76(4): 209–215.

Mallette, B. I., & Cabrera, A. F. (1991). Determinants of withdrawal behavior: An exploratory study. *Research in Higher Education* 32(2): 179–194.

McMillan, J. H., & Schumacher, S. (2001). *Research in education: A conceptual introduction*, 5th ed. New York: Longman.

Metzner, B. S., & Bean, J. P. (1987). The estimation of a conceptual model of nontraditional undergraduate student attrition. *Research in Higher Education* 27(1): 15–38.

Milem, J. F., & Berger, J. B. (1997). A modified model of college student persistence: Exploring the relationship between Astin's theory of involvement and Tinto's theory of student departure. *Journal of College Student Development* 38(4): 387–400.

Moline, A. E. (1987). Financial aid and student persistence: An application of causal modeling. *Research in Higher Education* 26(2): 130–147.

Ott, M. D. (1988). An analysis of predictors of early academic dismissal. *Research in Higher Education* 28(1): 34–48.

Pantages, T. J., & Creedon, C. F. (1978). Studies of college attrition: 1950–1975. *Review of Educational Research* 48: 49–101.

Pascarella, E. T., Duby, P. B., & Iverson, B. K. (1983). A test and reconceptualization of a theoretical model of college withdrawal in a commuter institution setting. *Sociology of Education* 5: 88–100.

Pascarella, E. T., & Terenzini, P. T. (1980). Predicting freshmen persistence and voluntary dropout decisions from a theoretical model. *Journal of Higher Education* 51(1): 60–75.

———. (1983). Predicting voluntary freshman year persistence/withdrawal behavior in a residential university: A path analytic validation of Tinto's model. *Journal of Educational Psychology* 75(2): 215–226.

Pascarella, E. T., Terenzini, P. T., & Wolfle, L. M. (1986). Orientations to college and freshman year persistence/withdrawal decisions. *Journal of Higher Education* 57(2): 156–175.

Perry, S. R., Cabrera, A. F., & Vogt, W. P. (1999). Career maturity and college student persistence. *Journal of College Student Retention: Research, Theory and Practice* 1: 41–58.

Peterson, S. L. (1993). Career decision-making self-efficacy and institutional integration of underprepared college students. *Research in Higher Education* 34(6): 659–685.

Pike, C. R., Schroeder, C. C., & Berry, T. R. (1997). Enhancing the educational impact of residence halls: The relationship between residential learning communities and first-year college experiences and persistence. *Journal of College Student Development* 38: 609–621.

Stage, F. K. (1988). University attrition: LISREL with logistic regression for the persistence criterion. *Research in Higher Education* 29(4): 343–357.

Task Force on Promotion and Dissemination of Psychological Procedures. (1995). Training in and dissemination of empirically-validated psychological treatments. *Clinical Psychologist* 48: 3–23.

Terenzini, P. T., Lorang, W. G., & Pascarella, E. T. (1981). Predicting freshman persistence and voluntary dropout decisions: A replication. *Research in Higher Education* 15(2): 109–127.

Terenzini, P. T., Pascarella, E. T., Theophilides, C., & Lorang, W. G. (1985). A replication of a path analytic validation of Tinto's theory of college student attrition. *Review of Higher Education* 8(4): 319–340.

Thomas, S. L. (2000). A social network approach to understanding student integration and persistence. *Journal of Higher Education* 71(5): 591–615.

Tinto, V. (1975). Dropout from higher education: A theoretical synthesis of recent research. *Review of Educational Research* 45: 89–125.

———. (1982). Limits of theory and practice in student attrition. *Journal of Higher Education* 53(6): 687–700.

———. (1986). Theories of student departure revisited. In *Higher education: Handbook of theory and practice*, ed. John C. Smart, Vol. 2: 359–384. New York: Agathon Press.

———. (1993). *Leaving college: Rethinking the causes and cures of student attrition.* 2nd ed. Chicago: University of Chicago Press.

# CHAPTER 6

# Student Persistence and Degree Attainment Beyond the First Year in College

## The Need for Research

*Amaury Nora, Elizabeth Barlow, and Gloria Crisp*

## INTRODUCTION

Student persistence is the product of a longitudinal process of varied lengths in students' lives. While some students may reenroll for a second or third year in college, dropping out is still a consideration for many students. Factors that have been found to impact student retention among first-year students may carry over to subsequent years, culminating in a decision to withdraw from college. Moreover, it is reasonable to assume that the strength and direction of those factors influencing dropout behavior may change over time (Ishitani & DesJardins 2002). New factors must also be taken into consideration as students proceed from one year to the next. While much has been written on student persistence over the past thirty years regarding the impact of different variables such as the academic and social integration of students on campus (e.g., Pascarella & Terenzini 1979; Terenzini & Pascarella 1980; Bean 1980), different sources and forms of support systems (e.g., Nora & Cabrera 1996; Nora 2004), student finances (e.g., Olivas 1986; Cabrera, Nora, & Castaneda 1992; St. John, Cabrera, Nora & Asker 2001), and even discriminatory behaviors and gestures (e.g., Nora & Cabrera 1996; Cabrera & Nora 1994) on the adjustment of students to college, their academic achievement, their first-to-second-year persistence, and ultimately their undergraduate degree attainment, major gaps in the persistence literature exist on student retention past the first year in college. It has been suggested that because of the intense focus by researchers and practitioners on the first year in college, problems with student attrition have shifted from the first year to subsequent years even when students successfully engage their initial collegiate experience.

The intent of this chapter is to provide an overview of findings in the literature on student persistence past the first year in college. Because very little has been investigated for the time period following a student's first year, this chapter will also attempt to provide a preliminary profile of student characteristics, academic performance, and attrition rates over a six-year period utilizing institutional records from a highly diverse student population enrolled at a major research university. To provide a context for comparison with what is known on the first-year experience, the conceptual framework for this chapter will be guided by current theoretical perspectives used in studying the persistence of first-time-in-college students.

As previously mentioned, much of what we know regarding student persistence has been focused on students as they move from the end of their first year in college to the beginning of their second year (e.g., Nora & Cabrera 1996; Nora, Cabrera, Hagedorn, & Pascarella 1996; Braxton & Lien 2000; Nora 2004). Many of these studies have used different, yet overlapping, frameworks. Much of the early work relied on Tinto's (1975) model of student integration. Subsequent studies modified Tinto's original model and led to the use of such models as Bean's (1985) student attrition model, Pascarella and Terenzini's (1980) interpretation of Tinto's (1975) theoretical framework, and even Astin's (1984) student involvement perspective.

During the thirty-year period of the persistence literature, numerous quantitative and qualitative studies have contributed to the literature base on student persistence. Studies by Braxton and Brier (1989), Rendon (1994), Hurtado and Carter (1997), Pascarella and Terenzini (1990), and others have modified and added an array of factors all found to impact the decisions of college students to remain enrolled in college or to drop out, temporarily or permanently. Among those efforts is research by Nora and associates (e.g., Nora & Cabrera 1996; Cabrera & Nora 1994; Cabrera, Nora, & Castaneda 1992; Nora & Garcia undated; Nora & Lang undated; Nora 2002, 2004). The culmination of those efforts has led to the conceptualization of the student engagement model (Nora 2004). Figure 6.1 displays the theoretical framework used in examining similar factors impacting withdrawal and persistence decisions of undergraduates past the first year in college.

# Figure 6.1
## Student/Institution Engagement Model Theoretical Framework

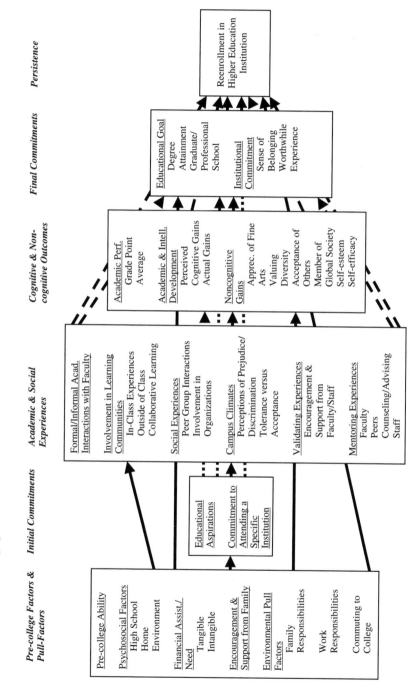

## CURRENT KNOWLEDGE OF STUDENT PERSISTENCE PAST THE FIRST YEAR

While it is not extensive, a body of literature does exist that examines student retention rates in the second and third years and, at times, factors that influence a student's decision to leave college altogether. Bartlett and Abell (1995) examined the number of first-time-in-college students retained over a ten-year period at a four-year institution in the Midwest. During that time period, the institution reported that between 72 and 80 percent of their beginning freshmen were retained to the second year (fall of first year to fall of second year). Furthermore, between 60 and 70 percent of students were retained to the third year and between 55 and 65 percent persisted to the fourth year. Data on sixty-seven U.S. colleges and universities (Smith 1995) and data from the National Center for Educational Statistics (NCES 1993) have documented that nearly 80 percent of first-time-in-college students continued to the second year and roughly 66 percent persisted to the third year. It is important to note that the percentages in those studies were specific to first-time students and did not include transfer students or students who may have taken a course or two prior to attending a four-year institution for the first time.

## PERSISTENCE RATES BY GENDER, ETHNICITY, AND SOCIOECONOMIC STATUS

A descriptive profile (albeit restricted by the number of studies) can be constructed that demonstrates differences by gender, ethnicity, and financial aid status in year-to-year persistence. DuBrock (1999) found that persistence among males and females during the first three years in college varies extensively. More specifically, the investigator found that females were more likely to return for their second and fourth years in college, and that male students were more likely to return for their third year in college. In contrast, Smith's (1995) earlier findings had revealed that female students were more likely to persist as compared to male students regardless of the academic-year-to-academic-year under consideration.

With regard to race or ethnicity, Smith (1995) found that after the second year, only 59 percent of Blacks, 62 percent of Hispanics, and 54 percent of American Indians were retained compared to 71 percent of other ethnic groups. More recently, however, DuBrock (1999) has noted that American Indians were significantly less likely to persist to the second year as compared to all other ethnic groups and that Hispanic students were more likely to persist to the fourth year.

Ishitani and DesJardins (2002) found that for students who come from low-income families, a mother's educational attainment significantly impacts student persistence in second-to-third-year reenrollment and in third-to-fourth-year return of students. Not surprising, being raised in a low-income family was found to more negatively influence student persistence at the end of the second and third years than it was in the first year. It is to be expected that circumstances associated with a family living in a low-income situation would put undue pressure on the part of the student to withdraw and help with family expenses. For those students coming from a low-income family, however, a mother's educational attainment had the largest impact on reducing student attrition in second-to-third-year rates. Specifically, at the end of the second year, students whose mothers had attained an undergraduate degree were 57 percent more likely to reenroll for a third year than students whose mothers did not complete a college education.

## PRE-COLLEGE FACTORS AND THEIR INFLUENCE ON SECOND- AND THIRD-YEAR ATTRITION RATES

### High School Curriculum

Differences in year-to-year persistence among college students who completed an advanced high school curriculum versus students who completed only a basic core curriculum have also been documented. Horn and Kojaku (2001) found that the level of a high school curriculum that was undertaken by a student was strongly related to third-year persistence in college. Specifically, at the beginning of the third year, 87 percent of the students who had completed an advanced high school curriculum were still enrolled in an institution of higher education compared to only 62 percent who completed simply a core curriculum.

### High School Academic Achievement

High school grades have been found to positively influence subsequent college academic performance, as measured by cumulative grade point averages (GPAs). However, academic performance in high school was also found to have very little influence on student persistence (Nora & Cabrera 1996; Cabrera & Nora 1994; Cabrera, Nora, & Castaneda 1993). In contrast to those findings, DuBrock (1999) found that high school

GPA exerted a significant effect on student persistence into the second and third years. The study found that a student with a GPA of one-tenth of a point higher is 8 percent more likely to persist to the second year. Similarly, the increased odds of persisting with a higher high school GPA are 7 percent for the second to third year, 8 percent for the third to fourth year, and 6 percent for the fourth to fifth year.

## Academic Ability

Differences among students identified as high ability or low ability as measured by standardized test scores have been shown to influence the withdrawal decisions of students enrolled in college (Ishitani & DesJardins 2002; DuBrock 1999). Over time, high ability students (as measured by SAT scores in the highest quartile) had lower risks of attrition relative to students who scored in the lower three quartiles (Ishitani & DesJardins 2002). Furthermore, students with SAT scores of 1010 or less that persisted to the fourth year were significantly more likely to graduate or persist to the fifth year (DuBrock 1999).

# INITIAL COURSE PERFORMANCE IN COLLEGE

In addition to a student's academic performance in high school, the academic achievement of undergraduates, as measured by a college GPA, may be relevant to the decisions of undergraduates to remain enrolled in college well into the first three years. Research on first-to-second-year persistence has revealed that how a student performs academically will impact his or her academic and social experiences, his or her commitment to attaining a degree, and ultimately his or her decision to withdraw from college, specifically for minority students (Nora & Cabrera 1996; Cabrera & Nora 1994). Even though minority students may not be required to withdraw from college because of their GPA, earning low grades introduces a sense of doubt related to academic performance and belonging in college for students of color.

Studies point to a lingering effect of poor first-year performance for first-time-in-college students (Maack 2002; Ishitani & DesJardins 2002; Bradburn 2002). Specifically, students are at very high risk of dropping out of college in year two of their college experience if their first-year GPA is below 2.0 (Ishitani & DesJardins 2002).

# FINANCIAL ASSISTANCE

Research on student persistence has indicated that finances play a major role in student withdrawal decisions (Cabrera, Nora, & Castaneda

1992; Nora & Cabrera 1996; Nora, Cabrera, Hagedorn, & Pascarella 1996). The stress associated with financing one's education was found to negatively impact the decisions of students to remain in college. Financial pressures—the pressures to meet the costs of tuition, fees, books, and room and board—overly affected a student's ability to integrate fully into his or her academic and social environment, ability to engage in in-class and out-of-class experiences, and ability to maintain a high level of aspirations toward earning a degree, and ultimately led to a student's decision to withdraw from college.

The effects of financial aid on persistence beyond the first year have also been documented. Research has shown that students are nearly twice as likely to persist between the second and third years if they receive financial aid (DuBrock 1999; Ishitani & DesJardins 2002). Specifically, Ishitani and DesJardins (2002) found that receiving financial aid reduced the risk of attrition the most in the third year. In contrast, needy students (operationally defined as receiving Pell Grants) were less likely to continue to the second year and were even less likely to return for the third year (DuBrock 1999).

An overlapping factor with student finances is the residency status of the student as that residency relates to out-of-state tuition. Not being able to establish residency in a state and having to pay nonresident tuition have a significantly negative effect on student persistence in the first two years of college. Specifically, undergraduates classified as out-of-state students are 1.93 times less likely to return for a second year and 2.04 times less likely to return for a third year (DuBrock 1999). The exceptionally high cost of tuition may outweigh any perceived benefits to students attending college outside their home state.

## STUDENT COMMITMENT

In many of the early studies on student persistence (e.g., Pascarella & Terenzini 1979, 1980; Bean 1980; Bean & Metzner 1985), the focus of the findings centered on the student's social integration into his or her environment. Throughout the years, the influence of this factor on a student's persistence decision has been confirmed and substantiated among different student groups at a variety of higher education institutions (Braxton & Lien 2000; Nora 1993, 2004). Higher educational aspirations have also been found to positively impact student attrition beyond the first year. Specifically, low educational aspirations were found to have the strongest negative effect on student retention in the first year (Ishitani & DesJardins 2002). Moreover, students were less likely to persist at their first institution if their educational goals did not include earning a bachelor's degree (Bradburn 2002).

## ENVIRONMENTAL PUSH FACTORS

Very early in the retention literature it was established that environmental influences in different forms negatively affected the student's ability to successfully engage in academic and social activities on campus, subsequently impacting academic performance and the student's desire to remain enrolled in college (e.g., Bean 1985; Nora 1987; Nora & Wedman 1993). Factors that pulled students away from college such as commuting, living off campus, and working off campus were found to push students into deciding not to return to college. DuBrock (1999) has noted that students with on-campus jobs, which permitted the students to remain in close proximity to faculty and an academic environment, were more likely to persist well beyond the first year. Similarly, those students who could afford to live on campus were much more likely to persist, even past the first year. Students living on campus were 1.73 times more likely to return the second year and 1.38 times more likely to persist to the third year.

## ACADEMIC AND SOCIAL EXPERIENCES

Among those factors that have been found to impact student persistence, two major components include formal and informal academic and social experiences of students (Braxton & Lien 2000; Cabrera, Nora, & Casteneda 1992; Cabrera, Nora, & Casteneda 1993; Nora 1987; Pascarella & Terenzini 1990). The engagement of the student in classroom discussion, collaborative learning experiences, student organizations, and contact with faculty are all part of an underlying process affecting the adjustment of students to college, their academic performance, and their decisions to remain enrolled to graduation.

Very little is known with regard to these aspects for students past the first year. A single institutional report found that the appropriate assessment of students as they entered college, seeking and receiving counseling (both academic and personal), and attending an official orientation session provided by the institution were significant factors associated with persistence to the second and third years (Maack 2002). While these factors are not fully representative of the academic and social experiences identified in the literature, they do represent valid proxies for those components.

# UNDERGRADUATE TRENDS: FIRST TIME IN COLLEGE (FTIC) DEMOGRAPHICS, SECOND- TO THIRD-YEAR STUDENT PERFORMANCE, AND SUBSEQUENT SIXTH-YEAR GRADUATION RATES

## National Databases: The Need for In-Depth Longitudinal Data

The lack of data on students past their first year in college is largely based on the shortcomings associated with large national databases. While those data sets are longitudinal in nature, the depth of information on individual students is limited. The next section of this chapter focuses on attrition rates, academic performance, specific course grades, and performance on core curricula, data that are available only at the institutional level and wanting in larger data sets. The profile that follows is based on first-time-in-college students at a large research university. The institution is the most highly diverse among research and comprehensive four-year institutions with regard to racial and ethnic student representation. It is believed that such a diverse student population can be used to begin to examine retention, academic performance, and graduation patterns past the first academic year, particularly since more and more students seeking higher education today reflect this diversity.

## DEMOGRAPHIC PROFILE

The population selected for examining the persistence rates of students past the first year in college consisted of the 2,906 "first-time-in-college students" (FTICs) entering in the fall 1997 semester at a major public, commuter, doctoral-granting institution. Students were considered as FTICs based on a record of no prior attendance at any other university or community college. Demographically, 46.5 percent of students were male and 53.5 percent were female. The ethnic breakdown of the cohort consisted of 35.3 percent White, 18.7 percent Black, 22.7 percent Hispanic, 21.1 percent Asian or Pacific Islander, less than 1 percent American Indian, and 1.8 percent international students.[1] The large majority of students were classified as full-time students. Only 11.8 percent of students were classified as part-time students, defined as students enrolled in fewer than twelve student credit hours for the semester.

Nearly a fourth (22.6 percent) of the FTIC cohort were classified as developmental students, defined as students who enrolled in at least one developmental course[2] in the first year. The majority (63.3 percent) of developmental students were Black or Hispanic. Although 35.3 percent of the FTIC cohort were White, only 15.8 percent were classified as such. Developmental students performed slightly below nondevelopmental students academically. For instance, the cumulative GPA of developmental students was only 2.09 compared to 2.43 for nondevelopmental students. In addition, the six-year graduation rate for developmental students (32.0 percent) was lower than for nondevelopmental students (37.9 percent).

## PROFILE OF ACADEMIC PERFORMANCE

### Pre-College Academic Performance

The mean high school GPA for the entering cohort was 3.17 and did not seem to impact college retention or graduation rates in subsequent years. As can be seen in Table 6.1, students retained to the third year[3] had only slightly higher mean GPAs than students who dropped out during their second year in college or did not return for their third year, 3.26 and 3.06, respectively. Furthermore, the mean high school GPA for students who graduated within six years was 3.31 compared to a mean GPA of 3.08 for students who had not graduated during that six-year period.

### Academic Ability

As for performance on entering standardized test scores, the average score on the Scholastic Aptitude Test (SAT) test for the FTIC cohort was 1,047 (with a large variation in the scores, $SD = 159$). The average SAT total score of students retained to the third year (1,054) was only slightly higher than those students not retained (1,036). However, the average SAT total score of students who graduated within six years (1,072) was much higher than the average total score of students who did not graduate (947). Furthermore, for those students who took at least one developmental course during their first academic year, the average SAT total score was only 922.

### Semester Hours Completed

In fall 1997, the entering cohort of students in college for their first time successfully completed an average of 91 percent of classes attempted at the beginning of their first academic semester in college. There is evidence to suggest that the ratio of student credit hours completed[4] may be associated

**Table 6.1**
**Demographic Profile FTIC Fall 1997 Cohort**

| | FTIC cohort (n = 2,906) | Retained to 2nd year (n = 2,101) | Retained to 3rd year (n = 1,614) | Graduated within six years (n = 1,063) |
|---|---|---|---|---|
| *Gender* | | | | |
| Male | 1,351 | 949 | 705 | 425 |
| Female | 1,555 | 1,152 | 909 | 638 |
| *Ethnicity* | | | | |
| White non-Hispanic | 1,026 | 681 | 509 | 365 |
| Black non-Hispanic | 544 | 409 | 295 | 174 |
| Hispanic | 659 | 470 | 366 | 223 |
| Asian or Pacific Islander | 613 | 508 | 414 | 280 |
| Am. Indian or Alaskan Native | 13 | 8 | 6 | 3 |
| International | 51 | 25 | 24 | 18 |
| *Tuition status* | | | | |
| In-state tuition | 2,703 | 1,970 | 1,504 | 984 |
| Nonresident tuition | 94 | 42 | 38 | 29 |
| Tuition exempt | 109 | 89 | 72 | 50 |
| *High school quartile* | | | | |
| Top 10% | 471 | 383 | 315 | 220 |
| 10–24% | 836 | 628 | 500 | 334 |
| 25–49% | 721 | 503 | 384 | 231 |
| 50–74% | 333 | 228 | 139 | 94 |
| Bottom 25% | 71 | 43 | 27 | 18 |
| *High school GPA* | | | | |
| Mean | 3.17 | 3.22 | 3.26 | 3.31 |
| 25th percentile | 2.80 | 2.85 | 2.92 | 3.00 |
| 50th percentile | 3.21 | 3.27 | 3.32 | 3.37 |
| 75th percentile | 3.58 | 3.62 | 3.66 | 3.70 |
| Total *N* | 2,675 | 1,959 | 1,503 | 986 |
| *SAT scores* | | | | |
| Mean total scores | 1,047 | 1,050 | 1,054 | 1,072 |
| Std. dev. total score | 92 | 94 | 95 | 161 |
| Total *N* | 2,656 | 1,960 | 1,507 | 991 |

with student retention. Students who persisted to the second year completed a larger proportion of their classes during their first semester in college (87 percent) than students not retained by the institution (81 percent), and students persisting from their second year to their third year had completed a larger proportion of their classes during their first academic semester in college (89 percent) than those students dropping out (74 percent). The pattern indicates that those students completing a larger proportion of their courses (for numerous reasons) maintained that pattern throughout their first and second years in college.

## Academic Performance in College

The academic performance of students during their first semester in college has been thought to influence not only subsequent academic performance but also student persistence, specifically for minority students (Nora & Cabrera 1996). The average GPA at the end of their first semester in college (fall 1997) for students retained to the second year[5] was 2.52 compared to 1.66 for students not retained. Similarly, the fall 1997 GPA for students retained to the third year (2.68) was much higher than students not retained (2.02). As anticipated, students who graduated within six years had an average GPA of 2.82 at the end of their first semester compared to an average GPA of 1.98 for nongraduates. The evidence reveals that how students perform academically during their initial semester in college may influence subsequent withdrawal decisions, specifically those decisions by minority student populations.

The impact of the academic performance of students extends past their first semester in college. The cumulative GPA for students retained to the second year was 2.57. The students' academic performance was substantially higher than the average GPA (1.75) for students not retained. Similarly, the cumulative GPA for students returning to the third year was 2.76 compared to an average GPA of 1.97 for students not reenrolling after the first two years following their initial enrollment in fall 1997.

## PROFILE OF ATTRITION RATES

### Racial or Ethnic Differences

Nearly three quarters, 72.3 percent, of the FTIC cohort were retained to the fall of the second year. Of the original entering cohort, 55.5 percent of them had persisted to the third year. While approximately 28 percent of the entering cohort withdrew from college at the end of their first year, an additional 16.8 percent of students were lost between the second and third year. Retention rates were higher for Asian students than for any other ethnic group, with 82.9 percent of Asian students retained to the second year and 67.5 percent persisting to the third year. Although 75.2 percent of Black students were retained to the second year, only 54.2 percent were still enrolled at the beginning of the third year. The attrition rate of Black students between the second and third year (21 percent) was higher than for any other ethnic group. Similarly, 71.3 percent of Hispanic students were retained to the second year, while only 55.5 percent were retained to the third year. Quite unexpected, the retention rate for White students was lower than for Black or Hispanic students. Only 66.4 percent of White students were retained to the second year, and 49.6 percent were retained to the third year.

## Educational Costs

Tuition and other college-related expenses have been found to affect both student academic performance and retention decisions (Nora & Cabrera 1996; Nora, Cabrera, Hagedorn, Pascarella, & Terenzini 1999; Nora & Lang 2000; St. John, Cabrera, Nora, & Asker 2002). In the current investigation, students who paid in-state tuition[6] were much more likely to reenroll in the following year when compared to students paying out-of-state or nonresident tuition. As expected, 72.9 percent of students paying in-state tuition returned to college for the second year compared to only 44.7 percent paying out-of-state or nonresident tuition. Of those FTICs in the original student cohort, 55.6 percent of students paying in-state tuition were retained to the third year compared to 40.4 percent of students paying out-of-state or nonresident tuition during that two-year period. Moreover, and more important, retention rates for students who were exempt from paying tuition[7] were higher than both of the above-mentioned groups, a finding that is consistent with previous research on persistence and financial assistance (e.g., Cabrera, Nora, & Castaneda 1993; Nora & Cabrera 1996; Nora 2004). The findings in the current study revealed that 81.7 percent of tuition-exempt students persisted to the second year and a total of 66.1 percent were retained to the third year.

## Enrollment Status

Part-time students or students enrolled with fewer than twelve student credit hours were less likely than full-time students to be retained to the second and third years; 19.5 percent of the students not retained to the second year and an additional 3.7 percent of students not retained to the third year were classified as part-time students. Among those students who reenrolled for a second and third year, 13.7 percent and 15.1 percent attended college part time, respectively. Moreover, students from the original FTIC cohort who persisted to the second and third years attempted taking more student credit hours in both years (M = 13.2) in fall 1998 and fall 1999 than students who dropped out of college (M = 12.1).

## PROFILE OF SIX-YEAR GRADUATION RATES

Of the 2,906 students who enrolled in college as first-time-in-college students, only 36.6 percent graduated within six years (fall 1997–spring 2003). Several interesting findings were associated with the population of graduating students. First, female graduation rates were 20 percentage points higher than males. A total of 60.0 percent of the graduates were female despite the fact that only 53.5 percent of the FTIC cohort were female. The evidence confirms that the overall performance of female students has surpassed that of males, from cumulative GPAs to persistence rates to graduation rates.

A second finding of interest indicated that although a smaller percentage of White students were retained to the second and third years, the graduation rates six years later for Whites (35.6 percent) were higher than those for Blacks (32.0 percent) and Hispanics (33.8 percent). And while a sizeable percentage of Asian (22.5 percent) and Hispanic (18.4 percent) students were retained to the sixth year, these students had not graduated.

## COURSE-TAKING PATTERNS

### Developmental Courses

Of the 656 developmental students who enrolled in the fall 1997 FTIC cohort, 60.8 percent enrolled in a developmental English course (ENGL 1300) during their first year. Successful completion of this course suggests a positive effect on graduation: 39.7 percent of the students who successfully completed the course during the first year graduated within six years. This figure compares to the overall FTIC cohort graduation rate of 36.6 percent. In contrast to those students who successfully completed a developmental English course during their first attempt, 8.5 percent of students who enrolled in the course did not complete the course in one semester. These students were required to reenroll in the same course the following semester, a condition that appeared to negatively affect academic progress. Only 17.6 percent of those students needing to take a developmental English course that required more than one semester to successfully complete that requirement graduated within six years. Similar outcomes were found with 15.3 percent of the FTIC cohort that enrolled in a developmental math course (MATH 1300) in their first year. A total of 42.4 percent of students who successfully completed the course during the first year graduated within six years. Of those students who took more than one semester to complete a developmental math course (47.8 percent), only 18.3 percent graduated within six years.

## Core Courses

As in all four-year institutions, students are required to enroll and successfully complete a set of general education requirements (or courses). The majority of the FTIC cohort (73.7 percent) enrolled in a core English course (ENGL 1303) during their first year of which 50.7 percent earned a grade of A, B, or C for the course while only 5.6 percent failed or withdrew. A total of 36.8 percent of the students who graduated within six years took this course in the first year. Not surprisingly, students who withdrew from or failed the course were less likely to graduate than students who took the course and earned a C or better. Only 7.4 percent of students who failed and 5.6 percent of students who withdrew from the course in the first year graduated within six years. In contrast, 42.3 percent of students who took the course and earned a grade of C or better graduated within six years.

Less than half (45 percent) of the FTIC cohort enrolled in a second core English composition course (ENGL 1304) during their first year. Of those students who completed the sequence, 63.3 percent earned an A, B, or C for the course, 0.5 percent failed, and 10.8 percent withdrew from the course. Once more, 43.9 percent of those students who enrolled in both English required courses during their first year in college graduated within six years. Of those students enrolled in the second required course in English, 51.5 percent earned a grade of C or higher and graduated within six years. In sharp contrast, not one of the six students who failed the course and 19.1 percent of the 141 students who withdrew from the course, requiring them to retake the course, graduated within six years.

Regarding a core algebra requirement (MATH 1310) in the curriculum, 63.6 percent of the FTIC cohort were enrolled in that course in their first year. Although nearly half (48.5 percent) of the students earned a grade of C or higher, 21.4 percent of those taking the course either failed or withdrew. Those FTIC students who enrolled in the course during their first year in college (38.6 percent) graduated within six years. Those students who earned a grade of C or better (50.1 percent) graduated within six years. In contrast, students who failed or withdrew from the course in the first year and were required to retake the course some time during their academic career were less likely to graduate within six years. Among that latter group of students, 17.1 percent took the course and failed and 29.1 percent of those students who withdrew from the class did not graduate.

Another required core course is an American history course. Nearly 68 percent (67.8 percent) of the FTIC cohort enrolled in the first core history course (HIST 1377) during their first year. Over half (54.0 percent) of those students enrolled in that course earned a grade of C or higher, while 19.8 percent of the students either failed or withdrew from the course. Once more, the link between completion of core courses during a student's first year in college and subsequent persistence and graduation were indicated in the data: 50.3 percent of students who took the course and earned a grade of C or better graduated within six years, while only 9.8 percent of students who took the course and failed and 19.2 percent who withdrew from the course graduated within six years.

As for those students who also enrolled in a second core history course (50.1 percent of the FTIC cohort in the first year), 39.3 percent of those students graduated within six years. In much the same fashion as with the other core courses previously mentioned, 51.0 percent of the students who took the class and earned a grade of C or better graduated within six years and students who failed or withdrew from this course in the first year were less likely to graduate. Only 15.3 percent of students who took the course in the first year and failed and 16.7 percent who withdrew graduated within six years.

## SOME PRELIMINARY FINDINGS AND DIRECTIONS

The literature on first-to-second-year persistence has provided a fairly robust picture of that portion of the persistence process taking place as students make the transition from home and high school to college. While each student is unique and each institution offers opportunities for a unique set of experiences, it has been informative to have an aggregate understanding of the transition and adjustment process and how the interconnectedness of different academic, social, and environmental factors in that longitudinal process points students toward persistence.

Beyond the first year, however, it may be especially important for institutions to gather and examine data on their individual students and their experiences. Factors pushing students forward or pulling students back become more localized in the experiences students have at a given institution, specifically as those experiences interact with personal circumstances (financial, familial, occupational, etc.). The longitudinal data previously discussed on students at one public, urban research university offer an opportunity to examine those issues that may drive research on persistence after the first year.

## MALE VERSUS FEMALE RETENTION PATTERNS: A SHIFT IN TRENDS

Prior research has shown different persistence rates among males and females depending on the year of progress. While this situation may reflect national trends, the persistence and graduation rates of females across six years were consistently higher in this preliminary investigation. One assertion that could be made regarding these specific patterns is that, within an institution, students are engaged in different academic and social experiences that impact females and males in different ways and result in quite different withdrawal and reenrollment decisions, as opposed to national trends. A different assertion may be that these specific patterns may reflect differences in the forces that drive students to enroll in higher education or attend a particular institution, forces such as financial status, and various support networks.

While institutions may find some satisfaction in knowing that their persistence and graduation rates among female and male students may reflect national trends or patterns at similar institutions, it is also just as important to examine the interaction between gender and institution-specific experiences and to determine whether such differences pose an improvement over national norms for some groups. If females experience greater success as reflected in the current data, does this mean that females bring characteristics with them that render them more likely to succeed, or is this pattern an indicator that the institution serves females more effectively than males?

## DIVERSITY OF RATES AMONG DIFFERENT STUDENT GROUPS

In line with existing research, the institutional data used for this chapter confirm that persistence and graduation rates are not consistent among different racial and ethnic groups, and that the pattern changes from year to year (see Figure 6.2). Overall, the trend for each group follows roughly the same pattern, that is to say, the largest proportion (slightly over 25 percent) of the cohort is lost between initial enrollment and year two, another 17 percent from year two to year three, and an additional 9 percent from year three to year four. The figures from year five and year six represent only those students who had not successfully graduated at those points in time; the trend for those years must be interpreted accordingly but are consistent with the pattern established in prior years. One conclusion that could be made and substantiated in future research is that because each group tracks in rough parallel over time, it is possible to suggest that similar issues influence reenrollment decisions at each stage. It may be also reasonable to assert that the examination of the experiences students have in common—the experiences at the institution—may yield insight into the phenomenon.

While the persistence trends of ethnic groups are parallel, they are not in close proximity. Asian students, for example, reveal a much higher persistence rate (83 percent) in year two than White students (66 percent). While the year-to-year change is roughly the same proportionally for both groups, a significantly larger proportion of the Asian cohort persists to year three (68 percent) than the White (50 percent), Hispanic (57 percent), and African American (55 percent) cohorts. Upon closer examination, other differences among groups are apparent. African American students, for example, show a slightly larger drop from year two to year three than other groups, and Hispanic students a smaller change overall from year two to year three and beyond. These differences may suggest that common factors may be interacting with institutional experiences at different levels, influencing persistence rates differently among the groups. The relatively more precipitous drop in African American persistence from year two to year three is unmistakably an area in much need of investigation. An accurate picture of what may appear to be small differences among ethnic groups may require disaggregating broadly delineated groups such as "Hispanic" or "Asian" into subcategories that better isolate the variety of experiences and reference points that might influence persistence in higher education.

## ENTERING ABILITY AND SUBSEQUENT WITHDRAWAL FROM COLLEGE

Standardized test scores such as the SAT have traditionally been used as the best predictor of future success in college. Research has consistently shown that SAT scores have a strong predictive value relative to grades during the first year in college, but no research exists that points to any substantive validity of SAT scores in predicting overall student adjustment to college, academic engagement in the classroom, retention rates, or graduation rates (Nora 1993; Pascarella & Terenzini 1990). The data in the current investigation reveal only a small difference in mean total SAT score for students who did and did not persist over time. The mean total SAT score for students who persisted to years two, three, and four climbed only 3–4 points per year, a difference that cannot be considered truly significant.

Among the pre-college factors available for examination, high school GPA and high school quartile are somewhat more illuminating, although the precise nature of the role they play in the persistence process remains unclear. A comparison of the high school GPA of the entering FTIC cohort with only those students who persisted to year two reveals only a 0.05 point difference on a 4.0 scale. From year two to year three the mean high school GPA is 0.04 higher in comparison to the entering cohort and 0.03 higher from year three to year four. While it is true that, for those students who persisted longer, a higher high school GPA is evident than for those who did not return to college over the six-year period, the difference becomes smaller over time. If entering academic ability in the form of a high school GPA is that influential in subsequent student persistence, then a much larger difference would exist between those who remained enrolled over the years versus those who withdrew from college.

Interpreting high school GPA within the context of high school quartile only introduces greater complexity to the role of high school academic achievement. The data indicate that students with higher high school class ranks persisted at a higher rate than those from lower ranks, but the pattern changes over time. Those students from the highest quartile persisted to year two at the highest rate (75 percent), but students from the second and third quartiles persisted at rates only slightly more than 1 percent apart (69.8 percent and 68.5 percent, respectively). From year two to year three, however, the pattern changes. While there is a drop in persistence rates of approximately fifteen percentage points among students who graduated from the top half of their high school class (75.1 percent to 59.8 percent among the top quartile, 69.8 percent to 53.3 percent among the second quartile), third quartile students fell at year three to only 41.7 percent of their original numbers, a drop of over 25 percent. It appears that students entering college who graduated in the third quartile from their high school class may keep up with their peers during their first year in college, but are less likely to continue during their second year. That SAT scores are not associated with a similar pattern of second-to third-year persistence warrants further scrutiny. It may be that SAT scores reflect the knowledge students have stored over time, but class standing is more contextual in nature, reflecting the grades students earn in situ, in a real academic environment that provides subtle forms of motivation, inspiration, and self-assessment, and that the habits students developed in response to that context change over time for some students in the college environment. If this is the case, then what factors cause that change, and what can be done to assist students during later years making the same or better academic progress as in the first year?

## FIRST-YEAR COLLEGIATE EXPERIENCES AND SUBSEQUENT PERSISTENCE DECISIONS

### Initial Academic Performance

It is especially important to examine the role that early academic experiences may have in persistence *beyond* the first year. Preliminary evidence suggests that academic success may indeed be pivotal to long-term persistence, but the data raise as many questions as those that they address. The mean GPA for those students who persist across the six-year time period rises steadily with each year of persistence. Six-year graduation figures support this trend; students who graduated within six years had earned a higher mean GPA during their first semester (2.79) than those who had not graduated (2.29). Clearly there is a connection between initial academic success and graduation, but further study is required to determine if academic success is a mediating variable, or if the same factors that result in good grades result in degree completion.

### Course Withdrawals

At the institution from which the data were gathered, academic policy allows students to drop courses without a grade as late as four weeks prior to the end of the semester, and there is no limit to the number of course withdrawals students may accumulate during their careers. An analysis of the ratio of credit hours students earned (complete the course with a passing grade) to the number of hours attempted (enrollment on the census date) indicated that unsuccessful course attempts may have played a significant role in persistence rates from year two to year three. Students who persisted to year two had successfully completed 92 per-

**Figure 6.2**
**Attrition Rates across Time for FTIC Students**

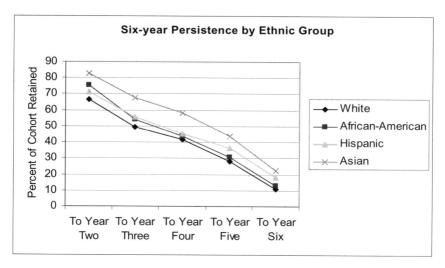

cent of the credits they attempted during the fall semester in year one, compared to only 81 percent among students who did not persist to year two. More striking is that students who persisted from year two to year three successfully completed 96 percent of the credits they attempted the fall semester of year two, compared to 74 percent among students who did not persist to year three. These data strongly suggest the need to examine the impact of course withdrawals over time and raise several questions: Can students who withdraw from courses recover? What resources enable them to do so? What role do policies that limit the number of withdrawal options have on student success?

Because students who persist attempt, on average, only slightly more credit hours than students who do not persist (an average of thirteen rather than twelve), the implication of the findings point less toward rate of progress (number of credits earned per semester) than to withdrawal behavior and the factors that influence and result from the decision to withdraw from courses. It is likely that withdrawal behavior mediates a relationship between background characteristics and environmental pull factors on the one hand, and students' sense of progress and commitment to continuing on the other. These issues may take a unique shape at institutions where program variations and student characteristics generate specific policies regarding withdrawal from courses on the part of the institution or certain withdrawal patterns or behaviors on the part of students.

## A FINAL NOTE: THE NEED FOR MORE PERCEPTUAL DATA

Finally, the data examined from the current institution should ideally be combined with perceptual data reflecting the academic and social experiences of students in the second year and beyond. The National Survey of Student Experiences provides an opportunity for many institutions to benchmark their students' experiences in these areas, but institutions need to develop their own instruments to fully capture the unique interactions between students and institutions, from student interactions with other students and faculty, to student finances, to student engagement with campus support systems. The structure of an institution, including academic policies, presence of research opportunities, faculty types, class sizes, and student demographics, will generate classroom environments, academic cultures, habits of faculty, and student interactions that will not be the same at all higher education institutions. Institution-specific experiences play a larger role in student persistence as time passes, so that a more fruitful understanding of the nature of these experiences and how institutions may influence them must be drawn not from data sets that combine data from many types of institutions, but from single-institution and like-institution studies that are designed to capture the persistence process over time within the unique context of an institution.

## NOTES

1. Note that students self-report their ethnicities, and it is probable that the international student population was underreported and the Asian population overreported.

2. Includes MATH 1300, READ 1300, and ENGL 1300.

3. Students still enrolled in fall 1998 and fall 1999.

4. Calculated by dividing the number of student credit hours attempted by the number earned.

5. Students still enrolled in fall 1998.

6. Students who have been Texas residents for at least the past twelve months.

7. Tuition-exempt students may include students who are blind or deaf, students who rank in the highest percentage of graduating high schools in Texas, children of disabled firefighters and peace officers, children of prisoners of war

or persons missing in action, veterans, and children of members of armed forces who were killed in action.

# REFERENCES

Astin, A. (1984). Student involvement: A developmental theory for higher education. *Journal of College Student Personnel* 25: 297–308.

Bartlett, C., & Abell, P. (1995, February). Understanding the transfer student—Or are we? Paper presented at the Annual National Transfer and Articulation Symposium, Tucson, AZ.

Bean, J. (1980). Dropouts and turnover: The synthesis and test of a causal model of student attrition. *Research in Higher Education* 12: 155–187.

———. (1985). Interaction effects based on class level in an explanatory model of college student dropout syndrome. *American Educational Research Journal* 22: 35–64.

Bean, J., & Metzner, B. (1985). A conceptual model of nontraditional undergraduate student attrition. *Review of Educational Research* 55: 485–540.

Bradburn, E. M. (2002). Short-term enrollment in postsecondary education: Student background and institutional differences in reasons for early departure, 1996–98. Postsecondary Education Descriptive Analysis Reports. National Center for Education Statistics, Publication No. NCES-2003–153.

Braxton, J., & Brier, E. (1989). Melding organizational and interactional theories of student attrition: A path analytic study. *Review of Higher Education* 13: 47–61.

Braxton, J. M., & Lien, L. A. (2000). The viability of academic integration as a central construct in Tinto's interactionalist theory of college student departure. In *Reworking the student departure puzzle*, ed. J. Braxton, 11–28. Nashville: Vanderbilt University Press.

Cabrera, A. F., & Nora, A. (1994). College students' perceptions of prejudice and discrimination and their feelings of alienation: A construct validation approach. *Review of Education/Pedagogy/Cultural Studies* 16(3–4): 387–409.

Cabrera, A. F., Nora, A., & Castaneda, M. B. (1992). The role of finances in the student persistence process: A structural model. *Research in Higher Education* 33(5): 571–594.

———. (1993). College persistence: The testing of an integrated model. *Journal of Higher Education* 64(2): 123–139.

DuBrock, C. P. (1999, May). Financial aid and college persistence: A five-year longitudinal study of 1993 and 1994 beginning freshmen students. Paper presented at symposium conducted at the AIR 40th Annual Forum, Cincinnati, OH.

Horn, L., & Kojaku, L. K. (2001). High school academic curriculum and the persistence path through college: Persistence and transfer behavior of undergraduates three years after entering four-year institutions. National

Center for Education Statistics, Publication No. NCES 2001–163. http://nces.ed.gov/pubs2001/2001163.pdf (accessed April 4, 2004).

Hurtado, S., & Carter, D. F. (1997). Effects of collage transition and perceptions of campus racial climate on Latino college students' sense of belonging. *Sociology of Education* 70: 324–345.

Ishitani, T. T., DesJardins, S. L. (2002, June). A longitudinal investigation of dropout from college in the United States. Paper presented at symposium conducted at the AIR 42nd Annual Forum, Toronto, Canada.

Maack, S. C. (2002). *Whatever happened to students who entered in the fall 1995? Persistence at Rio Hondo College.* ERIC Document Reproduction Service No. ED466878. http://www.eduref.org (accessed April 4, 2004).

National Center for Education Statistics (NCES). (1993). Persistence and attainment in postsecondary education for beginning AY 1989–90 students as of spring 1992. National Center for Education Statistics, Publication No. NCES 94-477. http://nces.ed.gov/pubs94/94477.pdf (accessed April 4, 2004).

Nora, A. (1987). Determinants of retention among Chicano college students: A structural model. *Research in Higher Education* 26(1): 31–59.

———. (1993). Two-year colleges and minority students' educational aspirations: Help or hindrance. In *Higher Education: Handbook of Theory and Research*, Vol. 9, ed. J. C. Smart. New York: Agathon Press.

———. (2002). A theoretical and practical view of student adjustment and academic achievement. In *Increasing access to college: Extending possibilities for all students*, ed. W. Tierney and L. Hagedorn, 65–77. Albany: State University of New York Press.

———. (2004). The role of habitus and cultural capital in choosing a college, transitioning from high school to higher education, and persisting in college among minority and non-minority students. *Journal of Hispanic Higher Education* 3(2): 180–208.

Nora, A., & Cabrera, A. F. (1996). The role of perceptions of prejudice and discrimination on the adjustment of minority students to college. *Journal of Higher Education* 67(2): 119–148.

Nora, A., Cabrera, A. F., Hagedorn, L., & Pascarella, E. T. (1996). Differential impacts of academic and social experiences on college-related behavioral outcomes across different ethnic and gender groups at four-year institutions. *Research in Higher Education* 37(4): 427–452.

Nora, A., & Garcia, V. (n.d.). The role of perceptions of remediation on the persistence of developmental students in higher education. Unpublished manuscript, University of Houston, Houston, TX.

Nora, A., & Lang, D. (n.d.). Precollege psychosocial factors related to persistence. Unpublished manuscript, University of Houston, Houston, TX.

Nora, A., & Wedam, E. (1993). Off-campus experiences: The pull factors affecting freshman-year attrition on a commuter campus. Unpublished manuscript, University of Illinois at Chicago.

Olivas, M. A. (1986). *Latino college students*. New York: Teachers College Press.

Pascarella, E., & Terenzini, P. T. (1979). Student-faculty informal contact and college persistence: A further investigation. *Journal of Educational Research* 72: 214–218.

————. (1980). Predicting freshman persistence and voluntary dropout decisions from a theoretical model. *Journal of Higher Education* 72: 214–218.

————. (1990). *How college affects students: Findings and insights from twenty years of research*. San Francisco Jossey-Bass.

Rendon, L. I. (1994). Validating culturally diverse students: Toward a new model of learning and student development. *Innovative Higher Education* 19(1): 23–32.

Smith, T. Y. (1995, May). The retention status of underrepresented minority students: An analysis of survey results from sixty-seven U.S. colleges and universities. Paper presented at symposium conducted at the AIR 35th Annual Forum, Boston, MA.

St. John, E. P., Cabrera, A. F., Nora, A., & Asker, E. H. (2001). Economic perspectives on student persistence. In *Rethinking the student departure puzzle*, ed. J. Braxton, Nashville: Vanderbilt University Press.

Terenzini, P., & Pascarella, E. (1980). Student/faculty relationships and freshman year educational outcomes: A further investigation. *Journal of College Student Personnel* 21: 521–528.

Tinto, V. (1975). Dropout from higher education: A theoretical synthesis of recent research. *Review of Educational Research* 45: 89–125.

# CHAPTER

# Pathways to a Four-Year Degree

## Determinants of Transfer and Degree Completion

*Alberto F. Cabrera, Kurt R. Burkum, and Steven M. La Nasa*

## INTRODUCTION

A bachelor's degree is no longer considered a potential stepping-stone to a better life. It is the gatekeeper to myriad social and individual benefits, ranging from income, employment stability, and occupational prestige to engagement in civic and political activities (e.g., W. Bowen & Bok 1998; Hossler, Braxton, & Coopersmith 1988; Leslie & Brinkman 1986; Lin & Vogt 1996; Pascarella & Terenzini 1991). Though the social and economic benefits of a college degree are numerous, acquiring them is tied to a single stepping-stone: completing a college degree (Adelman 1999).

As early as the 1960s, federal, state, and local governments have recognized that completion of a four-year degree can be an insurmountable step for individuals from disadvantaged socioeconomic backgrounds. Some student assistance programs like Chapter I, TRIO, and GEAR UP recognize the important role that academic preparation, awareness of opportunities for college, and assistance in completing the college application process play for low-income students whose parents are not college educated. However, most federal and state assistance programs focus on inability to pay as a deterrent for access to higher education and persistence to degree completion (College Board 2003).

The importance our society places in making a college degree an affordable option for able and willing low-income individuals is evidenced by the growth of college financial aid programs. In the early 1980s, the

cost of federal financial aid programs approached $20 billion per year
(Lewis 1989). By 2003, these federal financial aid program expenditures
were $66 billion (College Board 2003). As important as these need-based
programs have been in facilitating access to and success in college, economic need per se does not appear to explain fully why low-income individuals enroll (Hossler, Schmitt, & Vesper 1999) or persist in college
(e.g., Adelman 1999; Braxton 2000; Cabrera, Nora, & Castañeda 1992;
Choy 2002; Gladieux & Swail 2000; Swail 1995; Terenzini, Cabrera, &
Bernal 2001).

In addition to students' socioeconomic background, we know access to
and success in college as well as transferring from a two-year institution
to a four-year institution are the product of a complex set of factors, some
of which can be traced back to at least the eighth grade, while others
pertain to postsecondary experiences (e.g., Blecher, Michael, & Hagedorn 2002; Braxton 2000; Cabrera & La Nasa 2001; Hossler, Schmitt, &
Vesper 1999; McDonough 1997; Paulsen & St. John 2002; Tinto 1993).
In terms of what matters on the path to a four-year degree, we also know
individuals from low socioeconomic (SES) backgrounds are most disadvantaged.[1] Low-SES students tend to be raised by parents who are less
likely to be involved in school activities (Cabrera & La Nasa 2001).
Their parents are less knowledgeable about how to plan and pay for college (Flint 1992, 1993; King 1996). The middle schools that low-SES
students attend also compound the problem by lacking in enough certi-
fied teachers, adequate career counseling resources, and course offerings
(Venezia, Kirst, & Antonio 2003). By the end the senior year, low-SES
twelfth graders are less likely to have planned for and be academically
prepared for college (Adelman 1999; Cabrera & La Nasa 2000, 2001;
Terenzini, Cabrera, & Bernal 2001). If and when they enter college, they
do so often at readiness levels far below those of their better-off counterparts, while choosing public institutions and being clustered in community colleges (e.g., Kim 2004; McPherson & Shapiro 1998). Once
enrolled in postsecondary education, low-SES students' involvement
with the institution is similar to that exhibited by their better-off counterparts, with a few exceptions, including less involvement with faculty,
other students, clubs, and organizations and being more prone to work
longer hours (e.g., Cuccaro-Alamin & Choy 1998; Terenzini, Cabrera,
& Bernal 2001; Walpole 2003). Moreover, at the end of their first year,
low-SES students report greater learning gains in critical thinking and
enjoyment of arts than those reported by better-off students (Terenzini,
Cabrera, & Bernal 2001). In spite of the many similarities within college, low-SES students' degree completion rates lag substantially behind

those of their more affluent counterparts (Carroll 1989; Paulsen & St. John 2002; Terenzini, Cabrera, & Bernal 2001).

This chapter seeks to further our understanding of why postsecondary attendance and degree completion patterns differ markedly between socioeconomically disadvantaged students and their better-off peers. This is important as socioeconomically disadvantaged students are attending college in much greater numbers than in the past. Two milestones along the college path for members of the high school sophomore cohort of 1980 were examined. These two milestones are: (1) transferring from the two-year sector to the four-year sector, and (2) persistence to degree completion. This chapter also addresses three major shortcomings when examining socioeconomically disadvantaged students' path to a four-year degree. First, it examines the effect of financial aid *in addition to* other important determinants of degree completion. Second, it adheres to a more comprehensive definition of persistence by focusing on degree completion rather than persistence at the end of the first year. Third, it studies how determinants of degree completion vary across socioeconomic levels. When SES is brought to bear, with few notable exceptions (e.g., Paulsen & St. John 2002; St. John et al. 1996; Terenzini, Cabrera, & Bernal 2001; Walpole 2003), it is done with the purpose of controlling for an alternative explanation rather than with the explicit intention of highlighting differences between socioeconomically disadvantaged students and their better-off peers. Simply put: *we still do not know what specific factors lead some low-SES students to succeed on their path to a college degree despite overwhelming odds.* This study uses SES with the intention of highlighting differences between socioeconomically disadvantaged students and their better-off peers, an approach which has received little attention (Paulsen & St. John 2002; Walpole 2003).[2]

## PATHWAYS TO A FOUR-YEAR DEGREE

In examining the 1980 high school sophomore cohort, Adelman (1999) concluded that the quality and intensity of academic preparation secured in high school was one of the most important determinants of completing a four-year degree. Velez (1985) and Carroll (1989) found that postsecondary tracks also matter. Their findings suggest that high school students are more prone to obtain a bachelor's degree if their port of entry to postsecondary education was a four-year institution. When these two concepts are combined (preparation for college and first type of postsecondary institution attended),[3] it is possible to identify nine pathways to a college degree followed by the high school sophomore cohort of 1980 (see Figure 7.1).

By 1993, 58 percent of the high school sophomore cohort of 1980 had enrolled in a postsecondary institution. Of those enrolled, 47 percent first attended a four-year institution, 41 percent first opted for a two-year institution, and 12 percent first selected another type of institution. Only half were fully qualified for college. Figure 7.1 depicts the nine different paths to a four-year degree followed by the high school sophomore cohort of 1980, resulting from combinations of academic resource levels and the first type of institution attended. The type of institution students first enter correlates strongly with academic resources secured in high school ($r = 0.412$, $p < 0.001$). Seventy percent of those students highly prepared academically first enrolled at four-year institutions. In contrast, only 16 percent of the lowest prepared first enrolled at a four-year institution. For these academically deficient students, first institutional choice appears almost exclusively confined to institutions offering the associate's degree or less.

Academic Resources–Institutional Choice paths vary in their likelihood to produce a four-year degree. In the aggregate, successful pathways to a bachelor's degree appear to follow a logical progression: students who obtain the highest academic preparation and enter a four-year institution tend to secure a four-year degree. Conversely, students who are poorly qualified and choose a first institution other than a four-year college or university see their chances to graduate diminished. Seventy-eight percent of those students who pursued the first path graduated within ten years. In contrast, just 2.3 percent of those who were poorly qualified and first entered a two-year institution earned a four-year degree in the same timeframe. Although enrolling in a four-year institution exerts a powerful effect, academic preparation seems to provide better chances to graduate from college regardless of port of entry. Even when students begin their postsecondary careers in the two-year sector, those who are highly prepared have a 30 percent chance to earn a four-year degree (see Figure 7.1).

Securing different levels of academic preparation and choosing institutions of postsecondary education vary as one examines a student's socioeconomic status. Twenty-five percent of all lowest-SES students secure high academic resources. Moreover, only 30 percent of lowest-SES students first enrolled at a four-year institution regardless of academic resources (see Figure 7.2).

In contrast to the case of lowest-SES students, 59 percent of students from the highest-SES background obtained high academic resources. Ad-

**Figure 7.1**
**Degree Attainment by ACRES and First Institution Type for All Students**

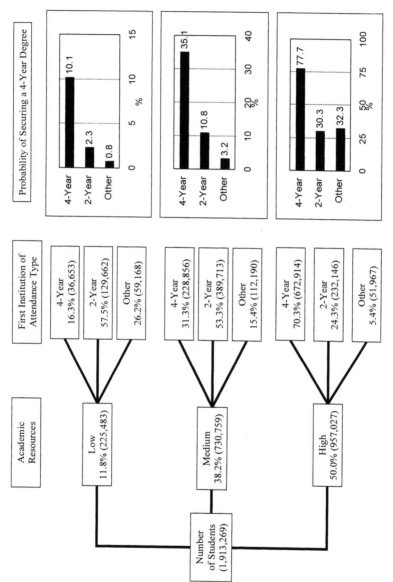

Note: Based on High School and Beyond, Sophomore Cohort (NCES 2000-194). Only cases with verified data were used.

**Figure 7.2**
**Degree Attainment by ACRES and First Institution Type for Lowest-SES Students**

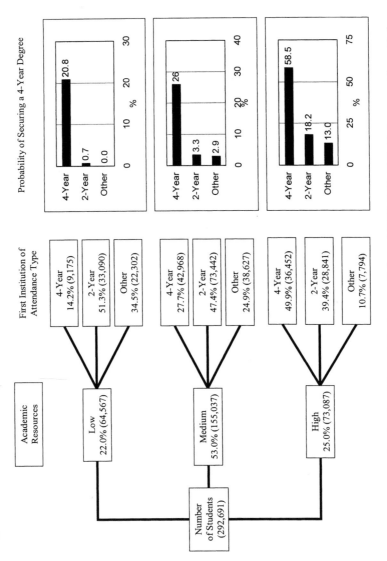

Note: Based on High School and Beyond, Sophomore Cohort (NCES 2000-194). Only cases with verified data were used.

ditionally, 58 percent of all highest-SES students first entered a four-year institution regardless of their academic resources (see Figure 7.3). These figures confirm a pervasive national trend documented more fully elsewhere (Cabrera & La Nasa 2000, 2001).

Paths pursued by students to earn a bachelor's degree do vary, in fact, by socioeconomic status. Lowest-SES students are most likely to journey on the path of medium academic resources and entrance at a two-year institution. The degree completion chances of those who journey on this path are only 3.3 percent (see Figure 7.2). At the opposite end is the case of highest-SES students who travel on the path of high academic resources and entrance in a four-year institution. Eighty-one percent of highest-SES students traveling on this path graduate with a bachelor's degree (see Figure 7.3).

Students from high socioeconomic backgrounds appear to have a relative advantage over students from the lowest socioeconomic levels for most of the pathways to a college degree. In all but one path, students from the highest socioeconomic backgrounds are more likely to secure a four-year degree than their disadvantaged peers, regardless of academic preparation or port of entry. Nevertheless, the results are not entirely dismal for disadvantaged students, because these students display remarkable success along a very important path. Lowest-SES students who secure only minimal academic resources and enter a four-year institution are approximately 11 percent more likely to secure a four-year degree than their better-off peers who follow the same path. This fact speaks highly to these students' resilience to overcome the high hurdles they face.

While our descriptive examination of the high school class of 1982 confirms an SES-based gap in postsecondary opportunities, the pathways to a four-year degree does not help us to form firm conclusions as to what helps lowest-SES students overcome their substantially low odds of degree completion. We know that collegiate experiences and curricular choices matter, irrespective of a student's SES (e.g., Adelman 1999; Montodon & Eikener 1997). Yet, the nature and role of collegiate experiences and their contribution to degree completion among socioeconomically disadvantaged students remain to be examined (Terenzini, Cabrera, & Bernal 2001; Walpole 2003). Examination of the high school sophomore cohort of 1980 database has already revealed much about the important role academic preparation has on persisting to degree completion (Adelman 1999). What remains is to uncover the role of academic preparation in facilitating transfer from the two-year sector to the four-year sector.

**Figure 7.3**
**Degree Attainment by ACRES and First Institution Type for Highest-SES Students**

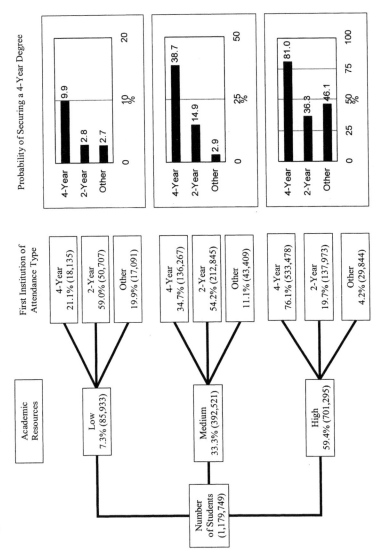

Note: Based on High School and Beyond, Sophomore Cohort (NCES 2000-194). Only cases with verified data were used.

The next sections, "Determinants of Transfer" and "Determinants of Degree Completion," examine critical factors enabling a student to transfer to the four-year sector and persist to degree completion. Each of these sections comprises two parts. The first part is an examination of each individual factor in the model using descriptive statistics, and the second part takes each of the separate factors into account simultaneously using more sophisticated statistical techniques.[4]

## DETERMINANTS OF TRANSFER

### First Type of Institution Attended and SES

Low-income students are more likely to enroll in two-year institutions than are their economically better-off counterparts (e.g., Blecher, Michael, & Hagedorn 2002; Hagedorn, Moon, Cypers, Maxwell, & Lester 2003; McPherson & Shapiro 1998). This institutional attendance pattern seems to support the claim of inequity of educational opportunities based on one's socioeconomic background (Karabel 1972, 1986).

Our examination of the college destinations for the high school sophomore cohort of 1980 supports McPhearson and Shapiro's findings, and is in line with Karabel's notion of SES-based inequity of higher education opportunity.[5] As shown in Table 7.1, a small but significant association between socioeconomic status and college destinations of high school sophomores exists ($X^2$ = 206,703. 6, $p < 0.001$, $r = 0.290$). Compared to the average high school sophomore, whose chances of enrolling at a four-year institution are almost 50 percent, the average poor sophomore's chance of enrolling at a four-year institution is only 30 percent. When comparing the enrollment rate at four-year institutions between the lowest-SES students and the highest-SES students, a huge disparity is evident. Highest-SES students are 37 percent more likely to enroll in a four-year institution than lowest-SES students.

### Transfer Patterns and SES

Compounding the problem of the moderate association between college destination and socioeconomic factors is the fact that few students enrolled in the two-year sector actually transfer to a four-year institution. Tinto (1987), while examining the high school class of 1972, estimated that only one out of four community college students eventually trans-

**Table 7.1**
**First Type of Postsecondary Institution Attended for the**
**High School Sophomore Cohort of 1980**

| Socioeconomic status | First type of postsecondary institution attended | | |
|---|---|---|---|
| | Other | 2-year | 4-year |
| Lowest | 22.3% | 47.8% | 29.9% |
| Medium low | 14.4% | 49.5% | 36.1% |
| Medium high | 13.7% | 42.5% | 43.9% |
| Highest | 3.9% | 29.2% | 66.9% |
| Overall | 12.0% | 40.4% | 47.6% |

Note: Estimates are based on the HSB/So panel weight PSEWT1.

ferred to a four-year institution. Other articles report that enrolling at a two-year institution substantially reduces one's chances of eventually securing a four-year degree (e.g., Astin 1975; Breneman & Nelson, 1981).

Our descriptive analyses of transfer rates among community college students enrolled during the 1983–84 academic year corroborate Karabel's contention: *community colleges do appear to help in perpetuating a system of unequal access to a college degree.* The overall transfer rate among this group was 29 percent, a transfer rate remarkably close to Tinto's estimates. We also found transfer to a four-year institution to be significantly associated with a student's SES ($X^2 = 13,380.9$, $p < 0.001$, $r = 0.164$). Differences in transfer rates by SES are vast. Lowest-SES community college students were 20 percent, 17 percent, and 6 percent less likely to transfer to a four-year institution than their counterparts in the highest-, medium high–, and medium Low–SES quartiles (see Table 7.2).

Despite these data, the role of the community college as an SES-based gatekeeper for eventual college degree attainment is debated. At the core of this controversy lie the level of analysis and the type of controls different studies employ. Experts on the community college sector have long believed that simple descriptive statistics obscure the role played by a variety of factors critical to a student's chances to eventually transfer to the four-year sector (e.g., Blecher, Michael, & Hagedorn 2002; Hagedorn et al. 2003; Kinnick and Kempner 1988; Breneman & Nelson 1981; Adelman 1999; Berkner & Chavez 1997; Hearn 1988, 1991; Lee & Frank 1990; Velez & Javalgi 1987). Their research suggests socioeconomic status plays a secondary role in transfer decisions when compared to other factors.

**Table 7.2**
**Transfer Rates by SES among Students Enrolled
in a Community College during the 1983–84
Academic Year**

| Socioeconomic status (in quartiles) | Percentage transferring |
|---|---|
| Lowest | 17.0% |
| Medium low | 22.9% |
| Medium high | 33.9% |
| Highest | 36.7% |
| Overall | 29.4% |

Note: Estimates are based on the HSB/So panel weight
PSEWT1.

## Educational Aspirations

Having clear educational aspirations along with strong high school
preparation for college seems to play a pivotal role in transfer decisions.
Kinnick and Kempner (1988) found that students entering a two-year institution were able to secure a four-year degree to the extent that they
had clear educational goals, were highly motivated, and were academically prepared. More recently, Adelman (1999) found the odds of eventually securing a four-year degree among community college students to
be highly associated with collegiate degree expectations. Lee and Frank
(1990) reported similar results when they examined transfer behavior for
a representative sample of the high school senior class of 1980.

## Degree Aspirations

When we examined those 1980 high school sophomores who entered
a community college between 1982 and 1983, we found striking differences in degree aspirations across SES quartiles. A moderate, but significant, correlation between SES and degree aspirations was observed,
where degree aspirations increased across SES. Lowest-SES students were
almost 30 percent less likely to aspire to a four-year degree than highest-
SES students (see Figure 7.4).

## Academic Resources

Securing academic resources in high school seems to be a determinant
of success in postsecondary education. Adelman (1999) found that the

**Figure 7.4**
**Proportion of Students Entering a Community College Aspiring to a Four-Year Degree by SES**

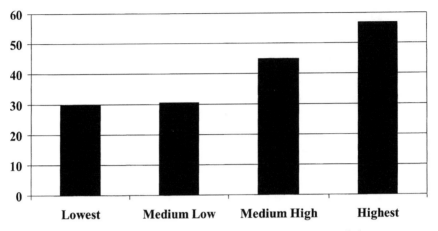

Note: Estimates are based on those high school sophomores who enrolled at a two-year institution between 1982 and 1983 ($r = 0.224$).

odds of earning a four-year degree increased in tandem with the academic resources the college student secured in high school: *the greater one's academic resources, the greater one's chances of four-year degree completion.* We find that the level of academic resources among community college is moderately associated with SES. Lowest-SES students were less prepared. While 42 percent of highest-SES students were highly academically prepared for college, merely 25 percent of lowest-SES students enjoyed the same level of academic preparation (see Figure 7.5).

## Community College Curricular Choice, Academic Success, and Collegiate Experiences

The type and quality of community college experiences are determining factors in decisions to transfer as well. Kraemer (1995) reported that academic performance in the community college affected a student's intent to transfer and actual transfer decisions. While examining factors that lead to transfer students' academic success at the four-year institution, Montondon and Eikner (1997) found academic performance at the two-year institution to be defining. In addition to academic performance, the quality of the interactions of community college students with faculty and peers matters. Nora and Rendón (1990) found intent to trans-

**Figure 7.5**
**Academic Resources among Community College Students across SES**

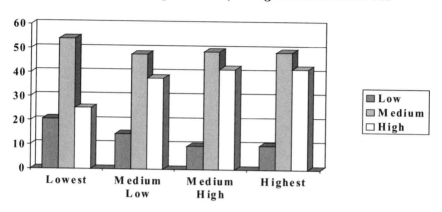

Note: Estimates are based on those high school sophomores who enrolled at a two-year institution between 1982 and 1983 ($r = 0.106$).

fer was most affected by the extent to which the community college student was satisfied with the academic and social components of the two-year institution. College curriculum also seems to play a role (e.g., Adelman 1999). Velez and Javalgi (1987) found that students enrolled in a community college in 1972 were more likely to transfer if they had an on-campus work-study position and lived on campus. They also found the effect of SES on transferring was negligible after controlling for background and collegiate experiences. Curricular choices and collegiate academic performance also seem to facilitate transfer. For instance, Lee and Frank (1990) found taking courses in math and science, along with having strong academic performance, to be among the strongest predictors of transfer for members of the 1980 high school class.

Table 7.3 highlights the degree of association between different collegiate experiences[6] and decisions to transfer for our student population. It is evident that transfer decisions are mostly associated with the number of courses earned in math and science, a finding consistent with Lee and Frank (1990). How well the student performs in the community college is also a factor associated with eventual transfer. Positive out-of-classroom experiences also matter. The degree of association between the remaining collegiate experiences, though positive, is small. We found no association between being satisfied with the cost of attending a community college and the likelihood of transferring to a four-year institution. Taken as a whole, our results suggest transfer is more likely to be associated with

Table 7.3
Degree of Association between Collegiate
Experiences and Transfer among 1980 High
School Sophomores

| Variable | $r$ |
|---|---|
| GPA | 0.178 |
| Out-of-classroom experiences | 0.123 |
| Quality of instruction | 0.088 |
| Counseling | 0.067 |
| Campus facilities | 0.078 |
| Institutional prestige | 0.088 |
| Number of math courses | 0.342 |
| Number of science courses | 0.332 |
| Satisfaction with cost of attendance | −0.043 |

a community college student's curricular choices and academic success than with any other collegiate experience measured.

## SES and Community College Curricular Choice, Academic Success, and Collegiate Experiences

The nature of collegiate experiences among socioeconomically disadvantaged students is an issue long neglected in the literature. Table 7.4 highlights specific SES-based collegiate differences. While there are significant mean differences between highest- and lowest-SES students within each collegiate experience, the largest differences are again seen in the number of math and science courses and grade point average (GPA). It is also noteworthy that these differences, though statistically significant, are rather small in absolute terms. For instance, lowest-SES students' academic performance in college was only a quarter of a grade lower than highest-SES students'.

### Remedial Education

The nature of remediation also plays a role in the likelihood of a community college student eventually attaining a four-year degree. Adelman (1998), while examining college transcripts of the 1980 high school sophomore cohort, found a negative relationship between taking remedial education and degree completion. However, in reviewing the data provided by Adelman (1998), Merisotis and Phipps (2000) reached an opposite conclusion. They found that the effectiveness, and eventual de-

**Table 7.4**
**Differences in Collegiate Experiences and Curriculum Patterns across SES**
**(Means and Proportions Comparison)**

| Variable | Socioeconomic status (in quartiles) | | | | $F/X^2$ | $r$ |
| | Lowest | Middle low | Middle high | Highest | | |
|---|---|---|---|---|---|---|
| GPA | 2.23 | 2.49 | 2.54 | 2.50 | 3,233.81** | 0.097 |
| Out-of-classroom experiences | 3.59 | 3.60 | 3.61 | 3.73 | 806.00** | 0.064 |
| Quality of instruction | 4.01 | 4.01 | 3.94 | 4.04 | 393.26** | 0.006 |
| Counseling | 3.36 | 3.37 | 3.31 | 3.49 | 670.08** | 0.039 |
| Campus facilities | 4.11 | 3.96 | 4.10 | 4.16 | 949.88** | 0.049 |
| Institutional prestige | 3.81 | 3.72 | 3.71 | 3.83 | 490.50** | 0.021 |
| Enroll in at least 1 math course | 21.4% | 28.5% | 32.9% | 38.4% | 7,740.35** | 0.124 |
| Enroll in at least 1 science course | 29.3% | 38.3% | 41.9% | 53.4% | 13,766.23** | 0.165 |
| Satisfaction with cost of attendance | 66.1% | 66.6% | 69.6% | 65.8% | 500.06** | 0.035 |

**$p < 0.001$.

gree attainment, among the least prepared students rested on the total number of remediation courses completed. Clearly, firm conclusions have not been reached regarding the role of remediation in transfer.

Our analysis indicates that the degree of association between SES and remediation is weak. Correlations between SES and remediation in English and in math were 0.125 and 0.084, respectively. However, it is evident that lowest-SES students are more likely to take remediation courses than are highest-SES students. Lowest-SES students were 9 percent and 4 percent more likely to take remedial English and math, respectively, than their highest-SES counterparts (see Figure 7.6).

## Family Responsibilities

Family responsibilities, particularly having a child prior to degree completion, have been found to diminish a student's chance of succeeding in college. For instance, Nora, Cabrera, Hagedorn, and Pascarella (1996)

**Figure 7.6**
**Percentage of Community College Students Taking Remedial English and Math Courses by SES**

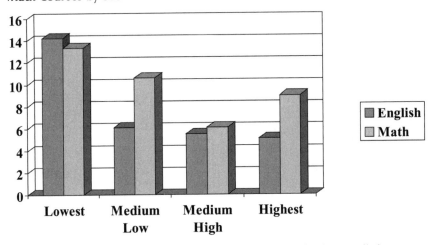

Note: Estimates are based on those high school sophomores who first enrolled at a two-year institution between 1982 and 1983 ($r = 0.125$ for English, $r = 0.084$ for math).

found family responsibilities decrease a student's likelihood to become involved with an institution, increasing the possibilities of dropping out of college. Similarly, Adelman (1999) identified lower long-term degree completion rates for students who had children while attending college.

Overall, we find that community college students who have children prior to degree completion are 24 percent less likely to transfer than are students without this type of responsibility. The degree of association between having a child and transfer was moderately small ($r = 0.148$). This impact is exacerbated within the lowest-SES quartile, as lowest-SES students are more prone to have children while attending college. As can be seen in Figure 7.7, lowest-SES students were 6 percent more likely to assume family responsibilities of this nature than highest-SES students. Though significant ($X^2 = 2,543.56$, $df = 3$, $p < 0.001$), the degree of association between SES and having children is rather small ($r = 0.073$).

## WHAT REALLY FACILITATES TRANSFER?

### Socioeconomic Status

From a purely descriptive basis, SES plays an important role in shaping transfer decisions for our student population. Yet, descriptive statistics can be misleading: they fail to account for the simultaneous effects

**Figure 7.7**
**Percentage of Students Having Children Prior to Degree Completion across SES**

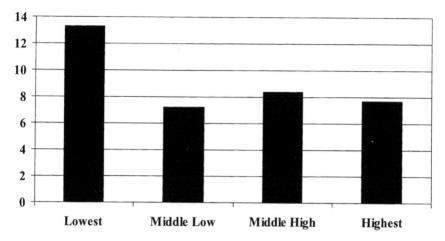

Note: Estimates are based on the High School and Beyond: 1980 (sophomore cohort). Panel weight PSEWT1 ($r = 0.073$).

of myriad other factors identified as critical to the transfer process. Once the joint effect of these factors is included in the analysis, the vast differences attributable to SES substantially decrease.[7] The 20 percent transfer gap between lowest-SES students and highest-SES students is reduced to 7 percent once demographic characteristics, encouragement, academic preparation, collegiate degree aspirations, performance in college, effort, remedial education, collegiate experiences, financial aid, and family status are controlled (see Table 7.5 and Figure 7.8).[8]

## Community College Curricular Choice

While aspirations, academic resources, remedial education, and family responsibilities were found to play a role in transfer, our analysis indicates taking math and science courses to be the most significant factor for all students. Community college students who took two science courses were 33 percent more likely to successfully transfer compared to those who took no science courses. Similarly, community college students who took two math courses were 19 percent more likely to transfer. The effect of taking science courses among lowest-SES students is even more pronounced. For this group, taking only one science course increases the likelihood of transferring 55 percent (see Table 7.5).

**Figure 7.8**
**Probabilities of Transferring to a Four-Year Institution by SES for the High School Sophomore Cohort 1980, Actual and Adjusted**

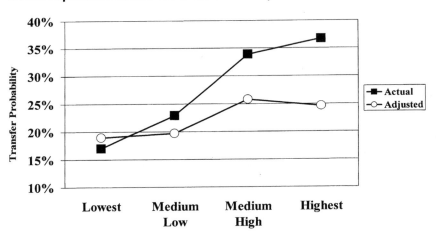

## Academic Resources

Sound preparation for college plays a key role in facilitating transfer. Compared to those students who had poor academic resources, middle and highly academically prepared community college students were 6 percent and 21 percent, respectively, more likely to transfer to a four-year institution. Among lowest-SES students, being highly academically prepared increases the chance of transferring by 21 percent (see Table 7.5).

## Educational Aspirations

Consistent with the extant literature (e.g., Adelman 1999), we find that aspiring to a four-year degree is a significant predictor of transfer. Net of other factors, such as academic ability, a community college student who aspired to a four-year degree while a high school sophomore had a 15 percent greater chance to transfer than high school sophomores holding lower educational aspirations. The literature also suggests that transfer rates are grossly underestimated by failing to account for the fact that not all community college students enroll with the intent to transfer (e.g., Adelman 1999; Kinnick & Kempner 1988). Isolating those students who aspired to a four-year degree, we find the adjusted probability of transfer substantially increases for the lowest- and middle low-SES groups (see Figure 7.9). This finding suggests that without controlling for

**Table 7.5**
**Changes in the Probability of Transferring due to Background, Encouragement, Academic Resources, Performance in College, Remediation, Collegiate Experiences, Financial Aid, and Family Responsibilities**

| Factor | All | Lowest | Middle low | Middle high | Highest |
|---|---|---|---|---|---|
| | | | Socioeconomic Status | | |
| SES | | | | | |
|   Middle low | — | | | | |
|   Middle high | 0.089* | | | | |
|   Highest | 0.073* | | | | |
| Female | — | −0.092** | −0.073** | — | −0.156** |
| Ethnicity | | | | | |
|   African American | — | −0.096** | — | −0.145** | 0.374** |
|   Hispanic | −0.084** | −0.079* | −0.107* | −0.229** | — |
|   Asian American | 0.052* | −0.152** | 0.514** | — | 0.188* |
| High school encouragement | | | | | |
|   From parents | — | — | 0.105* | 0.094* | — |
|   From high school professionals | 0.029* | — | — | — | 0.211* |
|   From friends | 0.062* | 0.249* | — | 0.166* | — |
| Academic resources | | | | | |
|   Moderately prepared | 0.063* | — | — | 0.101* | 0.149* |
|   Highly prepared | 0.210* | 0.207* | 0.117* | 0.075* | 0.386* |
| Collegiate aspirations | 0.154* | 0.073* | 0.284* | 0.175* | 0.262* |
| Grade point average | 0.085* | — | — | 0.095* | 0.303* |
| Earned hours | | | | | |
|   Three quarters and more of attempted | — | — | — | 0.104* | — |
|   Earned all hours attempted | — | — | — | — | — |
| Remediation courses | | | | | |
|   In mathematics | 0.040* | 0.031* | 0.041* | 0.026* | 0.104* |
|   In reading | — | 0.240* | — | — | — |
| Number of math courses | | | | | |
|   One course | 0.225* | 0.053* | 0.278* | 0.376* | 0.145* |
|   Two courses | 0.187* | 0.072* | 0.280* | 0.353* | 0.070* |
|   Three or more courses | 0.233* | 0.781* | 0.619* | 0.377* | — |
| Number of science courses | | | | | |
|   One course | 0.130* | 0.546* | 0.117* | 0.141* | 0.189* |
|   Two courses | 0.333* | — | 0.341* | 0.375* | 0.357* |
|   Three or more courses | 0.254* | 0.435* | 0.215* | 0.252* | 0.292* |
| Collegiate experiences | | | | | |
|   Out-of-classroom | 0.053* | 0.048* | — | 0.111* | 0.028* |
|   Quality of instruction | 0.061* | 0.147* | 0.228* | 0.049* | — |
|   Counseling | 0.025* | — | 0.133* | 0.031* | — |
|   Campus facilities | — | — | — | — | — |
|   Institutional prestige | — | — | — | — | 0.142* |

**Table 7.5 (continued)**

|  |  | Socioeconomic Status |  |  |  |
| --- | --- | --- | --- | --- | --- |
| Factor | All | Lowest | Middle low | Middle high | Highest |
| Satisfaction with costs | — | — | — | — | — |
| Financial aid |  |  |  |  |  |
| Loans | 0.113** | 0.217* | 0.209* | 0.125* | — |
| Grants/scholarships | 0.061** | 0.104* | 0.037* | — | 0.290* |
| Having children | −0.183* | −0.151* | — | −0.318* | −0.242* |

Note: Only marginal probabilities associated with significant betas are reported.

degree aspirations, along with other factors, observed probabilities of transferring are not reliable indicators of what really matters.

## Remedial Education

The merits of remediation have been debated. While Adelman (1998) questions its role, Merisotis and Phipps (2000) consider remediation important in facilitating transfer. Our results support both positions. Across all students, and controlling for SES, we find remediation plays either a mediocre or negative role. For all students, those taking math remediation courses were 4 percent more likely to transfer than those who did not. Taking remedial reading has a negative effect, by lowering the chances to transfer by 4 percent. However, among lowest-SES students, the effect of taking remedial reading is particularly noteworthy. For this group, taking remedial reading actually increases their likelihood of transferring by 24 percent (see Table 7.5).[9]

## Financial Aid

Financial aid facilitated transfer to the four-year sector. For all students, receipt of loans increased the chance to transfer by 11 percent, while receiving grants improved transfer chances by 6 percent. For lowest-SES students, receiving loans increased their chances to transfer by 22 percent (see Table 7.5).

## Parental Responsibilities

Adelman (1999) found that having family responsibilities plays a negative effect on a student's chance to succeed in postsecondary education.

**Figure 7.9**
**Adjusted Probabilities of Transferring to a Four-Year Institution by SES among 1980 High School Sophomores Aspiring to at Least a Four-Year Degree**

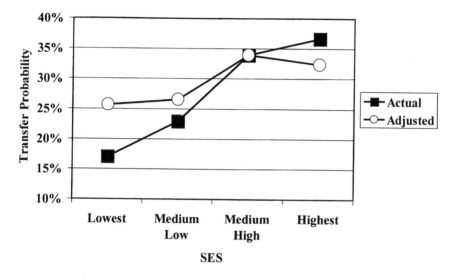

Our results are consistent with Adelman's. For all students, having children before completing a college degree reduces their chances to transfer to a four-year institution by 18 percent. Among lowest-SES students, this effect is about 15 percent (see Table 7.5).

## DETERMINANTS OF DEGREE COMPLETION

A growing body of literature that indicates what happens to students before and after they enroll in college helps explain four-year degree completion (e.g., Adelman 1999; Astin 1993; Cabrera, Nora, & Castañeda 1992; Gladieux & Swail 2000; Pascarella & Terenzini 1991; Terenzini, Cabrera, & Bernal 2001; Swail 1995; Tinto 1997). Factors associated with four-year degree completion include (a) background characteristics, (b) encouragement received in high school, (c) college preparation, (d) degree aspirations, (e) college path patterns, (f) academic involvement and success, (g) college curriculum, (h) collegiate experiences, (i) financial aid, and (j) parental responsibilities (Adelman 1999; Cabrera & La Nasa 2001; Hagedorn et al. 2003; Horn & Chen 1998; St. John, Cabrera, Nora, & Asker 2000; Velez & Javalgi 1987). As is the case with transfer, most degree completion studies use SES as a control factor, thereby neglecting examination of lowest-SES students' experiences within the postsecondary education system. In short, we do not know what specific factors lead some lowest-SES students to succeed on their path to a college degree despite overwhelming odds. This section examines degree completion by providing a synopsis of past research, descriptive statistics of the high school sophomore cohort of 1980, and results of our regression analyses for each factor.

## Degree Completion and SES

Terenzini, Cabrera, and Bernal's (2001) comprehensive review of the literature informs us that low-income students are already handicapped by a variety of adverse factors while attending college. These factors include low participation rates at the four-year sector; enrolling on a part-time basis; delayed enrollment after high school completion; working full-time; dropping, withdrawing from, or not completing college credits; and being a parent.

Of the 1980 high school sophomores who went on to postsecondary education, almost half first enrolled at a four-year institution (see Table 7.1). However, the four-year participation rate among lowest-SES students in this group is strikingly low compared to students for all other SES categories. The four-year college participation rate for lowest-SES students lags behind that of highest-SES students by 37 percent (see Table 7.1).

As we examine degree completion rates for the 1980 high school sophomore cohort, we find a moderate but positive association between a student's socioeconomic background and her chances of earning a bachelor's degree ($r = 0.335$). Two important trends underlying degree completion rates across SES quartiles are evident. First, the gap in degree completion rates across SES quartiles substantially increases as one moves up the SES ladder, and second, highest-SES students are 44 percent more likely to earn a college degree than lowest-SES students (see Figure 7.10).

## Encouragement

Development of degree aspirations as early as the eighth grade, securing high school academic qualifications, applying for college, and successful adjustment to college are related to the extent to which the student receives encouragement from parents, high school personnel, and important high school friends (e.g., Cabrera & La Nasa 2000, 2001; Cabrera, Nora, & Castañeda 1992; Flint 1992; Hossler, Schmitt, & Ves-

**Figure 7.10**
**Observed Probabilities of Degree Completion by 1993 for the High School Sophomore Cohort of 1980 (by SES)**

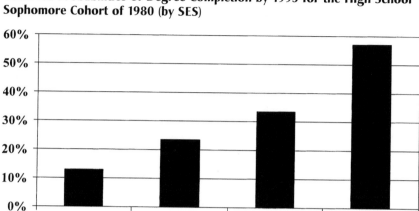

Note: Estimates are based on the High School and Beyond: 1980 (sophomore cohort). Panel weight PSEWTI ($r = 0.335$).

per 1999). This type of encouragement takes different forms, including motivational support, saving for college, and being involved in school activities (Cabrera & La Nasa 2001). Encouragement received while in high school is crucial for subsequent college enrollment. Perna (2000), for instance, noted that parental involvement in school activities predicts whether the student would enroll at a four-year college or university following high school graduation.

Some research suggests encouragement varies by SES. King (1996) observed that low-income high school seniors uncertain of whether their parents approved of their postsecondary plans were less likely than their better-off peers to aspire to attend a four-year institution. Saving for college provides the student a clear indication their parents are committed to their postsecondary education (Flint 1992, 1993). The amount of saving correlates with SES, as well. Miller (1997) reported that less than 33 percent of low-income parents saved enough money to cover more than 10 percent of their children's college education costs. Parental involvement also varies by SES. Cabrera and La Nasa (2000) reported that lowest-SES parents were less likely to participate in school activities.

Our analysis of the 1980 high school sophomore cohort reveals that a student's likelihood to receive encouragement to secure a college degree from parents, high school personnel, and high school friends was related

**Table 7.6**
**Differences in Encouragement across SES (Proportions Comparison)**

| | Socioeconomic status (in quartiles) | | | | | |
| Encouragement | Lowest | Middle low | Middle high | Highest | $F/X^2$ | $r$ |
|---|---|---|---|---|---|---|
| Parental | 68.8% | 71.1% | 83.6% | 92.7% | 131,125.46** | 0.248 |
| High school professionals | 61.3% | 63.5% | 68.9% | 76.7% | 35,994.37** | 0.130 |
| Friends | 47.7% | 54.2% | 64.9% | 75.5% | 98,770.08** | 0.216 |

** $p < 0.001$.

to his or her socioeconomic background. As a whole, highest-SES students received more encouragement, while the reverse is true for lowest-SES students. This encouragement-SES association ranged from 0.13 to 0.25. Ninety-three percent of highest-SES students reported their parents encouraged them to pursue a college degree. In contrast, 69 percent of lowest-SES students were similarly encouraged. While 77 percent of highest-SES students reported encouragement from high school professionals, only 61 percent of lowest-SES students reported receiving this sort of encouragement. The SES-based encouragement gap is even more pronounced when encouragement originates from high school friends. Less than 50 percent of lowest-SES students were encouraged by their high school friends to earn a college degree, whereas over three-fourths of highest-SES students were encouraged by their friends to become a college graduate (see Table 7.6). Given the connection between encouragement and success in college, this SES-encouragement association is troublesome.

## Academic Resources

Adelman (1999) demonstrated that securing high school–based academic resources substantially increases a student's chance to complete a bachelor's degree within eleven years of high school graduation. We find a moderate association between SES and the level of academic resources among 1980 high school sophomores who enrolled in higher education ($r = 0.216$). Lowest-SES students were less prepared. While 66 percent of highest-SES students were highly prepared academically for college, merely 23 percent of lowest-SES students enjoyed the same level of academic preparation (see Figure 7.11).

**Figure 7.11**
**Academic Resources among 1980 High School Sophomores across SES**

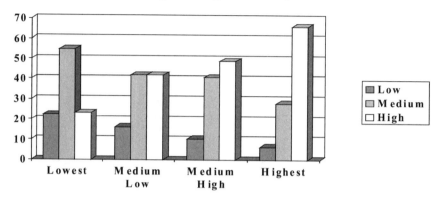

Note: Estimates are based on the 1980 High School Sophomores ($r$ = 0.216).

## Degree Aspirations

Aspiring for a four-year college degree as early as the eighth grade enables middle school students, high school students, and their families to ready themselves for college (Cabrera & La Nasa 2001). Students aspiring for at least a four-year degree are predisposed to take the appropriate course curriculum, complete high school, apply to college, enroll, and eventually graduate (e.g., Adelman 1999; Cabrera & La Nasa 2001). Some research indicates that SES moderates degree aspirations. While examining degree aspirations among 1988 middle school students, Terenzini, Cabrera, and Bernal (2001) found a difference of 29 percent between lowest-SES and highest-SES students' aspirations for at least a college degree.

As is the case for the 1988 middle school student cohort, we find significant SES-based differences in aspiring to a four-year degree among 1980 high school sophomores who entered postsecondary education during the 1982–83 academic year ($r$ = 0.335). As the SES level increases, so does the chance to develop college degree aspirations by the senior year in high school. The SES-based gap in degree aspirations is astounding. Seventy percent of the lowest-SES students who attended postsecondary education did not aspire to a college degree while a high school senior. This pattern is reversed among highest-SES students, whereby 74 percent of them had developed college aspirations before entering postsecondary education. In other words, lowest-SES students were 44 per-

**Figure 7.12**
**Degree Aspirations by SES for the 1980 High School Sophomores**

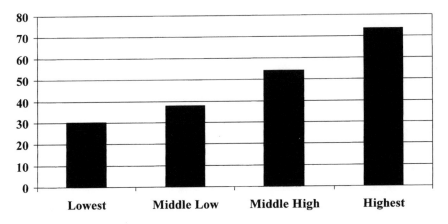

Note: Estimates are based on the High School and Beyond: 1980 (sophomore cohort). Panel weight PSEWT1 ($r = 0.335$).

cent less likely to aspire to a four-year degree than highest-SES students (see Figure 7.12).

## SES and Curricular Choice, Academic Success, and Collegiate Experiences

The degree to which a student engages with the different components of a college or university plays a key role in her cognitive and affective development (e.g., Kuh, Douglas, Lund, & Ramin-Gyurnek 1994). These positive collegiate experiences shape the extent to which a student successfully adjusts to college (e.g., Cabrera, Nora, & Castañeda 1992; Nora, Cabrera, Hagedorn, & Pascarella 1996; Pascarella & Terenzini 1991). Research has singled out several defining elements, including classroom experiences, interactions with faculty, interactions with peers, working on campus, involvement with college curriculum, and maintaining adequate academic performance (Pascarella & Terenzini 1991). The effort a student spends on academically related issues, such as maintaining adequate academic performance, seeking out and engaging faculty inside and outside the classroom, and curricular choices, is an important determinant of educational outcomes (Astin 1993; Cabrera, Colbeck, & Terenzini 2001; Kuh, Douglas, Lund, & Ramin-Gyurnek 1994). These important

**Table 7.7**
**Differences in Collegiate Experiences and Curriculum Patterns across SES (Means and Proportions Comparison)**

| Variable | Socioeconomic status (in quartiles) | | | | | |
| | Lowest | Middle low | Middle high | Highest | $F/X^2$ | $r$ |
|---|---|---|---|---|---|---|
| GPA | 2.33 | 2.51 | 2.49 | 2.65 | 11,143.99** | 0.112 |
| Out-of-classroom experiences | 3.61 | 3.64 | 3.65 | 3.83 | 9,114.92** | 0.108 |
| Quality of instruction | 4.05 | 4.11 | 4.04 | 4.09 | 961.74** | 0.007 |
| Counseling | 3.36 | 3.44 | 3.31 | 3.43 | 1,472.62** | 0.011 |
| Campus facilities | 3.97 | 3.97 | 9.97 | 4.06 | 1,155.36** | 0.035 |
| Institutional prestige | 3.81 | 3.81 | 3.81 | 3.94 | 2,451.29** | 0.051 |
| Worked on campus | 27.5% | 32.9% | 42.9% | 40.7% | 33,522.06** | 0.119 |
| Enroll in at least 1 math course | 23.7% | 33.6% | 41.5% | 59.3% | 164,528.54** | 0.264 |
| Enroll in at least 1 science course | 24.4% | 33.9% | 41.1% | 56.7% | 134,332.16** | 0.239 |

** $p < 0.001$.

outcomes include critical thinking, gains in competencies, clarity in vocational aspirations, and persistence.

Associated with these purely academic related activities, on-campus work positively impacts persistence and degree completion (Hossler 1984; Olivas 1985; Stampen & Cabrera 1986, 1988). Students who work on campus are more likely to interact with faculty and peers, develop transferable work skills, and become more integrated into the academic and social components of the institution. How the above factors play a role in degree completion is largely unknown. However, given the connection between persistence and collegiate experience on the one hand, and persistence and degree completion on the other, the connection between these collegiate experiences and degree completion is plausible.

The degree of association between SES and collegiate experiences ranges from 0.007 to 0.239, signifying a relationship ranging from nonexistent to moderately low (see Table 7.7). The degree of association between GPA and SES is significant, but rather small ($r = 0.112$). As a whole, lowest-SES students had a GPA one quarter lower than that exhibited by highest-SES students. Of the non–academically related collegiate experiences, whether the student had an on-campus work position was found to be somewhat significant ($r = 0.119$). SES-based differences are noted here as well, with lowest-SES students being 13 percent less likely to work on campus than highest-SES students. SES-based differences with out-of-classroom experiences, quality of instruction, counseling, and institutional prestige, though significant in absolute value, are almost nonexistent. What defines the nature of collegiate experiences between lowest-SES students and their better-off counterparts the most is the intensity of curriculum in math and sciences. The gap in the likelihood of taking at least one math and science course between lowest-SES and highest-SES is striking; on average, a lowest-SES student is 36 percent less likely to take college math courses and 32 percent less likely to take college science courses than his or her highest-SES counterpart.

## College Path

Popular belief holds that most students follow the same, straightforward path through college. Dubbed the "persistence track" by Carroll (1989), this path assumes entrance into a four-year institution the fall following high school graduation, enrolling full-time for four years, and then graduating with a four-year degree. Mounting research challenges this belief. Examining the college paths among members of the high school class of 1980, Carroll (1989) reported that one out of five students delayed entry into postsecondary education, entered less than four-year institutions, and enrolled part-time. Using the same cohort of students, Hearn (1992) identified thirteen college path patterns based on the combinations of three factors: delayed entrance, part-time versus full-time enrollment, and first type of institution attended. Furthermore, Hearn reported that the choice of one of these paths was highly conditioned by a student's socioeconomic background, degree aspirations, and academic preparation for college. In general, nontraditional college paths were chosen most by socioeconomically disadvantaged students with low degree aspirations who were poorly prepared for collegiate work.

Adelman's (1999) analysis of the college path patterns followed by the high school sophomore cohort of 1980 further demonstrates that students' trek through higher education is quite complex for a rather large number of students. Having examined college transcripts, Adelman found most college students do not graduate within four years. Moreover, a considerable proportion of high school students delay college entrance. Taking into account only those students who earned a minimum of ten college credits, Adelman reported that 19 percent of all high school graduates do not enroll in college immediately following high school graduation. Further examination by Adelman of the high school sophomore cohort of 1980 showed that only 53 percent initially enroll at a four-year institution, and only 46 percent remain solely within the four-year sector.

While a variety of college paths to degree completion exist (Adelman 1999; Carroll 1989; Hearn 1992), some paths are riskier than others. Challenging commonly held perceptions, Adelman (1999) did not find transfer per se to be a problematic college path behavior. He found many members of the high school sophomore cohort of 1980 transferred or alternated enrollment among institutions, yet still managed to secure a college degree within ten years of high school graduation. What matter, though, are part-time enrollment and the effort spent in earning college credits. Adelman demonstrated that failing to maintain continuous enrollment along with dropping, withdrawing from, and not completing college courses are the two riskiest college paths to a four-year degree.

Our examination of the college paths followed by members of the 1980 high school sophomore cohort shows lowest-SES students are, indeed, more prone to follow at-risk paths. Only 30 percent of lowest-SES students enter higher education at the four-year sector, a trend in sharp contrast to the 67 percent participation rate exhibited by highest-SES students (see Table 7.1). Slightly less than half of lowest-SES students enroll on a continuous basis, while 71 percent of highest-SES students do. Forty-one percent of lowest-SES students dropped, withdrew from, or left incomplete 10 percent or more of their college courses. This is in contrast to the 32 percent of highest-SES students who engaged in this at-risk behavior (see Table 7.8).

## Financial Aid

Some researchers have examined persistence in college as the by-product of economic decisions (e.g., Manski & Wise 1983; St. John 1990; St. John, Andrieu, Oescher, & Starkey 1994; Stampen & Cabrera 1986, 1988). Under this scenario, a student persists to the extent that social and economic benefits of attending college outweigh the costs and benefits associated with alternative activities (e.g., working full time). Higher costs of attendance relative to students' perceptions of their ability to pay could influence their decision to drop out, particularly if the costs of attending college far exceed future benefits (Becker 1964). Reduced tuition, direct grants, low-interest loans, and subsidized work-study programs all seek to equalize (if not increase) the benefits of attending

**Table 7.8**
**College Paths of the 1980 High School Sophomore Cohort across SES**

| Variable | Lowest | Medium low | Medium high | Highest | $X^2$ | $r$ |
|---|---|---|---|---|---|---|
| Continuous enroll-ment | 48.4% | 58.7% | 59.5% | 71.3% | 44,989.59** | 0.147 |
| Percentage of courses dropped, with-drawn from, or left incomplete | | | | | | |
| Less than 10% | 58.9% | 64.3% | 62.0% | 68.3% | | |
| 10%–20% | 14.7% | 15.8% | 14.8% | 15.0% | 17,288.64** | |
| More than 20% | 26.4% | 19.9% | 23.2% | 16.7% | | −0.066 |

college relative to its costs (H. Bowen 1977; Cabrera, Stampen, & Hansen 1990; St. John 1994).

Research into the effect financial aid plays on degree completion is contradictory. Nora (1990), Voorhees (1987), and St. John (1990) found all forms of federal support equally effective in preventing students from dropping out. However, Stampen and Cabrera (1986, 1988) found persistence rates were highest when student aid packages included work-study programs. More recently, Adelman (1999) reported grants-in-aid and loans had a small but positive contribution to the probability of securing a college degree. On the other hand, Astin (1975) found grants and work-study programs had positive effects on persistence, while loans had negative effects when directed to low-income students. St. John's (1991) comprehensive review of twenty-five years of research on the effect of financial aid led him to conclude reception of financial aid has a positive effect on persistence to graduation regardless of the type of financial aid. St. John also noted inconstancies could be attributed to methodological problems in terms of analytical models followed, the use of institutional databases versus national databases, and levels of controls.

We find SES differences in terms of financial aid received. Slightly more than half of lowest-SES students received grants-in-aid, whereas 36 percent of highest-SES students received this kind of aid (see Table 7.9). This finding is consistent with Stampen and Cabrera's (1988) study of the way in which student aid was targeted in the early 1980s. SES-based differences in the reception of loans are also noted ($r = 0.059$); however, these differences are rather small, and a clear trend is not seen. While

**Table 7.9**
**Financial Aid Factors for the 1980 High School Sophomore Cohort across SES**

| Variable | Lowest | Medium low | Medium high | Highest | $X^2$ | $r$ |
|---|---|---|---|---|---|---|
| Satisfied with cost of attending | 60.0% | 63.7% | 59.1% | 57.0% | 4,475.84** | 0.023 |
| Received grants between 1982 and 1986 | 53.5% | 44.6% | 41.3% | 36.2% | 34,095.21** | −0.118 |
| Received loans between 1982 and 1986 | 38.9% | 36.5% | 40.7% | 33.6% | 8,343.610** | 0.059 |

** $p < 0.001$.

lowest-SES students are as likely to rely on loans as are students from the middle two SES groups, highest-SES students receive loans to a lesser degree. Regarding satisfaction with cost of attending, the same mixed effect is seen: differences among SES groups are rather small, and no clear trend unfolds.

## Parental Responsibilities

Having children while attending college has been identified as another risk factor for persisting in college to degree completion. Nora, Cabrera, Hagedorn, and Pascarella (1996) reported family responsibilities had the effect of competing with the academic and social components of the institution, thereby lessening a student's engagement in the college experience, intellectual development, and subsequent persistence. Adelman (1999) adds that having children while attending college lessens one's chances of completing a college degree within ten years upon high school graduation.

For our student population, we find lowest-SES students are, indeed, more prone to having children prior to receiving a college degree. Twenty-four percent of lowest-SES students reported having at least one child by age 23 (see Figure 7.13). This number is 18 percent, 11 percent, and 5 percent greater than the ones reported by highest-SES, middle high–SES, and middle low–SES students, respectively.

**Figure 7.13**
**Percentage of 1980 High School Sophomore Cohort Enrolled in College
Who Had Parental Responsibilities by 1986 (by SES)**

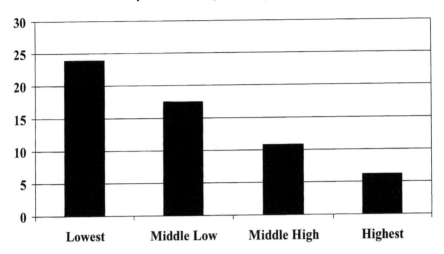

Note: Estimates are based on the High School and Beyond: 1980 (sophomore cohort).
Panel weight PSEWT1 ($r$ = 0.191).

## WHAT REALLY FACILITATES DEGREE COMPLETION?

### Socioeconomic Status

By 1993, 35 percent of the 1980 high school sophomore cohort earned a college degree. Among lowest-SES students, merely 13 percent managed to do so. In contrast, 57 percent of highest-SES students completed their college degree. Descriptive statistics underscore other significant differences between lowest-SES and highest-SES students in factors known or presumed to be critical in securing a four-year college degree. Once the effect of these degree-related factors is taken into account in a simultaneous manner, the 44 percent degree completion gap between highest- and lowest-SES students is reduced to 24 percent (see Table 7.10[10] and Figure 7.14).

### Encouragement

Encouragement matters in a student's chances of getting a college degree. Irrespective of SES, students who received encouragement from parents and friends to pursue a college degree while in high school were

**Table 7.10**
**Changes in the Probability of Degree Completion due to Background, Encouragement, Academic Resources, Performance in College, Remediation, Collegiate Experiences, Financial Aid, and Family Responsibilities**

| | | Socioeconomic status | | | |
|---|---|---|---|---|---|
| Factor | All | Lowest | Middle low | Middle high | Highest |
| SES | | | | | |
|   Middle low | 0.106* | | | | |
|   Middle high | 0.149* | | | | |
|   Highest | 0.235* | | | | |
| Female | −0.044* | −0.076** | −0.052** | −0.043** | −0.022* |
| Ethnicity | | | | | |
|   African American | — | — | −0.065* | −0.068* | 0.112** |
|   Hispanic | −0.038* | −0.055* | — | −0.088* | — |
|   Asian American | 0.192** | 0.369** | — | 0.105* | 0.209** |
| High school encouragement | | | | | |
|   From parents | 0.041* | — | — | 0.092* | — |
|   From high school professionals | — | — | — | — | 0.076* |
|   From friends | 0.052* | — | 0.140* | 0.152* | — |
| Academic resources | | | | | |
|   Moderately prepared | 0.044* | 0.191* | — | 0.081* | 0.075* |
|   Highly prepared | 0.120* | 0.319* | — | 0.274* | 0.087* |
| Collegiate aspirations | 0.229* | 0.223* | 0.425* | 0.155* | 0.255* |
| Type of first institution attended | | | | | |
|   2-year institution | 0.183* | 0.461* | 0.390* | — | 0.253* |
|   4-year institution | 0.459* | 0.686* | 0.496* | 0.311* | 0.391* |
| Continuous enrollment | 0.230* | 0.267* | 0.377* | 0.158* | 0.224* |
| DWI index | | | | | |
|   10–20% of courses | −0.132* | — | −0.086* | −0.172* | −0.208* |
|   At least 20% of courses | −0.267* | −0.124* | −0.156* | −0.270* | −0.364* |
| Number of math courses | | | | | |
|   One course | 0.274* | 0.031* | 0.422* | 0.339* | 0.193* |
|   Two courses | 0.292* | 0.340* | 0.296* | 0.221* | 0.296* |
|   Three or more courses | 0.419* | 0.567* | 0.622* | 0.497* | 0.268* |
| Number of science courses | | | | | |
|   One course | 0.206* | 0.245* | 0.219* | 0.196* | 0.085* |
|   Two courses | 0.208* | 0.262* | 0.249* | 0.192* | 0.151* |
|   Three or more courses | 0.287* | 0.420* | 0.355* | 0.355* | 0.148* |
| Collegiate experiences | | | | | |
|   Out-of-classroom | 0.083* | — | 0.157* | 0.114* | 0.037* |
|   Quality of instruction | 0.076* | 0.148* | — | 0.148* | 0.027* |
|   Counseling | 0.009* | 0.055* | — | 0.022* | 0.021* |
|   Campus facilities | — | — | 0.040* | — | — |
|   Institutional prestige | 0.012* | 0.057* | 0.023* | — | 0.018* |

**Table 7.10 (continued)**

| Factor | All | Lowest | Middle low | Middle high | Highest |
|---|---|---|---|---|---|
| | | | Socioeconomic status | | |
| Satisfaction with costs | — | 0.071* | — | — | — |
| Financial aid | | | | | |
| Loans | 0.104* | 0.112* | 0.296* | 0.036* | 0.051* |
| Grants/scholarships | 0.070* | 0.077* | 0.099* | 0.080* | 0.085* |
| *Worked on campus | 0.037* | 0.019* | 0.023* | 0.092* | 0.009* |
| College GPA | 0.320* | 0.279* | 0.493* | 0.190* | 0.328* |
| Having children | −0.221* | −0.126* | — | −0.229* | −0.458* |

Note: Only marginal probabilities associated with significant betas are reported.

**Figure 7.14**
**Adjusted Probabilities of Degree Completion by 1993 for the 1980 High School Sophomore Cohort (by SES)**

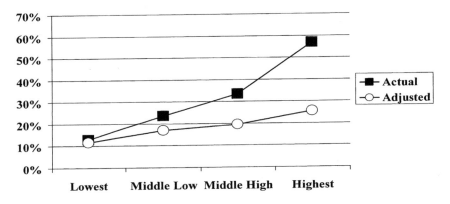

Note: Estimates are based on the High School and Beyond: 1980 (sophomore cohort). Panel weight PSEWT1 ($r$ = 0.335).

more likely to complete this goal. Compared with students whose parents did not encourage them to pursue a college degree, those who received parental encouragement increased their chance of degree completion by 4 percent. The impact of high school peer encouragement is similar, increasing degree completion chances by 5 percent (see Table 7.10).

## Academic Resources

Consistent with Adelman (1999), we find academic resources to have a substantial effect on degree completion across all SES groups. Compared to students poorly prepared academically, moderately and highly prepared students were 4 percent and 12 percent more likely to complete a college degree within ten years of graduating from high school, respectively (see Table 7.10). The effect of academic preparation among lowest-SES students is even more pronounced. Being moderately prepared or highly prepared for college increased their chances to secure a degree by 19 percent and 31 percent for this SES group, respectively (see Table 7.10).

## College Aspirations

Aspiring for a college degree is a good predictor of eventual college degree completion. Across all SES quartiles, students with college degree aspirations while still in high school were 23 percent more likely to do so, as compared with students without such aspirations. SES moderates the effect of collegiate aspirations. While all students benefit from this factor, middle low–SES students benefit the most. Lowest-SES students holding degree aspirations while in high school increase their chances of completing a degree by 22 percent. Middle low–SES, middle high–SES, and highest-SES students increase their degree completion chances by 43 percent, 16 percent, and 26 percent, respectively (see Table 7.10).

## Curricular Choice, Academic Success, and Collegiate Experiences

While most collegiate experiences increase the rate of degree completion across all students, academic performance in college (GPA) is the most significant factor. Across all students, every increasing grade change in GPA improves the chances to complete a college degree by 32 percent. SES also moderates the effect of GPA. For example, among lowest-SES students, changes in GPA increase degree completion rates by 28 percent, while among middle low–SES students the size of the effect is 49 percent (see Table 7.10).

Curricular choices are crucial too. Students who take only one college math course increase their degree completion chances by 27 percent. Those who take only one college science course increase their degree completion chances by 21 percent. Students who take three college math courses increase degree completion rates by 42 percent. Additionally, the impact of taking college math and science courses among lowest-SES students is striking. For this group, taking one, two, or three or more college science courses increases their chances of degree completion by 25 percent, 26 percent, and 42 percent, respectively. Lowest-SES students taking one, two, or three or more college math courses increase their chances of degree completion by 3 percent, 34 percent, and 57 percent, respectively (see Table 7.10).

Out-of-classroom experiences, quality of instruction, counseling, institutional prestige, and working on campus have small but significant effects on degree completion. For all students, positive out-of-classroom activities increase degree completion chances by 8 percent, while exposure to good classroom instruction does so by 8 percent. The quality of instruction is particularly relevant for lowest-SES students, whose probability to persist to graduation increases by 15 percent when taught effectively. Working on campus also helps. Every additional year of on-campus work increases a student's chances of completing a degree by 2 percent (see Table 7.10).

## College Path

The first type of postsecondary institution attended, continuous enrollment in college, and maintaining enrollment in college courses are also important factors in degree completion. For all students, those who first enroll in a two-year institution are 18 percent more likely to earn a college degree than those who enroll at a proprietary school. Those who enroll in a four-year institution are 46 percent more likely to earn a college degree. The effect of the first type of institution attended is particularly strong for lowest-SES students. For this group, enrollment at a two-year institution helps, but starting at a four-year institution helps even more. Lowest-SES students who started in a 2-year institution increase their chances by 46 percent. Lowest-SES students who first enroll in a four-year institution saw their chances to complete their four-year degree increase by 69 percent. Students who do not maintain continuous college enrollment are 23 percent less likely to earn a bachelor's degree. Those who drop, withdraw from, or fail to complete between 10 percent and 20 percent of their coursework are 13 percent less likely to secure a baccalaureate degree. Dropping, withdrawing from, or failing to complete more than 20 percent of the course work reduces a student's chances to complete a degree by 27 percent (see Table 7.10).

## Financial Aid

For all students, receiving grants-in-aid and loans increases chances of completing a four-year degree. Recipients of grants-in-aid are 7 percent more likely to earn a degree, while loan recipients are 10 percent more likely. SES also moderates the impact of financial aid, particularly for loan recipients. Lowest-SES and middle low–SES students receiving loans increase their degree completion chances by 11 percent and 30 percent, respectively (see Table 7.10).

## Parental Responsibilities

Incurring parental responsibilities while pursuing a college degree hampers one's chances of degree completion by 22 percent. This negative effect is felt most by highest-SES students for whom having children by age 23 decreases their degree completion chances by 46 percent (see Table 7.10).

## DiSCUSSION

## Pathways to a Four-Year Degree

A high school graduate faces nine pathways to a college degree. These pathways result from several degrees of academic preparation for college and the type of postsecondary institution first attended. Not all these paths are equally effective in leading to a four-year degree. When students follow the pathway of having high academic resources and choosing a four-year institution as their port of entry, their chances of eventually securing a four-year degree within a decade are considerable (78 percent). No other pathway is nearly as effective. When a student enters postsecondary education at the four-year sector and is only moderately academically prepared, his or her chances of earning a four-year degree are only 35 percent. Even more difficult is the pathway for those students with poor academic preparation who enter at a two-year institution. Their chance of earning a degree is only 10 percent.

Not all pathways are equally accessible to all students. Those traveling on the most successful pathways are most often highest-SES students. Almost 60 percent of all highest-SES sophomores have secured the highest level of academic resources before college enrollment. Of those, 76 percent enroll in a four-year institution. Overall, 45 percent of highest-SES 1980 high school sophomores followed the pathway defined by having high academic resources and enrolling at a four-year institution. For them, the chances of degree completion are almost certain (81 percent). Lowest-SES sophomores follow pathways opposite to those traveled by Highest-SES sophomores. They are 35 percent less likely to be highly academically prepared for college. Of those with high academic resources, less than half enter a four-year institution, and only 59 percent of these students earn a four-year degree. In other words, compared to equally prepared highest-SES students who followed the same path, the chances of lowest-SES sophomores to complete a degree are 22 percent less. However, lowest-SES high school sophomores are most likely to follow the pathway defined by medium academic resources and entrance at a two-year institution, a pathway where the chance of securing a four-year degree is only 3 percent.

## Determinants of Transfer

In following members of the high school sophomore cohort of 1980, we found that two out of five seniors selected a community college as their port of entry into higher education, regardless of SES. However, almost 50 percent of the lowest-SES students from this group attended a community college first, and only 17 percent of these students transferred to a four-year institution. The 20 percent transfer rate difference between lowest-SES and highest-SES students is reduced to just 7 percent once factors other than SES are considered simultaneously. What closes this SES-transfer gap is adequate preparation for college; degree aspirations; taking college math, science, and remedial reading courses; collegiate experiences; encouragement from peers; financial aid; and avoiding having children prior to transfer.

It has been argued the community college can be an obstacle in eventually securing a four-year degree because few community college students transfer (Karabel 1972, 1986). Underlying this argument is the assumption that community college students enroll while aspiring to a four-year degree. Our findings suggest enrollment at a community college per se plays little role in determining whether the student would eventually secure a four-year degree. First, only 42 percent of all community college students actually enter aspiring to a four-year degree. Second, net of other factors, community college students are 18 percent more likely to secure a four-year degree than are proprietary students (see Table 7.10).

Pre-college factors and collegiate experiences define a student's chances to transfer. Regardless of a student's socioeconomic background, securing appropriate academic resources in high school, coupled with degree aspirations, provides a foundation upon which transfer is facilitated.

The adjusted probability of transferring among highly prepared college degree seekers is 40 percent. What is striking is comparing this group of students to their exact opposites: those who are not academically prepared to perform college-level work and do not desire a bachelor's degree. Transfer rates for this group are only twelve percent. In short, for those individuals who planned and readied themselves for collegiate work as early as middle school, the community college can play a positive role in facilitating transfer.

Curricular choices at the community college are the second factor facilitating transfer. Students who take only one college-level math course increase their chances of transferring by 23 percent. Taking only one college-level science course increases transfer chances by 13 percent. When the pre-college factors of degree aspirations and high academic preparation are combined with taking one math and one science course in the community college, the adjusted probability of transferring is 60 percent. Thus, a college curriculum that includes math and science, combined with adequate academic preparation and a desire to attain a four-year degree, plays a pivotal role in facilitating transfer.

Merisotis and Phipps (2000) and Adelman (1999) have differing views of the role of remediation as a facilitator of transfer. Our findings support Adelman's contention when all students are considered in regard to remediation in reading. While remedial reading education was found not to play a significant role in facilitating transfer among all students, remediation in math is somewhat helpful for all students, increasing chances to transfer by four percent for each math remediation course completed. Our findings also support Merisotis and Phipps' contention as far as lowest-SES students are concerned. Indeed, lowest-SES students who take remedial reading see their chances to transfer increase by 24 percent.

Financial aid policies aimed at facilitating access to higher education seem to play a small but significant role in transferring. In this respect, our results are consistent with Adelman's (1999). Of all types of financial aid, loans are most beneficial. All students who received educational loans while enrolled at the community college were 11 percent more likely to transfer. The effect of this type of financial aid on lowest-SES students is even greater: receiving aid in the form of loans increases their chances to transfer by 22 percent.

## Determinants of Degree Completion

By 1993, three out of ten members of the 1980 high school sophomore cohort graduated from college with a baccalaureate degree. Out of 100 lowest-SES students, merely thirteen graduated with a four-year degree by 1993. In the same period of time, fifty-seven out of 100 highest-SES students graduated. The 44 percent SES-based gap between lowest- and highest-SES students decreased to 24 percent once demographics, collegiate aspirations, academic resources, collegiate experiences, college path, college curriculum, and financial aid factors are taken into account along with SES. However, factors other than SES help equalize chances to earn a bachelor's degree between lowest-SES students and their better-off counterparts. As in transfer, these mitigating factors produce significant effects for degree completion, regardless of SES.

Pre-college factors, college path factors, and collegiate-related factors play significant roles in facilitating degree completion. Of pre-college factors, high school–based academic resources and degree aspirations are the defining ones. The net added probability of earning a college degree by securing high school–based academic resources and aspiring for at least a bachelor's degree is 31 percent, irrespective of socioeconomic background.

Consistent with the literature (Adelman 1999; Carroll 1989; Hearn 1991, 1992), paths followed in postsecondary education greatly affect a 1980 high school sophomore's chances of getting a four-year degree. Opting for a four-year institution as the port of entry to postsecondary education yields a net benefit of 46 percent in one's chances of completing a degree, regardless of socioeconomic background. Among lowest-SES students, the effect of attending a four-year institution is more pronounced, yielding a 69 percent increase in the likelihood of graduating with a bachelor's degree within a decade (see Table 7.10).

Of the collegiate experience factors, continuous enrollment, academic performance, and a curricular emphasis on math and science are the most important determinants of degree completion. The effort a student spends in maintaining continuous enrollment in both postsecondary institutions and in his or her program courses enhances chances to graduate by 23 percent and 27 percent, respectively (see Table 7.10). For example, if a student maintains continuous enrollment and does not drop, withdraw from, or leave incomplete more than 10 percent of his or her courses, chances of degree completion increase 35 percent.

For every unit increase in GPA, a student's chances to secure a degree increase by 32 percent. Taking one, two, or three or more college math courses increases this probability by 27 percent, 29 percent, and 42 percent, respectively. For science courses, the corresponding effects are 21 percent, 21 percent, and 29 percent for one, two, or three or more courses, respectively (see Table 7.10). The joint effect of academic performance and curricular choices is particularly noteworthy. For example, a student who was academically prepared, aspired for college, maintained a C average, and took one math and science course has a net increase in the probability of degree completion of 36 percent. If that same student had maintained a B average, his or her chances of securing a degree increase to 68 percent. This is in stark contrast to a student who did not take any math or science courses while still maintaining a B average. His or her degree completion chances drop to only 23 percent. C average students with no math or science courses have only a 7 percent chance of graduating with a degree.

We also find financial aid policies enhanced 1980 high school sophomores' chances of securing a bachelor's degree by 1993. Net of SES, receiving loans increases the chances to complete a bachelor's degree by 10 percent, while grants had a net added benefit of 7 percent. Interestingly, the effect of loans is particularly strong among middle low–SES sophomores. For this group, receiving loans increased the probability of completing a degree by 30 percent (see Table 7.10).

Positive experiences with the academic and social domains of the postsecondary institutions contributed to the students' chances of earning a four-year degree. Students satisfied with their out-of-classroom experiences are 8 percent more likely to persist to graduation. Students satisfied with the quality of instruction feel the same level of benefit. Every year of working on campus yields a net benefit on this probability by 4 percent (see Table 7.10).

## Limitations

Readers should bear in mind the following when forming their own conclusions about the validity and usefulness of our findings.

Our conclusions are based on just one generation of students, those who were high school sophomores in 1980. During the last twenty years, school reform initiatives, changes in the composition of financial aid, and substantial technological and economic transformations have produced new generations for which the determinants of transfer and degree completion may be qualitatively different. We can tell the story of one single cohort; we cannot presume that all their experiences are applicable to subsequent cohorts.

Our study does not take into account some factors that affect the adjustment of the student with the institution, including the frequency and quality of the interactions with faculty and peers, exposure to different teaching practices, out-of-classroom experiences, and the nature of the curriculum (Astin 1993; Chickering & Reisser 1993; Hurtado, Milem, Clayton-Pedersen, & Allen 1999; Kuh, Douglas, Lund, & Ramin-Gyurnek 1994; Pascarella & Terenzini 1991; Tinto 1993, 1997). The lack of measures on these factors may lead to an underestimation of the effect of collegiate experiences on transfer and degree completion.

During the last twenty years, a number of valid measures of collegiate experiences have emerged. These measures capture academic and intellectual development, commitments to the institution, engagement with different elements of the campus life, student effort, campus and classroom climates, and classroom experiences (Pace 1980; Kuh 2000; Pascarella & Terenzini 1980; Cabrera & Nora 1994; Nora & Cabrera 1993; Kuh, Pace, & Vesper 1997; Cabrera, Colbeck, & Terenzini 2001). Though most of those measures were not available at the time the database was designed, future designers of national databases may want to consider their incorporation.

## Strengths

The strengths of this study derive primarily from its theoretical framework and research design.

All factors included in examining determinants of transfer from the two-year sector to the four-year sector were selected after a careful review of the literature (see references). This literature review led us to conclude that studies seeking to bring a comprehensive perspective in examining decisions to transfer ought to consider the following factors: (a) demographic characteristics of the high school student, (b) encouragement and support provided in high school, (c) a high school student's early degree aspirations, (d) acquisition of high school–based academic resources, (e) performance in college, (f) collegiate experiences, (g) remediation courses taken, (h) satisfaction with cost of attendance and type of financial aid received, and (i) acquiring family responsibilities before completing a college degree.

Our study uses degree completion as the measure of collegiate success. As shown by Adelman (1999), persistence to degree completion is a more valid and reliable measure of a student's success in college than are year-to-year persistence rates. The economic benefit a student receives due to his or her collegiate experience is predicated on his or her completing a degree, not on persisting from the first to second year of college.

Our use of a national database allowed us to track students from their sophomore year in high school to ten years post–high school graduation.

The HS&B/So database contains a sufficiently large number of student cases allowing for generalization of results on a national level.

Our measures of academic resources, enrollment patterns, curricular choices, financial aid, and academic performance are based on verifiable student records, such as high school and college transcripts and financial aid records (Adelman 1999). This feature increases the internal validity of our study while also ensuring the reliability of the relationships observed between these performance measures and transfer and degree completion.

Our conclusions regarding the nexus between SES and transfer and degree completion rest on sophisticated statistical analyses, rather than on simple descriptive statistics. Descriptive statistics tend to overestimate the connection between variables and fail to take into account the simultaneous effects of those factors also known to affect transfer and degree completion.

Data regarding satisfaction and student engagement with postsecondary education institutions were secured while the student was enrolled. We included statistical controls to make certain this was the case.

## Conclusions and Implications

This chapter underscores the importance of understanding the complex interaction of those factors shaping transfer and degree completion decisions as a precondition to developing intervention strategies. It also draws attention to the value of advanced statistical methods that single out the net effects of each of these factors. Though commonly used to inform policymaking, descriptive statistics may blind policymakers as to the importance of socioeconomic status as the sole determinant of transfer and degree completion. The real danger of using descriptive statistics as the basis of policy analysis is that the choice of variables automatically defines the problem and the solution.

Our study suggests that factors other than socioeconomic status play a larger role in successfully navigating the pathway to a college degree. As with countless generations, the path to a four-year degree for members of the 1980 high school sophomore cohort began as early as the eighth grade (Cabrera & La Nasa 2001; Wallace, Abel, & Ropers-Huilman 2000). At this time, aspirations for college triggered the need to secure the academic preparation necessary to succeed in college. Those who met this task had ample choices in their quest for a college degree, regardless of their socioeconomic status. In view of the fact that preparation for college and degree aspirations are so intertwined (Cabrera & La Nasa 2001), it stands to reason that strategies addressing these two critical factors simultaneously are more likely to enable students and their families to navigate the right path to a college degree. Programs such as TRIO and GEAR UP, which recognize that academic readiness and degree aspirations are the by-product of the connections between a student's family with peers, the K–16 school system, and the larger community, seem most appropriate (Cabrera & La Nasa 2001; Gladieux & Swail 2000).

Curriculum is at the heart of academic preparation for college (Adelman 1999). Academic preparation for college should begin as early as the eighth grade. Our results suggest curriculum should be articulated to foster the development of critical competencies, values, and skills known to prepare the student to successfully undertake collegiate work. The competencies acquired through math and science courses made a difference for members of the 1980 high school sophomore cohort by fostering their chances to transfer and earn a college degree. Current emphasis on the use of testing to hold elementary and secondary institutions accountable will be successful only if the tests themselves are valid measures of collegiate academic resources (National Research Council 1999). Without this orientation, the testing regime will produce countless children able to answer test questions, but unable to perform successfully in college. While the important nexus between high school and college is based on a single cohort who began their path to a four-year degree more than two decades ago, their story is remarkably similar to the one recently told by the most comprehensive study on the condition of K–12 across six states: socioeconomically disadvantaged middle and high school students aspire to college at rates similar to those exhibited by their better-off counterparts, but lacking adequate preparation for college denies them this dream (Venezia, Kirst, & Antonio 2003).

Accountability of public higher education, particularly for community colleges, needs revising on two fronts. First, policies aimed at holding community colleges accountable for low transfer rates need to be reconsidered. The community college as a potential funnel to a four-year degree is facilitated to the extent to which the student is academically prepared and aspires for at least a baccalaureate degree. Only 47 percent of the 1980 high school sophomore cohort who entered community college aspired to a college degree, and only 38 percent were highly academically prepared. It seems disingenuous to hold community colleges accountable for low transfer rates for those students who are not academically prepared for college-level coursework, do not want to transfer, and do not want a bachelor's degree. Second, holding community colleges responsible for creating academic resources, which evolve throughout middle and high school, is misplacing a responsibility that lies at the middle and high school levels.

Policies that stress year-to-year persistence within one institution should be revised to emphasize persistence to degree completion across the entire higher education system. We join Adelman (1999) in this recommendation. After all, the benefits of a college degree are universal, regardless of where the degree was ultimately obtained (Pascarella & Terenzini 1991). This change in policy would also recognize the increasingly transient nature of today's college student population. As Adelman (1999) noted, only 43 percent of all college students remained at the first institution attended; however, 63 percent of the same students persisted to degree completion in the entire higher education system.

The use of the year-to-year persistence rate as a criterion of success leads institutions to enact intervention strategies with short-term gains which miss the real causes of disengagement with the postsecondary system. Simply counting all students who failed to return to a specific institution for their second year as dropouts ignores the multidimensional nature of college withdrawal behavior (Tinto 1987, 1993). Mallette and Cabrera (1991) estimate that about two-thirds of all students counted as dropouts actually transferred to another institution. Counting nonreturnees as dropouts also ignores the fact that factors influencing withdrawal, transfer, and stopout decisions are different (Mallette & Cabrera 1991). Emphasis on first-year persistence has another drawback: it detracts attention from the realization that degree completion is the result of a longitudinal process. For many students, the roots of the first-year dropout rate go back as far as the eighth grade (Adelman 1999; Cabrera & La Nasa 2001).

Enrollment management should begin in grade school and be patterned after the complex process students undergo for readying themselves for college, a process whose main stages are college choice, collegiate experiences, and college outcomes (see Figure 7.15). In this longitudinal view to persistence, interventions can be designed with at least three groups in mind: students, their families, and K–12 school personnel. Community colleges and four-year institutions can help educate students and their parents about the benefits associated with college degree completion. They can advise students and parents about K–12 curricular choices that position a student to be academically prepared for

Figure 7.15
Degree Completion as a Longitudinal Process

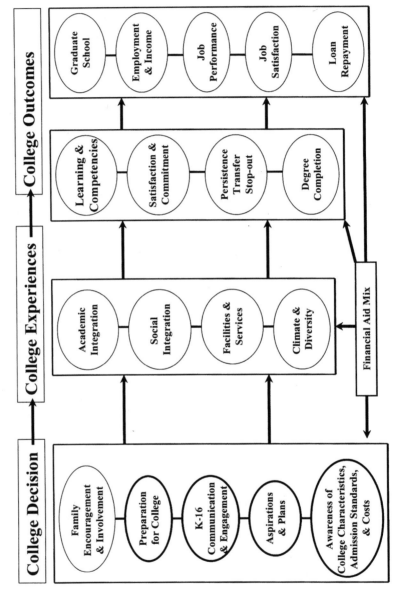

college. College personnel can best provide information about the college application process, including financial aid. Colleges and universities are also best equipped to tell parents and children what college is all about. Summer camps, summer bridge programs, and targeted visits are some strategies already in place for eleventh and twelfth graders. Making these opportunities available as early as the eighth grade is one mechanism to bring early awareness for college, particularly among lowest-SES students and their families.

Intervention strategies aimed at K–12 can touch several key domains. To begin, colleges and universities can work with elementary and secondary schools in aligning curriculum with competencies, experiences, values, and skills deemed essential for future collegial work. Universities can also assist impoverished school districts with faculty and resources to teach higher level math as well as foundations in sciences (Adelman 1999). K–12 personnel can also profit from the research and technical assistance colleges and universities can provide regarding effective instructional techniques and parental support mechanisms. These and other collaborative efforts are currently facilitated by initiatives such as GEAR UP, a federal program that supports multiple partnership initiatives targeted to low-income seventh graders.

Learning and academic performance in college leads to degree completion. These outcomes are best fostered when university personnel create contexts and environments that enhance student engagement with the academic and social components of the institution (Astin 1993: Kuh, Douglas, Lund, & Ramin-Gyurnek 1994; Tinto 1987, 1993). Learning communities are one of the promising intervention strategies. They seek to maximize student engagement in academically purposeful ways by increasing academic and social involvement through collaborative learning (Gablenick, MacGregor, Matthews, & Smith 1990; Lenning & Ebbers 1999; Tinto 1987, 1993; Zhao & Kuh 2004). Our study shows that taking college-level math and science courses significantly influences degree completion. What better way to foster a student's involvement with math and science than incorporating these two disciplines as part of the block scheduling underlying the use of learning communities?

Providing grants and loans on a need basis eases the pursuit of a four-year degree. Because involvement in academic and social areas matters, institutions should develop finance mechanisms to help pay for college which also increase opportunities for student involvement (St. John, Cabrera, Nora, & Asker 2000). Our results indicate that well-crafted forms of working on campus can be a viable way for students to pay for college while simultaneously being involved in academically purposeful activities.

## NOTES

1. Socioeconomic status, as defined by the National Center for Educational Statistics' data sets, includes the following measures: parental education, parental occupation, items in the home (i.e., dishwasher, books, etc.), and family income. This variable was built upon the respondent's socioeconomic status at the time he or she was a tenth grader in 1980, ranging from 1 (lowest SES) to 4 (highest SES).

2. General methods guiding the results reported in this chapter are included in footnotes. Contact the chapter authors for a full accounting of the research methods used.

3. Adelman (1999) created a composite measure of academic resources, dubbed ACRES, capturing students' abilities, high school graduation rank, and quality and intensity of high school curriculum. Adelman reported ACRES to be one of the best predictors of degree completion for members of the 1982 high school class. To facilitate comparisons, ACRES quintiles were transformed into thirds (low, medium, and high) by collapsing the two quintiles at both ends of the scale.

4. This study is based on the expanded college-choice persistence model (Blecher, Michael, & Hagedorn 2002; St. John, Cabrera, Nora, & Asker 2000; St. John, Paulsen, & Starkey 1996). The nexus model posits that college persistence is the by-product of a longitudinal process linking factors that predispose a high school student to select a college with his or her collegiate experiences and ability to pay for college. Our data analysis strategy was twofold. First, we examined the path to a four-year degree followed by members of the 1980 high school sophomore cohort. Second, we examined determinants of degree completion among four distinct SES groups.

5. The sample for this study was drawn from the National Longitudinal High School and Beyond 1980 Sophomore Cohort (HS&B/So), which tracks almost 15,000 high school sophomores over an eleven-year span (Zahs, Pedlow, Morrissey, Marnell, & Nichols 1995). The database also contains extensive college transcripts, financial aid records, and other verifiable information regarding college destinations (see Adelman 1999). The Postsecondary Education Participation Panel Weight (PSEWT1) was used to approximate the sample to the population of 1980 high school sophomores who enrolled in postsecondary education ($n = 2,155,164$).

6. The five indicators of collegiate experiences chosen were found by Cabrera (1987) to have moderate correlations with Pascarella and Terenzini's (1980) scales of academic and social integration.

7. Two logistic regression models were used to assess the effect of demographic, school-based, degree aspirations, collegiate experiences, college paths,

and family responsibilities on the probability of transferring and securing a four-year degree. Since a panel weight was employed to approximate the sample to the population of 1980 high school seniors who participated in Postsecondary Education (PSE), the average design effect of 1.5 was used for adjusting the standard deviations of the parameters in the regression models.

8. Adjusted probabilities were estimated using a logistic regression model controlling for background, high school academic resources, degree aspirations, collegiate experiences and financial aid. All independent variables were held constant at their mean value.

9. Using the formula developed by Petersen (1985), Table 7.5 reports incremental changes in the probability of transferring due to a unit change in the independent variable. Interpretation of marginal probabilities varies as a function of the metric of the independent variable under examination. In the case of GPA, a continuous variable, the marginal probability of 0.085 signifies that the probability of transferring increases by nine percentage points for every unit increase in GPA. The probability of 0.073 associated to the highest-SES group indicates that this group is seven percentage points more likely to transfer in relation to the lowest-SES group holding other factors constant.

10. Table 7.10 reports incremental changes in the probability of degree completion.

# REFERENCES

Adelman, C. (1998). The kiss of death? An alternative view of college remediation. *National Crosstalk* 6(3): 11. San Jose, CA: National Center for Public Policy and Higher Education.

―――. (1999). *Answers in the tool box: Academic intensity, attendance patterns, and bachelor's degree attainment.* Document No. PLLI 1999-8021. Washington, DC: U.S. Department of Education, Office of Educational Research and Improvement.

―――. (2000). More than 13 ways of looking at degree attainment. New Jersey State Department of Higher Education, Trenton. Office of Community Colleges. Programs. Trenton, NJ.

Aldrich, J. H., & Nelson, F. D. (1986). *Linear probability, logit, and probit models,* 3rd Ed. Beverly Hills, CA: Sage Publications.

Alexander, K. L., & Eckland, B. K. (1975). Basic attainment processes: A replication and extension. *Sociology of Education* 48: 457–495.

Alexander, K. L., Riordan, C., Fennessey, J., & Pallas, A. M. (1982). Social background, academic resources, and college graduation: Recent evidence from the national longitudinal survey. *American Journal of Education* 90(4): 315–333.

Armistead, L. P., Moore, D. M., & Vogler, D. E. (1987). Selected general education influences affecting degree completion for community college occupational students. *Community College Review* 15(3): 55–59.

Astin, A. W. (1975). *Preventing students from dropping out.* San Francisco: Jossey-Bass.

———. (1993). *What matters in college.* San Francisco: Jossey-Bass.

Attinasi, L. C. (1989). Getting in: Mexican Americans' perceptions of university attendance and the implications for the freshman year persistence. *Journal of Higher Education* 60(3): 247–277.

Baldwin, A. (1994). Indicators of the university success of associate degree recipients in the fields of business, computer science, and engineering. *Journal of Applied Research in the Community College* 1(2): 113–128.

Becker, G. S. (1964). *Human capital.* New York: National Bureau of Economic Research.

Berkner, L. K., & Chavez, L. (1997, October). *Access to postsecondary education for the 1992 high school graduates.* Statistical Analysis Report, NCES 98–105. Washington, DC: U.S. Department of Education, Office of Educational Research and Improvement, National Center for Education Statistics.

Bernal, E. M., Cabrera, A. F., & Terenzini, P. T. (1999). Class-based affirmative action admission policies: A viable alternative to race-based programs. Paper presented at the annual meeting of the Association for the Study of Higher Education, San Antonio, TX.

Bers, T., & Smith, K. (1991). Persistence of community college students: The influence of student intent on academic and social integration. *Research in Higher Education* 32(5): 539–556.

Birnbaum, R. (1970). Why community college transfer students succeed in 4-year colleges—the filter hypothesis. *Journal of Educational Research* 63(6): 247–249.

Blecher, L., Michael, W., & Hagedorn, L. (2002). Factors related to the "system" persistence of students seeking the bachelor's degree at four-year institutions. Paper presented at the annual meeting of the American Educational Research Association, New Orleans.

Bowen, H. R. (1977). *Investment in learning: The individual and social value of American higher education.* San Francisco: Jossey-Bass.

Bowen, W. G., & Bok, D. (1998). *The shape of the river: Long-term consequences of considering race in college and university admissions.* Princeton, NJ: Princeton University Press.

Boyer, E. (1987). *College: The undergraduate experience in America.* New York: Harper & Row Publishers.

Brauer, W. (2000). What happens to industrial technology alumni? A comparative look at two universities' graduates. *Journal of Technology Studies* 26(1): 44–48.

Braxton, J. M. (2000). *Reworking the student departure puzzle.* Nashville: Vanderbilt University Press.

Breneman, D. W., & Nelson, S. C. (1981). The future of community colleges. *Change* 13(5): 17–25.

Cabrera, A. F. (1987). Ability to pay and college persistence. Doctoral dissertation, University of Wisconsin–Madison.

———. (1994). Logistic regression analysis in higher education: An applied perspective. In *Higher education: Handbook for the study of higher education*, ed. John C. Smart, Vol. 10: 225–256. New York: Agathon Press.

Cabrera, A. F., Colbeck, C. L., & Terenzini, P. T. (2001). Developing performance indicators for assessing classroom teaching practices and student learning. *Research in Higher Education* 42(3): 327–352.

Cabrera, A. F., & La Nasa, S. M. (2000). Understanding the college choice of disadvantaged students. *New directions for institutional research*. San Francisco: Jossey-Bass.

———. (2001). On the path to college: Three critical tasks facing America's disadvantaged. *Research in Higher Education* 42(2): 119–150.

Cabrera, A. F., and Nora, A. (1994). College students' perceptions of prejudice and discrimination and their feelings of alienation: A construct validation approach. *Review of Education, Pedagogy, and Cultural Studies* 16(3–4): 387–409.

Cabrera, A. F., Nora, A., & Castañeda, M. B. (1992). The role of finances in the persistence process: A structural model. *Research in Higher Education* 33(5): 571–593.

Cabrera, A. F., Stampen, J. O., & Hansen, W. L. (1990). Exploring the effects of ability to pay on persistence in college. *Review of Higher Education* 13(3): 303–336.

Carroll, C. D. (1989). *College persistence and degree attainment for 1980 high school graduates: Hazards, for transfers, stopouts, and part-timers*. Survey Report #CS-89-302. Washington, DC: U.S. Department of Education, National Center for Education Statistics.

Cejda, B. (1999). The role of the community college in baccalaureate attainment at a private liberal arts college. *Community College Review* 27(1): 1–12.

Cejda, B., & Kaylor, A. (2001). Early transfer: A case study of traditional-aged community college students. *Community College Journal of Research and Practice* 25(8): 621–638.

Chen, X., & Kauffman, P. (1997). Risk and resilience: The effects of dropping out of school. Paper presented at the annual meeting of the American Association of Education Research, Chicago.

Chickering, A. W., & Reisser, L. (1993). *Education and identity*. 2nd Ed. The Jossey-Bass Higher and Adult Education Series. San Francisco: Jossey-Bass.

Choy, S. P. (2002). *Access & persistence: Findings from 10 years of longitudinal research on students*. Washington, DC: American Council on Education.

Choy, S. P., & Bobbitt, L. (2000). Low-income students: Who they are and how they pay. *Opportunity Outlook* 11: 9–11.

Choy, S. P., Horn, L., Nunez, A., & Chen, X. (2000). Transition to college: What helps at-risk students and students whose parents did not attend college. *New Directions for Institutional Research* 27(3): 45–63.

Choy, S. P., & Premo, M. D. (1996). *How low-income undergraduates financed post-secondary education: 1992–93.* Statistical Analysis Report #NCES 96–161. Washington, DC: U.S. Department of Education, National Center for Education Statistics.

Cohen, A. M. (2003). The community colleges and the path to the baccalaureate. Paper prepared for the Center for Studies in Higher Education Research Paper Series.

Colbeck, C. L., Cabrera, A. F., & Terenzini, P. T. (2001). Learning professional confidence: Linking teaching practices, students' self-perceptions, and gender. *Review of Higher Education* 24(2): 173–191.

College Board. (2003). *Trends in student aid.* Washington, DC: The College Board.

Conklin, M. E., & Dailey, A. R. (1981). Does consistency of parental educational encouragement matter for secondary students? *Sociology of Education* 54(4): 254–262.

Cross, K. P. (1998, July/August). Why learning communities, why now? *About Campus* 3(3): 4–11.

Cuccaro-Alamin, S., & Choy, S. P. (1998). *Postsecondary financing strategies: How undergraduates combine work, borrowing, and attendance.* Statistical Analysis Report, No. NCES 98-088. Washington, DC: U.S. Department of Education, National Center for Education Statistics.

Davies, T., Gray, C., & Karen, L. (1998). Student perceptions of the transfer process: Strengths, weaknesses, and recommendations for improvement. *Journal of Applied Research in the Community College* 5(2): 101–110.

DesJardins, S., McCall, B., Ahlburg, D., & Moye, M. (2002). Adding a timing light to the "tool box." *Research in Higher Education* 43(1): 83–114.

Dougherty, K. (1992). Community college and baccalaureate attainment. *Journal of Higher Education* 63(2): 188–214.

Dworkin, S. L. (1996). Persistence by 2-year college graduates to 4-year colleges and universities. *Community College Journal of Research and Practice* 20(5): 445–454.

Edstrom, R. B. (1991). *Undergraduate debt and participation in graduate education: The relationship between educational debt and graduate school aspirations, applications, and attendance among students with a pattern of full-time, continuous postsecondary education.* Princeton, NJ: Graduate Record Examinations Board.

Endo, J. J., & Harpel, R. L. (1982). The effect of student-faculty interaction on students' educational outcomes. *Research in Higher Education* 16(2): 115–138.

Farmer, E. I., & Fredrickson, J. C. (1999). Community college students transferring from technical and college transfer programs to four-year institutions. *Journal of Vocational Education Research* 24(2): 77–85.

Fleetwood, C., & Shelley, K. (2000). The outlook for college graduates, 1998–2008: A balancing act. *Occupational Outlook Quarterly* 44(3): 2–9.

Flint, T. A. (1992). Parental and planning influences on the formation of student college choice sets. *Research in Higher Education* 33(6): 689–708.

———. (1993). Early awareness of college financial aid: Does it expand choice? *Review of Higher Education* 16(3): 309–327.

Fredrickson, J. (1998). Today's transfer students: Who are they? *Community College Review* 26(1): 43–54.

Gablenick, F., MacGregor, J., Matthews, R., & Smith, B. L., Eds. (1990, Spring). *Learning communities: Creating connections among students, faculty, and disciplines; New directions for teaching and learning, 41.* San Francisco: Jossey-Bass.

Gladieux, L. E., & Swail, W. S. (2000). Beyond access: Improving the odds of college success. *Phi Delta Kappan* 82(9): 688–692.

Glass, J., Jr., Conrad, B., & Catherine, E. (1998). Length of time required to graduate for community college students transferring to senior institutions. *Community College Journal* 22(3): 239–261.

Hagedorn, L. S., Moon, S. H., Cypers, S., Maxwell, W. E., & Lester, J. (2003). Transfer between community colleges and four-year colleges: The all American game. Paper presented at the annual meeting of the Association for the Study of Higher Education, Portland, OR.

Hearn, J. C. (1988). Attendance at higher-cost colleges: Ascribed, socioeconomic, and academic influences on student enrollment patterns. *Economics of Education Review* 7(1): 65–76.

———. (1991). Academic and nonacademic influences on the college destinations of 1980 high school graduates. *Sociology of Education* 64(3): 158–171.

———. (1992). Emerging variations in postsecondary attendance patterns: An investigation of part-time, delayed, and nondegree enrollment. *Research in Higher Education* 33(6): 657–687.

Heller, D. E. (1997). Student price responses in higher education: An update to Leslie and Brinkman. *Journal of Higher Education* 68(6): 624–659.

Heubert, J. P., & Hauser, R. M., Eds. (1999). *High stakes: Testing for tracking, promotion, and graduation.* Washington, DC: National Academy Press.

Hilmer, M. J. (1997). Does community college attendance provide a strategic path to a higher quality education? *Economics of Education Review* 16(1): 59–68.

Horn, L., & Kojaku, L. (2001). High school academic curriculum and the persistence path through college: Persistence and transfer behavior of undergraduates three years after entering four-year institutions. *Education Statistics Quarterly* 3(3): 65–72.

Horn, L. J., & Chen, X. (1998). *Toward resiliency: At-risk students who make it to college.* Washington, DC: U.S. Department of Education.

Hossler, D. (1984). *Enrollment management: An integrated approach.* New York: The College Board.

Hossler, D., Braxton, J., & Coopersmith, G. (1989). Understanding student college choice. In *Higher education: Handbook of theory and research*, ed. J. Smart, Vol. 5: 231–288. New York: Agathon.

Hossler, D., Schmit, J., & Bouse, G. (1991). Family knowledge of postsecondary costs and financial aid. *Journal of Financial Aid* 21: 4–17.

Hossler, D., Schmit, J., & Vesper, N. (1999). *Going to college: How social, economic, and educational factors influence the decisions students make*. Baltimore: Johns Hopkins University Press.

Hossler, D., & Vesper, N. (1993). An exploratory study of the factors associated with parental saving for postsecondary education. *Journal of Higher Education* 64(2): 140–165.

House, J. D. (1999). The effects of entering characteristics and instructional experiences on student satisfaction and degree completion: An application of the input-environment-output assessment model. *International Journal of Instructional Media* 26(4): 423–434.

Hoyt, J. E. (1999). Promoting student transfer success: Curriculum evaluation and student academic preparation. *Journal of Applied Research in the Community College* 6(2): 73–79.

Hurtado, S., & Carter, D. F. (1996). Latino students' sense of belonging in the college community: Rethinking the concept of integration on campus. In *College students: The evolving nature of research*, ed. F. K. Stage, G. L. Anaya, J. P. Bean, D. Hossler, & G. Kuh, 123–136. Needham Heights, MA: Simon & Schuster Publishing.

Hurtado, S., Milem, J. F., Clayton-Pedersen, A., & Allen, W. R. (1998). Enhancing campus climates for racial/ethnic diversity: Educational policy and practice. *Review of Higher Education* 21(3): 279–302.

———. (1999). *Enacting diverse learning environments: Improving the climate for racial/ethnic diversity in higher education*. Washington, DC: George Washington University, Graduate School of Education and Human Development.

Jackson, G. (1978). Financial aid and student enrollment. *Journal of Higher Education* 49(6): 548–574.

Jacoby, B. (1996). *Service learning in higher education: Concepts and practices*. San Francisco: Jossey-Bass.

Jones, J. C., & Lee, B. (1992). Moving on: A cooperative study of student transfer. *Research in Higher Education* 33(1): 125–140.

Kahlenberg, R. D. (1996). *The remedy: Class, race, and affirmative action*. New York: Basic Books.

Karabel, J. (1972). Community college and social stratification. *Harvard Educational Review* 42: 521–562.

———. (1986). Community college and social stratification in the 1980's. In *The Community College and Its Critics. New Directions for Community Colleges*, ed. L. S. Zwerling, 54: 12–30. San Francisco: Jossey-Bass.

Keller, M., & Williams-Randall, M. (1999). The relationship between assessment of remedial need and student success in college. *MAHE Journal* 22: 48–55.

Kemp, A. D. (1990). From matriculation to graduation: Focusing beyond minority retention. *Journal of Multicultural Counseling and Development* 18(3): 144–149.

Kim, D. (2004). The effect of financial aid on student's college choice: Differences by racial groups. *Research in Higher Education* 45(1): 43–70.

King, J. E. (1996). *The decision to go to college: Attitudes and experiences associated with college attendance among low-income students.* Washington, DC: The College Board.

Kinnick, M., & Kempner, K. (1988). Beyond "front door" access: Attaining the bachelor's degree. *Research in Higher Education* 29(4): 299–318.

Koker, M., & Hendel, D. (2003). Predicting graduation rates for three groups of new advanced-standing cohorts. *Community College Journal of Research and Practice* 27(2): 131–146.

Kraemer, B. (1995). Factors affecting Hispanic student transfer behavior. *Research in Higher Education* 36(3): 303–322.

Kuh, G. (1995). The other curriculum: Out-of-class experiences associated with student learning and personal development. *Journal of Higher Education* 66: 123–155.

———. (2000). *The national survey of student engagement: The college student report.* Bloomington: Indiana University Center for Postsecondary Research and Planning.

Kuh, G., Douglas, K. B., Lund, J. P., & Ramin-Gyurnek, J. (1994). *Student learning outside the classroom: Transcending artificial boundaries.* ASHE-ERIC Higher Education Report 23(8). Washington, DC: The George Washington University, Graduate School of Education and Human Development.

Kuh, G., Pace, R. C., & Vesper, N. (1997). The development of process indicators to estimate student gains associated with good practices in undergraduate education. *Research in Higher Education* 38(4): 435–454.

Laanan, F. S., ed. (2001). *Transfer students: Trends and issues; New Directions for Community Colleges, No. 114.* San Francisco: Jossey-Bass.

Lee, V., & Frank, K. (1990). Students' characteristics that facilitate the transfer from two-year to four-year colleges. *Sociology of Education* 63(3): 178–193.

Leigh, D., & Gill, A. (2003). Do community colleges really divert students from earning bachelor's degrees? *Economics of Education Review* 22(1): 23–30.

Lenning, Q. T., & Ebbers, L. H. (1999). *The powerful potential of learning communities: Improving education for the future.* ASHE-ERIC Higher Education Report 26(6). Washington, DC: George Washington University, Graduate School of Education and Human Development.

Leslie, L. L., & Brinkman, P. T. (1986). Rates of return in higher education: An intensive examination. In *Higher Education: Handbook of Theory and Research*, ed. J. C. Smart, 207–234. New York: Agathon Press.

Leslie, L. L., Johnson, G. P., & Carlson, J. (1977). The impact of need-based student aid upon the college attendance decision. *Journal of Education Finance* 2: 269–285.

Lewis, G. L. (1989). Trends in student aid, 1963–64 to 1988–89. *Research in Higher Education* 30: 547–562.

Lin, Y., & Vogt, P. (1996). Occupational outcomes for students earning two-year college degrees: Income, status and equity. *Journal of Higher Education* 67(4): 446–475.

Litten, L. H. (1982). Different strokes in the applicant pool: Some refinements in a model of student college choice. *Journal of Higher Education* 53(4): 383–401.

Lowman, K. K. (1998). Comparison of time to B.A. degree attainment by transfer and nontransfer status. *Visions: The Journal of Applied Research for the Florida Association of Community Colleges* 2(1): 6–13.

Mallette, B. I., & Cabrera, A. F. (1991). Determinants of withdrawal behavior: An exploratory study. *Research in Higher Education* 32(2): 179–194.

Manski, C. F., & Wise, D. A. (1983). *College choice in America*. Cambridge, MA: Harvard University Press.

McDonough, P. (1997). *Choosing colleges: How social class and schools structure opportunity*. Albany: State University of New York Press.

McDonough, P. M., Antonio, A. L., Walpole, M., & Perez, L. X. (1998). College rankings: Democratized college knowledge for whom? *Research in Higher Education* 39(5): 513–538.

McPherson, M. S., & Schapiro, M. O. (1998). *The student aid game: Meeting need and rewarding talent in American higher education*. Princeton, NJ: Princeton University Press.

Menard, S. (1995). *Applied logistic regression analysis*. Sage University Paper series on Quantitative Applications in the Social Sciences, 07–106. Thousand Oaks, CA: Sage.

Merisotis, J., & Phipps, R. (2000). Remedial education in colleges and universities: What's really going on? *Review of Higher Education* 24(1): 67–86.

Miller, E. I. (1997). Parents' views on the value of a college education and how they will pay for it. *Journal of Student Financial Aid* 27(1): 20.

Montondon, L., & Eikner, A. E. (1997). Comparison of community college transfer students and native students in an upper level accounting course. *Community College Review* 25(3): 21–38.

Mortenson, T. (2000a, November). Private economic benefit/cost ratios of a college investment for men and women, 1967 to 1999. *Postsecondary Education Opportunity*, no. 101.

———. (2000b, December). Undergraduate degree completion by age 25 to 29 for those who start college, 1992 to 2000. *Postsecondary Education Opportunity*, no. 102.

Murguia, E., Padilla, R. V., & Pavel, M. (1991). Ethnicity and the concept of social integration in Tinto's model of institutional departure. *Journal of College Student Development* 32: 433–439.

National Center for Education Statistics (NCES). (1998). *High school and beyond sophomore cohort: 1980–92 postsecondary education transcripts; restricted file.* NCES 98-135. Washington, DC: U.S. Department of Education, Office of Educational Research and Improvement.

———. (2000). *High school and beyond sophomore cohort: 1980–92 postsecondary education transcripts and supplement; restricted file.* NCES 2000-194. Washington, DC: U.S. Department of Education, Office of Educational Research and Improvement.

National Center for Public Policy and Higher Education. (2000). *Measuring up: The state-by-state report card for higher education.* Washington, DC: National Center for Public Policy and Higher Education.

National Research Council. (1999). *Testing, teaching, and learning: A guide for states and school districts.* Committee on Title I Testing and Assessment, Richard F. Elmore and Robert Rothman, eds. Board on Testing and Assessment, Commission on Behavioral and Social Sciences and Education. Washington, DC: National Academy Press.

Nora, A. (1990). Campus-based aid programs as determinants of retention among Hispanic community college students. *Journal of Higher Education* 61(3): 312–331.

Nora, A., & Cabrera, A. F. (1992). Measuring program outcomes: What impacts are important to assess and what impacts are possible to measure? Paper prepared for the Design Conference for the Evaluation of Talent Search. Washington, DC: U.S. Department of Education, Office of Policy and Planning.

———. (1993). The construct validity of institutional commitment: A confirmatory factor analysis. *Research in Higher Education* 34(2): 243–262.

Nora, A., Cabrera, A. F., Hagedorn, L. S., & Pascarella, E. T. (1996). Differential impacts of academic and social experiences on college-related behavioral outcomes across different ethnic and gender groups at four-year institutions. *Research in Higher Education* 37(4): 427–752.

Nora, A., & Rendón, L. (1990). Determinants of predisposition to transfer among community college students: A structural model. *Research in Higher Education* 31(3): 235–256.

O'Brien, C., and Shedd, J. (2001). *Getting through college: Voices of low-income and minority students in New England; The New England student success study.* Washington, DC: Institute for Higher Education Policy.

Olivas, M. A. (1985). Financial aid packaging policies: Access and ideology. *Journal of Higher Education* 56(4): 462–475.

Olson, L., & Rosenfeld, R. A. (1984). Parents and the process of gaining access to student financial aid. *Journal of Higher Education* 55(4): 455–480.

Ose, K. (1997). Transfer student involvement: Differences between participators and nonparticipators in extracurricular activities. *College Student Affairs Journal* 16(2): 40–46.

Pace, R. C. (1980, April). Measuring the quality of undergraduate education. Paper presented at the annual meeting of the American Educational Research Association, Los Angeles.

Palmer, J. C. (2000). What do we know about transfer? An overview. *Peer Review* 2(2): 8–11.

Pascarella, E. T. (1985). Racial differences in factors associated with bachelor's degree completion: A nine-year follow-up. *Research in Higher Education* 23(4): 351–373.

Pascarella, E. T., & Terenzini, P. T. (1980). Predicting freshman persistence and voluntary dropout decisions from a theoretical model. *Journal of Higher Education* 51: 60–75.

———. (1991). *How college affects students.* San Francisco: Jossey-Bass.

Paulsen, M. B., & St. John, E. P. (2002). Social class and college costs: Examining the financial nexus between college choice and persistence. *Journal of Higher Education* 73(2): 189–236.

Perna, L. W. (2000). Differences in the decision to attend college among African Americans, Hispanics, and Whites. *Journal of Higher Education* 71(2): 117–141.

———. (2002). Precollege outreach programs: Characteristics of programs serving historically underrepresented groups of students. *Journal of College Student Development* 43(1): 64–83.

Petersen, T. (1985). A comment on presenting results from logit and probit models. *American Sociological Review* 50(1): 130–131.

Press, S. J., & Wilson, S. (1979). *Choosing between logistic regression and discriminant analysis.* Santa Monica, CA: Rand Corp.

Quanty, M. B., Dixon, R. W., & Ridley, D. R. (1999). The course-based model of transfer success: An action-oriented research paradigm. *Community College Journal of Research and Practice* 23(5): 457–466.

Rickinson, B. (1998). The relationship between undergraduate student counseling and successful degree completion. *Studies in Higher Education* 23(1): 95–102.

St. John, E. P. (1990). Price response in persistence decisions: An analysis of the high school and beyond senior cohort. *Research in Higher Education* 31(4): 387–403.

———. (1991). The impact of student financial aid: A review of recent research. *Journal of Student Financial Aid* 21(1): 18–32.

———. (1994). *Prices productivity, and investment: Assessing financial strategies in Higher Education.* ASHE-ERIC Higher Education Reports, No. 3. Washington, DC: George Washington University.

St. John, E. P., Andrieu, S., Oescher, J., & Starkey, J. B. (1994). The influence of student aid on within-in year persistence by traditional college-age students in four-year colleges. *Research in Higher Education* 35(4): 455–480.

St. John, E. P., Cabrera, A. F., Nora, A., & Asker, E. H. (2000). Economic influences on persistence reconsidered: How can finance research inform the reconceptualization of persistence models? In *Reworking the student departure puzzle*, ed. J. M. Braxton, 29–47. Nashville: Vanderbilt University Press.

St. John, E. P., Paulsen, M. B., & Starkey, J. B. (1996). The nexus between college choice and persistence. *Research in Higher Education* 37(2): 175–220.

Stage, F. K., & Hossler, D. (1989). Differences in family influences on college attendance plans for male and female ninth graders. *Research in Higher Education* 30(3): 301–315.

Stampen, J. O., & Cabrera, A. F. (1986). Exploring the effects of student aid on attrition. *Journal of Student Financial Aid* 16: 28–40.

———. (1988). The targeting and packaging of student aid and its effect on attrition. *Economics of Education Review* 7(1): 29–46.

Suarez, A. L. (2003). Forward transfer: Strengthening the educational pipeline for Latino community college students. *Community College Journal of Research and Practice* 27(2): 95–118.

Surette, B. (2001). Transfer from two-year to four-year college: An analysis of gender differences. *Economics of Education Review* 20(2): 151–163.

Swail, W. S. (1995). The development of a conceptual framework to increase student retention in science, engineering, and mathematics programs at minority institutions of higher education. Doctoral dissertation, George Washington University, Washington, DC.

Terenzini, P. T., Cabrera, A. F., & Bernal, E. M. (2001). *Swimming against the tide: The poor in American higher education.* College Board Research Report No. 2001-1. New York: The College Board.

Terenzini, P. T., & Pascarella, E. T. (1977). Voluntary freshman attrition and patterns of social and academic integration in a university: A test of a conceptual model. *Research in Higher Education* 6: 25–43.

Thayer, P. B. (May 2000). Retention of students from first generation and low income backgrounds. *Opportunity Outlook* 11: 2–8.

Thomas, G. E. (1992). Participation and degree attainment of African-American and Latino students in graduate education relative to other racial and ethnic groups: An update from Office of Civil Rights Data. *Harvard Educational Review* 62(1): 45–65.

Tierney, M. S. (1980). The impact of financial aid on student demand for public/private higher education. *Journal of Higher Education* 51(5): 527–545.

Tinto, V. (1987). *Leaving college: Rethinking the causes and cures of student attrition.* Chicago: University of Chicago Press.

———. (1993). *Leaving college: Rethinking the causes and cures of student attrition,* 2nd Ed. Chicago: University of Chicago Press.

———. (1997). Classrooms as communities: Exploring the educational character of student persistence. *Journal of Higher Education* 68: 599–623.

Townsend, B. (2001). Redefining the community college transfer mission. *Community College Review* 29(2): 29–42.

Veldman, C., et al. (1997). Baccalaureate and beyond longitudinal study: Second follow-up field test report, 1996. Technical Report: NCES-97-261.

Velez, W. (1985). Finishing college: The effects of college type. *Sociology of Education* 58: 191–200.

Velez, W., & Javalgi, R. G. (1987). Two-year college to four-year college: The likelihood of transfer. *American Journal of Education* 96(1): 81–94.

Venezia, A., Kirst, M. W., & Antonio, A. L. (2003). *Betraying the college dream: How disconnected K–12 postsecondary education systems undermine student aspirations.* Stanford University: Stanford Institute for Higher Education Research.

Volkwein, J., King, M., & Terenzini, P. T. (1986). Student-faculty relationships and intellectual growth among transfer students. *Journal of Higher Education* 57: 413–430.

Voorhees, R. (1987). Toward building models of community college persistence: A logit analysis. *Research in Higher Education* 26(2): 115–129.

Wallace, D., Abel, R., & Ropers-Huilman, B. (2000). Clearing a path for success: Deconstructing borders through undergraduate mentoring. *Review of Higher Education* 24(1): 87–102.

Walpole, M. (2003). Socioeconomic status and college: How SES affects college experiences and outcomes. *Review of Higher Education* 27(1): 45–73.

Windham, P., & Perkins, G. (2000). An investigation of the highest degree held by community college students. *Journal of Applied Research in the Community College* 7(2): 57–66.

Working, S. L. (1996). Persistence by two-year college graduates to four-year colleges and universities. *Community College Journal of Research and Practice* 20(5): 445–454.

Zahs, D., Pedlow, S., Morrissey, M., Marnell, P., & Nichols, B. (January 1995). *High school and beyond: Fourth follow-up; Methodology report.* Chicago: National Opinion Research Center.

Zhao, C. M., & Kuh, G. D. (2004). Adding value: Learning communities and student engagement. *Research in Higher Education* 45(2): 115–138.

# CHAPTER

# Nine Themes of College Student Retention

*John P. Bean*

## INTRODUCTION

Student retention can be studied from at least four perspectives. From the *theoretical* perspective, retention is something to be explained. Theoretical models contain factors linked by explanatory theories that lead to decisions to remain in college or leave. From the *policy* perspective, governments and others study policies related to access to college and how different types and amounts of funding affect retention. Institutional policies are made based on judgments about how academic and other programs or activities affect retention. From the *institutional research* perspective, retention research focuses on students attending single institutions. The research attempts to determine the effectiveness of retention programming or the reasons why students stay at or leave a particular institution. From an *individual* perspective, studies are conducted to identify how background characteristics, institutional experiences, student behavior, and attitudes interact to affect retention decisions. Of course, any given study can have more than one of these perspectives and can be used for more than one purpose.

The purpose of this chapter is to describe nine themes of college student retention. For each of these nine themes, the theme or factor is described, ways it is expected to affect retention are discussed, and programs related to this theme that might increase retention are identified. This approach emphasizes theoretical, institutional research, and individual perspectives. Governmental policymaking is largely ignored and institutional policies are reflected through the implementation of programs or activities. There are nine themes that affect retention: the student's background, money and finance, grades and academic performance, social factors, bureaucratic factors, the external environment, psychological and attitudinal factors, institutional fit and commitment, and intentions. In this chapter the terms *school, college, university,* and *institution* are used more or less interchangeably.

This chapter is based on empirical and theoretical studies of college student retention conducted between 1978 and the present. During that time I was engaged in a series of studies related to student retention or associated topics such as student satisfaction. These included eleven empirical studies published in research journals, four conceptual pieces in research journals, ten conceptual or applied works as book chapters, twelve empirical studies reported at conferences but not published, ten consulting reports based on empirical research, and seven dissertations which I directed on retention or other student outcomes from college. The publications and conference papers are included in the list of references at the end of this chapter.

I make few demographic distinctions in the themes. Being African American or Hispanic may be correlated with higher levels of student attrition at certain institutions, but it is not the cause for leaving. A chilly or hostile racist atmosphere on campus would result in a clear sense of minority students not fitting in or feeling alienated, and this lack of fit or alienation leads to leaving. If students in a racial minority at a university came from high schools that did not prepare them for college-level work, then academic ability, not race, is the factor at play. The factors and processes that influence leaving are assumed to be the same for all students: a student who does not fit in or who does not get passing grades will likely leave college regardless of his or her demographic status. The factors that have important effects on retention can be substantially different for different groups, but the overall set of relationships is assumed to be similar for all groups. For example, family approval is probably more important for a Chinese than a Caucasian student, but that factor could affect retention for either student.

Braxton, Hirschy, and McClendon (2004) have evaluated Tinto's (1993) retention model by enumerating studies that found a statistically significant relationship between constructs in Tinto's model. For example, they found a strong connection between social integration and retention. In statistics, the general does not apply to the specific. At a particular institution, or for the student in front of me in my office, social integration may have no relationship to leaving college. Social connections are not relevant in their personal retention equation. Knowing that most studies found a statistically significant relationship between two variables does not guarantee that improving the variable in question (e.g., increasing social integration) will increase retention at a given college. For students with a bookish orientation, increasing social interaction can be seen as diffusing academic quality, resulting in lower levels of retention. A statistically significant relationship suggests action an institution could undertake to help increase retention. It does not tell an institution what it must do, but suggests an area that might be beneficial.

This chapter provides a discussion of themes in the same spirit: acting on these themes is not a guarantee for success, but an institution might benefit from trying certain courses of action more than others. These themes also provide an understanding of why manipulating the variable in question might improve or fail to improve retention. In terms of utility, all research, regardless of being of a high or low quality, empirical or theoretical, or well or poorly presented, is valuable in its ability to provide new ways of thinking about and therefore acting to alleviate a problem—in this case, leaving college.

## THEORETICAL STRUCTURE OF THE RELATIONSHIPS

The themes are presented in the overall context of attitude-behavior theory (Fishbein & Ajzen 1975; Bentler & Speckart 1979). Bean and Eaton (2000) previously described the structure of this model:

> The model posits that behavior is the result of the intention to perform the behavior. Intention has two antecedents. First, intention is linked to an attitude toward the behavior, where attitude is based on beliefs about the consequences of the behavior. Second, intention is based on subjective norms which come from normative beliefs about the behavior. A feedback loop from the behavior to beliefs completes the model. Over time, beliefs lead to attitudes which lead to intentions which lead to behavior. Bentler and Speckart (1979) added the variable of past behavior to this process, showing that past behavior, attitudes, and norms all influence intention. All four of these variables then have direct effect on future behavior. (50)

This general model is adapted and adjusted for use in the context of student retention. The retention model posits that student departure is the result of the intention to leave. Intention is based on prematriculation attitudes and behaviors that affect the way a student interacts with the institution. On the basis of this interaction, the student develops attitudes toward their experiences and norms related to student behavior. The flow of the model over time is as follows: prematriculation behavior and attitudes→student interaction with the institution and external environment after enrollment→attitudes about school experiences→intention to leave→departure from college.

These themes are presented opposite the temporal flow and in a sequence consistent with the presumed importance of the effects of a factor on retention. Themes will be presented in the following order: intentions, institutional fit and commitment, psychological processes and key attitudes, academics, social factors, bureaucratic factors, the external environment, the student's background, and money and finance.

## INTENTIONS AND ATTITUDES

### Intentions

One element of the Fishbein and Ajzen (1975) model is that intentions to behave in a certain manner precede that behavior. In every study of residential students I have participated in, the intent to leave (or stay) variable was the best predictor of actual student departure from college. In empirical studies, after controlling statistically for intent, it was rare that other variables were significantly related to leaving. The variable is important as an indicator of who is going to leave and is useful in validating theory.

The effect of the variable decays over time; that is, the less time between ascertaining the student's intention and the behavior in question, the more accurate the prediction. Most students drop out between the end of the freshman year and the beginning of the sophomore year, and it is desirable to gather information about intent to return to school during the second half of the second semester. The variable is valuable for identifying who is going to leave and is thus helpful to an institution in better targeting retention efforts.

For older, commuter, and part-time students, the variable is less valuable. There are two probable reasons for this finding. First, students might *intend* to return to college but, for some other reason in the environment (lack of funding, shift in job responsibilities, moving to a new location, change in family responsibilities) are unable to do so. Second, the heterogeneity of the part-time nonresidential student makes any statistical relationship difficult to obtain. Statistically significant relationships are most likely in homogeneous populations, and these groups of students vary in age, educational experience, reasons for attending, obligations outside of school, and so on in a way very unlike 18-to-24-year-old full-time residential students. While the intentions of these students might be important, this importance is difficult to demonstrate.

By itself, intention is of little value in understanding the retention process. It is an *empty* variable because it does not help explain why students leave. It only predicts who will leave. Intentions are the by-product of the interaction of the student and the institution, especially the faculty, other students, administrators, and staff members. Researchers are left with finding out what factors affect intentions, and, according to theory, they need to look no further than attitudes.

## Institutional Fit and Institutional Commitment (Loyalty)

Two sets of attitudes are important for retention: attitudes about attachment to the institution, and attitudes about being a student. Institutional fit is a sense of fitting in with others at a college, and institutional commitment is a commitment to a specific institution as opposed to higher education in general. These attitudes are closely associated with intent to stay or leave. A second set of attitudes is related to satisfaction with being a student, feeling a sense of self-efficacy as a student, knowing the value of one's education for getting a job, and feeling stress as a student. These four variables can influence intent to leave directly or indirectly by affecting institutional fit and commitment.

The notion of "fitting in" with a group is not based on analytical jargon but with the common sense notions of being similar to other members of a group and having a sense of belonging to that group. Institutional fit extends that common sense notion to fitting in with others who share the role of being a student in a particular institution at a particular moment in time. It has a clearly social component—that is, fitting in with *others*—and can also have a value component related to Durkheim's (1951) shared values that formed the core of the Spady (1970) and subsequently the Tinto (1993) models of retention. A student is likely to fit in if that student shares values with other students. The values in question could be social (we're here to party), academic (we're here to study), or of any other area of interest (we're here to become lawyers or actors) or activity (we're here to play basketball). The important thing is that the student *feels* that he or she belongs at the college or university.

Many institutions have made it a priority to increase the demographic diversity of their student bodies. When students from varied racial, ethnic, and economic backgrounds enter college, their heritage may or may not represent a difficulty fitting in. If a group of students believe that they are being discriminated against for any reason, including race, ethnicity, sexual preference, or gender, they are not likely to feel that they fit in at the institution. Economically disadvantaged students may feel similar kinds of discrimination.

The second central attitude influencing intent to leave is institutional commitment. Institutional commitment indicates the extent to which a student is attached to the college or university. It parallels the common sense notion of loyalty or, as the Beach Boys would say, "Be true to your school." Similar to satisfaction or motivation, loyalty can be judged only by inquiring about a student's attitudes, not by observing their behavior (Price and Mueller 1986).

A major difference between institutional fit and institutional commitment is that fit has a primarily social component and is affected by social integration variables, while loyalty seems to be more of a psychological component and is affected by other psychological dispositions. Because both are attitudes, they are the result of other attitudes and experiences at school. While not subject to direct intervention, *those interested in affecting retention rates need to be profoundly aware that they are not just in the business of delivering services, but in delivering services in such a way that students develop a positive attitude toward school and toward their continued enrollment in school.* This condition pertains to the secondary set of attitudes as well.

## Psychological Processes and Key Attitudes

In the overall context of the Fishbein and Ajzen attitude-behavior theory, Bean and Eaton (2000) describe the way in which three psychological processes affect social and academic factors that influence retention decisions. These are the theory of self-efficacy, approach/avoidance behavioral theory as part of coping theory, and locus of control as a part of attribution theory. To briefly summarize, students who are self-efficacious believe in their ability to survive and adapt in an academic environment. They believe that they can perform in a way to achieve goals they set for themselves, and as a result they increase their self-confidence as students and their aspirations for academic success and finishing college. Personal accomplishments and feedback about these successes increase a student's self-efficacy, and in a cyclical fashion, an increase in self-efficacy raises educational goals and the likelihood of persistence.

The central task of an educational institution is academic achievement, and it is in that realm that a student's achieving self-efficacy is desired. Self-efficacy is task-specific (Mone, Baker, & Jeffries 1995), and achievement in one area, such as academic work, is not necessarily related to self-efficacy in another area, such as social interaction. Those working to improve student performance need to recognize the compartmentalized aspect of self-efficacy. Any interaction between students and an institution's faculty and other employees that increases the students' sense of self-efficacy is likely to improve their attitudes toward school and increase their likelihood of remaining enrolled.

Approach and avoidance are ways of coping with an environment to reduce the stress that the environment creates. Positive adaptations are likely to lead to behaviors that increase the likelihood of a student staying enrolled. Approach and avoidance in and of themselves do not assure increased retention. It is what is approached that is important. As Marsilio Ficino, a fifteenth-century Florentine doctor of philosophy, wrote in his *Book of Life*, the "five principal enemies of students [are]: phlegm, black bile, coitus, over-eating, and sleeping late" (Ficino 1489). Approaching those activities and avoiding studying will not lead to academic success no matter what the century. Avoiding excesses and approaching academic activities (learning to use academic libraries and computers, disciplined study habits, informed note-taking, using math or writing workshops) can provide skills that reduce stress and increase a sense of self-efficacy that can result in a positive self-image and positive attitudes about one's college.

Students with an internal locus of control are more likely to participate in beneficial activities because they believe that they are potent actors in the world they inhabit, and not acted upon by others. Such students believe, for instance, that good grades are the result of good study habits. Students with an external locus of control believe that they get good grades due to good luck or a beneficent teacher. In most cases, an internal locus of control leads to academic approach behaviors, reduced stress, improved performance, an increased sense of self-efficacy and self-confidence, and a series of positive attitudes toward the institution. When an institution acts in such a way that the student's locus of control shifts from external to internal, the result will usually be increased attachment to the school and increased retention.

The exception to this process is where the system is discriminatory. If, for example, an African American woman does A work and receives C grades, her perception of external locus of control is accurate. Grading is based on prejudicial assumptions, not performance. Where external locus of control exists and a student thinks, "I can only get a good grade if the professor wants to give me one no matter how good my work is," this situation is likely to lead to the student's alienation, negative attitudes toward the institution, and intent to leave.

In addition to these three psychological processes, attitudes play an important role in retention. Three important attitudes are a sense of satisfaction with being a student, a sense of self-development, and self-confidence as a student. These attitudes are related to each other and positively related to institutional fit, loyalty, and intent to stay. Confidence, competence, and satisfaction go hand in hand in many circumstances—I am good at riding a bicycle, I am confident that I can ride one, and it's fun. It should not be surprising that being competent at academic work, confident that one can get good grades, and enjoying this competence and these good grades as a reward are similarly related.

There are two other attitudes that are often important assessments of one's education. The first of these is thinking that one's education will lead to employment. The practical value of an education comes from learning skills or getting good grades in courses that will provide access to jobs requiring these skills. Students who make no connection between what they study and their future plans for employment are less likely to be loyal to a school or feel that they fit in. Of course, this statement is premised on the idea that the majority of students who are enrolling in college in the first place are doing so in order to get a job of their choice. More sophisticated students might engage in a cost-benefit analysis, but such sophistication is rare. The costs, including opportunity costs, are sometimes clear, but the benefits are largely guesswork. On the average, obtaining a college degree has substantial economic value over one's lifetime earnings, but an individual may guess that they will earn substantially more or substantially less than they actually will. Again, it is their attitude that is important in affecting their intentions to stay or leave. Believing their courses and major will get them to a job they will like can be a powerful motivating force to get good grades and stay enrolled in college regardless of whether or not such preparation actually leads to a particular kind of employment. The number of students who find careers in their final undergraduate major, a major that might change several times during college, is relatively small. Under such circumstances a student has to renew his or her belief in the major-employment connection several times during college.

The second attitude toward assessing one's education is the degree to which being a student at a given school is perceived as stressful. Coping mechanisms affect the level of stress a student experiences, students have a greater or lesser tolerance for this stress, and certain highly competitive college environments are usually more stressful than other environments. While some stress can provide motivation, high levels of stress have a negative influence on retention, reducing one's institutional fit and commitment. Programs aimed at stress reduction may help reduce attrition by improving students' attitudes toward their school.

A student's attitude toward the quality of the school can have important effects on fitting in, loyalty, and intent to leave. Perceived institutional quality affects the choice of which college to attend, and when a student thinks the product they are purchasing, their education, is of low quality, they might choose to leave that institution. Quality affects different students in different ways. A first-generation student attending an elite institution may leave because he does not fit in academically, whereas a very accomplished physicist might choose to leave her public comprehensive college because it was not challenging enough. After matriculation, an exciting learning environment is often associated with high institutional quality and for the high ability student, fitting in. As colleges use merit-based aid to attract academically elite high school graduates, they will need academic programs of equally high quality or the student will likely transfer.

Faculty members, more than any other group of employees at the university, shape the psychological processes and attitudes that have the greatest effect on retention. Faculty members' in-class and out-of-class contacts with students affect the students' sense of fitting in, loyalty, institutional quality, satisfaction, sense of self-development, self-confidence, and self-efficacy, the connection between course work and later employment, and stress. Others certainly have a role in these attitudes, not the least of which are other students, and in particular cases staff members can provide services and shape attitudes that are key in retention decisions. In my research I have consistently found that students' interaction with faculty members has had a much greater effect on important attitudes than interactions with professional staff or administrators.

## STUDENTS INTERACTING WITH THE INSTITUTION AND THE EXTERNAL ENVIRONMENT

Three themes related to student attitudes develop when students interact with the institution. These themes are academics, social factors, and bureaucratic factors. Simultaneously, the environment in which students are embedded outside of college affects students' attitudes.

## Academics

In the folklore of retention, academic abilities, usually reflected in grade point average (GPA) or class rank, is second only to money as the most acceptable excuse for leaving college. Academic performance is typically measured by class rank, standardized test scores, and GPA. A high GPA indicates that a student has met faculty expectations. One might assume that students with the highest IQs would have the highest GPAs. Emotional intelligence, manifest in the maturity to repress impulsive behavior and delay gratification, and social intelligence, manifest as the ability to understand what is expected in a class and act accordingly, undoubtedly affect a student's GPA. An individual's need for achievement and other motivations also can be important. GPA is much more complicated than a "High IQ = High GPA" formulation. The role of GPA in retention is not as straightforward as folklore would have us believe.

Institutions enrolling students with the highest academic achievements have the highest rates of retention. Selectivity might legitimize involuntary departure, as suggested by Laden, Milem, and Crowson (2000), by making sure some students flunk out to create solidarity among those who stay. I am more concerned with the way in which academic factors affect students at a given school, and not differences in retention rates between schools.

Voluntary and involuntary turnover is differentiated in the organizational literature (Price & Mueller 1986). An organizational member can quit or can be fired. Tinto (1975) distinguished between involuntary departure from college, where a student is dismissed due to a low GPA, and voluntary departure, where a student is permitted to stay but decides to leave. This distinction is important when the student is not capable of the academic performance required to maintain an acceptable GPA. Many students flunk themselves out of school, acting out because they do not know how else to get out of a situation they find uncomfortable.

A student might be classified as an academic failure when the student left for other reasons. Low grades were the mechanism for departure, not the cause. For example, a young woman might be sent by her parents to attend her mother's alma mater where she does not fit in. She wants to attend another college to be with her best friend from high school. Unable to reason with her parents, she fails her courses so that she is dismissed and then can join her friend and resume her education. This is an example of an academic dismissal with nonacademic roots. I have been hesitant to separate voluntary from involuntary dismissals because what appears to be involuntary leaving might come from the same sources as voluntary leaving. In either case, departure resulted from the student not being socialized to the values of the institution she was leaving.

Academic and social integration are key to Tinto's (1975, 1993) modeling of the departure process. I discuss academics in connection with institutional interaction that has both precursors and antecedents. The academic theme of retention begins with prematriculation academic experiences and performance. These are indicated by high school grades, rank in a high school class, and the extent to which the student took a college preparatory curriculum. A student brings to college the student's academic preparation as part of his or her cultural capital (Bourdieu 1973, 1977), assets that can be used in negotiations with the institutional environment.

There are four major ways in which a student interacts with academic resources. First, and most obvious, is through the courses taken. Does the institution, and do the courses, provide the student with the substantive information and skills that the student wants from his or her education? Courses are the most important vector by which a faculty interacts with students to promote their education. The commodity the student is purchasing from the school is this education, nebulous as the concept may be. An institution that does not provide courses that students want to take will have difficulty retaining its students.

As the poet William Butler Yeats has written, "How can we know the dancer from the dance?" and by analogy, "How can we know the course from the faculty member who teaches it?" A faculty member presents substantive material in a course in a way that promotes or does not promote students to be socialized to academic values and choose a particular major. Professors affect the student's self-image and self-efficacy assessments. Faculty members deliver the institution's product, education. When students feel faculty members do not care about the students' development, their bonds to the institution weaken.

Faculty members can reinforce or challenge a student's self-image as a person or a major outside of class as well. Many proclaim this informal connection between professor and student to be an important one. At teaching-oriented or student-centered institutions, it may be, but at large research universities, lower division students may not expect or receive much out of class attention from faculty members. Since students think little about it, the faculty-student connection has minimal effects on other aspects of their academic work.

Academic advising is another area where there is much blame and spotty evidence. Where evidence exists (Metzner 1989), advising helps retention. Many students use poor advising as an excuse for leaving. Good advising should link a student's academic capabilities with his or her choice of courses and major, access to learning resources, and a belief that the academic pathway a student is traveling will lead to employment after college. Whether lower division academic advising should be done by a professional advising staff or by faculty members is an unnecessary debate. Advising should be done well so students recognize their abilities and make informed academic choices. Either staff or faculty can provide this resource. When a student is certain of his or her major and close to graduation, the major advisor has the potential to make the most important contributions to advising. Simultaneously, staff members are more likely to be in touch with the market for graduates, outside of academia, than the faculty. The placement of current graduates symbolizes the likelihood that a lower division student will find work in a given field and helps them associate their course work with employment.

Two outcomes of these interactions are a belief that the student's education will be of practical value to the student in getting work and the development of self-confidence about the student's academic abilities. The combination of the student's background, interaction with the institution related to academic matters, and a belief in one's abilities to perform academic work have a cumulative mutual influence resulting in academic integration. When students' academic integration improves, so do their academic performance and their grades.

A low GPA has a negative effect on retention, and failing to achieve some minimum level of performance, students are asked to leave and do so involuntarily. A high GPA does not assure continued enrollment. In statistical studies, GPA alone typically explains only a small percentage of the variance in retention. There are several possible explanations for this finding. First, with grade inflation, the variance in grades is reduced, and this effect limits the ability of the variable to predict anything. Inflation also means that students can get high grades even though they are not performing well in their courses. In this case, GPA is not related to academic integration. Second, students with the highest GPAs might transfer to another institution. From the individual perspective this is not departure, but from the institutional perspective it is. Third, retention is based on many more factors than academic performance. Differences in social connectivity, attitudes toward the school, and financial and other factors external to the school can have profound effects on retention.

These effects diminish the comparative importance of academic performance in retention decisions.

To summarize the academic theme, a student enters college with a record of academic performance and cultural capital, interacts with faculty members, advisors, and other students in formal and informal academic settings, forms the attitudes that their education is of practical value for getting work, develops a sense of academic self-efficacy, approaches academic work, develops an internal locus of control related to academic achievement, gets good grades, feels loyal to the school, and chooses to continue enrollment there. The importance of the effects of academic performance in college on retention should not be underestimated. Neither should it be overestimated.

## Social Factors

The twin pillars of Tinto's modeling of the retention process are academic and social integration. Few would deny that the social lives of students in college and their exchanges with others inside and outside the institution are important in retention decisions. Braxton et al. (2004), in an extensive review of the literature using Tinto's model, found that relationship in Tinto's model best supported by existing empirical studies was the effect of social integration on institutional commitment and retention. Students' modes of social interaction are extremely varied, as they would be for any group of people. Traditionally aged students are confronted with developmental tasks that are heavily laced with social interaction (Chickering 1969; Perry 1970). Students of any age form social bonds with others at the college and such attachments, when strong and focused on the positive aspects of learning and developing, help a student fit in with others at the school. Weak social attachments, or those that reinforce destructive or avoidant behavior, can hurt retention.

Spady's (1970) initial conceptual model considered family origin, specifically father's education, to influence completion rates from college. Prior to this time, SES or socioeconomic status was considered to affect retention rates. For example, Sewell and Shaw (1967) found that family status had a major influence on graduation rates. Bourdieu's (1973, 1977) description of cultural capital and social capital reflect a similar belief. Where a student comes from affects how the student interacts with the institution and the likelihood of survival. In my own research, parents' education consistently had a more important influence on retention than the other aspects of socioeconomic status, parents' occupation and income. Parental exposure to college should provide additional cultural and social capital for students increasing the intensity of their interaction with the institution and adjustment to college.

It was surprising that Braxton, Hirschy, and McClendon (2004) found little support for parental approval of the institution or encouragement to attend college as an important contributor to retention for full-time residential students. I first noticed the importance of this variable in a study comparing Black and White student retention at a southern university in the early 1980s (Bean & Hull 1984). In this study, parents' approval had significant statistical effects on eight of thirteen intervening variables: academic integration, goals, utility, reduced alienation, social integration, finances, reduced opportunity to transfer, and institutional fit. Such findings were similar to other empirical studies I conducted including the last one in 1997 where encouragement was significantly related to nine of seventeen intervening variables. Social support before and during college from important people inside and outside the institution is important for retention.

Besides support for attending college, friendships with other members of the institution are an important part of the social integration. Friendship is notoriously difficult to measure ("I got a million friends"). The number of friends seems less important than a student having one or a small number of close friends at the college. By close friends I mean a friendship that contains care, empathy, concern, affect, spending time, and so on. People one "hangs out with" may be called friends, but casual friendships are not substitutes for close friendships. Social support and close friendships form the core components of social integration.

Students derive satisfaction from these social attachments. Having close friends on campus and feeling supported increase a student's self-confidence. Where satisfaction and self-confidence are found, students believe that they fit in. Friendships and fitting in are tightly coupled. Students can feel that they fit in for a variety of reasons at a college—academically, financially, racially, ethnically, linguistically, due to shared interests—but the social aspects of "fit" are consistently the most important ones. Social factors are also associated with loyalty to the alma mater, but there are more important influences on loyalty.

Many factors affect the social connections students feel at college. The student's expectations from parents, siblings, and high school friends who went on to college before them and the information and encouragement received from these people affect the way the student will interact with the social resources of the institution. These social resources include faculty, staff, and particularly other students. Social connectedness leads to satisfaction, self-confidence, loyalty, fitting in, and remaining enrolled. The social world of students is important to retention decisions, and there are many potential sources of social support.

An institution can do much to structure the social world of students without intruding upon it. Social activities that contain academic and intellectual components can simultaneously promote academic and social integration. It is important that there is opportunity for social interaction in the form of leisure time, and places, events, and others willing to interact. The particular form of social engagement can vary widely depending on the norms, traditions, and values of the student culture. Given institutional encouragement, appropriate forms of social interaction will emerge. Housing arrangements, placement in sets of classes with the same students, and special academic, athletic, and interest groups can aid in developing a social attachment to the school. It is important for institutional officials to recognize that social connectedness is important for retention. Programming that fosters such connections is valuable. There are abundant examples of such programs in the literature. Students leave college for a variety of reasons, and a variety of interventions can help them decide to stay.

## Bureaucratic Factors

The somewhat pejorative term *bureaucratic* as opposed to *organizational* was chosen in order to emphasize the role of offices in retention. I used organizational constructs at the beginning of my research on college students (Bean 1980). These reflected the organizational situation at a college and more than the interaction between students and service providers at the school. The interaction described here starts as a bureaucratic one but may grow to include other interpersonal aspects. Bureaucratic factors are defined as the way in which formal exchanges of resources (time, money, effort, information) between a student and the institution take place. A common pattern of such exchange would be between a student and offices or programs that handle outreach programs, admissions information, the application process, financial aid applications and awards, the bursar's office, housing, advising, the academic calendar, orientation, registration and the registrar's office, class attendance, resident advisors, study skills programs, departmental offices that define major requirements, recreation programs, athletic programs, special interest groups, formal convocations, social and athletic events, and so on. Students bring documents, money, completed application forms, papers, and the like, and exchange these things for access to institutional resources and activities. Exchanges requiring the completion of forms are formal by definition, and other activities may be based on institutional norms.

A failure to negotiate the formal requirements can be disastrous. Violating rules (failure to pay tuition, failure to attend class, failure to behave appropriately in a residence hall) can result in reprimand or expulsion. If too much emphasis is placed on these exchanges, the student can be greatly disheartened. The bureaucratic aspects of the academy are soulless, deadening students whose spirits should be lifted by their academic experiences. For more pragmatic students, rules and regulations represent obstacles of a greater or lesser magnitude. Successful accomplishment of these bureaucratic activities is required for graduation, many of which have nothing to do with academic development.

Colleges and universities could not exist without a bureaucratic mantel. Goal displacement occurs when getting the form filled out correctly is more important to employees than helping the student. The way in which bureaucratic activities are carried out can lead to greater social integration for students on the one hand and greater alienation on the other. Students who feel helped and empowered by these exchanges are likely to feel loyal to the school and remain enrolled. Students who feel powerless in the face of this bureaucratic maze can become alienated, a situation that seems to pertain particularly to African American students at traditionally White institutions (Bean & Hull 1984).

Institutional members need to figure out how to provide these services in a way that students appreciate. These exchanges represent an opportunity for the staff to affect student attitudes toward the college in a positive fashion. As with all retention programming, these activities are labor intensive. Caring for individual students is at the opposite end of a continuum that starts with the efficient processing of large groups. Institutions have to balance the costs of not caring and the associated negative attitudes toward the school with the costs of reducing the number of forms completed per hour.

The admissions office is particularly important because it often marks the first formal interchange between the student and the college. Admissions policies are working well when they yield large numbers of graduates, not large numbers of first-year students. Admissions can be viewed as setting the tone for other agents of the institution: are you processing another student ID as a source of revenue or welcoming a new member of the campus community? Students can tell the difference. Students who feel they have been misled will find it especially difficult to form positive attitudes toward the institution.

While the curriculum is the centerpiece of academic integration, it also involves the student obeying rules and fulfilling requirements, including required courses and prerequisites, requirements for admission to and graduation from majors, and required times of course attendance. Students who are not able to take the courses they want because they are not offered, they are offered but are full, or they are offered at a time when the student cannot attend them feel less loyalty and believe their education is of less practical value. Adjusting a curriculum is not a trivial undertaking. Creating a pleasing smorgasbord of "Surveys of Everything" might have short-term appeal but will lack the depth associated with institutional quality. Courses that are perceived to be of low quality will hurt the image of the institution no matter how conveniently they are offered.

The curriculum also has an array of rules and regulations regarding transferring credits, distribution requirements, prerequisites, maintenance of an overall GPA and the GPA in the major, academic dishonesty, major requirements, and so on. Helping students understand what is important and what is possible may be unnecessary for some and vital for others. If this curriculum represents an academic challenge to students, a wide variety of programs are available to help students respond positively to these challenges. Basic skills programs or study skills programs could be necessary conditions for these students to stay enrolled. Social or emotional support for these students can be essential for improving their self-confidence.

Freshman interest groups, residential programs, and mentoring programs are all formal ways an institution can integrate students into campus life (Bean & Eaton 2001). As with any programs, an emphasis on rules and regulations diminishes the value of the interaction for student development.

Financial aid offices are places most students frequent, and there is plenty of angst associated with paying for college. Financial aid forms can seem to some as complicated as Internal Revenue Service tax forms and are met with equal trepidation. Along with admissions officers, the staff involved in helping students apply for financial aid can also provide a caring or an antagonistic experience for students at the beginning of their interaction with campus offices.

The situation at many colleges and universities might be due to the litigiousness of our society, our preference for bureaucratic order, or a notion that unless everything is recorded and assessed resources will not be distributed properly. Whatever the reason, an emphasis on following rules, on meeting the letter of the law and not the spirit of the law, can make a student feel trapped and alienated by the institutional offices. Where students feel alienated, they are more likely to be under stress and less likely to develop positive attitudes toward or to graduate from a college or university. When the bureaucracy of a school errs more on the side of ad hoc solutions to student problems and less on the side of rigidity, students for whom reasonable exceptions are made are likely to feel a stronger attachment to the institution. Students who feel trapped by unreasonable rules want out.

## The External Environment

These variables were first identified as "environmental variables" with direct effects on leaving college in Bean and Creswell (1980). While recognized by Tinto (1975) and initially excluded from his model, environmental variables were firmly imbedded in his thinking by 1993. Students can be pulled out of school by forces beyond their control and beyond the control of the institution. They can also be attracted to other roles as students, employees, or significant others which require that they leave their current institution. The external environment is a catch-all phrase meant to indicate forces beyond the control of the student or institution that can affect retention decisions at any time. Besides finances, which is treated separately, the external environment contains significant others, opportunities to transfer, opportunities to work, and family responsibilities. These factors often are directly related to retention, although sometimes they affect intent to leave and institutional fit. With the exception of finances, the institution can do little to retain a student if these factors come into play.

Significant others, which usually indicates having a boyfriend or girlfriend at another college, can be potent attractants. An institution can do everything right in terms of retention, and a student can love being enrolled there, but if he or she loves another person and wants to be with that person, then the holding power of the institution is weak by comparison.

Family responsibilities, such as raising children or taking care of a sick or aging parent, can take precedence over academic pursuits. If these are short-term arrangements, the student may stop out to take care of them and then return to school. For younger students, it may be their parent's family that is of concern, while for older students, it can be issues related to children, a spouse, or parents. Students who are married to someone who is employed might leave school when their spouse is transferred or finds another job. In each case, the student and institution may have done everything right in their relationship.

When a student believes that it would not be difficult to transfer to another college or university, the institution is at risk of losing the student. A student who is socially and academically anchored at a college will find it difficult to transfer because it involves severing both social and academic ties. When transfer is perceived to be easy, the student has not developed a sense of loyalty to the college. Of the environmental variables, an institution, by making itself attractive, can make transfer more difficult, reducing the likelihood of a student's leaving.

## The Student's Background

A general way of looking at a traditional-aged college student's background is to understand the social capital (networks and connections a student has which often have to do with who one's parents are) and the human capital (personal abilities, capabilities, and skills) a student brings to college. The more practical way of looking at students' backgrounds has been in terms of educational goals, high school grades, class rank, standardized test scores, success in a college preparatory curriculum, and parents' education, occupation, and income.

For traditional, residential college students entering college after high school, retention is greatest where students of very high ability enroll in very high quality academic programs. Similarly, college completion is lowest at low-status institutions with open admission policies. When the student and institution are matched, so that the institution wants what the student has to offer and the student wants what the college has to offer, retention is likely to improve.

Given this situation, one could change retention rates if one could change the student body or change the staff and faculty of an institution, or both. If students with dramatically different backgrounds than current students enroll in a college in large numbers, then retention rates are likely to change. Retention rates and institutional status are usually in alignment, and increasing the number of students with a high-survival profile will likely raise retention rates. This profile is typified by high levels of past academic performance in a college preparatory curriculum, ambitious educational goals, college educated parents with high incomes and high-status occupations, and parents who support their children financially, practically, and emotionally in attending the college. Few institutions have the luxury of choosing a high proportion of their students from this kind of background.

The match between the student and the institution affects retention rates. Few institutions can quickly and dramatically change the profile of the students attending the institution, and it is the institution that must change in order to improve retention rates. An institution that admits larger and larger freshman classes of lower and lower ability can reasonably expect retention rates to decline unless the institution simultaneously increases its support for basic skills or other appropriate academic support programs. Retention programming is labor intensive, and labor is the chief expense of most colleges and universities. Colleges in financially precarious situations may not have the resources necessary to fund programs to increase retention and thus tuition income.

## Money and Finance

In a capitalist society, and we certainly are one, few things capture the imagination like money. Institutions cannot survive without monetary resources. Students can rarely attend college without paying substantial sums of money for the opportunity. As a result, institutions spend a considerable amount of energy trying to figure out how to extract resources from the environment in the form of tuition, state appropriations, philanthropic gifts, funded research, and the like. Students look for resources from gainful employment, savings, parents and relatives, loans, grants, and scholarships.

A few colleges in this country charge no tuition. Some students have full scholarships that pay for their tuition, room, and board. Some students are given grants and can attend college without using their own money. These are exceptions. Most students pay a great deal for their education. Students, parents, institutional policymakers, and the federal and state governments share a concern about who should pay for college and how much they should pay. Actually understanding the role of money in retention is difficult.

There are several complicating factors in understanding how money affects retention. First, running out of money is probably the best excuse for leaving college that there is, because it places the reason for leaving outside the locus of control of the student. Running out of money is normatively accepted; it represents no academic or motivational failure on the part of the student. Many students who leave college for other reasons blame their departure on money problems.

Second, students who have money, if it came from their parents, also probably have high levels of social and human capital. Isolating the effects of money from cultural capital is difficult. These factors are likely to be mutually supportive in terms of retention, and a student who has both money and cultural capital will benefit in terms of social integration and institutional fit. Demonstrating the unique contribution of each factor is more difficult. Institutions that are able to attract wealthy students are likely to have high retention rates because such students have educational advantages, have cultural advantages, can pay for the direct costs of their education, and can fully participate in the social life and material culture of the college they attend.

Third, finding out the amount of resources actually available to a student is difficult. Financial aid offices can have excellent information about parental income for students who depend on their parents for tuition, but due to privacy laws, such information might not be available to researchers. On questionnaires, students might underreport available resources thinking that if they report having less money, they might get more resources from the college they attend. Fourth, in surveys that attempt to relate parental income to retention, students, when asked about how much money their parents make, may not know the answer, or may not want to tell if they do know. Fifth, because retention decisions are complicated and students can leave for any number of reasons, isolating the effects of a single factor, like money, is difficult.

Some issues associated with money are clear. From a retention perspective, lower tuition is preferable to higher tuition. Grants are preferable to loans. If an institution can reduce tuition for students with little money, it will likely increase retention. Larger numbers of students providing fewer tuition dollars is a situation few institutions can tolerate. Some institutions have raised tuition and applications have increased because more expensive institutions are presumed to be of higher quality. Institutions that provide grants instead of loans will likely retain higher numbers of students, particularly African American students who do not like to take out loans. In a multi-institution study, Pascarella, Pierson, Wolniak, and Terenzini (2004) found evidence that financial aid may not have been found to affect retention because it was "*insufficient* rather than ineffective" (280) for first-generation students. Lower costs were related to higher rates of retention.

Most research on money and college students has to do with the direct costs of an education: tuition, room, and board. Student lifestyles can also be expensive. It is common at some institutions for students to have technological devices (computers, stereos, TVs, cell phones, media collections), clothing, sports equipment, and a car, the total value of which might exceed $50,000. Students with little money are excluded from the status and bonds that form around wealth. It costs money to participate in the social life of a college, and social integration and institutional fit have an economic basis. Students with far less or far more wealth than the average might not fit in and as a result might leave school.

Students who work to make money for college are likely to be more motivated to complete college than students who earn money to maintain their lifestyles. Regardless of why a student is working, working more than twenty hours a week can have negative consequences for the student's academic and social life. Part-time students with full-time jobs are, of course, another question. For them, retention may be less a question of finding tuition dollars and more a problem of time constraints, balancing their job with their schooling and other commitments in their lives.

Institutions have a certain amount of discretion about who should receive financial aid and how much a student should receive, and college represents a major cost to most students. The greater the subsidies for students, the higher the retention rates, and the fewer resources the institution has. It is difficult to establish policies that achieve the appropriate equilibrium between financial aid and tuition, but institutions that do so are likely to prosper.

To recap, then, students from wealthy or moderately wealthy backgrounds are likely to possess high levels of social and human capital and have money to pay for the direct costs of their education and additional costs associated with social integration. Their advantaged position is also likely to be associated with institutional fit. However, very wealthy or very poor students may not fit in with others. Students with less money are less likely to fit in than students with more money. Institutions can adjust direct costs and types and amounts of student aid. They rely on tuition income from students, and there is a limit to the amount of resources institutions can spend to reduce direct costs to students.

## SENSIBLE RESPONSES TO RETENTION NEEDS

Changes in retention rates come from changes in institutional personnel or the way they do their jobs, changes in the composition of the student body, and changes in the way these two groups interact. Policies and programs can be important for retaining particular students, but major changes in the overall rates of retention usually involve major changes in the institution's social, academic, and economic condition. An institution needs to change what it is or what it does in order for retention rates to change.

Institutions have to ask themselves, "How much can we change?" The question is one of ability to change, motivation to change, and forms of resistance to change. Assuming a relatively stable external environment, is change likely to occur? If an institution has neither the academic nor the professional staffing necessary to implement a change, it will remain the same. If an institution has no motivation to change, it will remain the same. If each move to make a change is blocked by one or many powerful individuals, the institution will not change.

Student retention is a win-win situation: the student gains an education and increased lifetime earnings and the institution educates a student, fulfilling its mission, and gains tuition income. For these reasons, it makes sense for institutions to invest in retention programming. Because students leave for a wide variety of reasons, the institution can sensibly invest in a wide variety of programs intended to increase retention. Development programs that change faculty and staff's understanding about why students leave college and what faculty can do in their classes and staff can do in their programs can help increase retention. There is a one-time cost and, with luck, long-term payoffs. Programs that require increased staffing and thus increased cost to the institution can rarely prove their worth. Assessment usually is most effective when the causes and effects of programs are clearly understood and easily measured. Such is rarely the case in retention.

Changes in retention rates should be thought of in terms of how collective efforts produce overall changes. Institutions that set up a retention office and reward or punish the office based on changes in retention rates live in a bureaucratic fantasy world. It's bureaucratic because responsibility is assigned to an office or individual, and it's a fantasy because changes in retention occur when the institution changes, not when a new program is added. That is not to say that there should be no retention office or enrollment management office, only that to assign to one office rewards and punishments based on something they could not possibly control is a fantasy. If a student leaves because of a sour run-in with a departmental secretary, an unpleasant room-mate, inadequate funds for tuition, an abusive professor, an insensitive bursar, a desire to be with a friend at another college, or all of these reasons at once, what exactly is this retention office supposed to do? Retention offices should help fund and coordinate particular programs that meet the needs of particular students.

Students are less likely to leave when they understand what will be expected from them in terms of academic work and when they are capable of succeeding in the college classroom. They are less likely to leave when the academic and social environments are familiar to them. They are less likely to leave when the atmosphere on campus is attractive—physically, emotionally, intellectually, socially. Being attractive doesn't mean fancy; it means appealing to some part of the student's psyche.

Institutions that treat students as customers—those who generate custom—are faced with the standard business norm that the customer is always right. While this attitude might lead to grade inflation ("I paid for the course now give me an A"), it is not likely to lead to transformative learning. A sense of entitlement does not involve the student in the difficult study necessary for deep learning. The best education isn't very efficient, because it involves the whole student learning, in fits and starts, with individual feedback, how to learn. The administrative culture of efficiency is in conflict with the faculty culture of learning, and retention programming in that context is problematic.

Assessment is concerned with standardization, costs, efficiency, and improvement based on measurable standards. Retention is quite measurable. A percentage of the students who enroll are still enrolled or have graduated at some later date. The reasons why students leave are poorly understood. A retention program might have direct effects on retention rates, but proving that a student stayed in school due to one program is practically impossible. Students' experiences are complex, and their reasons for departure are complex. Collective efforts are likely to produce results, but measuring the effects of individual programs is difficult at best. The good effects of a retention program may have to be taken on faith, something antithetical to assessment norms.

The nine themes of student retention suggest many areas where institutions can sensibly apply their resources. Benchmarking is valuable in providing possibilities for retention programs, for example, how to organize freshman interest groups or orientation activities. The fact that College A has a higher retention rate than College B and a great freshman interest group program does not tell an observer if College B has an appropriate retention rate or whether the retention rate would improve with a freshman interest group program. What works at other institutions with other faculty members and other students might not work in one's own institution. A wide variety of retention programming seems preferable to an extensive program in a single area. An institution would do well to develop programs that respond to many if not all of the nine retention themes described in this chapter. College officials could begin addressing campus retention issues by answering the following questions:

- If students come from a background that is academically or socially unusual for your institution, what programs are in place to help the student adjust to life on campus?

- What is the optimal balance between tuition and financial support? Do students understand the total cost of their education? Is there a free social life on campus, or are social events expensive for students?

- Are resources in place so that all admitted students can succeed in their classes? Is there a culture on campus that seeks to involve students in academic endeavors both inside and outside the classroom?

- Can the institution develop an atmosphere where students are respected as people and valued as friends and not just a source of revenue? Does the social atmosphere revolve around activities that reinforce learning or reinforce escapism? Are there places, events, and people who model care for students so students learn to care about themselves and others?

- Are the institution's bureaucratic offices user friendly? Do staff and faculty members know that the competent provision of their services is necessary for retention but not sufficient? Do they understand that their role in shaping the attitudes of students can have a profound effect on student retention?

- Does the college make itself as attractive as possible so that students who are capable of transferring to another school are not interested in doing so? Do staff and faculty members understand students' responsibilities to employers, family members, or significant others outside of the institution?

- Do faculty and staff members understand the importance of not just providing their services but providing them in a way that students appreciate so that students develop positive attitudes toward the college?

- Does the institution anticipate the importance of students feeling that they fit in at college? Are rites and rituals in place so that students identify and bond with the institution? Sporting events are the most obvious of these activities, where students can identify with the team, but sporting events do not appeal to all students. Other institutional events include events that open the school year, mark graduation, pay tribute to current and past heroes of the college—events that recur on an annual basis, that are endorsed at the highest level, that provide meaning to the student about what it means to attend this college.

- Ask students if they intend to leave, and if they do, are there things the college could do that would make students change their minds and stay?

These recommendations for rethinking retention programming at a college or university based on the nine themes in retention are similar to what others have written. When I compare the recommendations I made for improving retention twenty years ago (Bean 1986a) with the summary in Braxton et. al. (2004) of the research that has taken place since that time, there is some difference in language, but little disagreement about what should be done to improve retention. Colleges and universities better understand that different kinds of students leave for different reasons. Because leaving college is not a monolithic process, different retention programs can all benefit some but not all students. There is no magic bullet. Perhaps the greatest contribution to research in the past twenty years has been an improved understanding of retention for different minority groups, part-time nonresidential students, and first-generation students.

The one major difference between my approach to studying student retention and that based on Tinto's model is related to attitudes. I have found that students evaluate their experiences and form attitudes toward the college that influence their intentions to stay enrolled and their decision to stay or leave. Anyone and everyone on campus can affect these attitudes, and for this reason everyone on campus is responsible for retention. While this is a bureaucratic nightmare, since retention successes and failures cannot be accurately attributed to any single office, it means everyone on campus can and should work to improve students' experience. The assessment of retention programs needs to be based not only on what these academic or co-curricular programs are supposed to accomplish, but on whether, in providing their services, staff and faculty members shape students' attitudes toward the institution in a positive fashion.

## REFERENCES

Bean, J. P. (1979). Path analysis: The development of a suitable methodology for the study of student attrition. Paper presented at the annual meeting of the American Educational Research Association, San Francisco.

———. (1980). Dropouts and turnover: The synthesis and test of a causal model of student attrition. *Research in Higher Education* 12: 155–187.

———. (1981, April). Synthesis of a theoretical model of student attrition. Paper presented at the annual meeting of the American Educational Research Association, Los Angeles.

———. (1982a). Conceptual models of college dropout: How theory can help the institutional researcher. In *Studying student attrition*, ed. E. Pascarella, 17–33. San Francisco: Jossey-Bass.

———. (1982b, March). The interaction effects of GPA on other determinants of student attrition in a homogeneous population. Paper presented at the annual meeting of the American Educational Research Association, New York.

————. (1982c). Student attrition, intentions, and confidence: Interaction effects in a path model. *Research in Higher Education* 17: 291–320.

————. (1983). The application of a model of turnover in work organizations to the student attrition process. *Review of Higher Education* 6: 127–148.

————. (1985). Interaction effects based on class level in an explanatory model of college student dropout syndrome. *American Educational Research Journal* 22: 35–64.

————. (1986a). Assessing and reducing attrition. In *Managing college enrollments*, ed. D. Hossler, 47–61. San Francisco: Jossey-Bass.

————. (1986b). The Clark-Trow typology revisited: Its conceptual validity and a comparison of threshold and valence theories in explaining students' outcomes from college. Paper presented at the annual meeting of the Association for the Study of Higher Education, San Antonio, TX.

————. (1990a). Strategic Planning and Enrollment Management. In *The strategic management of college enrollments*, ed. D. Hossler & J. P. Bean, 21–43. San Francisco: Jossey-Bass.

————. (1990b). Using retention research in enrollment management. In *The strategic management of college enrollments*, ed. D. Hossler & J. P. Bean, 170–185. San Francisco: Jossey-Bass.

————. (1990c). Why students leave: Insights from research. In *The strategic management of college enrollments*, ed. D. Hossler & J. P. Bean, 147–169. San Francisco: Jossey-Bass.

————. (1991a, November). Improving retention through institutional change. Paper presented at the annual meeting of the American Association of Collegiate Registrars and Admissions Officers, Atlanta.

————. (1991b, November). Ethical considerations in effective retention. Paper presented at the annual meeting of the American Association of Collegiate Registrars and Admissions Officers, Atlanta.

————. (2002). College student retention. In *The encyclopedia of education*, 2nd Ed., ed. J. Guthrie, New York: Macmillan Reference USA.

Bean, J. P., & Bradley, R. K. (1986). Untangling the satisfaction-performance relationship for college students. *Journal of Higher Education* 57: 393–412.

Bean, J. P., & Creswell, J. W. (1980). Student attrition among women at a liberal arts college. *Journal of College Student Personnel* 21: 320–327.

Bean, J. P., & Eaton, S. (2000). A psychological model of college student retention. In *Rethinking the departure puzzle: New theory and research on college student retention*, ed. J. M. Braxton, 48–61. Nashville: Vanderbilt University Press.

Bean, J. P., & Eaton, S. B. (2002). The use of psychological factors in effective retention programs. *Journal of College Student Retention: Research, Theory and Practice* 3(1): 73–90.

Bean, J. P., & Hossler, D. H. (1990). Tailoring enrollment management to institutional needs: Advice to campus leaders. In *The strategic management of college enrollments*, ed. D. Hossler & J. P. Bean, 285–302. San Francisco: Jossey-Bass.

Bean, J. P., & Hull, D. F. (1984). Determinants of black and white student attrition at a major southern state university. Paper presented at the annual meeting of the American Educational Research Association, New Orleans.

Bean, J. P., & Kuh, G. D. (1984). The reciprocity between student-faculty informal contact and the academic performance of university undergraduate students. *Research in Higher Education* 21: 461–478.

Bean, J. P., & Metzner, B. S. (1985). A conceptual model of nontraditional undergraduate student attrition. *Review of Educational Research* 55: 485–540.

Bean, J. P., & Plascak, F. D. (1987). Traditional and nontraditional undergraduate student attrition at an urban liberal arts college. Paper presented at the annual meeting of the American Educational Research Association, Washington, DC.

Bean, J. P., & Vesper, N. (1990). Quantitative approaches to grounding theory in data: Using LISREL to develop a local model and theory of student attrition. Paper presented at the annual meeting of the American Educational Research Association, Boston.

———. (1992, October). Student dependency theory: An explanation of student retention in college. Paper presented at the annual meeting of the Association for the Study of Higher Education, Minneapolis.

———. (1994, November). Honors students' satisfaction with being a college student. Paper presented at the annual meeting of the Association for the Study of Higher Education, Tucson.

Bennett, C., & Bean, J. P. (1984). A conceptual model of black student attrition at a predominantly white university. *Journal of Educational Equity and Leadership* 4: 173–188.

Bentler, P., & Speckart, G. (1979). Models of attitude-behavior relations. *Psychological Review* 86: 452–464.

Bourdieu, P. (1973). Cultural reproduction and social reproduction. In *Knowledge, education, and cultural change*, ed. R. Brown, 487–510. London: Tavistock.

———. (1977). *Outline of a theory of practice*. Trans. R. Nice. Cambridge, UK: Cambridge University Press.

Braxton, J. M., ed. (2000). *Rethinking the departure puzzle: New theory and research on college student retention*. Nashville: Vanderbilt University Press.

Braxton, J. M., Hirschy, A. S., & McClendon, S. A. (2004). *Understanding and reducing college student departure*. Vol. 30, No. 3. San Francisco: Wiley Periodicals.

Chickering, A. W. (1969). *Education and identity*. San Francisco: Jossey-Bass.

Durkheim, E. (1951). *Suicide*. Trans. J. A. Spaulding & G. Simpson. Glencoe, IL: The Free Press.

Eaton, S., & Bean, J. P. (1995). An approach/avoidance behavioral model of college student retention. *Research in Higher Education* 36: 617–645.

Hossler, D., & Bean, J. P. (1990). Principles and objectives. In *The strategic management of college enrollments*, ed. D. Hossler & J. P. Bean, 3–20. San Francisco: Jossey-Bass.

Ficino, M. (1489). *The book of life*. Florence: Filippo Valori. Published as: Ficino, Marsillo. Marsilio Fincino: The Book of Life. (1980) Translated by Charles Boer. Dallas, TX: Spring Publications.

Fishbein, M., & Ajzen, I. (1975). *Belief, attitude, intention, and behavior: An introduction to theory and research*. Reading, MA: Addison-Wesley.

Janis, I. (1972). *Victims of groupthink*. Boston: Houghton Mifflin.

Laden, B. V., Milem, J. F., & Crowson, R. W. (2000). New institutional theory of undergraduate retention. In *Rethinking the departure puzzle: New theory and research on college student retention*, ed. J. M. Braxton, 235–256. Nashville, TN: Vanderbilt University Press.

Metzner, B. S. (1989). Perceived quality of academic advising: The effect on freshman attrition. *American Educational Research Journal* 26: 422–442.

Metzner, B. S., & Bean, J. P. (1987). The estimation of a conceptual model of nontraditional undergraduate student attrition. *Research in Higher Education* 27: 15–38.

Mone, M. A., Baker, D. D., & Jeffries, F. (1995). Predictive validity and time dependency of self-efficacy, self-esteem, personal goals, and academic performance. *Educational and Psychological Measurement* 55(5): 716–727.

Pascarella, E. T., Pierson, C. T., Wolniak, G. C., & Terenzini, P. T. (2004). First-generation college students: Additional evidence on college experiences and outcomes. *Journal of Higher Education* 75(4): 249–284.

Perry, W. G. (1970). *Forms of intellectual and ethical development in the college years: A scheme*. Troy, MO: Holt, Rinehart and Winston.

Plascak-Craig, F. D., Stage, F. K., MacLean, L. S., & Bean, J. P. (1990). Successful retention programs at two institutions. In *The strategic management of college enrollments*, ed. D. Hossler & J. P. Bean, 202–223. San Francisco: Jossey-Bass.

Price, J. L., & Mueller, C. W. (1986). *Handbook of organizational measurement*. Marshfield, MA: Longwood Press.

Spady, W. (1970). Dropouts from higher education: An interdisciplinary review and synthesis. *Interchange* 1(1): 64–85.

Swell, W. R., & Shaw, V. P. (1967). Social class, parental encouragement, and educational aspirations. *American Journal of Sociology* 73: 559–572.

Thomas, R. O., & Bean, J. P. (1988). Student retention at liberal arts colleges: The development and test of a model. Paper presented at the annual meeting of the Association for the Study of Higher Education, St. Louis.

Tinto, V. (1975). Dropout from higher education: A theoretical synthesis of recent research. *Review of Educational Research* 45(1): 89–125.

———. (1993). *Leaving college: Rethinking the causes and cures of student attrition*. 2nd Ed. Chicago: University of Chicago Press.

# CHAPTER

# Pre-College and Institutional Influences on Degree Attainment

*Alexander W. Astin and Leticia Oseguera*

## INTRODUCTION

Degree completion is one of the few student outcomes in higher education in which virtually all constituencies have a stake. Most students and parents, for example, view attainment of the degree as an essential step in realizing the student's career aspirations. Parents, in addition, have an economic stake in the student's being able to complete the degree in a timely fashion. Institutional faculty and staff view the retention and graduation of each student as a sign that their efforts have been successful, while legislators and policymakers are inclined to see an institution's degree completion rate as an indicator of its "performance."

From any of these perspectives, empirical studies of college student retention have at least two very practical applications: *prediction* and *control*. When we speak of predicting a dichotomous outcome such as degree completion (versus noncompletion), what we really have in mind is our capacity to *estimate* the student's chances of completing a degree within a specified period of time: "What are the odds that this student will complete a bachelor's degree within six years after entering?" Such information is obviously of potential value to college officials who are responsible either for admitting students or for designing special programs for high-risk students. The issue of control refers to our capacity to *enhance* students' chances of completing a degree: "What type of college, or what particular conditions of attendance, offer this student the best chances of completing the degree?" Such information is of obvious value not only to prospective students, but also to college officials or policy-makers who wish to improve degree completion rates.

The principal purpose of this chapter is to assess what recent empirical studies of degree completion can tell us about the prediction and control of undergraduate degree completion. We shall focus on three types of information that can be useful in estimating any student's chances of completing college: (1) pre-college characteristics of the student, (2) the characteristics of the college that the student attends, and (3) environmental contingencies of attendance (e.g., whether the student lives at home or on campus, financial aid, work status, and so on). While the bulk of the chapter will focus on findings from a recent large-scale national longitudinal study, we shall first present a brief overview of other recent studies of degree completion.

## PREVIOUS RESEARCH

A substantial portion of the empirical research on undergraduate degree completion during the past thirty years has focused on the development and testing of theoretical models for explaining degree attainment. These range from status attainment models (Sewell, Haller, & Ohlendorf 1970), in which researchers examine the role of ascribed status in the degree attainment process, to holistic models (Tinto 1987), whereby researchers examine pre-college attributes and within-college experiences that might explain degree attainment, to comprehensive models integrating multiple theoretical frameworks for explaining variations in success among different groups (Cabrera, Castaneda, Nora, & Hengstler 1992). Given our emphasis on prediction and control, this brief review will necessarily be circumscribed to focus on the three categories of predictors noted above: (1) individual characteristics (including prior experiences) of the entering college student, (2) institutional characteristics, and (3) environmental contingencies (place of residence, etc.).

## Pre-College Characteristics

Researchers have repeatedly found that students' chances of degree attainment are to a substantial degree a function of their own individual backgrounds (Astin 1993a; Carter 2001; Pascarella & Terenzini 1991; Tinto 1993). These variables include school grades, gender, ethnicity, parental income and education, standardized test scores, and age. Although the predictive power of traditional admissions criteria varies somewhat from study to study, standardized test scores and high school grades have consistently been shown to be among the strongest predictors of degree attainment among undergraduates (Astin 1993b; Astin, Tsui, & Avalos 1996; Astin & Oseguera 2003; Pascarella, Smart, & Ethington 1986; Stoecker, Pascarella, & Wolfe 1988; Titus 2003). There is some evidence to suggest, however, that standardized test scores may not be as predictive of degree completion as originally posited, especially for students of color. Fleming and Garcia (1998) reviewed twelve studies of predictive validity and showed that test scores and grades differed in their ability to predict retention among non-White students. Over the last thirteen years, Fleming and Garcia have concluded that SAT scores and high school grades are consistent predictors of degree completion for White students but that their predictive power for Black students is inconsistent.

Both parental education and parental income have been shown to affect college completion directly and indirectly (Astin 1993b; Astin & Oseguera 2003; Mow & Nettles 1990; Oseguera 2004). The student's initial aspirations and goals have also been shown to be significant predictors of college completion (Astin 1975; Bean 1982; Pascarella, Smart, Ethington, & Nettles 1987). Generally, the higher the level of one's educational or occupational aspirations, the greater the likelihood of college completion.

Studies also provide some support to suggest that social integration is useful in examining degree completion. D. F. Allen and J. M. Nelson's (1989) and Cabrera, Nora, and Castaneda's (1992) single-institution studies both reported that a student's level of social integration is significantly and positively related to eventual degree completion. This finding was also confirmed in multi-institutional studies which defined social integration in terms of measures such as peer relations, participation in extracurricular activities and student clubs, participation in student government, and satisfaction with social life (Astin 1993b; Braxton, Vesper, & Hossler 1995; House 1996; Munro 1981). With respect to gender differences, Stage (1988) found that social integration, as measured by peer group relations, residency, and hours spent engaged in social activities and intercollegiate athletics, was more influential in degree completion among men than among women.

In separate, national studies of degree completion using data from the Cooperative Institutional Research Program (CIRP),[1] degree completion was found to be enhanced by expecting to join a fraternity or sorority, participating in volunteer or community service, being elected to student office, maintaining a social activist agenda (i.e., desire to be a community leader, desire to influence social values), and participating in student groups. However, the student's chances of persisting toward a degree were negatively affected by engaging in hedonistic activities (i.e., smoking cigarettes, drinking beer, partying) and socializing with friends (Astin 1993b; Dey & Astin 1989; Astin & Oseguera 2003).

In a national study of college students using CIRP data, Dey and Astin (1989) found that commitment to goals such as raising a family and influencing social values were positive predictors of degree completion. Wanting to write original works, expecting to develop a meaningful philosophy of life, and wanting to get involved in programs to clean up the environment were negative predictors. In another multicampus study of college freshmen, Astin and Oseguera (2003) found that self-ratings of academic ability, drive to achieve, and intellectual self-confidence are positively predictive of degree completion.

## Institutional Characteristics

This literature is necessarily limited to multi-institutional studies. Several researchers have found that institutional control, size, costs, and selectivity affect a variety of educational outcomes, including degree attainment (Astin 1993a; McClelland 1990; Smith 1990). The available research on institutional control (public vs. private) is not entirely consistent, but it does suggest that attending a private rather than a public college or university has a net positive influence on bachelor's degree attainment, even after controlling for pre-college characteristics (Astin 1977; Thomas & Bean 1988). In a national longitudinal study of undergraduates, Astin and Oseguera (2003) and Oseguera (2004) confirmed an earlier national study by Astin, Tsui, and Avalos (1996) that found that small institutional size, private control, and selectivity all have positive effects on degree completion.

In a later study, Astin (1993b) found that degree completion was positively affected by the percentage of resources invested in student services, the percentage of graduate students in the student body, the percentage of Catholics in the student body, and the percentage of students majoring in physical sciences, and negatively affected by institutional size. Also, as reported in earlier studies (Astin 1977, 1982), the percentage of men enrolled in the student body had a negative effect on degree attainment.

Attending institutions with a large percentage of student commuters negatively influences both four-year and six-year degree completion (Astin 1993b; Oseguera 2004; Sjoberg 1999). In all likelihood, having a lot of commuting students detracts from the institution's ability to create a climate that encourages student engagement with campus resources, facilities, and personnel.

Student retention is also enhanced in institutions that have relatively large expenditures on instruction and academic support services and a lower student faculty ratio (Oseguera 2004; Sjoberg 1999).

## Environmental "Contingencies"

Evidence on the effect of the entering student's preferred academic major tends to be mixed because, according to Hearn (1987), the study of academic majors is "complex and multidimensional." Nevertheless, college major has been shown to influence degree completion (Hartnett & Centra 1977; Astin & Oseguera 2003; Oseguera 2004). Specifically, students in engineering and the hard sciences are less likely to attain a baccalaureate degree within four years (Astin 1975, 1993b; Oseguera 2004), while students in the social sciences have the highest rates of degree completion (Mow & Nettles 1990; Pascarella, Ethington, & Smart 1988).

Financial concerns are commonly cited in the research literature as important reasons students give for their departure from college. In a meta-analysis of thirty-one studies of the effect of financial aid on college persistence, Murdock (1987) showed that family influences play a small yet significant influence on college persistence. Murdock reported that students from lower socioeconomic[2] (SES) levels consistently report that financial burdens influence the decision to withdraw from college. Additionally, among the noncompleters, Murdock reported that concerns about financing college were often cited as a greater influence for students who dropped out earlier in their degree programs compared to students who dropped out at the later stages of their degree programs. These findings were later confirmed by Cabrera, Stampen, and Hansen (1990) in their analysis of financial aid utilizing a combination of theoretical frameworks and financial aid literature. Some research, however, suggests that there are trivial or no significant effects of financing college on eventual degree completion (Stampen & Cabrera 1986).

Working full time clearly appears to impede persistence among traditional age students (Astin 1975; K. Anderson 1981). Part-time work, however, does not appear to produce similarly negative effects, and employment on campus can positively influence degree completion (Anderson 1981; Astin & Oseguera 2003; Oseguera 2004). Related factors that have been posited to influence degree completion are students' commitments that are external to the institution (Tinto 1993). Having responsibilities off campus and having outside family commitments, for example, have been shown to negatively influence degree attainment of undergraduates (Tinto 1993; Astin & Oseguera 2003).

There is another class of environmental contingencies that we might call "post-entry" contingencies that will not be included in the present study because they cannot be known at the time the student first enters college (i.e., they cannot be used in computing pre-college estimates of the student's chances of completing the degree). However, since these post-entry contingencies are often included in retention models and have been shown to have substantial relationships with degree completion, we shall briefly review some of the recent research that utilizes them.

Past research has demonstrated, for example, that academic achievement during college powerfully influences degree attainment (Astin 1975, 1993a; Carter 2001; Tinto 1987, 1993; Titus 2003). (In the current study, pre-college *expectations* for academic success can be viewed as a kind of proxy for actual college achievement.) Other post-entry contingencies that positively affect degree completion include involvement and interactions with faculty and peers (Gurin & Epps 1975; Stoecker, Pascarella, & Wolfe 1988; Astin 1993a) as well as involvement in extracurricular activities (Pascarella & Chapman 1983; Waldo 1986). Involvement in either the academic or social aspects of college has also been shown to positively influence degree attainment of undergraduates (Grosset 1991; Tinto 1993). In sum, the past twenty years of research on undergraduates suggests that involvement with academics, faculty, and peers is the most potent form of positive involvement and that degree completion, in particular, is negatively affected by noninvolvement (Astin 1993a; Pascarella & Terenzini 1991; Tinto 1993).

## METHOD

The data for this study were drawn from a national sample of baccalaureate-granting institutions that participated in the Cooperative Institutional Research Program's annual survey of entering freshmen in the fall of 1994 (Astin, Korn, Sax, & Mahoney 1994). Four-year and six-year degree attainment data were obtained in the summer of 2000 by sending to the registrar at each institution rosters containing names of randomly selected entering freshmen who had completed the 1994 survey. A total of 90,619 students (an average of about 210 per institution) were selected at random from each of 424 institutions in the original national sample. In order to obtain more reliable results by race, all Mexican American/Chicana/o, Puerto Rican, Asian American, and American Indian students as well as 50 percent of all African American students who had participated in the original 1994 survey were included.

Degree attainment data were eventually received on 56,818 cases at 262 institutions. Since data were obtained on virtually 100 percent of the students at each of the institutions that responded to our request, any nonresponse bias would be entirely attributable to institutions (rather than students) that did not comply with the request for data. However, a careful comparison of curricular, financial, and other institutional data between responding ($N = 262$) and nonresponding ($N = 162$) institutions within stratification cells failed to reveal any institutional self-selection bias within stratification cells (as already noted, the CIRP sample is stratified by type, control, race, and selectivity level; see the following text as well as Astin, Korn, Sax, & Mahoney 1994).

The data for this study have been weighted. The CIRP weighting scheme is designed to allow us to approximate the results that would have been obtained if all students from all baccalaureate-granting institutions had participated in both the 1994 entering freshman and 2000 registrar's follow-up surveys. This weighting scheme initially inflates the number of respondents within each institution to the total first-time, full-time freshman enrollment by gender, then compensates for differential sampling of institutions within stratification cells. The CIRP stratification scheme compensates for any institutional sampling bias associated with institutional type (four-year vs. university), control (public, private nonsectarian, Roman Catholic, Other Christian), race (historically Black versus non-Black), and selectivity level (institutions are stratified by selectivity separately within type and control; see Astin, Korn, Sax, & Mahoney 1994). Differential weights were also used to compensate for the oversampling of certain minority groups (see the preceding text). All data reported here are weighted to approximate the national norms for all first-time, full-time entering freshmen in the fall of 1994.

The Higher Education Research Institute (HERI) collects extensive pre-college data on the characteristics of full-time, first-time entering freshmen, including demographic and biographical information, high school grade point averages (GPAs), standardized test scores, degree and career aspirations, self-concept, attitudes, values, and expectations for college. Characteristics of the student's institution that are also collected include size, control, selectivity, region, and type of institution. Environmental contingency data from the CIRP entering freshman survey include the student's place of residence (campus residence hall, private room, with parents), choice of major, and type and amount of financial aid.

For the current analyses we included measures of all pre-college characteristics, institutional characteristics, and environmental contingencies that the persistence literature has identified as potentially having an effect on the baccalaureate degree completion of college students. For a complete list of the variables included in the analyses, see Appendix A.

## Data Analysis

A series of weighted descriptive analyses were run to examine degree attainment differences by institutional type, gender, and academic achievement. To more thoroughly explore the potential value of each variable in estimating the student's chances of completing the baccalaureate degree, we employed a series of stepwise linear regression analyses. The dichotomous dependent variables used in the analyses were either (a) degree completion within four years or (b) degree completion within six years. Our dependent variables were selected based on earlier research (Astin, Tsui, & Avalos 1996) suggesting that time-to-degree is prolonged among certain student subgroups and at certain institutional types. Thus it is important to identify factors that contribute to degree completion within the traditional four-year time frame, as well as factors that contribute to this "delayed" degree completion.

Although logistic regression analysis is often recommended over Ordinary Least Squares (OLS) regression in the study of dichotomous outcomes, extensive empirical comparisons of the two methods using CIRP data show that they yield essentially identical results (Dey & Astin 1993; Oseguera & Vogelgesang 2003). Accordingly, we chose to use OLS regression because the Statistical Package for the Social Sciences (SPSS) program includes important options (e.g., "beta in" for variables not in the equation) not available in the Stata logistic regression program.

In each regression analysis the independent variables were organized into three blocks according to their presumed temporal order of occurrence: (1) pre-college entering student characteristics, (2) environmental contingencies, and (3) institutional characteristics. Within each block, variables were entered in forward stepwise fashion until no additional variable within that block was capable of producing a reduction in the residual sum of squares exceeding $p = 0.0001$. Given the large number of independent variables, the $p$ value was set at this extreme level to minimize Type I errors. And, given the large $N$ available for each regression (56,818), Type II errors were also minimized.

A final set of regressions was run to provide a means of comparing variables that predicted degree completion within four and six years. The procedure was as follows. Separate regressions were first run for each of the two dependent variables, as previously described. Then, the two regressions were rerun with the following modification: all independent variables that entered *either* of the first set of regressions were force entered into both regressions. In this way, both regressions contained exactly the same set of independent variables.

## RESULTS

The results are presented in four sections. First, we examine the descriptive results, which show weighted differences in degree attainment by institutional type, gender, and secondary school achievement. In the next three sections we review factors that entered the regression analyses as the strongest predictors of degree attainment within four and six years of college entry.

### Degree Attainment by Institutional Type, Gender, and High School Grades

Table 9.1 shows the overall degree attainment rates using two different time periods. Only about one in three students (36 percent) was able to complete a bachelor's degree within four years of entering college. However, this number rises by a remarkable 22 percent (to 58 percent) if we allow six years for degree completion.[3] These four-year results reinforce the popular conception that four-year degree completion rates in American higher education have been declining. Looking at both time periods makes it clear that students today may also be taking longer to graduate.

Today, degree attainment rates vary substantially by type of institution. The highest six-year rate is in the private university (80 percent), with the lowest rate in the public college (47 percent). These differences by institutional type are no doubt partially attributable to the varying preparation levels of the students entering different types of institutions. For example, nearly 70 percent of the students entering private universities, compared to only about 30 percent of those entering public four-year colleges, have an A grade average from high school (Sax, Astin, Korn, & Mahoney 2000). Similarly, while each of the three types of private four-year colleges enrolls freshmen who are better prepared than those entering the four-year public colleges (39–42 percent versus only 30 percent

**Table 9.1**
**Four-Year and Six-Year Degree Attainment Rates, by Institutional Type**

| | Unweighted N | | Weighted percent completing bachelor's degree within | |
| Institutional type | Students | Institutions | 4 years | 6 years |
|---|---|---|---|---|
| Public university | 6,650 | 20 | 28 | 58 |
| Private university | 4,931 | 18 | 67 | 80 |
| Public college | 7,457 | 27 | 24 | 47 |
| Nonsectarian college | 17,610 | 75 | 56 | 66 |
| Catholic college | 5,436 | 38 | 46 | 60 |
| Other Christian college | 14,734 | 84 | 51 | 61 |
| All institutions | 56,818 | 262 | 36 | 58 |

Note: Weighted to approximate national norms for 1994 freshmen.

have an A grade average from high school), four-year college freshmen in general are substantially less prepared than are freshmen entering private universities (where 70 percent have an A grade average from high school). The public university is the only type of institution that does not follow this pattern: while their entering freshmen are better prepared (50 percent have an A average from high school) than freshmen at all other types of institutions except private universities, their four-year degree attainment rates continue to be much lower than the rates at all three types of private colleges, and even their six-year rates remain slightly lower. Apparently, the relatively low degree completion rate shown by students attending public universities cannot be attributed to the students' level of academic preparation at the time of college entry. Multivariate analyses (see the following text) will shed more light on these issues.

The data in Table 9.1 also suggest that certain types of institutions are especially likely to prolong the time students spend in obtaining a bachelor's degree. For example, the absolute differences in four-year and six-year degree attainment rates are 30 and 23 percent, respectively, for public universities and public colleges, compared to only 10 percent for nonsectarian and Christian (non-Catholic) colleges. Why the students at public institutions should be taking so long to complete their degrees is not clear, but given the rapidly declining state support for public institutions, this would certainly appear to be an important topic for future

**Table 9.2**
**Four-Year and Six-Year Degree Attainment Rates, by Gender**

|            | Weighted percent completing bachelor's degree | | |
|            | Men | Women | Total |
|------------|-----|-------|-------|
| 4 years    | 33  | 40    | 36    |
| 6 years    | 55  | 60    | 58    |

Note: Weighted to approximate national norms for 1994 freshmen.

research. In other words, if public institutions could find ways to help more students complete their degrees in four years, they could substantially increase their "throughput" of students without significant additional resources.

Table 9.2 shows the four-year and six-year degree attainment rates for men and women. Women are more likely than men are to attain the bachelor's degree, regardless of the time period or category. This finding confirms and extends earlier national studies (Astin 1971, 1975, 1982, 1993b; Astin, Tsui, & Avalos 1996), which have consistently shown that women, as compared to men, are more likely to complete their bachelor's degrees. These data show that such gender differences decrease slightly with time. Nevertheless, a 5 percent gender gap remains six years after college entry.

Table 9.3 shows the effect of high school grades on each degree attainment measure. School grades are indeed a major determinant of the student's chances of completing college, regardless of whether degree completion is set at four or six years. Thus, if we look at degree completion within six years, we find that students who enter college with A grade averages are four times more likely to finish college than are students with C grade averages or less. When it comes to completion within four years, the ratio is more than seven to one. Despite the relatively crude nature of our seven-letter grade categories, differences between categories are quite similar, ranging from a low of about 7 percent to a high around 12 percent for those completing within six years. This would suggest that the relationship comes reasonably close to being linear (especially for six-year completion), despite the arbitrary nature of letter grades.

Table 9.3
**Four-Year and Six-Year Degree Attainment Rates, by Average High School Grade (HSG)**

| Average high school grade | Unweighted N | Percentage of students who receive bachelor's degree within | |
| --- | --- | --- | --- |
| | | 4 years | 6 years |
| A, A+ | 12,112 | 58 | 78 |
| A− | 12,261 | 47 | 68 |
| B+ | 12,090 | 35 | 59 |
| B | 11,434 | 25 | 48 |
| B− | 4,527 | 19 | 40 |
| C+ | 2,582 | 15 | 33 |
| C or lower | 1,212 | 8 | 20 |

Note: Weighted to approximate national norms for 1994 freshmen.

## Pre-College Characteristics Influencing Degree Attainment

The results of the second set of regressions are summarized in Table 9.4. Clearly, the pre-college characteristic that carries the most weight in estimating the student's chances of completing college is the high school GPA. Its unique predictive power (i.e., after taking into account all other pre-college characteristics) is almost identical for both four-year and six-year degree completion: betas of 0.15 and 0.16, respectively. This contrasts with the results for admissions test scores (SAT or ACT Composite), which produced betas (after all other pre-college characteristics were controlled) of 0.12 and 0.08. Further, while the betas for high school grades do not change when institutional and contingency variables are controlled, controlling these additional variables further shrinks the betas for test scores to only 0.05 and 0.03. These contrasts are all the more interesting in light of the fact that the *simple* correlations of GPA and test scores with degree completion are quite similar: 0.30 versus 0.29, respectively (four-year completion), and 0.27 versus 0.24 for six-year completion. An inspection of the step-by-step results indicates that in addition to high school grades, the other entering variables that attenuate the relationship between test scores and degree completion are father's educational level, years of foreign language study in high school, living in a residence hall, and institutional selectivity. In other words, *the main reasons why admission test scores are related to college degree comple-*

**Table 9.4**
**Summary of Four- and Six-Year Regressions (N = 48,277)**

| | Simple $r$ | | Beta after inputs | | Final beta | |
|---|---|---|---|---|---|---|
| | 4 year | 6 year | 4 year | 6 year | 4 year | 6 year |
| *Entering characteristics* | | | | | | |
| Gender: female | 0.09 | 0.05 | 0.04 | <u>0.01</u> | 0.04 | <u>0.01</u> |
| High school grades | 0.30 | 0.27 | 0.15 | <u>0.16</u> | 0.15 | <u>0.16</u> |
| Standardized test scores | 0.29 | 0.24 | 0.12 | 0.08 | 0.05 | 0.03 |
| Race: American Indian | −0.06 | −0.06 | −0.02 | −0.03 | −0.01 | −0.02 |
| Religion: Catholic | 0.01 | 0.02 | 0.02 | 0.03 | 0.03 | 0.03 |
| Religion: Jewish | 0.07 | 0.05 | 0.03 | 0.03 | 0.02 | 0.02 |
| Years study: foreign language | 0.23 | 0.18 | 0.10 | 0.08 | 0.06 | 0.05 |
| Activity: smoked cigarettes | −0.10 | −0.12 | −0.06 | −0.07 | −0.06 | −0.07 |
| Activity: overslept & missed class | −0.09 | −0.09 | −0.04 | −0.04 | −0.05 | −0.04 |
| Self-rating: artistic ability | −0.01 | 0.00 | −0.03 | <u>−0.01</u> | −0.02 | <u>−0.01</u> |
| Self-rating: creativity | −0.01 | −0.01 | −0.02 | <u>−0.02</u> | −0.02 | <u>−0.02</u> |
| Self-rating: emotional health | 0.07 | 0.07 | 0.04 | 0.04 | 0.05 | 0.04 |
| Self-rating: understanding of others | 0.01 | 0.00 | −0.03 | −0.02 | −0.03 | −0.02 |
| Parental income | 0.14 | 0.12 | 0.02 | 0.02 | 0.02 | <u>0.01</u> |
| Father's educational level | 0.19 | 0.16 | 0.05 | 0.05 | 0.04 | <u>0.04</u> |
| Mother's educational level | 0.16 | 0.14 | 0.03 | 0.04 | 0.02 | 0.03 |
| Hours per week: studying/ homework | 0.18 | 0.15 | 0.05 | 0.04 | 0.03 | 0.03 |
| Hours per week: student clubs | 0.13 | 0.10 | 0.04 | 0.02 | 0.02 | 0.02 |
| Hours per week: reading for pleasure | 0.02 | −0.01 | −0.03 | −0.04 | −0.03 | −0.04 |
| Future activity: work full-time | −0.12 | −0.10 | −0.04 | −0.04 | −0.02 | −0.02 |
| Future activity: play intercollegiate athletics | 0.00 | −0.01 | 0.03 | <u>0.00</u> | −0.01 | −0.02 |
| Future activity: need extra time for degree | −0.12 | −0.06 | −0.06 | <u>−0.01</u> | −0.03 | <u>0.00</u> |
| Future activity: participate in volunteer work | 0.15 | 0.12 | 0.04 | 0.03 | 0.02 | 0.02 |
| Parents alive and living together | 0.08 | 0.09 | 0.02 | 0.03 | 0.02 | 0.03 |
| *Environmental Contingencies* | | | | | | |
| Major: engineering | −0.06 | 0.00 | −0.07 | −0.02 | −0.07 | −0.03 |
| Major: health professions | −0.03 | −0.02 | −0.04 | −0.03 | −0.04 | −0.03 |
| Major: fine arts | −0.03 | −0.02 | −0.01 | <u>−0.01</u> | −0.03 | <u>−0.01</u> |
| Aid: parents or family | 0.14 | 0.11 | 0.05 | 0.04 | <u>0.01</u> | 0.02 |
| Aid: summer savings | 0.06 | 0.06 | 0.03 | 0.04 | 0.02 | 0.03 |

**Table 9.4 (continued)**

|  | Simple r | | Beta after inputs | | Final beta | |
|---|---|---|---|---|---|---|
|  | 4 year | 6 year | 4 year | 6 year | 4 year | 6 year |
| Aid: other savings | 0.07 | 0.07 | 0.03 | 0.03 | 0.02 | 0.02 |
| Aid: part-time work on campus | −0.12 | −0.10 | −0.05 | −0.05 | −0.03 | −0.03 |
| Aid: full-time work | −0.06 | −0.06 | −0.01 | −0.02 | 0.00 | −0.02 |
| Live plan: residence hall | 0.18 | 0.13 | 0.10 | 0.07 | 0.04 | 0.04 |
| *Institutional characteristics* | | | | | | |
| Type: public university | −0.18 | −0.07 | −0.13 | −0.04 | −0.15 | −0.04 |
| Type: private university | 0.10 | 0.09 | 0.02 | 0.02 | −0.02 | −0.01 |
| Type: public 4-year college | −0.19 | −0.12 | −0.12 | −0.06 | −0.11 | −0.04 |
| Selectivity | 0.32 | 0.26 | 0.16 | 0.12 | 0.16 | 0.11 |

Note: All variables significant at $p < 0.0001$ unless otherwise noted.
Underlined coefficients: $0.01 > p > 0.0001$.
Underlined coefficients: $p > 0.01$.

tion is that students with high test scores also tend to get good grades and take more years of foreign language in high school, have well-educated parents, attend selective colleges, and live in campus residence halls during their freshman year. Once these other factors are taken into account, admissions test scores are only weakly related to degree completion.

After high school grades, the two pre-college variables showing the strongest unique effects on degree completion are smoking cigarettes (final betas of −0.06 and −0.07, respectively, for four-year and six-year completion) and years of foreign language study in high school (betas of 0.06 and 0.05).[4] In other words, even after other pre-college and institutional characteristics are controlled, the data show that nonsmokers and students who take a lot of foreign language courses have higher-than-average rates of college completion.

Other pre-college factors that contribute to our ability to estimate a student's chances of completing a bachelor's degree can be briefly summarized as follows:

Positive Factors (final betas for four-year and six-year degree completion):

- Father's educational level (0.04, 0.04)
- Mother's educational level (0.02, 0.03)
- Parents alive and living with each other (0.02, 0.03)

- Parental income (0.02, 0.01*)
- Gender: female (0.04, 0.01*)
- Religion: Roman Catholic (0.03, 0.03)
- Religion: Jewish (0.02, 0.02)
- Self-rated emotional health (0.05, 0.04)
- Plan to participate in community service (0.02, 0.02)
- Time spent in student clubs and groups (0.02, 0.02)

$p < 0.0001$, *$p > 0.0001$

Negative Factors:

- Race: American Indian (−0.01, −0.02)
- Will need extra time to get degree (−0.03, 0.00*)
- Plan to work full time (−0.02, −0.02)
- Overslept and missed a class or appointment (−0.05, −0.04)
- Hours spent reading for pleasure (−0.03, −0.04)
- Self-rated understanding of others (−0.03, −0.02)
- Self-rated artistic ability (−0.02, −0.01*)
- Self-rated creativity (−0.02, −0.02)

$p < 0.0001$, *$p > 0.0001$

Two patterns stand out from these lists. First, it seems clear that coming from an intact and socioeconomically advantaged family facilitates degree completion, even when prior achievement, test scores, and various motivational factors are taken into account. Second, students who are prone to become involved (who participate in community service or student clubs or groups) enjoy a greater likelihood of degree completion, whereas indicators of noninvolvement in college (full-time work, missing classes) are negatively related to degree completion. The fact that the student's self-rated emotional health at the time of entry is also positively related to degree completion suggests that student counseling and health services might well be able to play an important role in helping to enhance degree completion rates. Finally, it should be noted that several of the findings that might seem counterintuitive—the negative effects of reading for pleasure and self-rated artistic ability, creativity, and understanding of others—have been reported in previous studies (Astin 1975, 1977, 1993b).

## Environmental Contingencies Affecting Degree Attainment

The contingency showing the strongest positive effect on degree completion is living in a residence hall during the freshman year. Although the final beta was 0.04 for both four-year and six-year retention, these coefficients were substantially larger—0.10 (four-year) and 0.08 (six-year)—before other environmental and institutional variables were controlled. The shrinkage in these coefficients occurred primarily because students who live in residence halls tend to attend selective institutions and to finance college primarily through personal savings and parental support. Other contingency variables showing significant positive effects on degree completion all had to do with financing college: the amount of support provided by savings from summer work (final betas of 0.02 and 0.03, respectively, for four-year and six-year degree completion), other savings (0.02 and 0.02), and parents (0.01 and 0.02). While this next-to-last coefficient (i.e., four-year degree completion) is not significant at the extreme level we have set ($0.0001 < p < 0.01$), it is highly significant (beta = 0.05) prior to the entry of institutional characteristics.

Environmental contingencies showing negative effects on degree completion included one financial variable—off-campus employment (betas = −0.03 for both four-year and six-year degree completion)—and three fields of study: engineering (−0.07, −0.03), health professions (−0.04, −0.03), and fine arts (−0.03 and −0.01) (this last coefficient is not significant [$0.0001 < p < 0.01$]). Given that the six-year coefficients tend to be much smaller than the two-year coefficients, these results suggest that engineering and fine arts students are more likely than other students to take more than four years to complete their baccalaureate degrees.

In sum, these findings once again underscore the importance of student involvement: students are more likely to finish college if they are able to live in a campus residence hall during their freshman year and if they do not have to work off campus. Both findings, incidentally, have been replicated in numerous earlier studies (e.g., Astin 1975, 1977, 1993b; Chickering 1974; Pascarella & Terenzini 1991).

## Institutional Characteristics Affecting Degree Completion

The institutional characteristic showing the strongest effect on degree completion is selectivity: final betas = 0.16 and 0.11, respectively, for four-year and six-year completion. For four-year completion, the unique effect of selectivity (final beta = 0.16) is as strong as the unique effect of high school grades (final beta = 0.15). (Indeed, the simple correlations of high school grades and institutional selectivity with four-year degree completion—0.30 and 0.32, respectively—slightly favor selectivity.) Highly selective institutions, of course, tend to have more resources than less selective institutions do, but their most important asset is more likely to be the student peer group, which tends to be better prepared academically, to be more highly motivated, and to come from higher socioeconomic levels than are the peer groups at less selective institutions. Again, this is a finding that has been reported in many earlier studies (e.g., Astin 1982, 1993b).

Two other institutional characteristics also showed substantial effects on degree completion, but in this instance the effects were both negative: public university (final betas = −0.15 and −0.04 for four-year and six-year retention, respectively) and public four-year college (−0.11 and −0.04). Once again, this negative effect of attending a public institution replicates earlier studies (Astin 1975, 1977, 1982, 1993b). Note, however, the sharp decline in the size of the coefficients when we switch from four-year to six-year degree attainment, a finding that suggests that many students will take longer to complete their degrees if they attend a public rather than private college or university. Although there are many possible reasons for this effect, the large size and impersonal atmosphere of many public institutions no doubt play a significant role (Astin 1993b).

## CONCLUSION

The national longitudinal study discussed in this chapter is concerned with the prediction and control of baccalaureate degree completion. The four-year and six-year degree attainment data used in this study, which involves more than 50,000 undergraduates attending 262 colleges and universities, suggest that fewer and fewer students today are graduating from institutions of higher education within four years of college entry. Even if some of these students manage to complete their degrees within six or more years, these trends should cause concern to higher education personnel and policymakers, given that colleges and universities throughout the country are becoming increasingly overcrowded and underfunded. With the swell of enrollment that is expected in the years to come, especially in the public institutions (where retention is declining and time-to-degree is increasing), it is especially important to identify the reasons why so many students are either not being retained or taking longer and longer to graduate.

Multivariate analyses indicate that degree completion is a complex phenomenon that can be affected by a variety of student pre-college characteristics, environmental contingencies, and institutional characteristics. Although the secondary school grade average continues to be the strongest pre-college predictor of the student's chances of completing a bachelor's degree within four or six years after starting college, a number of other demographic and personal characteristics contribute significantly to our ability to estimate the student's chances of completing college. Those students with the best chances of finishing college thus tend to have good grades in high school, to come from intact families that are affluent and well educated, and to show a propensity to become highly involved or engaged in the social and academic life of the institution. Of particular interest is the finding that once these factors are taken into account, scores on standardized admissions tests add little to our ability to estimate the student's degree completion chances.

The student's chances of completing college can also be affected by a number of environmental contingencies. Degree completion chances can be enhanced if the student lives in a residence hall during the freshman year and is able to finance a good proportion of college expenses through parental support or personal savings. Chances are reduced if the student has to work off campus or starts college with plans to major in engineering, fine arts, or allied health professions. Majoring in such fields also tends to prolong the time to a degree. Among other things, these findings suggest that degree completion rates can be enhanced if (a) more students are provided with opportunities to live on campus and (b) more opportunities are created for part-time employment on the campus.

The institutional characteristic that has the strongest effect on the student's chances of completing the bachelor's degree is the selectivity of the college or university attended: the more selective the institution, the better the student's chances of finishing. Attending a public college or university, on the other hand, reduces the student's chances of finishing and prolongs the time to the degree. These finding present a special challenge for public institutions to find more effective ways to help students complete their undergraduate studies in four years.

# APPENDIX A:
## Variables Used in Full Regressions

### I. ENTERING CHARACTERISTICS

**Background**

- Father's education
- Mother's education
- Parents' income
- Student's sex: female/male
- Parents' status
    *Both alive—living together
    *Both alive—divorced or separated
    *One or both deceased
- Student's age
- Student native English speaker
- Student's religion
    *Catholic
    *Protestant
    *Jewish
    *Other religion
    *No religion
- Student's race
    *African American
    *American Indian
    *Asian American
    *Mexican American/Chicano
    *Puerto Rican American
    *Caucasian
- Citizenship status
    *U.S. citizen
    *U.S. resident

## Academic

- High school GPA
- SAT composite
- Degree aspirations

## Activities in Past Year

- Attended a religious service
- Was bored in class
- Participated in organized demonstrations
- Studied with other students
- Was a guest in a professor's home
- Smoked cigarettes
- Drank beer or wine or liquor
- Performed volunteer work
- Came late to class
- Played a musical instrument
- Overslept and missed class or appointment
- Discussed politics
- Discussed religion

## Self-Ratings

- Academic ability
- Artistic ability
- Competitiveness
- Cooperativeness
- Creativity
- Drive to achieve
- Emotional health
- Leadership ability
- Mathematical ability
- Physical health
- Popularity
- Public speaking ability
- Self-confidence (intellectual)

- Self-confidence (social)
- Understanding of others
- Writing ability

## Reasons for Attending College

- Parents wanted me to go
- Could not find a job
- Wanted to get away from home
- Get a better job
- Gain a general education
- Improve reading and study skills
- Nothing better to do
- Become a more cultured person
- Make more money
- Learn more about the things that interest me
- Prepare for graduate or professional school
- Role model/mentor encouraged me

## Student Opinions

- Too much concern for the rights of criminals
- Abortion should be legal
- Abolish death penalty
- Activities of married women best at home
- Marijuana should be legalized
- Prohibit homosexual relations
- Employers can require drug testing
- Federal government should do more to control handguns
- College should prohibit racist/sexist speech
- Wealthy people should pay more taxes

## Hours per Week in Last Year Spent

- Studying or doing homework
- Socializing with friends
- Talking with a teacher outside of class

- Exercising or sports
- Partying
- Working for pay
- Volunteer work
- Student clubs or groups
- Watching TV
- Household or childcare duties
- Reading for pleasure

## Goals and Values

- Become accomplished in performing arts
- Become authority in own field
- Obtain recognition from colleagues
- Influence the political structure
- Influence social values
- Raise a family
- Have administrative responsibility
- Be very well off financially
- Help others in difficulty
- Make theoretical contribution to science
- Write original works
- Create artistic work
- Be successful in own business
- Develop meaningful philosophy of life
- Participate in community action program
- Promote racial understanding
- Keep up to date with political affairs
- Be a community leader

## Possible Future Activities

- Change major field
- Change career choice
- Get job to help pay expenses
- Graduate with honors

- Work full-time while attending college
- Play varsity or intercollegiate athletics
- Make at least a B average
- Need extra time for degree
- Get a bachelor's degree
- Participate in student protests
- Drop out temporarily
- Drop out permanently
- Participate in volunteer or community service work

## II. ENVIRONMENTAL CONTINGENCY VARIABLES

### Sources of Financial Aid

- Parental or family aid
- Savings from summer work
- Full-time job while in college
- Part-time job while in college
- Pell grant
- State scholarship or grant
- College work-study grant
- Other college grant
- Other private grant
- Federal guaranteed student loan
- National direct student loan
- Other college loan

### Undergraduate Student Majors

- Agriculture
- Biological sciences
- Business
- Education
- Engineering
- English

- Health professional
- History or political science
- Humanities
- Fine arts
- Mathematics or statistics
- Physical science
- Social science
- Other technical
- Other nontechnical
- Undecided

**First Year Living Arrangements**

- Plan to live: home
- Plan to live: college dormitory
- Plan to live: other on campus, not dorm
- Plan to live: off campus, not at home

# III. INSTITUTIONAL CHARACTERISTICS

**Institutional Size**

**Institutional Selectivity**

**Type/Control**

- Public university
- Private university
- Public 4-year college
- Nonsectarian 4-year
- Catholic 4-year
- Other Christian 4-year
- Historically Black college
- Hispanic serving institution
- Women's college

## IV. DEPENDENT MEASURES

- Retention within four years
- Retention within six years

# Appendix B
## Complete Variable List of Four-Year and Six-Year Regressions

| | Four-year regression | | | | Six-year regression | | | |
|---|---|---|---|---|---|---|---|---|
| | Simple r | Beta after inputs | Beta after contingency | Final beta | Simple r | Beta after inputs | Beta after contingency | Final beta |
| *Entering characteristics* | | | | | | | | |
| Gender: female | 0.0876 | 0.0437 | 0.0322 | 0.0359 | 0.0506 | 0.0090 | 0.0067 | 0.0083 |
| High school grades | 0.3025 | 0.1545 | 0.1556 | 0.1537 | 0.2745 | 0.1633 | 0.1641 | 0.1565 |
| Standardized test scores | 0.2914 | 0.1236 | 0.1099 | 0.0513 | 0.2368 | 0.0840 | 0.0732 | 0.0288 |
| Race: White | 0.0713 | 0.0262 | 0.0110 | 0.0020 | 0.0457 | 0.0046 | −0.0067 | 0.0020 |
| Race: American Indian | −0.0626 | −0.0243 | −0.0248 | −0.0145 | −0.0582 | −0.0290 | −0.0292 | −0.0224 |
| Religion: Catholic | 0.0093 | 0.0243 | 0.0266 | 0.0275 | 0.0192 | 0.0311 | 0.0313 | 0.0294 |
| Religion: Jewish | 0.0652 | 0.0318 | 0.0335 | 0.0227 | 0.0497 | 0.0258 | 0.0268 | 0.0173 |
| Years study: foreign language | 0.2261 | 0.0951 | 0.0829 | 0.0565 | 0.1820 | 0.0779 | 0.0698 | 0.0550 |
| Activity: smoked cigarettes | −0.1048 | −0.0579 | −0.0571 | −0.0604 | −0.1182 | −0.0724 | −0.0716 | −0.0738 |
| Activity: overslept & missed class | −0.0949 | −0.0409 | −0.0417 | −0.0454 | −0.0945 | −0.0430 | −0.0425 | −0.0442 |
| Self-rating: artistic ability | −0.0076 | −0.0286 | −0.0204 | −0.0197 | −0.0022 | −0.0123 | −0.0082 | −0.0088 |
| Self-rating: creativity | −0.0087 | −0.0167 | −0.0184 | −0.0183 | −0.0138 | −0.0217 | −0.0233 | −0.0235 |
| Self-rating: emotional health | 0.0697 | 0.0419 | 0.0445 | 0.0451 | 0.0683 | 0.0412 | 0.0422 | 0.0414 |
| Self-rating: intellectual self-confidence | 0.0728 | −0.0287 | −0.0284 | −0.0144 | 0.0607 | −0.0287 | −0.0261 | −0.0190 |
| Self-rating: understanding of others | 0.0056 | −0.0269 | −0.0272 | −0.0281 | 0.0005 | −0.0214 | −0.0205 | −0.0209 |
| Parental income | 0.1439 | 0.0244 | 0.0224 | 0.0155 | 0.1217 | 0.0223 | 0.0168 | 0.0119 |
| Father's educational level | 0.1878 | 0.0528 | 0.0451 | 0.0356 | 0.1612 | 0.0513 | 0.0447 | 0.0391 |
| Mother's educational level | 0.1641 | 0.0337 | 0.0264 | 0.0207 | 0.1401 | 0.0353 | 0.0291 | 0.0258 |
| Reason for college: become more cultured | 0.0874 | 0.0266 | 0.0204 | 0.0132 | 0.0653 | 0.0166 | 0.0131 | 0.0090 |
| Reason for college: gain general education | 0.0887 | 0.0237 | 0.0184 | 0.0100 | 0.0708 | 0.0209 | 0.0174 | 0.0128 |
| Hours per week: studying/homework | 0.1750 | 0.0513 | 0.0501 | 0.0302 | 0.1491 | 0.0437 | 0.0418 | 0.0295 |
| Hours per week: student clubs | 0.1258 | 0.0367 | 0.0243 | 0.0220 | 0.0968 | 0.0239 | 0.0160 | 0.0157 |
| Hours per week: housework/childcare | −0.0376 | −0.0324 | −0.0258 | −0.0155 | −0.0344 | −0.0232 | −0.0191 | −0.0132 |

| | | | | | | | | |
|---|---|---|---|---|---|---|---|---|
| Hours per week: reading for pleasure | 0.0214 | −0.0259 | −0.0288 | −0.0300 | −0.0078 | −0.0413 | −0.0421 | −0.0424 |
| Goal: make theoretical contribution to science | −0.0191 | −0.0286 | −0.0086 | **−0.0103** | −0.0022 | −0.0142 | −0.0037 | −0.0072 |
| Future activity: change career choice | 0.0801 | 0.0326 | 0.0168 | 0.0085 | 0.0716 | 0.0294 | 0.0192 | **0.0121** |
| Future activity: work full-time | −0.1229 | −0.0422 | −0.0251 | −0.0201 | −0.1048 | −0.0392 | −0.0253 | −0.0234 |
| Future activity: play intercollegiate athletics | −0.0030 | 0.0267 | **0.0114** | −0.0147 | −0.0078 | 0.0050 | −0.0045 | −0.0156 |
| Future activity: need extra time for degree | −0.1234 | −0.0609 | −0.0532 | −0.0293 | −0.0630 | −0.0098 | −0.0072 | 0.0040 |
| Future activity: participate in volunteer work | 0.1495 | 0.0391 | 0.0268 | 0.0172 | 0.1171 | 0.0281 | 0.0216 | 0.0193 |
| Parents alive and living together | 0.0822 | 0.0184 | 0.0164 | 0.0218 | 0.0865 | 0.0280 | 0.0255 | 0.0297 |
| *Environmental contingency* | | | | | | | | |
| Major: engineering | −0.0619 | −0.0736 | −0.0772 | −0.0705 | −0.0016 | −0.0199 | −0.0226 | −0.0268 |
| Major: health professions | −0.0319 | −0.0395 | −0.0505 | −0.0395 | −0.0213 | −0.0307 | −0.0343 | −0.0289 |
| Major: fine arts | −0.0347 | −0.0148 | −0.0259 | −0.0265 | −0.0217 | −0.0052 | **−0.0111** | **−0.0119** |
| Major: other technical | −0.0316 | **−0.0126** | −0.0198 | −0.0157 | −0.0255 | −0.0128 | −0.0152 | **−0.0138** |
| Aid: parents or family | 0.1400 | 0.0533 | 0.0363 | **0.0143** | 0.1134 | 0.0404 | 0.0276 | 0.0176 |
| Aid: summer savings | 0.0622 | 0.0341 | 0.0227 | 0.0220 | 0.0626 | 0.0382 | 0.0307 | 0.0284 |
| Aid: other savings | 0.0720 | 0.0304 | 0.0236 | 0.0223 | 0.0673 | 0.0323 | 0.0256 | 0.0248 |
| Aid: part-time work on campus | −0.1193 | −0.0525 | −0.0377 | −0.0285 | −0.1024 | −0.0462 | −0.0389 | −0.0343 |
| Aid: full-time work | −0.0557 | **−0.0135** | −0.0052 | −0.0021 | −0.0568 | −0.0216 | −0.0166 | −0.0160 |
| Aid: college grant | 0.1511 | 0.0651 | 0.0538 | **0.0137** | 0.1035 | 0.0274 | 0.0195 | **0.0135** |
| Live plan: residence hall | 0.1847 | 0.0988 | 0.0775 | 0.0446 | 0.1350 | 0.0672 | 0.0493 | 0.0351 |
| *Institutional characteristics* | | | | | | | | |
| Type: public university | −0.1847 | −0.1330 | −0.1175 | −0.1455 | −0.0743 | −0.0354 | −0.0281 | −0.0353 |
| Type: private university | 0.1004 | 0.0232 | 0.0283 | −0.0237 | 0.0920 | 0.0214 | 0.0209 | −0.0055 |
| Type: public 4-year college | −0.1917 | −0.1159 | −0.0877 | −0.1079 | −0.1211 | −0.0586 | −0.0395 | −0.0352 |
| Selectivity | 0.3223 | 0.1634 | 0.1643 | 0.1570 | 0.2581 | 0.1210 | 0.1144 | 0.1080 |
| Percent of Asian Students at institution | **0.1107** | 0.0058 | 0.0213 | −0.0313 | 0.1136 | 0.0252 | 0.0325 | −0.0006 |

Note: All variables significant at $p < 0.0001$ unless otherwise noted. Bold coefficients: $p < 0.01$. Underlined coefficients: not significant.

# NOTES

1. CIRP is an ongoing national longitudinal study of student development; see the "Method" section for more details.

2. SES is generally defined in terms of some combination of parental income and parental education.

3. These figures compare favorably with a five-year rate of 47 percent (with an additional 9 percent still enrolled) derived from the Beginning Postsecondary Student (BPS) Longitudinal Study, which followed up 1989–1990 entering freshmen in 1994 (Choy 2002).

4. These latter two coefficients would be significantly larger—0.08 and 0.10, respectively—if it were not for the fact that students who take a lot of foreign language study in high school tend to be concentrated in selective institutions.

# REFERENCES

Allen, D. F., & Nelson, J. M. (1989). Tinto's model of college withdrawal applied to women at two institutions. *Journal of Research and Development in Education* 22(3): 1–11.

Allen, W. R. (1992). The color of success: African American college student outcomes at predominantly White and Historically Black colleges and universities. *Harvard Educational Review* 62(1): 26–44.

Anderson, J. (1984). *Institutional differences in college effects.* Boca Raton: Florida Atlantic University Press.

———. (1986). College contexts, student involvement, and educational attainment. Paper presented at the annual meeting of the American Education Research Association, San Francisco.

Anderson, K. (1981). Post high school experiences and college attrition. *Sociology of Education* 54: 1–15.

Astin, A. W. (1971). *Predicting academic performance in college.* New York: The Free Press.

———. (1975). *Preventing students from dropping out.* San Francisco: Jossey-Bass.

———. (1977). *Four critical years.* San Francisco: Jossey-Bass.

———. (1982). *Minorities in American higher education.* San Francisco: Jossey-Bass.

———. (1984). Student involvement: A developmental theory for higher education. *Journal of College Student Personnel* 25: 297–308.

———. (1991). *Assessment for excellence: The philosophy and practice of assessment and evaluation in higher education.* New York: Macmillan/Oryx.

———. (1993a). College retention rates are often misleading. *Chronicle of Higher Education* (22 September): A48.

———. (1993b). *What matters in college: Four critical years revisited.* San Francisco: Jossey-Bass.

————. (1996). How "good" is your institution's retention rate? *Research in Higher Education* 38(6): 647–658.

Astin, A. W., & Henson, J. W. (1977). New measures of college selectivity. *Research in Higher Education* 6: 1–9.

Astin, A. W., Korn, W. S., Sax, L. J., & Mahoney, K. M. (1994). *The American freshman: National norms for fall 1994.* Los Angeles: Higher Education Research Institute, UCLA.

Astin, A. W., & Oseguera, L. (2003). Degree attainment among Latino undergraduates: Rethinking time-to-degree. Berkeley: California Policy Research Institute, UC Latino Policy Institute.

Astin, A. W., Tsui, L., & Avalos, J. (1996). *Degree attainment rates at American colleges and universities: Effects of race, gender, and institutional type.* Los Angeles: Higher Education Research Institute, UCLA.

Avalos, J. (1996). The effects of time-to-degree completion, stopping out, transferring, and reasons for leaving college on students' long term retention, educational aspirations, occupational prestige, and income. Doctoral dissertation, University of California, Los Angeles.

Bean, J. P. (1982). Student attrition, intentions, and confidence. *Research in Higher Education* 12: 155–187.

Braxton, J., Sullivan, A. S., & Johnson, R. (1997). Appraising Tinto's theory of college student departure. In *Higher education: Handbook of theory of research*, ed. J. Smart, Vol. 12: 107–163. New York: Agathon Press.

Braxton, J. M., Vesper, N., & Hossler, D. (1995). Expectations for college and student persistence. *Research in Higher Education* 36(5): 595–612.

Cabrera, A. F., Castaneda, M. B., Nora, A., & Hengstler, D. (1992). The convergence between two theories of college persistence. *Journal of Higher Education* 63: 143–164.

Cabrera, A. F., Nora, A., & Castaneda, M. B. (1992). The role of finances in the persistence process: A structural model. *Research in Higher Education* 33: 571–593.

————. (1993). College persistence: Structural equation modeling of an integrated model of student retention. *Journal of Higher Education* 64(2): 123–139.

Cabrera, A. F., Stampen, J. O., & Hansen, W. L. (1990). Exploring the effects of ability to pay on college persistence. *Review of Higher Education* 13: 303–336.

Carter, D. F. (2001). *A dream deferred? Examining the degree aspirations of African American and White college students.* New York: RoutledgeFalmer Press.

Chickering, A. W. (1974). *Commuting versus resident students: Overcoming educational inequalities of living off campus.* San Francisco: Jossey-Bass.

Choy, S. P. (2002). *Access and persistence: Findings from ten years of longitudinal research on students.* Washington, DC: American Council on Education.

Dey, E. L., & Astin, A. W. (1989). *Predicting college student retention: Comparative national data from the 1982 freshman class.* Los Angeles: Higher Education Research Institute, UCLA.

————. (1993). Statistical alternatives for studying college student retention: A comparative analysis of logit, probit, and linear regression. *Research in Higher Education* 34(5): 569–581.

Grosset, J. M. (1991). Patterns of integration, commitment, and student characteristics and retention among younger and older students. *Research in Higher Education* 32(2): 159–178.

Gurin, P., & Epps, E. (1975). *Black consciousness, identity, and achievement: A study of students in Black colleges*. New York: Wiley Press.

Fleming, J. (2002). Who will succeed in college? When the SAT predicts Black students' performance. *Review of Higher Education* 25(3): 281–296.

Fleming, J., and Garcia, N. (1998). Are standardized tests fair to African Americans? *Journal of Higher Education* 69: 471–495.

Hartnett, R. T., & Centra, J. (1977). The effects of academic departments on learning. *Journal of Higher Education* 48: 491–507.

Hearn, J. C. (1987). Impacts of undergraduate experiences on aspirations and plans for graduate and professional education. *Research in Higher Education* 27(2): 119–141.

House, D. J. (1996). College persistence and grade outcomes: Non-cognitive variables as predictors for African American, Asian American, Hispanic, Native American, and White students. Paper presented at the annual meeting of the Association for Institutional Research, Albuquerque, NM.

Leppel, K. (2002). Similarities and differences in the college persistence of men and women. *Review of Higher Education* 25(4): 433–450.

Maclay, K. (2000). Higher education faces flood of students: UC, counterparts nationwide cope with rising enrollments, tighter space. *Berkeley* (Office of Public Affairs, Regents of the University of California).

Mallete, B. I., & Cabrera, A. F. (1991). Determinants of withdrawal behavior: An exploratory study. *Research in Higher Education* 32(2): 179–194.

McClelland, K. (1990). Cumulative disadvantage among the highly ambitious. *Sociology of Education* 63: 102–121.

Mow, S., & Nettles, M. (1990). Minority student access to, and persistence and performance in college: A review of the trends and research literature. In *Higher education: A handbook of theory and research*, ed. J. C. Smart, Vol. 6: 35–105. New York: Agathon Press.

Munro, B. H. (1981). Dropouts from higher education: Path analysis of a national sample. *American Educational Research Association* 18(2): 133–141.

Murdock, T. A. (1987). It isn't just about money: The effects of financial aid on persistence. *Review of Higher Education* 11: 75–101.

Oseguera, L. (2002). Degree aspiration changes during the college years. Paper presented at the annual meeting of the Association for the Study of Higher Education, Sacramento.

————. (2004). Institutional and environmental influences on the baccalaureate degree attainment of African American, Asian American, Caucasian, and Mexican American undergraduates. Doctoral dissertation, UCLA.

Oseguera, L., & Vogelgesang, L. (2003). Statistical alternatives for studying college student retention: Logistic versus linear regression—an update. Unpublished manuscript, UCLA.

Pachon, H., de la Garza, R., Bhargava, A., & Salazar, K. V. (1999). Differential access to advanced placement courses: Implications for the University of California admissions policies. Claremont, CA: Tomas Rivera Policy Institute.

Pascarella, E. T. (1980). Student faculty informal contact and college outcomes. *Review of Educational Research* 50: 545–595.

———. (1984). College environmental influences on educational aspirations. *Journal of Higher Education* 55(6): 751–771.

Pascarella, E. T., & Chapman, D. W. (1983). Validation of a theoretical model of college withdrawal. *Research in Higher Education* 19(1): 25–48.

Pascarella, E. T., Ethington, C., & Smart, J. (1988). The influence of college on humanitarian/civic involvement values. *Journal of Higher Education* 59: 412–437.

Pascarella, E. T., Smart, J., & Ethington, J. (1986). Long term persistence of two-year college students. *Research in Higher Education* 24: 47–71.

Pascarella, E. T., Smart, J., Ethington, J., & Nettles, M. (1987). The influence of college on self-concept. *American Educational Research Journal* 24: 49–77.

Pascarella, E. T., Smart, J., & Stoecker, J. (1989). College race and the early status attainment of Black students. *Journal of Higher Education* 60: 82–107.

Pascarella, E. T., & Terenzini, P. T. (1991). *How college affects students: Findings and insights from twenty years of research.* San Francisco: Jossey-Bass.

Perna, L. W. (2000). Racial and ethnic group differences in college enrollment decisions. In *Understanding the college choice of disadvantaged students: New directions for institutional research*, ed. A. F. Cabrera & S. M. La Nasa, 45–63. San Francisco: Jossey-Bass.

Sax, L. J., & Astin, A. W. (1997). The benefits of service: Evidence from undergraduates. *Educational Record* 25–32.

Sax, L. J., Astin, A. W., Korn, W. S., & Mahoney, K. M. (2000). *The American freshman: National norms for fall 2000.* Los Angeles: Higher Education Research Institute, UCLA.

Sedlack, W. (1987). Black students on White campuses: Twenty years of research. *Journal of College Student Personnel* 16: 214–219.

Sewell, W., Haller, A. O., & Ohlendorf, G. W. (1970, December). The educational and early occupational attainment process: Replication and revision. *American Sociological Review* 35: 1014–1027.

Sjoberg, C. E. (1999). The relationship of environmental predictors and institutional characteristics to student persistence. Doctoral dissertation, Oklahoma State University, Stillwater.

Smith, D. G. (1990). Women's colleges and coed colleges: Is there a difference? *Journal of Higher Education* 61(2): 181–195.

Smith, D. G., Morrison, D., & Wolf, L. (1994). College as a gendered experience: An empirical analysis using multiple lenses. *Journal of Higher Education* 65(6): 696–725.

Stage, F. K. (1988). University attrition: LISREL with logistic regression for the persistence criterion. *Research in Higher Education* 29(4): 343–357.

Stampen, J. O., & Cabrera, A. F. (1986). Exploring the effects of student aid on attrition. *Journal of Student Financial Aid* 16: 28–40.

Stoecker, J., Pascarella, E., & Wolfe, L. (1988). Persistence in higher education: A nine year test of a theoretical model. *Journal of College Student Development* 29: 196–209.

Thomas, R. O., & Bean, J. P. (1988). Student retention at liberal arts colleges: The development and test of a model. Paper presented at the annual meeting of the Association of the Study of Higher Education, St. Louis, Missouri.

Tinto, V. (1987). *Leaving college: Rethinking the causes and cures of student attrition.* Chicago: University of Chicago Press.

————. (1993). *Leaving college: Rethinking the causes and cures of student attrition.* 2nd ed. Chicago: University of Chicago Press.

Titus, M. A. (2003). An examination of the influence of institutional context on persistence at four-year colleges and universities: A multilevel approach. Doctoral dissertation, University of Maryland, College Park.

Waldo, M. (1986). Academic achievement and retention as related to students' personal and social adjustment in residence halls. *Journal of College and University Student Housing* 16: 19–23.

# CHAPTER

# Finances and Retention

## Trends and Potential Implications

*John H. Schuh*

### INTRODUCTION

A volume on issues related to student retention would be incomplete without a discussion about the relationship between student retention and finance. Financing higher education has become a complex, high-stakes activity for students and their institutions. Many students, in effect, are betting their economic future on their college experience. In turn, colleges, their benefactors, and various governmental authorities, especially the federal government, have made and are likely to continue to make significant commitments to students so that they can attend college. Thus, this chapter will examine some of the salient issues related to how students finance their education, the amount of debt that they incur to finance their education, and the implications for institutions of higher education when students do not persist to graduation.

### CURRENT FISCAL ENVIRONMENT

Contemporary financing of higher education has involved an increasing reliance on students and their families to provide revenues for colleges and universities. Students, in turn, are relying on financial aid to finance their education. Loans have become an important aspect of financial aid. These conclusions will be discussed in detail in the next section of this chapter.

## HOW INSTITUTIONS OF HIGHER EDUCATION ARE FINANCED

One of the most important trends in higher education finance over the past two decades is the ever-increasing reliance that institutions of higher education have on tuition and fee revenue. This is true for publicly assisted institutions as well as not-for-profit institutions. The following data illustrate this trend.

## Public Institutions

In reporting year 1980–1981, public degree-granting institutions received 12.9 percent of their revenue from tuition and fees. This has grown to 18.5 percent of their income in reporting year 1999–2000, the most current year for which data are available (U.S. Department of Education 2003, Table 330). Data are available across public institutional types and demonstrate another aspect of the revenue picture. While doctoral extensive institutions received just 16.1 percent of their revenue from tuition and fees, master's and baccalaureate institutions received 21.9 percent and 26.7 percent of their income, respectively, from tuition and fees (Table 334). Thus, students who do not persist represent significant revenue loss for their institution, particularly those institutions that have less emphasis on research activities. The situation is even more pronounced at private not-for-profit institutions.

## Private, Not-for-Profit Institutions

Because of changes in accounting procedures, longitudinal data are not as current for these institutions, but the trends are just as dramatic. In 1980–81, private not-for-profit institutions relied on tuition and fees for 35.9 percent of their income. By 1995–96, tuition and fees accounted for 41.5 percent of their income (U.S. Department of Education 2003, Table 332). Looking at a cross-section of these institutions for the 1999–2000 reporting year, doctoral extensive institutions received just 12.9 percent of their income from tuition and fees, but master's and baccalaureate institutions received 53.1 percent and 32.5 percent of their income from tuition and fees (Table 335). Again, significant financial implications result for each student who does not stay to complete a baccalaureate degree.

# HOW STUDENTS PAY FOR THEIR EDUCATION

Students use a variety of sources to pay for their postsecondary education, including savings, work, assistance from their parents, and financial aid. The following discussion will identify the sources of support that students use to pay for their education. It will also look at how such factors as family income and work influence students' ability to pay for college.

The federal government has published a number of reports that examine how students pay for their education, among them, *Student Financing of Undergraduate Education: 1999–2000* published by the U.S. Department of Education (2002) (referred to hereafter as NCES 2002-167). This report provides the foundation for the discussion in this chapter of how students finance their education.

All undergraduate students do not attend college on a full-time basis, being defined as enrolling in twelve credits in an academic term. In fact, according to the report previously cited, 47.9 percent of all students during the 1999–2000 reporting year attended college on a part-time basis, while just over 52 percent attended full time (NCES 2002-167, Table 5.1-B). Attendance status affects financial aid dramatically, a point we will return to later in this section.

## Cost of Attendance

The average cost of attendance for students ranges considerably, depending on the type of institution they attend. According to NCES 2002-167, the price of attendance (which includes tuition and fees as well as other costs such as room and board) ranged from $9,100 per year for public two-year institutions to $23,600 per year at a private not-for-profit four-year institution. The difference, $14,500, is more than the average price of attendance at a public four-year institution. Hence, as one looks at the price of attendance, it is important to remember that the range is substantial, and that students have a wide variety of financial choices when they select their college.

The largest percentage of full-time students (37 percent) choose to attend institutions with a price of attendance of $8,000–11,999 per year, according to NCES 2002-167 (Figure 3). Thirty percent attended colleges with a cost of $16,000 or more per year, followed by 21 percent who attended a college with a cost of $12,000–15,999 per year. As students attend more expensive institutions, they are more likely to receive financial aid, and an increasing proportion of their aid comes from loans. For example, according to NCES 2002-167 (Figure 4), just 25 percent of students who attend institutions with a cost of $4,000 per year or less receive any aid, and only 2 percent of all students receive aid with loans. At the other end of the continuum are students who attend institutions that cost $12,000 per year or more. Seventy-eight percent of these students receive financial aid, and 60 percent of students who attend these colleges receive aid with loans. So, it can be concluded that as the price of attendance increases, students rely more on loans as part of their financial aid package.

## Family Income

Family income also has an influence on student financial aid. Students are divided into two categories for reporting purposes: those who are considered financially dependent on their parents and those who are considered financially independent. Those who are dependent are slightly more likely to receive financial aid, depending on the family income, which is divided into three categories: low (under $30,000 per year), middle ($30,000 to $80,000 per year) and high (over $80,000 per year). Seventy-five percent of dependent students from low-income families receive aid, while 73 percent of independent students with low income receive aid. About half of these students receive loans as part of their aid package. As family income increases, the percentage of students who receive aid declines. Just 34 percent of independent students with high income receive aid (including 9 percent who receive aid with loans), whereas 48 percent of dependent students from high-income families receive aid, 26 percent of whom receive loans as part of their financial aid package (NCES 2002-167, Figure 5).

## Institutional Type

The type of institution students attend is relative to the aid they receive. Students attending private institutions (both for profit and not for profit) are more likely to receive aid than students who attend public institutions. While students who attend private institutions are more likely to receive financial aid, they are also more likely to receive loans than those who attend public institutions (NCES 2002-167, Figure 7). The range of students receiving loans is particularly dramatic. Just 17 percent of students who attend public two-year colleges receive loans, while 75 percent of students who attend private for-profit institutions receive loans.

## Sources of Financial Aid

Typically, four sources are available for student financial aid: the federal government, state governments, institutions themselves, and private sources. All sources of financial aid except the federal government are more likely to provide grants to students than loans as sources of financial aid. Borrowing from all sources (federal and other) increased during the 1990s. In 1992–1993, 32.3 percent of all students receiving aid borrowed, while in 1999–2000, 45.4 percent of all students receiving aid took out loans (U.S. Department of Education 2003).

## Student Borrowing

The final foundational element in this discussion has to do with who borrows and of those who borrow, how much they borrow. In terms of undergraduates at public four-year institutions, 38 percent received no aid in 1999–2000 according to NCES 2002-167 (Figure 13). Another 23 percent received aid, but took out no loans. Another 12 percent received loans only, on average $4,800. Finally, 28 percent received loans and other aid, totaling $8,900. Those who borrowed had an average federal cumulative debt of $11,000. Financial aid for undergraduates at private not-for-profit institutions had a somewhat different picture in 1999–2000. Twenty-four percent received no aid. Aid but no loans was received by 26 percent and loans (averaging $7,000) but no other aid was received by 6 percent. Loans and other aid were received by 44 percent. For those who borrowed, the average federal cumulative debt was $12,000 (NCES 2002-167, Figure 14).

## Influence of Price Increases on Student Attendance

The financial environment described to this point does not report what happens to certain groups of students when the price of attendance changes. Specially, when the price of attendance increases, students from various income groups are affected in different ways. Heller (1997) observed that students from lower-income families are more sensitive to changes in tuition and financial aid than students who come from middle-income or upper-income families. African American students are more sensitive to price changes than Caucasian students. Heller also reported that the evidence is more mixed for Hispanic students. He observed that as the federal government has shifted its financial aid policy from grants to loans, the higher education community increasingly has been concerned about the impact of this change on access.

Paulsen and St. John (2002) found similar results in their study of social class and college choice. They concluded, "[L]ow-income and lower-middle-income students are far more responsive to prices than students upper-middle and upper-income families" (228). They added, "The high-tuition, high-loan environment is clearly problematic for poor and working-class students. For such students, the cost of tuition, net of available aid, is clearly not affordable" (230). In some cases, such students are particularly at risk in terms of defaulting on their loans. One of the options that students have to help defray their costs is work.

## Students Who Work

The percentage of full-time students (age 16–24) who work has increased steadily according to data published by the U.S. Department of Education (1997). These data indicated that 33.8 percent of all students worked in 1970, but the percentage of working students grew to 47.2 percent for all students in 1995. Additionally, the percentage of students who reported working twenty hours or more, or more than thirty-five hours per week, also has increased over the same time period, from 14.1 percent to 26.8 percent and from 3.7 percent to 6.5 percent, respectively.

Another U.S. Department of Education report (1998) examined some of the effects of working on students. Thirty percent of the students included in this study reported that working limited their number of classes, 40 percent indicated that working limited their class schedule, 26 percent reported that working limited their access to the library, and 36 percent indicated that working reduced their class choices (8). The greater the number of hours students worked, the more restricted their schedules and choices were. Did working affect academic performance negatively? Thirty-seven percent reported that it did, while 15 percent indicated that working had a positive effect on their performance. The balance (48 percent) reported that working had no effect on their performance (9).

On the other hand, students who worked more hours borrowed less. For example, students who worked from one to fifteen hours per week had an average loan of $4,344, but those who worked thirty-five hours or more borrowed $3,810. So, if one assumes that loan debt is undesirable, then working more hours is a way to reduce a student's loan. However, working full time has a negative relationship with persistence. The report observed, "Even when controlling for related factors such as attendance status, income, and institution type, students who worked full time had lower persistence than those who worked 1–15 hours" (1998, 16). That brings us to the next topic: Who is at risk for defaulting on student loans?

## Factors That Contribute to Loan Default

Flint (1997) examined a number of variables to determine their influence on the repayment of student loans. He found that the potential for default was increased by the following characteristics: being male, Black, and each year of age beyond 21. Higher grade point averages were associated with avoiding default. Finally, two characteristics after college were associated with default: lower disposable income and greater incongruence between undergraduate major and current employment.

Volkwein, Szelest, Cabrera, and Napierski-Pranci (1998) also examined factors related to loan default. Their analysis resulted in several conclusions. First, they found that default rates are based more on the nature of borrowers and their achievements than on the types of institutions they attended. Second, such factors as having a parent who attended college, completing a degree, being married, and not having dependent children are associated with reduced default rates for all those included in their study, and these factors were even more powerful on the African Americans included in the study. Third, regardless of racial or ethnic group, Volkwein et al. concluded that borrowers who have similar earned degrees, marital status, and family income exhibit almost identical records of earned income and loan repayment.

## SPECIFIC STUDENT INCOME GROUPS

The next section is devoted to how students from low- and middle-income backgrounds finance their education.

## Low-Income Students

The U.S. Department of Education released a report in 2000 (referred to hereafter as NCES 2000-169) that focused on low-income students and how they paid for college. Low income for the purpose of the study was described as a student "whose family income was below 125 percent of the federally established poverty level for their family size" (2). Of all the undergraduates who attended college in 1995–1996, 26.4 percent met this definition. The majority of these students were female (56.8 percent), less than 24 years of age (54.7 percent), White (70.55 percent), and separated or not married (79.0 percent). These students were not single parents (89 percent), and most typically attended a public community college (43.2 percent) or public four-year college (30.3 percent). They did not delay attending college after finishing high school (67.9 percent) and lived off campus (61.1 percent), and just 32.2 percent did not work while they attended college.

Focusing just on dependent students, 87.9 percent applied for financial aid and 84.7 percent of the students received aid. Included in their aid packages were grants (80.1 percent), Pell grants (67.3 percent), loans (47.7 percent), work study (14.8 percent), and other sources of aid (7.0 percent). For those students who attended public community colleges, the average amount of grant aid received by these students who were enrolled full time for the entire year was $2,536, out of a total aid package of $3,067. For students who attended public four-year colleges, the typical aid package was $6,533, including $4,203 in grants with the balance in loans and other forms of aid.

Low-income students most commonly did not borrow the maximum amount of Stafford loan money for which they were eligible. For those who attended public two-year colleges, just 5.1 percent borrowed the maximum, and for those who attended public four-year colleges, 12.6 percent borrowed the maximum. Student who were classified as "not low income" who attended public four-year colleges were more likely to borrow the maximum (18 percent), while just 3.6 percent of such students who attended public two-year colleges borrowed the maximum according to this study.

This study found that low-income students were likely to work. A total of 67.8 percent of these students worked during the academic year, for an average of 22.6 hours per week. These students worked a comparable number of hours as those from not-low-income if they attended public two-year or four-year institutions. As one might expect, students from low-income families were far less likely to receive parental contributions than those from not-low-income families. For example, 29.8 percent of low-income students who enrolled in public two-year colleges received a direct contribution from their parents (for tuition, housing, meals, or books) compared with 58.3 percent of students from not-low-income families. Just 34.4 percent of students from low-income families received family contributions compared with 69.2 percent of students from not-low-income families.

Finally, this report concluded that low-income students are at a greater risk than other students of not completing college: "After controlling for student background characteristics . . . and other factors thought to affect persistence . . . low income students who began their postsecondary education in 1995–1996 were less likely than not-low-income students to have attained a degree or certificate or be still enrolled" (NCES 2000-169, 52).

## Middle-Income Dependent Students

Another important study of how students pay for their education focused on middle-income undergraduates. This study, referred to hereafter as NCES 2001-155, focused on students with family incomes between $35,000 and $69,999 in 1994 and is the source of the statistical information contained in this section. This cohort included 37 percent of full-time, full-year students during the time period studied. Most commonly, these students were female (52.9 percent), White (80.8 percent), and from families with four persons (38.4 percent), lived on campus (36.5 percent), and worked while they were enrolled (77.8 percent). These students most likely attended public institutions of higher education (over 70 percent), and 64.2 percent of these students received financial aid. Most commonly these students received grants (46.1 percent), followed closely by students who received loans (42.8 percent). Some students received work study (13 percent), and a few (3.6 percent) received other forms of aid.

Grants most often came from their institution (31.1 percent) or through state grant programs (16.9 percent). A few students received other grant aid (12.0 percent) or federal (6.6 percent) grant aid. A substantial percentage (43.9 percent) of middle-income students also received loans, receiving on average $3,930.

The vast majority of the parents of these students (91.1 percent) provided some contribution to their students and 74.4 percent made a direct contribution to their educational costs. This is substantially more than students from lower-income families (52.6 percent contributed directly to their students' education) but less than the percentage of upper-income families (89.1 percent) who contributed directly to their students' education.

Students in this income group were more likely to work while they were enrolled than those from the other income groups. As was mentioned previously, 77.8 percent worked while they were enrolled compared with 74.5 percent of lower-income students and 68.1 percent of higher-income students. Typically, middle-income students worked about the same number of hours as lower-income students, and slightly more than higher-income students.

## STUDENT ECONOMIC CIRCUMSTANCES AND DEBT

Students who complete a college degree, on average, have greater earnings than those individuals who do not complete a college degree, as was illustrated by the *Digest of Education Statistics 2002* (U.S. Department of Education 2003, 448–49). These data are consistent with the findings of two inquiries that studied the relationship between completing a college degree and income. Sanchez, Laanan, and Wiseley (1999, 107–8) examined the relationship between a community college education and earnings. Their conclusion was, "as students complete more education, they increase the likelihood of experiencing greater gains in their post college earnings. However, completing a vocational certificate or associate degree greatly increases students' postcollege earning compared with taking a handful of units." Paulsen (1998) arrived at essentially the same conclusion. He observed, "This research demonstrates significant economic payoffs or returns to various types of investment in sub-baccalaureate postsecondary education, findings that are quite timely and of considerable importance for decision makers at federal, state—local, and institutional levels" (476). Paulsen provided similar conclusions about the economic value of a baccalaureate degree. He observed, "The magnitude of earnings differentials between college and high school graduates—which has increased substantially since the mid-1970s—is clearly one of the most striking and straightforward demonstrations of the value of a college education. Another is the substantial difference between the unemployment rates of college and high school graduates" (474).

## DEBT AFTER GRADUATION

About 50 percent of all full-time, full-year undergraduate students borrow money to help defray the costs of their education. According to the U.S. Department of Education (NCES 2002-167, 25), about 60 percent of graduating seniors from public four-year institutions had incurred a cumulative debt averaging $16,100. The same authors reported that 66 percent of graduating seniors from private not-for-profit institutions had borrowed an average of $18,000 in college loans (26). How do students manage this debt after they graduate? Several reports provide insight into this question.

About half of the students who graduated from college in 1992–1993 had borrowed money to help pay for college, according to an earlier U.S. Department of Education report, hereafter referred to as NCES 2000-188

(U.S. Department of Education 2000a). A smaller percentage of students graduating from public institutions (46.8 percent) had borrowed than those who graduated from private institutions (54.6 percent), and they borrowed a smaller amount of money, $8,633 compared with $10,382. Fewer than half of the students, regardless of institutional type, according to this report had borrowed more than $10,000, although this amount has grown according to more recent reports (see, for example, NCES 2002-167, 25–26).

Four years after graduation, 39 percent of 1992–1993 graduates still owed money on their college loans. The balance had either paid off their loans (16 percent) or had never borrowed (46 percent) (NCES 2000-188, 18). Of those borrowers who had not enrolled in further education (around 53 percent), 33 percent still had debt in 1997 (NCES 2000-188, 55). Their average amount of student loan debt was $7,100, they paid about $151 per month, and their median debt burden (monthly payments as a percentage of monthly income) was 5 percent (NCES 2000-188, 55). The report concluded, "Based on reported spending for major noneducation items such as rent or mortgage, car payments, and other debt, there was no evidence that borrowers who had not enrolled for further education degree[s] were on a tighter budget than nonborrowers or that their outstanding debt was inhibiting their current spending. Nor did education debt appear to cause delays in marrying, owning a car, buying a home or saving" (NCES 2000-188, 55). Those who had borrowed for education beyond a bachelor's degree (about half) had borrowed an average of $26,458 (NCES 2000-188).

Nevertheless, some who borrow ultimately experience problems repaying their loans. Scherschel (2000) concluded that delinquency rates of subsidized Stafford loans, where interest does not accrue while students are enrolled, had been trending downward from 1995 through 1997 on a quarter-by-quarter basis. On the other hand, she found that the rate of seriously delinquent loans of unsubsidized Stafford loans, whereby interest accrues while students are enrolled, had been increasing over the same period of time.

Graduating from college is a crucial factor in whether or not a borrower defaults on college loans. As has been established earlier, those who graduate from college earn higher incomes than those who do not. According to the work of Volkwein and Cabrera (1998), the default rate of college graduates by racial group ranges from 7 percent to 10 percent. Those who do not have a college degree have default rates from 35 percent to 43 percent. In rough terms, not finishing college increases the potential of defaulting on existing college loans by about five times or more. So, graduating from college is absolutely crucial in limiting the potential for defaulting on college loans.

One other aspect of borrowing is worthy of note, that is, the extent to which borrowing discourages attendance in graduate school. Heller (2001, 32) has explored this issue and concluded that "undergraduate borrowing appears to have little impact on whether students attend graduate school." Heller added, however, that the students in his sample "attended college before the large increase in borrowing limits under the federal loan programs enacted as part of the 1992 Reauthorization of the Higher Education Act" (2001, 32).

## INSTITUTIONAL COSTS OF NONPERSISTENCE

To this point, this chapter has examined the costs to individual students when they do not persist. These costs can be substantial, ranging from the costs associated with attending college but not graduating, to a potential lifetime of lower income, a more modest lifestyle, and an inability to repay debt. Institutions also incur costs when students do not persist to graduation, although the research on this point is scarce. To address this question, the balance of this chapter will present a conceptual framework that could be applied at specific institutions to consider the costs associated with students not persisting to graduation. This framework has three elements:

- Immediate direct institutional costs
- Immediate indirect institutional costs
- Long-term institutional costs after students leave their institution

## DIRECT COSTS

Institutions have a number of direct costs associated when students fail to graduate. Four of these are identified in this section of this chapter, and they reflect the investment that is made in students who do not persist as well as income that is not realized when students leave their college before graduating.

### Student Recruitment

Institutions spend substantial resources to recruit students whether they are highly selective or have an open admissions policy. Suppose, hypothetically, that the admissions budget for College A is $1 million and the college enrolls 500 new (first-year students and transfers) students per year. The cost of recruitment, simply calculated by dividing the budget by the number of new students, is $2,000. But, if the students persist to graduation and, on average, finish in four years, then the cost per student per year is reduced to $500. To replace each student who drops out, the college must spend $2,000, based on the preceding figure. So, it is quite obvious from this rather antiseptic example that the institutional cost of students dropping out is substantial when calculated on a per student basis.

Suppose that College A's persistence rate is 80 percent. If the entering first-year class consists of 400 students, an 80 percent persistence rate means that eighty students will leave after the first year. In gross terms, then, the college will have spent $160,000 on the recruitment of these eighty students, but will have received only one year's worth of income from them. The net loss is substantial. In purely economic terms, then, institutions are served far better when their students persist to graduation.

## Financial Aid

The costs to institutions are far more than just the costs associated with recruitment. Institutions also invest money in financial aid that does not have to be repaid. Whether this is a discount on the amount of tuition students pay or actual dollars given to students to help them defray their costs, this is money invested in students that simply is lost if they do not persist.

Using our example of College A, if half of the students receive some form of college-based merit aid, and the average award is $5,000, then an investment of $200,000 has been lost if forty students do not persist to their second year. This college-based aid could have been invested in other students who attended the college, or it could have been used to provide an incentive to other students who were recruited by the college but did not attend because financial aid was not available to them (and awarded to students who did not persist). The point is that institutionally based merit aid that is invested in students who do not persist is an investment that is lost. It can be used in succeeding years to attract and retain students, but the aid invested in students who leave the college cannot be recovered.

## Lost Tuition Income

One of the obvious financial implications of students not persisting is that after students drop out, they will not pay tuition and fees. This lost income cannot be recouped. Suppose College A charges students $18,000 per year for tuition and fees. In our class of 400, if eighty drop out, then the gross amount of tuition lost for the second year is $1,440,000 less any institutionally provided merit aid. We estimated that $200,000 of institutional merit aid was invested in the students who did not return for their second year, so the net tuition loss was $1,240,000. Unless the college can replace the students who leave with transfer students, this income stream is lost. Add in the third and fourth years, and the total income lost from the eighty students who left is $3,720,000, not taking into account any tuition adjustments for increasing costs. So, it certainly is in College A's interest to retain as many students as possible.

## Other Lost Income

College A is a residential institution, where more than 95 percent of the student body live on campus for all four years of their education, so when students leave, payments to the institution for other services also cease. College A charges $7,000 per year for room and board. If 95 percent of the eighty students who left lived in campus housing, then the amount of gross revenue lost is $532,000. To be sure, expenses are reduced in campus housing when students leave, including food costs, some maintenance costs, and potentially some utility costs (such as telephone line charges or cable television hookups), but costs such as debt service, staffing to a great extent, and other utility costs (such as HVAC) will not be reduced appreciably.

The $532,000 in lost income will be multiplied by the three years that the students would have lived in the residence halls had they attended College A until graduation. Gross revenues lost to the residence system, unadjusted for cost increases, would be $1,596,000.

Other income also would take into account textbook and supply purchases, money spent by guests who come to campus, and other ancillary income. The primary loss, however, to College A for these eighty students leaving at the end of the first year is estimated to be $5,316,000, using these simple measures. That is a substantial amount of income for a college of 1,500, and it simply is lost unless transfers replace the students who leave. Even then, replacing the students who leave with transfers will not generate a similar amount of income, since it costs approximately $2,000 to recruit each new student.

Admittedly, these measures are illustrative and are only rough approximations of the costs to an institution if students leave and are not replaced. This example does, however, underscore how dramatic the costs can be if students leave their institution. Some institutions have higher persistence rates than 80 percent, but many more have lower persistence rates. As persistence rates fluctuate, the financial implications are more or less dramatic, depending on how much revenue is forgone. In any event, each student who leaves can represent substantial income lost to an institution of higher education.

## INDIRECT INSTITUTIONAL COSTS

In addition to the direct costs to institutions of students not persisting are some indirect institutional costs, particularly if one considers the value of the time that faculty and staff devote to students.

### Faculty and Staff Indirect Costs

Faculty time is both direct and indirect. Faculty devote time preparing for their courses, delivering courses, grading papers and other student work products, and counseling and advising students. One could make the case that by registering and paying for their courses, students have a right to expect that faculty will devote a certain amount of time to them. That is as it should be. If one thinks of education as process, and that learning builds on learning, then the additive dimension is lost when students do not persist. Moreover, the time that faculty members devote to students outside the formal learning process, by having lunch with them in the residence halls, having a cup of coffee in the departmental lounge, or talking with them over the telephone, is time that could be spent with other students or time that could be spent in other ways. This time cannot be quantified, because it will vary from faculty member to faculty member, but what is certain is that the time that faculty spend with students who leave may be better spent on students who persist or on other faculty activities such as scholarship, grant preparation, and so on. This assertion certainly can be debated, but the point is that faculty time is finite and that when it is spent on students who leave, it cannot be reclaimed and redirected to other tasks.

Similarly, staff devote time to students, be it the academic advisor, career counselor, financial aid coordinator, or other staff members. Again, students, by virtue of their paying their tuition and fees, have a reasonable expectation that such staff members will devote time to them. But if these staff spend additional time on students who do not persist, that time could have been spent with students who persist to graduation.

## Long-Term Potential Institutional Costs

One other category of institutional costs is worthy of note. This has to do with a set of outcomes that are difficult to predict or quantify but certainly have the potential to be harmful to institutions when students do not persist. While one may be able to point to some anomalies, typically institutional benefactors do not emerge from those who do not achieve their educational goals. There may be some notable exceptions, but in the main, graduates are more likely to serve as benefactors of their institutions than those who drop out are. So, one way of thinking about those who do not persist is that they are unlikely to donate time or money to their former institution in the future.

Those who do not persist also may be less inclined to recommend to others that they should attend their former institutions. Siblings, children, friends, or others may be the recipients of such advice. Whether it is persuasive or not is beside the point. Nonpersisters are less likely to be "friends" with their institution than those who graduate. They also might be less likely to support candidates for office who express interest in helping the college they left. In short, if the old adage "you can never have too many friends" has any validity, then those who do not persist represent individuals who have less potential for being a friend to their institution than those who graduate.

## CONCLUSION

This chapter has examined such issues as how students finance their education, the financial implications that students who do not persist face, and the costs to institutions when students do not persist. In addition to the loss of talent development and loss of human capital that occur from students who do not persist, the financial implications of students who do not persist are noteworthy. The effect is negative for both the students who do not persist and the colleges that they left.

## REFERENCES

Flint, T. A. (1997). Predicting student loan defaults. *Journal of Higher Education* 68: 322–354.

Heller, D. E. (1997). Student price response in higher education. *Journal of Higher Education* 68: 624–660.

———. (2001). *Debts and decisions: Student loans and their relationship to graduate school and career choice*. Indianapolis: Lumina Foundation.

Paulsen, M. B. (1998). Recent research on the economics of attending college: Returns on investment and responsiveness to price. *Research in Higher Education* 39: 471–489.

Paulsen, M. B., & St. John, E. P. (2002). Social class and college costs. *Journal of Higher Education* 73: 189–236.

Sanchez, J. R., Laanan, F. S., & Wiseley, W. C. (1999). Postcollege earnings of former students at California colleges: Methods, analysis, and implications. *Research in Higher Education* 40(1): 87–113.

Scherschel, P. M. (2000). *Student debt levels continue to rise*. Indianapolis: USA GROUP Foundation.

Thomas, S. L. (2000). Deferred costs and economic returns to college major, quality and performance. *Research in Higher Education* 41: 281–313.

U.S. Department of Education. (1997). *The condition of education, 1997*. NCES 97-388. Washington, DC: National Center for Education Statistics.

———. (1998). *Undergraduates who work*. NCES 98-137. Washington, DC: National Center for Education Statistics.

———. (2000a). *Debt burden four years after college*. NCES 2000-188. Washington, DC: National Center for Education Statistics.

———. (2000b). *Low-income students: Who they are and how they pay for their education*. NCES 2000-169. Washington, DC: National Center for Education Statistics.

———. (2001a). *The condition of education 2001*. NCES 2001-072. Washington, DC: National Center for Education Statistics.

———. (2001b). *Middle income undergraduates: Where they enroll and how they pay for their education*. NCES 2001-155. Washington, DC: National Center for Education Statistics.

———. (2001c). *Study of college costs and prices, 1988–89 to 1997–98*. NCES 2002-157. Washington, DC: National Center for Education Statistics.

———. (2002). *Student financing of undergraduate education: 1999–2000*. NCES 2002-167. Washington, DC: National Center for Education Statistics.

———. (2003). *Digest of education statistics, 2002*. NCES 2003-060. Washington, DC: National Center for Education Statistics.

Volkwein, J. F., & Cabrera, A. F. (1998). Who defaults on student loans? In *Condemning students to debt*, ed. R. Fossey & M. Bateman, 105–125. New York: Teachers College Press.

Volkwein, J. F., Szelest, B. P., Cabrera, A. F., & Napierski-Pranci, M. R. (1998). Factors associated with student loan default among different racial and ethnic groups. *Journal of Higher Education* 69: 206–238.

# CHAPTER 11

# Where We Go from Here

## A Retention Formula for Student Success

*Alan Seidman*

*For intervention programs and services to be successful they must
be powerful enough to effect change.*

## INTRODUCTION

The study of college student retention goes back decades (see Chapter 1, "Past to Present: A Historical Look at Retention"). Over the years colleges and universities have designed programs and services to help retain students. The programs and services try to ease student transition into the academic and social systems of the institution. These programs and services consist of orientation programs (Green 1987), counseling and student development (Seidman 1992a, 1992b), assessment, remedial and academic support services (Seidman 1993, 1995; Crockett 1984), and the development of educational communities within the classroom (Tinto et al. 1994; Tinto 1997, 1998), among others. Yet even with the implementation and strengthening of these programs and services, the retention data reveal that students are not retained at a higher rate than they were twenty years ago (see Chapter 2, "Measurements of Persistence"). The retention rate may have been influenced by student academic achievement; that is, student academic backgrounds may be weaker than they were twenty years ago.

The literature, however, gives the impression that a student can have a successful college experience if he or she chooses a college carefully and if the college is compatible with his or her individual characteristics. That is, if a student's background, both academic and social, and a college's characteristics, academic and social, are similar, then there is a likelihood of student success. Also, if a college provides a structure that integrates the student into the formal and informal academic and social systems of the college, then the student has a higher likelihood of success. This is consistent with the Tinto (1987, 1993) retention model, which posits that individual pre-entry college attributes (family background, skill and ability, prior schooling) form individual goals and commitments; the individual's goals and commitments then interact over time with institutional experiences (the formal and informal academic and social systems of an institution). The extent to which the individual is successful in becoming academically and socially integrated into the systems of an institution determines the individual's departure decision.

Positive experiences and interventions will reinforce persistence by heightening individual intentions and commitments, whereas negative experiences will weaken intentions and commitments. Intentions can include the desire to earn a degree in a particular field of study, whereas commitment is the student's desire to complete that degree and willingness to spend the time and energy necessary to obtain it (Astin 1985). Therefore, the greater the individual student's levels of integration into the social and academic systems of the college, the greater his or her subsequent commitment to the college (Baumgart & Johnston 1977; Terenzini et al. 1981; Pascarella et al. 1986).

## SEIDMAN RETENTION FORMULA

The Tinto (1987, 1993) model has served as the foundation upon which retention programs and services have been based. The Seidman retention formula is built on this foundation too and provides a college with a course of action to follow. The formula states:

$$RET = E_{ID} + (E + I + C)_{IV},$$ that is, RETention = Early $_{IDentification}$ + (Early + Intensive + Continuous)$_{InterVention}$.

### Retention Defined

Retention is defined as student attainment of academic and/or personal goal(s). A student may attain his or her academic and/or personal goals prior to graduation or may graduate without meeting those goals. Therefore it is important for a college to ascertain the reason(s) a student enrolls in the first place and whether the reason(s) for college attendance changes over time.

Additionally, defining retention in accordance with college mission is essential. Chapter 4, "How to Define Retention: A New Look at an Old Problem," deals with this issue. For discussion purposes, program, course, and student retention will be used in this chapter. Program retention and attrition will be the current federal government college definition requirement to measure retention. It looks at the full-time, first-time student and tracks him or her over a period of time (six years for four-year colleges and three years for two-year colleges) to determine whether or not the student graduated in the intended major at entry. Course retention and attrition measure the number of students enrolled in each college course after the course census date and how many students successfully complete the course with an A–D grade at the end of the term. Using the census date, usually the tenth to twentieth day of the term, gives time for a student to determine whether or not to stay in a specific class. After the census date it is assumed that the student has made a commitment to the class.

Course retention and attrition give an overall picture of retention by course, and do not distinguish between the full-time and part-time student or year of attendance. Using course retention, a college can look at all courses, regardless of whether the student is enrolled full-time or part-time, or is a first-, second-, third-, or fourth-year student. Some course sections (i.e., Accounting 101) with higher than average retention and attrition rates can be examined to determine the reason(s). Perhaps a larger than average attrition rate in a course section is due to inappropriate course placement, or advisement, or course content, or other factors. Student retention and attrition data would discover whether or not the student attained his or her academic and/or personal goal(s) at exit. If a student misses two consecutive terms, excluding summer sessions, then he or she would be sent a questionnaire or called to try to determine if academic and/or personal goal(s) were achieved while enrolled. These data can be matched with student goal data collected at college entry.

## Early Identification

Early identification is identification at the earliest possible time of a student who is potentially at risk for being unsuccessful at the college, either academically or personally. The identification can take place at the time of application, through the thorough examination of academic records and types of courses taken in high school, difficulty of courses, grades received, and scores received on standardized assessment

(SAT/ACT). The review of written recommendations may reveal non-course-related academic or personal issues.

Paradoxically, many colleges already have the information to help identify a student who is at risk for not completing his or her program. Using past student data, a profile of prior unsuccessful students can be developed. When a student applies and is accepted with a similar profile, logic dictates that that student may also have difficulty. If profile information is not readily available either in the college database or through regular data gathering, then a file should be started right away. Gathering all necessary student information may require developing or buying a form and database program or having existing databases linked.

## Early Intervention

Early intervention means starting an intervention at the earliest time possible after identification of a problem. Intervention programs and services should be available as early in a student's college career as possible. A college does not have to wait until a student enrolls to begin intervention programs and services; rather, it can be a part of the student's acceptance to the college. Intervention(s) can begin while the student is still enrolled in high school or during the summer months prior to the beginning of the first term. Admission can be contingent upon the student taking part in the intervention process and successfully completing it prior to actual enrollment. The intervention should continue until the student has demonstrated that the deficiency has been overcome.

## Intensive Intervention

Intensive intervention is creating an intervention that is intensive or strong enough to effect the desired change. This can result in a student spending five days per week, two to four or more hours per day, in an intervention program. The student must demonstrate that he or she has mastered the skill(s) or social factor(s). Specific deficiencies in skill sets may be identified, and the student must demonstrate mastery of each skill set to continue at the college. The intervention program must provide the student with an experience powerful enough to be effective and to make the desired change in the student academic and/or personal behavior.

## Continuous Intervention

Continuous intervention means an intervention that persists until the change is effected. The intervention can continue throughout the student's college career (in the case of a social issue) and beyond. No time limit should be established for the student to complete the intervention program and process. Upon graduation, if the student continues with the intervention, the college can charge a modest fee for the service based on ability to pay. A relationship with the student becomes a lifelong commitment between the student and the college, and the college and the student.

It should be noted that most often a student with a particular deficiency is put into a remedial class for a full term. Suppose your college gives a student a writing assessment and the student demonstrates mastery in ten of fifteen necessary skills. Instead of putting the student into a class that teaches all fifteen skills, individualize the program and concentrate only on the deficient skills. A student may demonstrate mastery of the five skills in a shorter time than a full term and be able to move back into regular classes more quickly. A student should not have to take a class that repeats skills he or she has already mastered and should be able to attain the needed skills through a flexible program. This should eliminate the student/parent complaint that the college has put the student into a remedial course regimen simply to receive more tuition money.

In sum, the aim of the Seidman formula is to identify a student in need of assistance academically and/or socially as early as possible, assess student needs, prescribe interventions, and monitor, assess, and adjust interventions where necessary. An intervention program can start prior to enrollment, actually having the acceptance contingent upon the student successfully completing the intervention. The intervention program must be intensive enough and continue until the desired change is effected.

The medical model can provide an analogy for the Seidman retention formula. A physical examination or prescreening for a specific condition can be completed before it becomes a problem. In the case of a student, a prescreening can be instituted before the student enrolls by using the student's past academic and/or social history or using college-specific data (past unsuccessful students) as a diagnostic tool.

If there is a history of a specific health problem in a family, a test can be conducted to determine whether or not a family member or relative is predisposed to the same or similar problem. In some instances, remedial action can be taken if the particular trait is found in the person. A pre-enrollment academic physical or assessment can find a potential academic and/or personal problem. A pre-enrollment physical can also uncover potential physical and/or emotional problem(s) before they surface. Neither the medical model nor the retention formula is punitive; rather, it is preventative. As such, students should know up front the reason(s) and purpose(s) for the pre-enrollment assessment and possible out-come(s) thereof. It is important that a potential student understand the process, the reason he or she is asked to participate in it, the expected outcomes, and the consequences.

A student or parent would think very favorably of a college that truly cares about a student's growth and development. Not making the process accessible and understandable to a student or parent will only cause anx-iety and may drive the student to another college. Letting a student or parent know up front the reasons for the assessment and intervention should help him or her understand and appreciate what the college is try-ing to accomplish—to give the best possible services to the student so he or she will be successful in his or her academic and social endeavors.

When a person becomes ill, sometimes medical help is not desired be-cause the person may believe the illness will pass or will get better in a short period of time. The illness is slight and the person does not have a temperature, although the throat is sore. Sometimes a person will not seek help because of the cost. When a student gets into academic diffi-culty, the student may not seek help because things may get better as the term progresses. The student believes that he or she will study more; the one big project due next week will receive an A and save the term grade; the student will complete and turn in back homework, and so on. Edu-cators have heard many excuses throughout their teaching careers for why a student has not completed work or has done poorly on an examination.

A student's unwillingness to seek help in college should not be a sur-prise to college administrators. After all, a student directly out of high school is used to having someone tell him or her that a problem exists and an intervention is needed. This is the high school model. A high school guidance counselor may call a student into the counselor's office to discuss academic or personal difficulties reported by a teacher, and to suggest or require a specific remedy. In college it is left up to the student to seek help when necessary. Sometimes a student will not seek help for a personal problem that can be embarrassing, although recent research shows that more students are using counseling services on campus. At other times, the student does not know whom to contact if in difficulty. A college needs to be proactive and facilitate this process.

After a time, the untreated illness lingers and may get worse. A per-son can tell that he or she is not getting better and that something has to be done to cure the illness. The student may get a D grade or fail the course before the realization sinks in that assistance is necessary. A per-son with a lingering illness will finally go to the doctor so that the na-ture of the illness can be diagnosed and a prescription can be given to help overcome the illness. The student will finally seek help because he or she has been put on academic probation or even been dismissed from the college.

Many students will not seek help because they may think that college personnel are keeping close tabs and will come to the rescue. That is far from reality. Students may deal with the problem simply by dropping out of college. The literature illustrates that a student will blame finances as the reason for failure even when they are not. When a student is contacted to find out why he or she has left an institution, research shows that the student is amazed that someone actually has taken the time to call. In some instances the student will talk about the problem, seek help, and reenroll in a subsequent term.

When a patient goes to the doctor, an examination is given and an assessment is made based on the patient's symptoms (given verbally and by the examination), or sometimes by using tests (blood, etc.; and, in the case of students, assessment). The doctor will then make a diagnosis. The diagnosis uses the knowledge gained through years of data gathering, since the patient with certain symptoms most likely will have a specific illness or ailment. The doctor will then prescribe a course of action or intervention such as bed rest, plenty of fluids, special diet, and nonprescription or prescription drugs. The key is to give the patient an intervention that is powerful enough to make the patient well. That is the reason a doctor will tell patients to take all of their medicine. If the patient does not take the medicine for the prescribed period of time, often the illness will come back and may even be prolonged. If the drug that the doctor gives the patient is not powerful enough, or the diagnosis was wrong, then the patient will remain ill, and may have to return to the doctor, who will prescribe an alternative medication or course of action.

A similar occurrence may affect a student who is at risk academically or socially. The problem may not be caught in time, or may be misdiagnosed, or the intervention may not be powerful enough to make a difference. The point here is that early identification, proper diagnosis of the problems (both academic and social), and prescription of an intervention(s) over a period of time, with periodic check-ups, is the key to the successful student/college retention program. The diagnosis must be accurate and must use an appropriate assessment. The prescription must be powerful and long enough to affect change.

There is evidence that the preceding approach shows promise. Reisberg (1999), in the *Chronicle of Higher Education* states, "Ohio State University, for example, has turned to a high-priced consultant to identify incoming freshmen who are most at risk of dropping out before their sophomore year, and to suggest ways to keep them on campus" (54). He continues that the consultant "[used] admissions applications, high-school transcripts, and surveys of freshmen . . . students who enrolled at Ohio State in 1996 and 1997 and noted the common characteristics of the students who returned, as well as those of students who did not. The company used that data to assign "at-risk" scores to freshmen who en-rolled in 1998" (56).

Although the increase in retention for this group was slightly greater than for those who were identified as at-risk but not given additional ser-vices, 75 percent versus 72 percent, the results are promising. Perhaps the interventions were not powerful enough to effect change.

To date there is a paucity of research that tests the Seidman formula and its applicability and utility. However, Young (1999) reports some of his findings using the Seidman retention formula. He concludes:

> The second research question asked if Seidman's (1996) equation for retention—R = E(Id) + (E & In)(Iv) or Retention equals Early Iden-tification and Early and Intensive Intervention—applied to com-munity college students. The TASP requires that all Texas public colleges test students using standard exams to determine their readi-ness for college-level course work. This was the primary method used by all of the colleges to identify students at risk.
>
> Only the two colleges with high retention had any intervention programs that could be called intensive, and both colleges started the interventions early in a student's college career. The two col-leges with relatively low retention did not start interventions until students started to miss classes, and the interventions applied were not intensive. Based on this study, it appears that Seidman's (1996) equation of retention did apply to the colleges in the study. In re-cent correspondence, the researcher learned that Seidman has up-dated the retention equation to read: "Retention equals Early Identification and Early, Intense, and Continuous Intervention" (A. Seidman, January 15, 1999). Since college A's intervention lasted only one term, and college B's interventions continue until the stu-dent completed remediation, college B may more closely have fol-lowed this updated model.

## Implementing the Formula

To set the stage to implement the Seidman retention formula, a college-wide retention committee should be formed. Implementation of the retention program varies with each college depending upon the amount and type of pre-enrollment information that has been collected about the student, assessment of academic and personal goals, and programs currently available for student development. Colleges that tap into their databases and develop a profile of the previous unsuccessful student will be ahead of those colleges that have not kept this information. Colleges should gather accurate information about their students and track them until they achieve their academic and/or personal goal(s), leave the institution prematurely, or graduate.

A retention program requires commitment from senior management. Without the active commitment and participation of senior management, efforts may not succeed. A broad-based, all-inclusive college community committee should be formed. Since faculty play such an important role, it would be appropriate for a respected senior faculty member to chair the committee.

In conjunction with the formation of the retention committee, a retention reading list should be developed and books and articles put on reserve in the learning resource center (library). This gives committee members and the college community a common understanding of this complicated topic. The college community at large should be encouraged to also take advantage of the readings. Having a retention expert provide a reading list, come to the campus, and give a presentation or workshop can be helpful to set the tone for the committee's work.

The college mission statement is the guiding principle for the college's educational processes, programs, and services. The college mission statement tells students, faculty, staff, and the public why the college exists and how it will serve its students.

An example of how a committee might work is as follows. Key committee questions that should be asked first are: What is the problem we are trying to solve? How do we define retention and attrition? How do we compare with our peers? Are we satisfied with our results?

These initial questions may seem simple, but they are not. Simply stating that the problem is to keep students through graduation may not be sufficient. The question that follows, that is, what are your current retention rates, will depend on your retention definition and whether it is at a level of comfort and/or satisfaction. Defining retention can also be a challenge, since students enter, leave, take different numbers of courses a term, and so on. For example, are part-time, nontraditional, distance learning students included in your definitions? For how long a period of time do you want to track students? How do you compare with your peers? Do you know who your peers are? Do they define retention and attrition similarly? (See Chapter 4, "How to Define Retention: A New Look at an

Old Problem.") After comparison with peers, how does the college stack up? Are the results satisfactory or can the college do better? Are the results consistent with the college mission statement?

It is assumed that the college wants to improve retention rates. The next step is to choose a model (Tinto model) for college intervention(s), decide what plan to use (Seidman formula), assign responsibility, design an evaluation plan, keep the college community informed (retention newsletter), and modify where necessary after an evaluation period.

The college retention committee will spend its first period of time learning about college student retention through readings, and perhaps having a college-wide retention presentation or workshop. Key committee questions may be answered with these results: What is the problem the college is trying to solve? Improve the retention rate of all first-time, full-time students from the first to second year by 3 percent for the next three years, for a total of 9 percent more students retained from the first to second year. Improve second to third year retention rates by 2 percent and third-year to fourth-year retention rates by 2 percent. Increase four-year graduation rates by 3 percent per year each of the next three years, so the rate is 78 percent, and increase the five-year graduation rate by 2 percent, for a cumulative retention rate after five years after three years of 84 percent, and a six-year graduation rate of 2 percent for a cumulative retention rate after six years after three years of 90 percent.

We will assume that the retention committee has defined retention as the first-time, full-time student. Using that retention definition, the committee examines the retention and attrition rates after each term and graduation rates for four, five, and six years. The committee compares results with peer institutions and comes up with goals listed in the preceding paragraph.

The committee has decided to use the Tinto (1987, 1993) retention model as the foundation for retention efforts and the Seidman retention formula to improve college student retention (see Figure 11.1).

## Identification of the Student at Risk Prior to Enrollment

As early as possible in the admissions process, a college needs to identify a student who may need intervention(s) to succeed. Past institutional-specific data of an unsuccessful student can be used as an initial screening tool. These data can be used to develop a profile of the student at risk. Common factors will emerge, such as SAT or ACT score average, high school grade point average, socioeconomic level, parents'

Figure 11.1
The Seidman Retention Formula

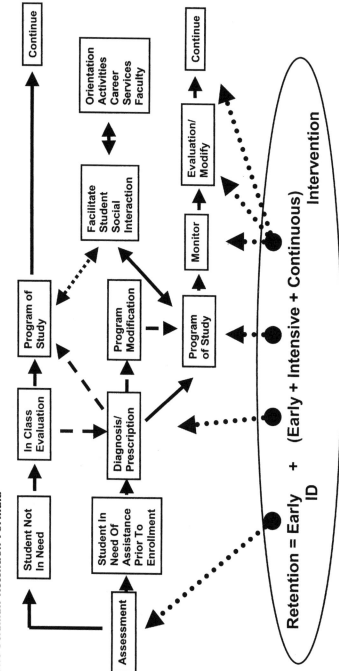

education level, distance from the college, and specific curriculum choice.

If a student with a similar profile of an unsuccessful student applies and is accepted to the college, then it should be no surprise that this particular student has a higher than normal chance that he or she will not persist. The more data collected and the more varied those data are, the better. Additional data could include the student's academic and personal goals; family background information (single-parent family, parental education, economic level); work plans during college; and plans to join clubs and participate in activities. Additional data can broaden the student profile and provide additional service combinations for the student. The point here is to use existing data to identify a potential student at risk or to collect additional information that will be helpful in developing the profile.

Data collection can be achieved through items on the application, obtained as supplemental information, from standardized assessment (SAT or ACT), from college assessment at time of acceptance or program planning, or through a questionnaire included with the acceptance letter, or gathered during assessment of basic skills, over the Internet, during orientation, or at any other events prior to the start of the first term. A college concerned with inundating a potential student with too many requirements can collect data after the acceptance deposit is received.

For a variety of reasons a national database would be fitting. Perhaps regional accreditation agencies, in conjunction with colleges, can develop the most pertinent data collected. These data would not only identify the student at risk, but would also provide colleges with information about students and their behaviors. For comparison or peer review purposes, these data could be accessed by college affiliation, size, region, state, or other characteristics. The possibilities are endless on the use and study opportunities of this type of data collection. This would only work as long as the central purpose of the data collection is established: to help students to overcome specific academic and social deficiencies that hinder their ability to accomplish academic and personal goals. The data would not be used to judge colleges against each other, since all colleges are unique. The idea is to give a college comparable data to judge how well interventions are working term to term and year to year and how those interventions are affecting graduation trends. Mainly, the college mission statement will drive the way in which a college compares itself with another similar college.

The federal and state governments need to assure colleges that collection of universal data will not be used to compare states and regions of the country. Rather, the data will be used to help a college identify the student at risk and to provide early, intensive, and continuous interventions. All segments of the educational enterprise (colleges and the state and the federal governments) should be working together in partnership to help a student achieve his or her academic and personal goals.

As part of the demographic information, family structure and background are helpful. These areas include information such as whether the student is from a single-parent family and whether that family is headed by a mother or father. It is clear that a student from a single-parent family, particularly headed by a mother, achieves at a different level than a student from a nuclear family (Hewlett 1991).

Tors (1995) cites numerous studies over the years that clearly indicate that children in father-absent households score lower on standardized tests (ACT's, SAT's). This, Tors said, is due to the lack of financial resources available to women to adequately provide for their children. In fact, "female-headed households make up a disproportionate and increasing share of persons in poverty" (7).

Further, Tors (1995) says, "A lack of educational attainment can result in diminished critical reasoning ability in ascertaining cause and effect relationships, analyzing any media information and objectively assessing various choices at the personal, community and national levels" (9).

## Identification of the Student at Risk after Enrollment

Even though a college identifies a student at risk early, some students in need of assistance will not meet the profile criteria and will be excluded from very early identification. What can be done to identify this student? Identification of a student at risk must occur as soon as possible so interventions can be instituted early on. Remediating academic deficiencies or social behavioral problems once they have occurred may prove to be difficult.

Although some faculty believe that retention is not their responsibility, faculty play a central role in the identification and remediation of the student at risk after enrollment. Faculty are the key to successful retention programs. A student needs to be identified as a student at risk early in the first term. Some colleges currently use academic probation to define a student at risk, but academic probation is usually designated at the end of the term, after the student has experienced the problem, for the entire term. The longer a problem persists, the longer it may take to remediate. Since academic probation takes place after the term, the student may already be off campus. This will make it difficult to begin an intervention program. A student on academic probation may have been academically advised for the upcoming term and may have scheduled courses as though he or she passed the present term's work. What kind of signal are we sending to this student?

In addition, a college that has put a student on academic probation usually has a process that students must complete to reenroll for the next term. This type of student is less likely to seek help in the first place to overcome difficulties or is less able to navigate the probationary process. Consequently, the student will not follow through and probably not return. This seems a waste of human capital, especially when the problem may not be very critical and may be remediated with a minimum of services.

Early warning or midterm notification of academic difficulty is a step in the right direction. The earlier a deficiency can be identified, the sooner an intervention can begin. Since faculty work with students on an ongoing basis throughout the term, using them to help identify the student at risk during a term makes a lot of sense. Faculty know their students. Faculty know if the student is exhibiting poor attendance or poor writing skills (grammatical errors, etc.), is not attentive in class, seems to be distracted easily, fails quizzes, is not handing in work, is failing or exhibits poor work by a specific date, is falling asleep in class, has the appearance of being tired all of the time, and other warning signs.

Use faculty knowledge of student behaviors to help define the problem. A faculty subcommittee of the retention committee can collect anecdotal data to develop a profile of the student at risk during the first term in attendance. This profile is similar to the data-driven profile the college has for the unsuccessful student. Once a student at risk is defined during the first term, that student must be identified. This is where the faculty performs another central role. An early warning or alert Web-based system should be instituted. A feedback loop to the faculty member is desirable so the faculty member knows that participation is taken seriously and the college is beginning an intervention with the referred student. In addition, the student may even be the faculty member's advisee. Keeping the faculty member informed of interventions is another way to facilitate communication between the student and faculty member. College administrators would be very surprised to learn that faculty members can probably identify a student at risk after the first week of class, since faculty members recognize an unsuccessful student as soon as that student arrives in their class.

Since faculty know their students well, they should meet with students individually on a regular basis. Faculty can use the campus email system to identify students whom they feel may be having academic or social difficulties or simply to communicate with a student. An acknowledgment to the faculty member who identifies a student at risk should be built into the system, as well as follow-up reports on the student. If the student is hard to contact or not abiding with the intervention, then the faculty member can be contacted to personally meet with the student. Additionally, the faculty member can develop a class discussion listserv where students can ask questions and interact with each other, perhaps facilitating a classroom community. The faculty member can come into the discussion list at any time to clarify points or discuss other issues. The possibilities to help students are endless.

Encouraging faculty to interact with students in other than the formal classroom setting is also important. Perhaps faculty can be encouraged to eat in the cafeteria with students by subsidizing faculty food purchases. Faculty should be encouraged to attend cultural and sporting events at a discount and announce those upcoming events prior to the beginning of class to encourage student participation. Meeting students in other than the formal classroom setting has been shown to be significant in helping students persist. Departmental events (teas, coffee, pizza, job events) can bring students together to interact with each other and with departmental faculty.

## Academic and Personal Assessment

Once the student at risk is identified, either through pre- or post-enrollment, an extensive assessment should be given. A battery of academic assessment tools can be used and scored immediately using computer adaptive assessment. Other types of personality assessment or social assessment can also be given. It is important that assessment occur upon identification or referral and that the results are made available in a timely fashion so remedial action can commence at the earliest possible time. Again, if the assessment can be made prior to enrollment, then interventions can potentially start long before the beginning of the student's first term (see Figure 11.1).

## Diagnosis and Prescription

Directly after assessment, the student will need to meet with a professional who can interpret and diagnose the assessment results and develop a prescription for success. It is important that assessment results be given to and thoroughly discussed with the student. The student must realize there is indeed a problem(s) and if not corrected there is a very good chance that the student will not succeed at the college. Naturally, some students will be in denial, but nevertheless, the problem(s) needs to be identified and discussed with the student honestly and openly.

Once the diagnosis is made, then the prescription can be written. A contract between the counselor and the student may be developed. Peer intervention may be appropriate, as in the dropping of a class, use of existing campus programs where appropriate (tutorials, peer counseling, psychological counseling, Alcoholics Anonymous (AA), etc.), or referral to outside agencies. Remember, a student may be academically but not socially integrated. A brilliant student may be a social isolate, and may leave because of this isolation. A student may be so socially integrated that he or she parties to the detriment of going to class. The diagnosis is critical, and weekly meetings can be held where program progress is discussed. Interventions can be adjusted as the term progresses.

The intervention should be mandatory. If the student does not, or will not, abide by the diagnosis or prescription, then an appeals process can be built into the system. After the appeal, either the student abides by the decision, or the student can go to another college. This may sound draconian, but the college is trying to provide the student with the tools, both academic and social, to succeed. The college must be committed to providing the necessary services and the student must be willing to accept the prescription. Concentrating on the student who will benefit from the interventions will keep him or her through goal completion. Letting a student attend a college who is likely to be unsuccessful can seem as cruel as not letting the student enroll if he or she does not accept the intervention. Since assessment, diagnosis, and prescription are based on empirical data and an appeals process is built into the system, the acceptance should be withdrawn if the student does not want to partake in the prescription specified.

## Follow-Up

If a student takes a remedial program, then the college has the responsibility to make sure that the student is receiving and doing whatever was prescribed. Follow-up, where the professional counselor and the student meet regularly to assess and discuss progress and outcomes, is important. Email contact can be used, although face-to-face meetings are best, and checking with those providing the remediation is also important to get a sense of how the student is doing.

Remember, for intervention programs and services to be successful, they must be powerful enough to effect change. The prescription can, and in many instances will, take longer than one term in order to reme-diate problems. It is doubtful that a writing problem can be corrected in only one term, so the intervention must be longer. If specific deficiencies can be identified, then perhaps the remediation can be divided into mod-ules. Once one module is completed, the student can move on to the next one, and so on, until mastery is demonstrated. Suggested summer instruction can be encouraged and contingencies for the following term plan mapped out. Contacts during vacations and the summer will show the student that the college is indeed concerned with his or her academic and social growth and development. A summer newsletter can be sent to all students, and one may be sent specifically to the parent or guardian of a student to keep the parent or guardian informed of campus events and other topics.

If a number of skills can be identified (perhaps ten in writing, for ex-ample), then the student should only have to work on the specific skill deficiency instead of starting at the beginning of a course. In this ex-ample, the student lacks skills 7, 8, and 10. The remediation should be for skills 7, 8, and 10 and not 1–10, as is presently the case at most col-leges. The remediation may take only three weeks or it may take many more, depending on the identified problem(s) and student motivation. Since most colleges already have supplemental or remedial programs, ad-ditional cost is minimal. The idea is to identify problems early, diagnose them, and develop individual mandatory prescriptions. Student assess-ment will and should be ongoing to ensure that progress is being made and that the prescription is modified as necessary.

## Measuring Student Success Outcomes

Program evaluation should be ongoing to judge its effectiveness. The profile of the student at risk should be adjusted after each term or year, and programs should be strengthened in order to effect change. Faculty identification after enrollment should be updated periodically. Outcome measures are very important too. Looking at the data from course, pro-gram, and student retention perspectives can help a college determine whether or not courses are providing the necessary skills for students to succeed in the next level course. Program retention data will allow the college to determine the length of time, under various circumstances (i.e., after one year of remediation), it will take a full-time student to com-plete a program. Student retention data can provide the needed infor-mation for a college to know whether or not a student is reaching his or her educational and personal goals when he or she exits the college.

## Concluding Remarks

Education is a process that should be nurtured, cultivated, and developed. There should be a lifelong learning process for all citizens. It is a benefit to our nation and society if we can promote and encourage the thirst for knowledge. Anyone should feel comfortable seeking out answers to simple and complex questions using the skills gained through the education process. There are many benefits to the pursuit of lifelong learning opportunities. Keeping current in an ever-changing and complicated world is essential. Since job skills continue to evolve, employees should know how to access a variety of learning experiences. Our society should also encourage our populace to seek out learning simply for the joy of learning. The development of critical thinking skills is essential so that people can filter what they hear and read and make independent judgments.

The programs and services of colleges and universities should afford the individual the opportunity to develop new ideas, mature emotionally, experience the world around him or her, develop critical thinking skills, and learn to tolerate individual differences. Are colleges meeting the needs of students in this regard? Are programs and services integrated to give a student a sense of the world around him or her and the needed support to be successful? Does a college practice what it preaches in its literature, that a high value is placed on learning? Does a college demonstrate this to a student? Should everyone be given the opportunity for a college education? How much of its financial resources should the nation spend to help all students achieve academic and personal goals?

Students need to be able to complete programs that they are interested in pursuing. Students who are recruited and admitted to a college should have a reasonable expectation that programs and services will provide them with a chance for success.

How can we ensure that programs offered by a college are excellent and provide students with the needed skills in an area of specialization? To ensure academic program excellence, assessment, of course, and program offerings, and a good "fit" with future courses and programs are necessary. For instance, does the exit skill for a course meet the entry-level skills for the next progressive course? How does a program at the college effectively prepare the student for the next level program at another college or for a job? Does a community college program in accounting prepare a student to transfer to a four-year college and not lose credit because courses do not match up? Does the community college have transfer agreements or developed programs to match the first two years of the four-year college program? Has the four-year college program prepared the student with the skills necessary for the world of work? Have colleges received feedback from employers about whether or not programs have adequately prepared the student for the demands of the workplace? How flexible is a college to alter its curricula to meet changing industry and business needs? Has the four-year college prepared the student to pursue a graduate degree either directly after graduation or later?

The smooth transition and progression of courses and programs will enable the student to better achieve his or her academic and personal goals. Courses should complement each other and work in progression as a student learns about a particular area of interest. Outcome measures of achievement need to be considered along the way to ensure that the student is learning what the student is supposed to learn.

The exploration of creating classroom communities for commuter students may enable them to become integrated into the academic and social systems of a college. The research shows that commuters find it harder to become integrated into the social systems of a college. This occurs because, once finished with a class, the student goes home, back to relationships of the past. The transition from high school to college is a lot harder to accomplish in this instance. Developing classroom communities can help to overcome this barrier.

The establishment of learning communities makes a college look at different ways to deliver course content and programs to students. Grouping students with similar interests together in residence halls and classes establishes a bond within the group and should help the student become integrated into the academic and social systems of the college.

Therefore, it is incumbent on colleges and universities to recruit, accept, and enroll students who will succeed at their institution. Colleges should attempt to match student characteristics with those of the college. Accepting a student who does not meet college characteristics academically may be setting up the student for failure. If a college does accept a student, it is also important to provide the student with the programs and services to help the student succeed.

Retention rates have not improved over the years, in spite of the many and varied programs and services that colleges have instituted. Colleges have spent enormous sums of money and resources to help students integrate into the academic and social systems of the college. Individual programs, such as orientation and academic counseling, have been shown to have a positive impact on retention, but taken in isolation, individual programs may not provide an experience that is comprehensive and intensive enough to effect change. For retention programs and services to make a difference they must be powerful enough to effect change. It is evident from the research that colleges are taking retention seriously. As is evident by the money expended and resources committed to retention, retention continues to be an important issue on our campuses.

It is time to move forward in the quest to help students meet their academic and personal goals. While the Tinto model provides the foundation, the Seidman retention formula provides colleges with a method to achieve retention goals.

$$RET = E_{ID} + (E + I + C)_{IV},$$

that is,

RETention = Early $_{IDentification}$ + (Early + Intensive + Continuous) $_{InterVention}$,

gives a college a formula to help students succeed. Simply, the student at risk is identified as early as possible, using a variety of assessment tools, and once identified, the student and a professional meet to discuss the assessment outcome (diagnosis) and plan intervention(s) to remediate a deficiency. An honest discussion of area(s) of concern and how the college will assist the student in overcoming the deficiency is essential. The student needs to know that, as part of the admissions process, the remediation plan is mandatory. The student must follow the prescription specified with periodic assessment to check on progress and adjust the program where necessary. The college will have to commit the resources necessary to monitor and follow up with a student. The program must also be flexible enough to be modified where necessary and powerful enough to effect change. The college may also want to set time limits to complete the mastery of skills—but must give sufficient time to complete them.

Linkages with community agency services should be a part of the assistance offered to the student. Sharing resources can strengthen the bond between the college and local community, can cut costs, and can provide a positive exchange between colleges and local and governmental agencies. If a new program or service needs to be developed, these partnerships can help to minimize expenses. Sharing resources may overcome cost issues by providing enough clients to make the program cost effective.

Is this type of program people-intensive? It can very well be. Chapter 10, "Finances and Retention: Trends and Potential Implications," deals with this topic and demonstrates the cost benefit of keeping a student through academic and personal goal attainment.

Preparing a student for the challenges of the world in which he or she must live is the main mission of a college. Providing the student with programs and services to help students reach their academic and personal goals and aspirations is a small price to pay to accomplish this mission. An educated citizenry will keep the United States strong and vibrant. This, in essence, is what makes us a great nation and an example for others to follow.

## REFERENCES

Astin, A. (1985, July/August). Involvement: The cornerstone of excellence. *Change* 35–39.

Baumgart, N., & Johnston, J. (1977). Attrition at an Australian university: A case study. *Journal of Higher Education* 48(5): 553–570.

Crockett, D. S. (1984). *Advising skills, techniques, and resources.* Iowa City: ACT National Center for the Advancement of Educational Practices.

Green, E. (1987). At many colleges, orientation has become a serious introduction to campus life. *Chronicle of Higher Education* 34(6): 41–43.

Hewlett, S. (1991). *When the bough breaks: The cost of neglecting our children.* New York: Basic Books.

Pascarella, E. T., Terenzini, P. T., & Wolfe, L. M. (1986). Orientation to college and freshman year persistence/withdrawal decisions. *Journal of Higher Education* 57(2): 153–175.

Reisberg, L. (1999, October). Colleges struggle to keep would-be dropouts enrolled. *Chronicle of Higher Education* 46: 54.

Seidman, A. (1992a). Academic advising can have a positive impact on student enrollment: The results of an integrated admissions and counseling process on student enrollment. *Colleague* (State University of New York), 36–42.

———. (1992b). Integrated admission counseling: Impact on enrollment. *Freshman Year Experience Newsletter* 4: 6.

———. (1993). Needed: A research methodology to assess community college effectiveness. *Community College Journal* 63(5): 36–40.

———. (1995). The community college: A challenge for change. *Community College Journal of Research and Practice* 19(3): 247–254.

———. (1996). Retention revisited: $R = E_{ID} + (E + I + C)_{IV}$. *College and University* 71(4): 18–20.

———. (2004). *Retention slide show.* www.cscsr.org/docs/RetentionFormula2004a_files/frame.htm (accessed April 12, 2004).

Terenzini, P. T., Lorang, W. G., & Pascarella, E. T. (1981). Predicting freshman persistence and voluntary dropout decisions: A replication. *Research in Higher Education* 15(2): 109–127.

Tinto, V. (1997). Classrooms as communities. *Journal of Higher Education* 68(6): 599–623.

———. (1998). Colleges as communities: Taking research on student persistence seriously. *Review of Higher Education* 21(2): 167–177.

———. (1987). *Leaving college: Rethinking the causes and cures of student attrition.* Chicago: University of Chicago Press.

———. (1993). *Leaving college: Rethinking the causes and cures of student attrition.* 2nd ed. Chicago: University of Chicago Press.

Tinto, V., Russo, P., & Kadel, S. (1994). Constructing educational communities: Increasing retention in challenging circumstances. *Community College Journal* 64(4): 26–29.

Tors, B. (1995). *A preliminary investigation of factors affecting educational attainment of children of divorce.* ERIC Document Reproduction Service No. ED 391 121.

Young, R. J. (1999). An examination of factors influencing retention of developmental education students at selected Texas community colleges. Doctoral dissertation, University of Texas at Austin.

# EPILOGUE
## Moving from Theory to Action

*Vincent Tinto*

### INTRODUCTION

Despite many years of research on student retention and attempts at theory building, there is still much to do. Although significant strides have been made in constructing the broad dimensions of a theory of institutional departure, there is still a good deal of disagreement, if not confusion, over the details of such a theory. More important, there has been little significant development of a theory of action that would provide guidelines to institutions of higher education so that they can develop policies, programs, and practices to enhance student persistence. Consequently, while it can be said that we now know the broad dimensions of the process of student leaving, we know very little about a theory of action for student persistence. The goal of this concluding chapter is to continue the discussion started by Alan Seidman in Chapter 11; to lay out the broad outlines of such a theory and show how the theory might be used to guide institutional action.

To do so, we first must consider the nature of the current debate about existing retention theories, in particular as they are exemplified in the preceding chapters. Understanding some of the challenges that researchers and theorists face will not only help build a more effective theory of student departure but also aid our pursuit of a useful theory of institutional action.

## REFLECTION ON CURRENT DEBATES OF A THEORY OF INSTITUTIONAL DEPARTURE

### Defining Student Leaving

One of the challenges we face in developing social theory, regardless of its focus, lies in the complexity of defining the very object of our concern, namely, human behavior. We continue to struggle with the question of how we should define the human act. Is it what an external observer sees or what the actor intends? So too in considering student leaving: we have yet to be clear on what constitutes leaving. Is it the act that is seen by an institutional observer, or is it what the leaver intends? Though an institutional observer (e.g., administrator) may rightly feel that any departure represents a type of failure, if only because of the loss of revenue as described by John Schuh in Chapter 10, the departing individual may understand his or her departure quite differently. Among other possibilities, the leaver may understand leaving as enabling entry to another institution (transfer). In that case, it may be seen as a positive rather than negative act.[1] It may also be the case that some students leave to take on a job or accept a promotion that was in fact the goal of their initial entry. In this case, their attendance has led to the successful achievement of an occupational goal.[2] For other persons, leaving may represent a response to external commitments that pull them away from the institution. They would have preferred to stay but were obliged to leave at least for a period of time. For some this may result in stopout, while for others it may mean the end of their educational pursuit. In either case, their leaving may be seen as a form of involuntary behavior that has little to do with their experience on campus.

What is the point? The point is that among the behaviors an institutional observer may define as institutional departure, there are likely to be a range of behaviors that are quite different in character, intent, and causation. Unfortunately, most studies of institutional departure, and by extension attempts to construct and test theories of institutional departure, have typically lumped together, under the label "leaving," what often are very different behaviors.[3] The result is not only a restriction to explained variance, but more importantly a conceptual confusion that yields muddled if not contradictory and sometimes nonsensical conclusions. This, in effect, is the point Tom Mortenson makes in Chapter 2.

There are other challenges. Researchers have often ignored Weber's observation that the terms we employ in constructing social theory, such as social status, are abstractions that cannot be understood without specific reference to the behaviors and contexts from which they are derived. Nor can they be separated from the meanings individuals attach to their behaviors. People do not have social status. They have, among other things, income, education, occupation, and material possessions. Social status is merely an abstraction that allows us to talk about how the sum of those possessions can be used to understand patterns of human behavior. At the same time, though our analyses of human behavior often assume that people understand and respond to social status in very much the same ways, we know that this is not the case. We make that assumption to simplify what would otherwise be very complex analyses.

The same can be said of the abstractions "academic and social integration." The fact is that students are not integrated. They interact with a range of people and situations on campus, both academic and social, and they derive meaning from those interactions in ways that may lead them to feel at home or feel that they are a member of a place or community. They feel that they "belong." Of course, others may, in the process of interaction, come to feel at odds with those who make up the institution or feel that they are not welcomed by people in the institution. They feel as if they do not belong or that others do not want them to belong. This is what Hurtado and Carter (1996) were getting at in their use of the term *hostile climate*. In the final analysis, what matters in students' decisions to stay or leave are not their interactions, as objectively defined, but how they understand and draw meaning from those interactions. For researchers, what matters are not the abstractions such as academic or social integration that we use, but how we define and in turn measure the behaviors from which the abstractions are drawn, and the different meanings that people derive from those interactions.

Why does this matter? It matters because what we use for our construction and tests of theory are data that reflect a series of decisions involving both conceptualization and measurement that may vary from study to study, and may differentially represent differing behaviors. Although studies may be using the same abstraction, such as academic integration, their data are often drawn from very different measures. The result is more conceptual confusion that further muddies the water.

What's my point? My point is simply that we still have much to do to develop a more powerful theory of institutional leaving that captures the full range of behaviors that are lumped under the umbrella term of "student leaving." This does not mean that our existing theories are seriously flawed. Quite the contrary, we have more than ample evidence to support the broad outlines of existing theories of student institutional departure. Those theories are, in their current form, only rough predictors of leaving as currently measured. In their present formulation, they can tell us only so much about the forces that shape student leaving.

More important, theories of student leaving can tell us only so much about the forces shaping student persistence. Leaving is not the mirror image of staying. Knowing why students leave does not tell us, at least not directly, what institutions can do to help students stay and succeed. What matters are not our theories, but how those theories help us address pressing issues of persistence, especially among low-income and underrepresented students. Unfortunately, current theories of student leaving are not well suited to that task. This is not only because they focus on leaving, but also because they utilize abstractions and variables that are not clearly under the immediate control of the institution to influence. Take, for instance, the concept of academic integration. Though the concept may be useful to a theorist, it does not tell a practitioner what she or he would do to achieve academic integration. What is needed is a model of student persistence and in turn a model of institutional action that provide institutions guidelines to develop effective policies, procedures, and programs that enhance the persistence of students, especially those who continue to fare less well in higher education, namely low-income and underrepresented students.

## Moving Toward a Model of Institutional Action

Our goal here is modest. Rather than propose a full model—that is beyond the scope of this chapter—we will identify some of the major elements that such a model must include. We do so in the expectation that future work will begin to fill in the gaps and move toward the development and testing of a useful model and in turn a theory of institutional action for student success.[4]

In moving toward the identification of a possible model of institutional action, we will focus on the conditions within institutions in which we place students rather than on the attributes of students themselves. We will focus on the conditions within institutions because it is too easy to see the absence of student success as solely the responsibility of students. Too often we tend to blame the victim and avoid seeing our own actions as being at least partially responsible for the problems we face.

This is not to say that individual attributes do not matter. Of course they do. In some cases they matter greatly. We all know of stories of students who by sheer drive of personality succeed against what are for most students seemingly insurmountable barriers. Yet other students do not succeed even when placed in settings that favor success. Nevertheless, though some might argue otherwise, student attributes such as personality, drive, or motivation are, for the great majority of institutions, largely beyond immediate institutional control.[5] This is not the case, however, for the conditions or environments in which students are placed. Such environments are already within institutional control, reflecting as they do past decisions, and can be changed if institutions are serious in their pursuit of student success. Since our focus is on institutional action, it makes sense to begin our search for a model of action with those aspects of institutional environment that shape student success and that are within the capacity of institutions to change.

What are these conditions? What does research on student success tell us about the conditions within universities that promote success?[6] What it tells us is that there are at least five conditions that capture the nature of settings in which students are most likely to succeed. These conditions are institutional commitment, expectations, support, feedback, and involvement or engagement.

## Commitment

First and perhaps most clearly, institutional commitment is a condition for student success. Simply put, institutions that are committed to the goal of increasing student success, especially among low-income and underrepresented students, seem to find a way to achieve that end. But institutional commitment is more than just words, more than just mission statements issued in elaborate brochures; it is the willingness to invest the resources and provide the incentives and rewards needed to enhance student success. Without such commitment, programs for student success may begin, but they rarely prosper over the long term.

## Expectations

Second, expectations, specifically high expectations, are a condition for student success. Quite simply, no student rises to low expectations. Regrettably, too often universities expect too little of students, especially during the critical first year of college. Indeed, a recent national study by Kuh (2003) indicates that first-year students spend less time on their studies out of class than what we deem necessary for successful learning. They simply do not study enough. It is my view that this is the case in part because we do not expect enough of them or construct educational settings that require them to study enough.

At the same time, universities will sometimes hold different expectations for different students. This may be expressed in the labels we use to describe groups of students, as for instance contained in the term *remedial* students, or more subtly, but no less effectively, in the way we treat different students as sometimes happens among faculty and students of different gender or ethnicity. However expressed, research is clear that students quickly pick up expectations and are influenced by the degree to which those expectations validate their presence on campus. This is precisely what Rendon (1994) was referring to in her research on validation and success of nontraditional, first-generation college students and what Solorzano, Ceja, and Yosso (2000) were referring to in their study of microaggressions.

Expectations can also be expressed in concrete ways through formal and informal advising. Knowing the rules and regulations and the informal networks that mark campus life are part and parcel of student success. Yet formal advising remains a hit-and-miss affair; some students are lucky and find the information they need, while others are not. The same can be said of the informal advising, the sharing of accumulated knowledge that goes on within a campus among and between faculty, staff, and students. Again some students are able to locate that knowledge, often through informal networks of peers, while others are not (Attinasi 1989).

Advising is particularly important to the success of the many students who either begin college undecided about their major or change their major during college.[7] The inability to obtain needed advice during the first year or at the point of changing majors can undermine motivation, increase the likelihood of departure, and for those who continue, result in increased time to degree completion. Although students may make credit progress, they do not make substantial degree-credit progress.

## Support

Third, support is a condition that promotes student success. Research points to three types of support that promote success, namely, academic, social, and financial. As regards academic support, unfortunately more than a few students enter the university insufficiently prepared for the rigors of university study. For them, as well as for others, the availability of academic support, for instance, in the form of developmental education courses, tutoring, study groups, and academic support programs such as supplemental instruction, is an important condition for their continuation in the university. So also is the availability of social support in the form of counseling, mentoring, and ethnic student centers. Such centers provide much-needed support for individual students and a safe haven for groups of students who might otherwise find themselves out of place in a setting where they are a distinct minority. For new students, these centers can serve as secure, knowable ports of entry that enable students to safely navigate the unfamiliar terrain of the university.

As regards the nature of support, research has demonstrated that support is most effective when it is connected to, not isolated from, the learning environment in which students are asked to learn. Supplemental instruction, for instance, provides academic support that is directly attached to a specific class in order to help students succeed in that class. As a support strategy, it is most often used for key first-year "gateway" courses that are foundational to course work that follows in subsequent years.

## Feedback

Fourth, monitoring and feedback are conditions for student success. Students are more likely to succeed in settings that provide faculty, staff, and students frequent feedback about their performance. Here I refer not only to entry assessment of learning skills and early warning systems that alert institutions to students who need assistance, but also to classroom assessment techniques such as those described by Angelo and Cross (1993) and those that involve the use of learning portfolios. These techniques are not to be confused with testing; rather, they are forms of assessment, such as the well-known "one-minute" paper, that provide students and faculty alike information on what is or is not being learned in the classroom. When used frequently, such techniques enable students and faculty alike to adjust their learning and teaching in ways that promote learning. When implemented in portfolio form that requires continuous reflection, assessment can also deeply enrich learning.

## Involvement

Fifth, and finally, involvement, or what has been frequently been described as academic and social integration, is a condition for student success (e.g., Astin 1993; Tinto 1993). Quite simply, the more students are academically and socially involved, the more likely they are to persist and graduate. This is especially true during the first year of university study when student membership is so tenuous yet so critical to subsequent learning and persistence. Involvement during that year serves as the foundation upon which subsequent affiliations and engagements are built.

Nowhere is involvement more important than in the classrooms and laboratories of the campus, again especially during the first year of college. This is the case for two reasons. First, the classroom may be the only place students meet each other and the faculty. Lest we forget, most students commute to college and a majority work while in college. For them and for many others, the classroom is often the only place where they meet other students and the faculty. If involvement does not occur in those smaller places of engagement, it is unlikely it will easily occur elsewhere. Second, learning is central to the college experience and the root source of student success. Involvement in classroom learning, especially with other students, leads to greater quality of effort, enhanced learning, and in turn heightened student success (Tinto 1997). Even among students who persist, students who are more involved in learning, especially with other students, learn more and show greater levels of intellectual development (Endo & Harpel 1982). It is for these reasons that so much of the literature on institutional retention, student learning, and development speaks of the importance of building educational communities that involve all, not just some, students (Tinto 1993).

To sum up, students are more likely to succeed when they find themselves in settings that are committed to their success, hold high expectations for their success, provide needed academic, social, and financial support, provide frequent feedback, and actively involve them, especially with other students and faculty in learning. The key concept is that of educational community and the capacity of institutions to establish educational communities that involve all students as equal members.

## Moving Toward a Theory of Institutional Action

Two observations should be made about the current discussion. First, this discussion argues that student learning is central to student success and by extension that without learning, students are not successful regardless of whether or not they persist. The more students learn, the more value they find in their learning, the more likely they are to stay and graduate. This is true not only for those students who enter college academically underprepared, but also for the more able and motivated students who seek out learning and are, in turn, more likely to respond to perceived shortcomings in the quality of learning they experience on campus.

Second, our discussion leaves open, for the moment, the definition of success other than to imply that without learning there is no success and that at a minimum success implies successful learning in the classroom. By extension this discussion argues that one way of understanding stu-

## Figure E.1
## Elements of a Model of Institutional Action

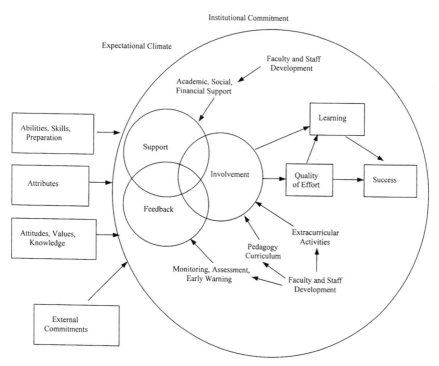

dent success as it may be influenced by institutional action is to see it as being constructed from success in one class at a time, one upon another in ways that lead to academic progress. A model of institutional action, whatever its final dimensions, must therefore treat student learning as part and parcel of the process of student success and that success, however it is defined and measured, must have at its core success in individual classes.

What then might a model of institutional action for student success look like? Following upon the prior discussion, Figure E.1 describes some of the elements that such a model would contain and some of the institutional actions that would shape those elements.

Students enter an institution with a variety of attributes (e.g., gender, social class, race, ethnicity), abilities, skills, and levels of prior academic preparation (e.g., academic and social skills), and attitudes, values, and knowledge about higher education (e.g., goals, commitments, motivations, and expectations). At the same time, they participate in a range of external settings (e.g., family, work, and community), each of which have their own demands on the students' time and energies. They enter an institution with specific attributes (e.g., level, mode of control, size, location, and resources). As argued here, both student and institutional attributes, within the time frame for institutional action, are considered fixed and therefore not immediate objects of institutional action.[8] What are not fixed are institutional commitments; the expectational climate established by members of the institution (faculty, staff, administrators, and other students); the academic, social, and financial supports provided by the institution; the feedback that is provided to and about students by the institution; and the educational and social activities that shape student academic and social involvements or engagements.

As depicted, the model argues that institutional commitments provide the overarching context for institutional action. As noted earlier, everything else being equal, institutions that are committed to student success are more likely to generate that success than institutions whose commitment to students may be of lower order than other competing commitments (e.g., research, athletics). Institutional commitment to student success in turn sets the tone for the expectational climate for success that students encounter in their everyday interactions with the institution— with its policies, practices, and various members (faculty, staff, administrators, and other students).

Within these nested climates, students encounter varying degrees of academic, social, and financial support, are provided varying types of feedback about their progress, and experience educational settings whose structure and practices result in differing degrees of academic and social involvement. These act together to influence the quality of student effort (Pace 1982), which in turn influences student learning, and both influence student success. That success and success in other classes generate credit and degree credit progress and, for some students, eventual degree completion.

The institution acts in a variety of ways through its policies, practices, and programs to shape those conditions. Although there are many possible courses of action, Figure E.1 notes several that must be part of any institutional strategy for student success. Two deserve comment here, namely, actions that shape pedagogy and curriculum and those that attend to faculty and staff development. The former actions play a direct role in shaping the learning environment within the class and in turn patterns of social and academic involvements. The latter actions, especially as they relate to faculty, play a direct role in influencing pedagogy and curriculum and, in turn, an indirect but very important role in student involvements, and therefore student learning and success. Faculty and staff development practices may also influence assessment practices and help shape the way support is provided to students.[9]

Several observations should be made about the model. First, in this model student effort and learning are central to student success. Second, in this model the classroom is the critical ground upon which student success is played out. This is especially true for nonresidential campuses and for commuter students because in those settings, and for those students, the classroom may be the only place where students engage faculty, staff, and other students in learning. Third, this model is intended to highlight those aspects of institutional environments that are amenable to direct institutional action, which have been shown to influence student success. As such, the model posits a chain of causation linking institutional action to environments in which students participate to student success. As a result, although it is evident that external events matter, for the purposes of this discussion, such events are treated as outside institutional control. Fourth, the model is preliminary. It is not intended to be a full model of institutional action. Clearly there is more that should be, and over time will have to be, added to this model to make it a more complete depiction of how institutional actions shape student success.

## Translating Theory into Action: A Case Study

To repeat, the model of institutional action presented here argues that students are more likely to succeed when they find themselves in settings that are committed to their success; hold high expectations for their success; provide needed academic, social, and financial support; provide frequent feedback; and actively involve students with other students and faculty, especially in learning. The key concept is that of educational community and the capacity of institutions to establish educational communities that involve all students as equal members.

Unfortunately, the educational experiences of most students are not involving; the time they spend on task disturbingly low (Kuh 2003). Learning, especially in the critical first year of college, is still very much a spectator sport in which faculty talk dominates and where few students actively participate. Most students experience learning as isolated learners whose learning is disconnected from that of others, where the curriculum is experienced as a set of detached, individual courses, one separated from another in both content and peer group, one set of understandings unrelated in any intentional fashion to the content learned in other courses. Although specific programs of study are designed for each major, courses have little academic or social coherence. It is little wonder that students seem so uninvolved in learning. Their learning experiences are not very involving.

## Pedagogies of Engagement

What should universities and colleges do? How should they reorganize themselves and construct educational environments that promote student learning? Fortunately there are a number of pedagogical, curricular, and support strategies for which evidence supports the claim that they can enhance student persistence and learning. These strategies include the use of cooperative or collaborative learning and problem-based learning strategies that require students to work together in cooperative groups: service learning, where students engage in service activities that are connected to learning in the classroom; the use of learning communities that require students to enroll in courses together and share the experience of learning a common coherent curriculum; classroom assessment techniques that provide students and faculty frequent feedback about student learning; and the use of supplemental instruction strategies where academic assistance is connected to specific courses and to specific student academic needs.

Although these reforms are different, they share a number of common attributes that capture the underlying sources of their success. First, they all focus on student learning and the places in which students are asked to learn. They are either located in classrooms or directed toward the task of learning in the classroom. Second, they all stress shared, connected learning and the importance of educational community. Students are asked to learn together in a coherent manner and form communities that provide social as well as academic support. Third, when assistance is provided, it is typically connected to the classroom, not isolated from it. In this way, assistance is contextualized so that students can utilize assistance for learning in the settings in which they are attempting to learn.

## Learning Communities and Student Success

Of these various possibilities, I will focus here on learning communities because accumulating evidence suggest that learning communities offer a particularly effective way of addressing the learning needs of a range of students while also providing a structure for collaboration among faculty and between faculty and student affairs professionals (Taylor et al. 2004). Equally important, for the purposes of the present discussion, learning communities provide institutions an integrated way of directing support, feedback, and involvement to the critical task of learning in the classroom.

Learning communities have a number of characteristics (Gablenick 1990). First, they require students to enroll in two or more courses together. In this way, students are asked to share the experience of taking courses together. But the courses students take are not random or coincidental; the courses must be linked by an organizing theme or problem that gives meaning to their linkage. This is necessary because an important attribute of learning communities is that they serve to build academic as well as social connections between what otherwise would be discrete academic and social experiences. Their purpose is to promote a deeper, richer multidisciplinary learning that is typically not possible when courses are unrelated one to another. To do so, learning communities require the faculty and staff who teach in them to collaborate. This collaboration will ensure that the experience of the learning community provides an academic coherence that crosses the borders of the linked courses. Finally, an increasing number of learning communities are altering the way students experience learning so that students not only share the curriculum; they also share the experience of learning the shared curriculum together. Faculty and staff are turning away from reliance on traditional lecture methods to more active learning strategies such as cooperative learning, collaborative learning, and problem-based or project-based learning.

Research has shown that learning communities, in particular those that are fully integrated, yield a number of important benefits for students (Tinto 2000). First, students tend to develop supportive peer groups and find personal support via the interactions that occur within those groups. As one student noted in an interview, the learning community in which she was enrolled was "like a raft running the rapids of her life." Second, students in learning communities tend to spend more time together, in particular more time studying together, and they do so in ways that extend beyond the borders of the classroom. As one student observed, "class continued even after class." The result is that students study more after class and they do so with other students with whom they share the learning community. Third, in finding more support and spending more time studying, students in learning communities become more involved in a range of learning activities, learn more, and persist more frequently than do students in more traditional learning settings (Tinto 1997, 2000; Zhao & Kuh 2004). This is true for regularly admitted students as well as those students who enter academically underprepared for college work (Tinto 1998; Malnarich et al. 2004). Finally, and perhaps most importantly, students in learning communities, in particular those communities employ active learning strategies, speak of "learning better together." They come to experience and, in turn, value the power of environments that provide for a multilensed, multivoice learning experience that requires students to "think, re-think, and even re-re-think" about what they are learning. As one student noted, "you not only learn more, you learn better" (Tinto 2003).

One of the many virtues of learning communities is that they can be applied to a variety of majors and fields of study and can be adapted to the needs of varying groups of students. For instance, they are being adapted to the needs of undecided students as well as students who require academic assistance (Tinto 1998; Malnarich et al. 2004). In the latter case, one or more of the linked courses is a developmental level or study skills course. In residential campuses, some learning communities have moved into the residence halls. These "living-learning communities" combine shared course work with shared living. However structured, the power of these and other arrangements is that they enable the institution to integrate the provision of academic assistance to the social and academic needs of students in ways that are connected to their needs as learners. In other words, as a form of institutional action, learning communities enable institutions to reshape several important conditions, each of which impact student learning and, in turn, student success.

One of the other benefits of learning communities is that they provide an academic structure within which collaboration among faculty and between faculty and professional staff is possible, and indeed often required (Engstrom & Tinto 2000; Taylor et al. 2004). For learning communities to succeed, faculty must work together to ensure that the linked courses provide a coherent, shared learning experience that is tailored to the needs of the students whom the community serves. In this way, learning communities can have an indirect yet powerful impact upon student success because they help reshape the nature of institutional arrangements and patterns of affiliation that in turn impact the experiences of students and eventually their success.

## Closing Thought

Though we have learned much over the past thirty years on why students leave colleges, we have not yet fully explored why students stay and succeed. More important, we have yet to develop an effective model of institutional action that provides institutions guidelines for the development of policies, programs, and practices to enhance student success. The goal of this book, in particular this chapter and that by Alan Seidman, is the development of such a model. Clearly there is still much to do in the development of an effective model, not the least of which is the testing of various proposed models to determine which model proves most useful to institutions seeking to enhance student success. In the final analysis, that is the test that matters.

## NOTES

1. Indeed more than a few students enter institutions with the unstated goal of transferring to another institution before graduation.

2. Lest we forget, a sizeable proportion of students enter higher education with no intention of completing a college degree. They may enter with the sole intent of obtaining a better job.

3. Given the likely variations in the patterning of differing types of leaving behaviors at different institutions, researchers who use multi-institutional data to study departure may inadvertently compound the problem by combining or comparing studies that reflect quite different patterns of leaving.

4. This is not to say that researchers have ignored this matter. In addition to a range of studies on the impact of specific programs on student success (e.g., Bowles & Jones 2003 study of supplemental instruction), several authors have written about strategies to increase retention (e.g., Braxton, Hirschy, & McClendon 2004). But only Swail, Redd, and Perna (2003) have sought to develop a comprehensive framework for student retention, specifically, for minority students.

5. Not surprisingly, many institutions see this issue as one of recruitment, of attracting more able and motivated students who themselves are more likely to graduate. But there are only so many able and motivated students, and it seems as if every university is seeking to attract the same group of students. In any event, such efforts leave untouched the learning environment and do little to ensure that the experience of students will in any way be changed by attracting more able students.

6. Here the term *research* must be understood more broadly as accumulated knowledge that includes research, institutional studies, and shared experience of many practitioners. Such research is often more reliable than the research cited in some of the chapters in this volume, because it involves the accumulation of evidence from differing sources and methodologies of knowledge making.

7. It is estimated that among four-year college students nearly two-thirds either begin undecided or change their majors at least once during college.

8. For the purposes of the present discussion, the time frame for institutional action is considered that which applies to the experiences of any entering student cohort, that is, three to five years. The longer-term time frame that would encompass several cohorts and therefore reflect long-term institutional actions is not considered in this discussion.

9. Some have argued that effective faculty and staff development practices are in fact essential for long-term institutional success because they shape the skills that faculty and staff bring to the task of helping their students succeed.

## REFERENCES

Angelo, T., & Cross, P. (1993). *Classroom assessment techniques: A handbook for college teachers.* San Francisco: Jossey-Bass.

Astin, A. (1993). *What matters in college.* San Francisco: Jossey-Bass.

Attinasi, L. C., Jr. (1989). Getting in: Mexican Americans' perceptions of university attendance and implications for freshman year persistence. *Journal of Higher Education* 60: 247–277.

Bowles, T. J., & Jones, J. (2003). The effect of supplemental instruction on retention: A bivariate probit model. *College Student Retention: Research, Theory and Practice* 5(4): 431–439.

Braxton, J., Hirschy, A., & McClendon, S. (2004). *Understanding and reducing college student departure.* San Francisco: Jossey-Bass.

Endo, J., & Harpel, R. (1982). The effect of student-faculty interaction on students' educational outcomes. *Research in Higher Education* 16: 115–135.

Engstrom, C., & Tinto, V. (2000). Building collaborative partnerships with student affairs to enhance student learning. In *Handbook for student affairs administrators*, ed. M. Barr. San Francisco: Jossey-Bass.

Gablenick, F., MacGregor, J., Matthews, R., & Smith, B. L. (1990). *Learning communities: Creating connections among students, faculty, and disciplines.* San Francisco: Jossey-Bass.

Hurtado, S., & Carter, D. F. (1996). Latino students' sense of belonging in the college community: Rethinking the concept of integration on campus. In *College students: The evolving nature of research*, ed. F. K. Stages. Needham Heights, MA: Simon and Schuster.

Kuh, G. (2003). What we're learning about student engagement from NSSE. *Change* 35(2): 24–32.

Malnarich, G., Dusenberry, P., Sloan, B., Swinton, J., & van Slyck, P. (2004). The pedagogy of possibilities: Developmental education, college studies, and learning communities. Olympia, WA: Washington Center for Improving the Quality of Undergraduate Education, Evergreen State College.

Pace, R. C. (1982). *Achievement and the quality of student effort.* Higher Education Research Institute, Graduate School of Education, University of California, Los Angeles.

Rendon, L. (1994). Validating culturally diverse students: Toward a new model of learning and student development. *Innovative Higher Education* 19: 13–52.

Solorzano, D., Ceja, M., & Yosso, T. (2000). Critical race theory, racial microaggressions and campus racial climate: The experiences of African American college students. *Journal of Negro Education* 69: 60–73.

Swail, S., Redd, K., & Perna, L. (2003). *Retaining minority students in higher education: A framework for success.* San Francisco: Jossey-Bass.

Taylor, K., Moore, W., MacGregor, J., & Lindblad, J. (2004). *Learning community research and assessment: What we know now.* Olympia: Washington Center for Improving the Quality of Undergraduate Education, Evergreen State College.

Tinto, V. (1993). *Leaving college: Rethinking the causes and cures of student attrition.* 2nd ed. Chicago: University of Chicago Press.

———. (1997). Classrooms as communities: Exploring the educational character of student persistence. *Journal of Higher Education* 68(6): 599–623.

———. (1998). Adapting learning communities to the needs of remedial education students. Paper presented at the Rethinking Remedial Education Symposium, Stanford University.

———. (2000). Linking learning and leaving: Exploring the role of college classrooms in student departure. In *Reworking the student departure puzzle,* ed. J. Braxton, 81–94. Nashville: Vanderbilt University Press.

———. (2003). *Learning better together.* Higher Education Monograph Series, No. 2. Syracuse: Higher Education Program, Syracuse University.

Zhao, C., & Kuh, G. (2004). Adding value: Learning communities and student engagement. *Research in Higher Education* 45(2): 115–138.

# INDEX

# ABOUT THE EDITOR AND CONTRIBUTORS

Some of the leading educators who study college student retention contributed to this book. I am grateful to each of them for their willingness to participate in this project. Each was enthusiastic with the endeavor and gave many helpful suggestions. All are truly dedicated to helping students achieve their individual academic and personal goals. The list and biographical sketch of each follows.

ALEXANDER W. ASTIN is Allan M. Cartter Professor of Higher Education at the University of California, Los Angeles, and senior scholar and founding Director of the Higher Education Research Institute at UCLA. He has authored twenty books and some three hundred other publications in the field of higher education. His books include *Preventing Students from Dropping Out, Predicting Academic Performance in College, Achieving Educational Excellence,* and *What Matters in College?: Four Critical Years Revisited* (1993). Major areas of inquiry include the outcomes of higher education, the role of values and spirituality in higher education, civic responsibility and service learning, institutional quality, equality of opportunity and access, assessment, and citizenship. Dr. Astin has been a recipient of awards for outstanding research and service from ten national educational associations, is a member of the National Academy of Education, has been a fellow at the Center for Advanced Study in the Behavioral Sciences, and is the recipient of ten honorary degrees. A 1990 study in the *Journal of Higher Education* identified Dr. Astin as the most frequently cited author in the field of higher education. In 1985 readers of *Change* magazine selected Dr. Astin as the person "most admired for creative, insightful thinking" in the field of higher education. Dr. Astin serves on the editorial board of the *Journal of College Student Retention: Research, Theory & Practice*.

ELIZABETH BARLOW is Executive Director of Institutional Research at the University of Houston, Houston, Texas. Her studies have focused on the adjustment and academic performance of first-time-in-college students and first-year transfer students at receiving institutions, and transforming the experience of at-risk undergraduate students on educational campuses. Dr. Barlow has published several institutional reports that have helped to uncover the underlying patterns among factors that positively and negatively affect undergraduate student performance. Currently, she has in press a refereed journal article on covariance structural modeling in the *American Educational Research Journal*.

JOHN P. BEAN, Associate Professor of Higher Education at Indiana University–Bloomington, has studied college student retention since writing his dissertation on the subject at the University of Iowa twenty-five years ago. He has been involved in about twenty empirical studies of college student retention, wrote with Don Hossler the classic *The Strategic Management of College Enrollments* (1990), and has served on the editorial board of the *Journal of College Student Retention: Research, Theory & Practice* since its inception. He is best known for his theoretical models of student retention which were based on organizational theory and psychology and provided plausible alternatives to the Durkheim/Spady/Tinto sociological approach to retention. According to Web of Science, his work has been cited by scholars in the field over 500 times. Miscellaneous activities include having written the lyrics for five songs on Tad Robinson's 2004 CD *Did You Ever Wonder*, making nine Cremonese-style violins, selling one of his oil paintings to John Mellencamp, and placing third in the 18-and-under Eastern U.S. Kayak Slalom Championships in 1964.

JOSEPH B. BERGER is an Associate Professor of Education and Chair of the Department of Educational Policy, Research, and Administration in the School of Education at the University of Massachusetts Amherst. He earned his B.A. in anthropology and sociology from Lawrence University; his M.A. in College Student Personnel from Bowling Green State University; and his Ph.D. in Education and Human Development, specializing in Higher Education Administration, from Vanderbilt University. He is the author of numerous book chapters, research reports, and journal articles, and has received several national awards for his research. He also serves on the editorial boards of journals such as *Research in Higher Education* and *Journal of College Student Development* and is the book review editor for the *Journal of College Student Retention: Research, Theory & Practice*.

JOHN M. BRAXTON is Professor of Education in the Higher Education Leadership and Policy Program in the Department of Leadership, Policy and Organizations at Peabody College, Vanderbilt University. His research interests center on the college student experience, the sociology of the academic profession, and academic course-level processes. He has published over sixty refereed journal articles and book chapters on topics related to these areas of research interest. His current scholarly interests include research and theory development pertaining to college student departure, scientific misconduct, and the normative structure of undergraduate college teaching. Recent articles and book chapters on these topics have appeared in the *Journal of Higher Education, Research in Higher Education, Science, Technology and Human Values,* and *Higher Education: Handbook of Theory and Research*.

Professor Braxton also has edited four books: *Reworking the Student Departure Puzzle, Perspectives on Scholarly Misconduct in the Sciences*, and *Faculty Teaching and Research: Is There Conflict?* He is also the author of three books: with Alan E. Bayer, Braxton wrote the book *Faculty Misconduct in Collegiate Teaching*; with William Luckey and Patricia Helland, he wrote *Institutionalizing a Broader View of Scholarship Through Boyer's Four Domains*; and with Amy S. Hirschy and Shederick A. McClendon, he wrote *Understanding and Reducing College Student Departure*.

Professor Braxton serves as a Consulting Editor for the *Journal of Higher Education* and *Research in Higher Education* and is on the editorial board of the *Journal of College Student Retention: Research, Theory & Practice* where he guest edited a special issue. He is also the Immediate-Past President of the Association for the Study of Higher Education.

KURT R. BURKUM is a doctoral student and Ostar Fellow in the Center for the Study of Higher Education at The Pennsylvania State University. He currently works with Dr. Carol Colbeck on institutional, state, and federal higher education policy initiatives for the center. His dissertation focuses on the role state higher education governance structures have in state-level higher education lobbying. Previous research at the center includes working with Dr. Colbeck on an examination of how faculty integrate work and family responsibilities, sponsored by the Alfred

P. Sloan Foundation, and a study with Dr. Alberto Cabrera of the factors that facilitate successful student transfer from the two-year to the four-year sector and subsequent degree completion, funded by the Association for Institutional Research. Before coming to Penn State, Kurt served as a student affairs administrator at Luther College in Decorah, Iowa, where he also received a bachelor's degree in psychobiology.

ALBERTO F. CABRERA specializes in research methodologies, college choice, college students, classroom experiences, minorities in higher education, and economics of education. He is a member of Pathways to College Network, which is dedicated to increasing college opportunities for underrepresented student populations. Dr. Cabrera has consulted with the Pell Institute, the Hispanic Association of Colleges and Universities (HACU), the Cooperative Institutional Research Program at the University of California, Los Angeles, the American Council on Education, Western Interstate Commission on Higher Education, United States Department of Education, the National Postsecondary Education Cooperative, the Argentinean Minister of Education, and with several universities in the United States and abroad. He has served on the editorial boards of *Journal of Higher Education*, *Review of Higher Education*, and *Research in Higher Education*. His work on classroom practices, the role of finances on college persistence, and determinants of default behavior has received several awards.

GLORIA CRISP is a doctoral student in educational leadership with a focus on higher education in the department of Educational Leadership and Cultural Studies, College of Education at the University of Houston, Texas. Ms. Crisp is also an instructor at San Jacinto Community College. Her research interest is in the area of student persistence at both two-year and four-year educational institutions.

LINDA SERRA HAGEDORN is an associate professor and the associate director of the Center for Higher Education Policy Analysis (CHEPA), as well as the program chair for the Community College Leadership program in the Rossier School of Education at the University of Southern California. She came to USC in 1996 from the University of Illinois at Chicago, where she was a visiting assistant professor and research associate for the National Center for Teaching, Learning, and Assessment (NCTLA). Dr. Hagedorn earned her Ph.D. in public policy analysis with an emphasis in higher education from the University of Illinois at Chicago. She has experience as a community college instructor.

She has published numerous articles and chapters on various aspects of higher education including student retention, student gains, faculty salary, and sexual harassment on campus. Dr. Hagedorn teaches courses in higher education curriculum and administration as well as applied statistical analyses. She was the 1999–2000 recipient of the Socrates Award from the Graduate Student Association of the Rossier School of Education. She was elected Vice President of Division J of the American Education Research Association (AERA) and will serve in this capacity from 2004 to 2007. She received the 2000 Promising Scholar/Early Career Achievement Award from the Association for the Study of Higher Education. She is also a Fulbright Senior Specialist and has taught seminars in Vietnam.

AMY S. HIRSCHY is an assistant professor in the Department of Educational and Counseling Psychology and the Department of Leadership, Foundations, and Human Resource Education at the University of Louisville. Her research interests include the college student experience in general and, more specifically, factors that positively and negatively influence student persistence.

STEVEN M. LA NASA is currently Assistant Vice Provost for Academic Planning at the University of Missouri—Kansas City, where he is responsible for outcomes assessment, planning, and program evaluation. Steve has served in various administrative and academic roles for over twelve years, and holds a Ph.D. in Higher Education from Penn State. Steve's research interests and projects focus on college-going decisions, student persistence, and faculty roles.

STEPHANIE D. LEE is a doctoral student in the Department of Leadership, Policy, and Organizations at Peabody College of Vanderbilt University in Nashville, Tennessee. Focusing on higher education policy, her research interests include issues of access and the academic preparedness of students of color for higher education.

SUSAN C. LYON works in the Office of Student Affairs in the School of Engineering at the University of Massachusetts, Amherst. She is also a doctoral candidate at the University of Massachusetts, Amherst. She previously earned a B.S. from the State University College at Oswego, New York, and an M.B.A. from the University of Massachusetts. Her professional interests focus on student affairs administration and the recruitment and retention of underrepresented groups in science and engineering.

THOMAS G. MORTENSON is Senior Scholar at The Pell Institute for the Study of Opportunity in Higher Education in Washington, DC, and an independent higher education policy analyst living in Oskaloosa, Iowa. Tom's policy research focuses on opportunity for postsecondary education and training and the ways public policy fosters or impedes access to that opportunity. He has special concern for populations that are underrepresented in higher education. His studies have addressed academic and financial preparation for college, access, choice, persistence, attainment, and labor force entry of college graduates. He is particularly interested in public and private finance of higher education opportunity and the enrollment consequences of the cost shift from taxpayers to students that has been underway for the last twenty years. He has been employed in policy research and budget analysis roles for the University of Minnesota, Illinois Board of Higher Education, Illinois State Scholarship Commission, and American College Testing Program.

Currently Tom is editor and publisher of *Postsecondary Education OPPORTUNITY*, a monthly research letter devoted to analysis and reporting on the demographics, sociology, history, politics, and economics of educational opportunity after high school. He provides consulting services on higher educational opportunity policy to state and national organizations and makes presentations on opportunity throughout the country. In 2003 Tom received the Arturo Alfonso Schomberg Award from the Association for Equality and Excellence in Education for his work on behalf of populations that have been denied access and opportunity in the pursuit of higher education. In 2000 Tom was awarded the Shirley Chisholm Award by the New England Educational Opportunity Association for his research and policy analysis of issues facing TRIO students. In July of 1999 Tom was awarded the Robert P. Huff Golden Quill Award by the National Association of Student Financial Aid Administrators for his research on financial aid for college students. In 1990 he received the same award for earlier student financial aid research. Tom is the only person to receive this award twice.

AMAURY NORA is Professor of Higher Education and Associate Dean for Research and Faculty Development in the College of Education at the University of Houston, Texas. His research focuses on student academic achievement, pre-college and collegiate psychosocial factors impacting adjustment to college and student persistence, the role of college on diverse student populations across different types of institutions, academic and social experiences influencing cognitive as well as noncognitive student outcomes, and theory building and testing. His inquiries have contributed to the development of theoretical perspectives related to traditional lines of research on college persistence and have helped to focus on research related to minorities in both two-year and four-year institutions. Dr. Nora has served as consultant to the American Council of Education, the Ford Foundation, the Hispanic Association of Colleges and Universities, and the United States Department of Education, and he is currently a reviewer for the National Research Council in Washington, DC.

Nora has served on the editorial boards of *Research in Higher Education*, the *Review of Higher Education*, the *Journal of Higher Education*, *Journal of Hispanic Higher Education*, and *Journal of College Student Retention: Research, Theory & Practice*. He assumed the role of editor for the *Review of Higher Education* in January 2004. Nora has published numerous book chapters and articles in refereed journals, including the *Review of Higher Education*, the *Journal of Higher Education*, *Research in Higher Education*, *Higher Education: Handbook of Theory and Research*, *Community College Review*, *Education and Urban Society*, *Journal of College Student Development*, *Journal of Hispanic Higher Education*, *American Educational Research Journal*, *Journal of College Student Retention: Research and Theory*, and *Educational Record*.

LETICIA OSEGUERA earned her doctorate in the University of California, Los Angeles School of Education's Higher Education and Organizational Change program. She is a postdoctoral fellow at the Higher Education Research Institute (HERI) at UCLA. Her research focuses on the stratification of American higher education, the civic role of higher education, and baccalaureate degree attainment for underrepresented groups. She is coauthor (with Alexander W. Astin) of *Degree Attainment Rates at American Colleges and Universities* (2002). She is presently serving as the assistant editor for an upcoming special issue of the *Journal of College Student Retention: Research, Theory & Practice*. Beginning in spring of 2004 she will begin work as a postdoctoral scholar at HERI working with Sylvia Hurtado.

JOHN H. SCHUH is distinguished professor of educational leadership at Iowa State University in Ames, Iowa, where he is also department chair. Previously he has held administrative and faculty assignments at Wichita State University, Indiana University (Bloomington), and Arizona State University. Schuh is the author, co-author, or editor of over 190 publications, including nineteen books and monographs, fifty book chapters, and ninety-five articles. Currently he is editor in chief of the *New Directions for Student Services Sourcebook* Series and is associate editor of the *Journal of College Student Development* and on the editorial board of the *Journal of College Student Retention: Research, Theory & Practice*. Schuh received a Fulbright award to study higher education in Germany in 1994.

ALAN SEIDMAN is the creator and editor of the *Journal of College Student Retention: Research, Theory and Practice*. The journal is the only scholarly journal devoted exclusively to college student retention issues. In addition to the journal, Dr. Seidman created the Center for the Study of College Student Retention (CSCSR) Web site (www.cscsr.org). The Web site contains information about the *Journal*, a retention discussion list (retentionlist) with over 1,000 members worldwide, a retention reference list with over 800 retention references, and a retention slide show featuring Dr. Seidman's retention formula, Retention = Early Identification + (Early + Intensive + Continuous) Intervention which is featured in this book.

Alan Seidman has contributed a book chapter on minority student retention and published articles in scholarly journals in the area of retention and attrition, student services, the community college, and enrollment management and has given presentations on these topics at local, state, regional, and national conferences. Alan has also served as a consultant to colleges in the area of enrollment management and retention.

Alan Seidman has over thirty years of experience in education as a college administrator, educational consultant, and elementary school teacher. Dr. Seidman earned his B.A. and M.A. from Glassboro State College, New Jersey (Rowan University) and his Ed.D. in educational administration from Syracuse University, New York.

VINCENT TINTO received his Ph.D. in education and sociology from the University of Chicago. He is currently Distinguished University Professor at Syracuse University and chair of the higher education program. He has carried out research and has written extensively on higher education, particularly on student retention and the impact of learning communities on student growth and attainment. He has consulted widely with federal and state agencies, independent research firms, foundations, and two-year and four-year institutions of higher education on a broad range of higher educational issues, not the least of which concern the retention and education of students in higher education. His current research, funded by a grant from the Lumina Foundation for Education, focuses on the impact of learning communities on the academic achievements of underprepared college students in urban two-year and four-year colleges.